The Bloomsbury Reader in Religion and Childhood

EDITED BY
ANNA STRHAN, STEPHEN G. PARKER
AND SUSAN B. RIDGELY

Bloomsbury Academic
An imprint of Bloomsbury Publishing Plc

BLOOMSBURY
LONDON · OXFORD · NEW YORK · NEW DELHI · SYDNEY

Bloomsbury Academic
An imprint of Bloomsbury Publishing Plc

50 Bedford Square	1385 Broadway
London	New York
WC1B 3DP	NY 10018
UK	USA

www.bloomsbury.com

BLOOMSBURY and the Diana logo are trademarks of Bloomsbury Publishing Plc

First published 2017

British Library Cataloguing-in-Publication Data
A catalogue record for this book is available from the British Library.

ISBN:	HB:	978-1-4742-5110-5
	PB:	978-1-4742-5109-9
	ePDF:	978-1-4742-5111-2
	ePub:	978-1-4742-5112-9

Library of Congress Cataloging-in-Publication Data
Names: Strhan, Anna, editor.
Title: The Bloomsbury reader in religion and childhood / edited by Anna Strhan,
Stephen G. Parker, and Susan B. Ridgely.
Description: New York : Bloomsbury Academic, 2017. |
Includes bibliographical references and index.
Identifiers: LCCN 2016037876| ISBN 9781474251105 (hb) | ISBN 978147425112 (epub)
Subjects: LCSH: Religions. | Children–Religious aspects. |
Children–Religious life. | Religious education of children.
Classification: LCC BL85 .B56 2017 | DDC 200.83–dc23 LC record available at
https://lccn.loc.gov/2016037876

Cover design by Olivia D'Cruz
Cover image © Manchester Daily Express/Getty Images

Typeset by Integra Software Services Pvt. Ltd.
Printed and bound in Great Britain

Contents

Acknowledgments

An initial catalyst for this volume was a research seminar, "Religion and Childhood: Theory, Research and Pedagogy," held at the University of Kent in July 2013. Several of the contributors to the reader participated in this seminar, which was funded by the Leverhulme Trust as part of Anna Strhan's Early Career Fellowship Award (Grant Number ECF-2012-605). We are very grateful to the Leverhulme Trust for their support of this, and also for their funding for Stephen Parker's research on the history of religious educational broadcasting (Grant Number RPG-2013-162). This led to productive conversations between the editors on work which opened up new avenues between those working on childhood and religion in historical and contemporary contexts. Alongside the authors in this volume, we would like to thank those who have given permission to include pre-published material in this book. Many thanks also to Lalle Pursglove, Lucy Carroll, and Anna MacDiarmid at Bloomsbury Academic for their help, enthusiasm, and encouragement with producing this volume. We are also very grateful to Sarah Hutton for all her help with copyediting and to Manikandan Kuppan (Project Manager), Jothilakshmi Ganesh and Gowthaman Subramanian likewise for their work on copyediting.

On a personal note, we would also like to thank our families for providing space for working on this collection, so a particular thank you to Martin, Fiona, Nathanael, Steve, Amelia, and Andersen.

Permissions Details

"Learning to Be a Muslim" by Jonathan Scourfield, Sophie Gilliat-Ray, Asma Khan and Sameh Otri, from "Islam and Middle Childhood" and "Conclusion" in *Muslim Childhood: Religious Nurture in a European Context* (Oxford University Press, 2013). Reprinted by permission of Oxford University Press.

Excerpts from "Becoming Muslim in a Danish Provincial Town" by Marianne Holm Pedersen originally published in "Islam in the Family: The Religious Socialization of Children in a Danish Provincial Town" in *Making European Muslims: Religious Socialization Among Young Muslims in Scandinavia and Western Europe*, ed. Mark Sedgwick, pp. 21–38, Routledge.

"Training Children in Religion", by John G. Williams, from "Training Children in Prayer" in *Worship and the Modern Child* (1957), pp. 58–65. Reprinted by permission of SPCK.

"A World of Their Own Making," by John R. Gillis, from *A World of Their Own Making: Myth, Ritual and the Quest for Family Values* (Harvard University Press, 1997), pp. 68–78, reprinted by permission of Perseus Books.

"'No matter how small': The Democratic Imagination of Dr. Seuss," in *Hop on Pop*, Henry Jenkins, Jane Shattuc, Tara McPherson, eds., pp. 187–208. Copyright, 2002, Duke University Press. All rights reserved. Republished by permission of the copyright holder.

"Autumn Days" and "One More Step Along the World I Go" (in "The BBC's *Religious Service for Schools, 'Come and Praise'*, and the Musical Aesthetic and Religious Discourse Around the Child"). Reprinted by permission of Stainer and Bell.

"A Crisis About the Theology of Children," by Robert A. Orsi, from Harvard Divinity Bulletin Spring 2002, reprinted by permission of the author.

"Mitzvah Girls," by Ayala Fader, from "Defiance" in *Mitzvah Girls: Bringing Up the Next Generation of Hasidic Jews in Brooklyn* (Princeton University Press, 2009), pp. 76–78. Reprinted by permission of Princeton University Press.

"Child Labour and Moral Discourse in Brazil," by Maya Mayblin, from "Learning Courage: Child Labour and Moral Discourse in Brazil," *Ethnos* 75.1 (2010): 23–48, reprinted by permission of Taylor and Francis.

Images of the model Sunday School classroom at Westhill, Birmingham supplied courtesy of the Cadbury Research Library, University of Birmingham, UK, reference: WC Box 217.

Introduction

Anna Strhan, Stephen G. Parker, and Susan B. Ridgely

From First Communions and Bar Mitzvahs to novices entering Buddhist monasteries, children are often some of the most visible participants in religious life. For adults, children's involvement or non-involvement in religion can often raise particularly strong feelings, as children seem to represent the possible futures of religious and secular communities, even of society itself. Debates about the place of religion in contemporary societies often become particularly heated when these concern children, as we have seen in recent years across arguments about faith schools and religious indoctrination or radicalization to the sex abuse scandals in the Roman Catholic Church and tensions surrounding the politics of the family. The intensity of such debates reflects the ways in which childhood has, from the late 1960s onward, been brought to the forefront of political, personal, and academic agendas. Demographic shifts to an ageing population and changes in family structure have intensified focus on children, imbuing the "priceless" child with a unique scarcity value (Zelizer 1994). At the same time, complex, entangled ideational currents sharpen this focus: the repositioning of personhood as societies move away from traditional categories of identity; the fast pace of social change readjusting orientations toward time and mortality; the desire for a moral center and investment in futures seeming increasingly pressing (James et al. 1998: 5). We live in an era that has been marked by both a heightened concern for children—in which children and the care of children have come to take on a sacred status (Lynch 2012)—and a sense of childhood as under threat. Childhood has become—and not only in the West—"popularized, politicized, scrutinized and analysed in a series of interlocking spaces in which the traditional confidence and certainty about childhood and children's social status are being radically undermined" (James et al. 1998: 4). This intensified focus on children also affects religion, and as control over what happens to children in many societies has moved away from religious bodies and is concentrated in structures of state education, the media, or commercial interests, childhood has become a site of particular struggle in relation to religion.

From the 1990s onward, a "new paradigm" of childhood studies[1] has placed the social, historical, and cultural conditions surrounding childhood and the experiences of children firmly on the map of a range of disciplines. This approach argues that scholars need to understand childhood as a social construction and as a variable of social analysis that intersects with other variables (such as class, race, gender), and emphasizes that children should be studied in their own right, rather than as refracted solely through the prism of their relationships with adults (Oswell 2016). An exciting body of work on religion and childhood is emerging, influenced by this approach. This, however, follows something of a historical neglect, with children often the "purloined letters" of religion: prominently displayed yet all too often overlooked (Bales 2005: 12). This doesn't mean that children were altogether absent in the study of religion: children's capacity to stand for the future of religion led to research focused on intergenerational continuities and changes in relation to religion, as well as studies of children's religious development. Yet critical analysis of the social construction of childhood and attention to children's experiences were not in themselves areas of scholarly attention.

The aim of this Reader is to move beyond this historical lacuna by drawing together readings that explore how children's lives and the meanings of childhood are shaped by particular social and cultural expectations and practices across different times and places, and to address the significance of religion within these processes. How, we ask, does religion figure in what childhood means and how does it affect children's experiences, from the intimate settings of the home and family to national, global, and existential scales? In bringing together a range of classic, contemporary, and specially commissioned readings to explore these questions, our aim is to open up understanding of the meanings of childhood for both adults and children, how these shape and are shaped by particular forms of religious life, and the wider social and cultural significance of this. Let us begin, however, with a brief inventory of the place of childhood within the study of religion.

Locating children in the study of religion

Historically, much of the research on children and religion has emerged from the disciplines of psychology, theology, sociology, and particular subfields within religious studies, especially the study of new religious movements. Yet within these literatures, children have often been silent, appearing "primarily as reflections of adult concerns about the present or as projections of adult concerns for the future" (Ridgely 2011: 1). The present realities of children's lives have all too often been obscured from scholarly focus as objects of interest in their own right. In developmental psychology, for example, approaches to religion mirrored and drew on cognitive developmental approaches within the discipline as a whole, through which children were measured, assessed, and judged in the context of "normal" religious development toward the ideal of adulthood. Exemplifying this approach, Goldman (1964) linked children's intellectual development to their understanding of religion by examining children's understandings of Bible stories, and proposed a developmental model, which presented intuitive thought as predominant from 5 to 7 years, "concrete operational thought" dominant between 8 and 10 years, as children developed a focus on particular details in religious stories and pictures, and then a third stage of "formal operational thought," when religion began to be seen in more hypothetical and abstract terms (Goldman 1964; see Carrette this volume, and Madge et al. 2014: 13). This developmental approach shaped the orientation of a body of work in psychology on children's religion and spirituality, which connected social with biological development. As a result, children's interactions, language, behavior, and thinking in relation to religion were taken as evidence marking progressive stages of development, with little account of the significance of these for children themselves or for their religious community as a whole. The 1990s saw something of a reaction against this kind of developmental approach, following the publication of Robert Coles' *The Spiritual Life of Children* (1990). Coles noted that psychological research tended to look for signs of children's "faith development," but that his own research with Hopi children in the United States who "are illiterate, never learned how to take a test…and clam up tightly even if approached by an investigator" (1990: 23) showed him the inadequacy of this. Cole's research thus included narratives of children which show their spirituality, "visionary moments," and metaphysical curiosity.

From the late 1990s onward, a number of sociologists also began to develop a sustained focus on young people's understandings of religion (e.g. Wuthnow 1999; Smith and Denton 2005). The 1990s also saw interest in children and religion emerging within history, for example, the edited *Church and Childhood* (Wood 1994), and the anthropologist Charlotte Hardman's edited *Children in New Religions* (Palmer and Hardman 1999) deepened the understanding of children within new religious movements. At the same time, there was growing interest in childhood from theologians, with Marcia Bunge's important edited volume *Child in Christian Thought* published in 2001, and in 2003, Bunge and her colleagues created the "Childhood Studies and Religion" consultation in the American Academy of Religion. Yet, as Ridgely notes (2011: 3), despite this growing interest in children and religion across disciplines, the prevailing construction of children as mirrors of adult hopes and concerns remained unchallenged, with research about children rather than informed by them. The pioneering 2009 edited volumes *Children and Childhood in World Religions* (Browning and Bunge 2009) and *Children and Childhood in American Religions* (Browning and Miller-McLemore 2009), as Ridgely notes (2011: 3), present important insights into how different religious traditions view children. Yet insofar as these focus mainly on adult-centred perspectives and the teachings on childhood from particular religious traditions and texts, these approaches offer only a partial account of social reality. A deeper understanding of the social realities of religion and childhood requires looking beyond official religious teachings to the everyday materialities and embodied practices of children's religion, to how "childhood" is socially constructed through particular cultural practices, and to how religious and secular desires, hopes, and concerns are interwoven throughout these. It also requires attending to children's own experiences and ideas.

The relative silence on the topic of children and religion reflects a broader historical silencing of children across the social sciences and humanities. Since the 1990s, this has been challenged by the emergence of what became known as the "new paradigm" or "new social studies of childhood," which has begun to influence a growing recent body of literature in the study of religion and has shaped the approach we have taken in this volume. The new paradigm began with Allison James and Alan Prout's edited *Constructing and Reconstructing Childhood*, originally published in 1990, which drew attention to both the agency of children and the social construction of childhood, as well as highlighting how previously dominant conceptualizations of childhood had inhibited attention to these areas.[2] The dominant developmental approach to childhood—which had extended far beyond its origins in psychology—delineated, they argued, a notion of personhood with rationality its universal mark, with childhood conceptualized as the period of apprenticeship for adulthood. Psychology presented an essentially evolutionary model of the child as developing into an adult, with this process seen as "a progression from simplicity to complexity of thought, from irrational to rational behaviour" (Prout and James 1997: 10). The notion of evolutionary progression from childhood simplicity to adult complexity was, James and Prout argued, influenced by earlier anthropologists' constructions of "other" cultures as "childish" and "simple" (1997: 10), as can be seen in the words of Tylor, for example, arguing that he could apply "the often-repeated comparison of savages to children as fairly to their moral as to their intellectual condition" (1871, cited in Prout and James 1997: 11). This binary construction of irrational child/rational adult also shaped socialization theories within sociology and anthropology from the 1950s onward. Socialization was conceptualized as "the key which turns the asocial child into a social adult," based on assumptions about the child's passivity: "[t]he child is portrayed, like the laboratory rat, as being at the mercy of external stimuli: passive and conforming. Lost in a social maze, it is the adult who offers directions…. In being constructed as unable to initiate interactions the child's nature is thus visualized as fundamentally different from an adult's" (Prout and James 1997: 13).

The stimulus for the challenge posed to these dominant concepts came in part, as Prout and James outline, from the training of a generation of sociologists in the theoretical frameworks of symbolic interactionism and social phenomenology. Symbolic interactionist approaches drew attention to the idea of social life as being created through social actors' everyday interactions and how these create possibilities for meaningful action, and sociologists' attention to the lifeworlds of those in more marginalized social locations eventually extended to children (Prout and James 1997: 15). The work of the historian Philippe Ariès was also significant in drawing attention to the idea of childhood as culturally constructed. In *Centuries of Childhood* (1962), originally published in French in 1960, Ariès made the bold claim that the idea of childhood did not exist in medieval society. Drawing on medieval iconography, Ariès argued that children were seen and depicted as miniature adults, and it was only from the fifteenth century onward that they were gradually removed from adult society and seen as children, through new "coddling" attitudes toward children and the development of long periods of formal education. Ariès's argument has since been fiercely debated and contested by other historians. Pollock, for example, argued that:

Many historians have subscribed to the mistaken belief that, if a past society did not possess the contemporary Western concept of childhood, then the society had no such concept. This is a totally indefensible point of view—why should past societies have regarded children in the same way as Western society today? Moreover, even if children were regarded differently in the past, this does not mean that they were not regarded as children. (1983, cited in Prout and James 1997: 17)

Despite the reaction against Ariès, this somewhat more understated claim that childhood is socially and culturally constructed has largely been accepted and was also supported by the earlier work of anthropologists such as Ruth Benedict (1935) and Margaret Mead (1928), who paid attention to cultural variations in child-rearing practices, albeit with little attention to children's agency in these processes.

Influenced by these approaches, the contributors to the new paradigm set out a programmatic approach to Childhood Studies, which emphasized that childhood is a social construction and that its construction takes place through the actions of both adults and children, and that childhood can never be separated from other variables of social analysis (James and Prout 1997a: 4). Children are, they argued, worth studying in their own right as "actively involved in the construction of their own social lives, the lives of those around them, and of the societies in which they live," rather than just as reflections of adults' concerns and "passive subjects of structural determinations" (1997a: 4). Ethnography was the favored method in this approach for allowing "children a more direct voice in the production of sociological data than is usually possible through experimental or survey styles of research," encouraging researchers to attend to the meanings children themselves attach to their lives (James and Prout 1997a: 4–5).

Temporality was an important element of this paradigm. Jens Qvortrup had earlier argued for the need to understand children as social beings rather than social becomings (Qvortrup 1985, discussed in Oswell 2016), and the new paradigm drew attention to the idea of social construction as realized in the present. James and Prout argued against the tendency in much sociological writing to locate childhood in "some timeless zone standing as it were to the side of the mainstream (that is adult) history and culture. Childhood appears to be, so to speak, lost in time, its present is continuously banished to the past, the future, or out of time altogether" (1997b: 234). Their critique of childhood as conceptualized through models of socialization and development was argued on the basis that children's agency to change social structures, as well as the shape of those structures, is materialized in the present. Thus, as Oswell argues, a particular political inflection underpinned the attention they gave to children's agency, "since a statement about what children are is also a statement about their capacity to change the organisation of the social world in which they live" (2016: 2–3). Much of the literature influenced by the new paradigm has taken up this idea of focusing on children's becoming and agency in the present, although attention has also been given to the ways in which children themselves think of their lives in terms of both being *and* becoming, so that children might be conceptualized as "being and becomings" (Uprichard 2008).

Alongside the new paradigm, there has also emerged, as Oswell describes (2016), an important body of writings on childhood from a different theoretical heritage, more influenced by Foucauldian ideas of power, knowledge and subjection, materiality, and notions of distributed agency from actor-network theory (e.g. Castañeda 2002; Prout 2005; Turmel 2008). There is, as Oswell notes, a methodological axiom of "no *a priori*" in this alternative paradigm, which focuses primarily on the practices and discourses through which childhood becomes marked off as a socially visible phenomenon. André Turmel, for example, frames his historical sociology of childhood (2008) as focused on the question: "what is childhood from a sociological standpoint if it is no longer either a residue of social theory or a peripheral phenomenon of adult society?" (Turmel 2008: 306). These approaches have focused less on the experiences and agency of children themselves, but nevertheless share with the new paradigm a close attention to the social construction of childhood by focusing on the processes and inscriptions through which children are produced as "other" to adults, both familiar and strange, seeming to inhabit another world, and yet also of the self.

In recent years, there has been a growing body of work across the disciplines of sociology, anthropology, history, geography, and religious studies influenced by this turn to childhood—in particular the new paradigm of childhood studies—and has been attentive to the social construction of childhood and to children's agency (e.g. Orsi 2005; Mintz 2006; Arweck and Nesbitt 2011; Madge, Hemming and Stenson 2014; Ridgely 2011; Bales 2005; Hemming 2015). In the Sociology of Religion and in Religious Studies, this focus on children's experiences has also been stimulated by the burgeoning literature on "lived religion." This body of work has encouraged attention to those such as the "women, children, and other illiterates" who have historically been silenced by predominant lenses in the study of religion, which have tended to focus more on the religion of elite social groups (McDannell 2011: 139), as well as to the everyday religious practices beyond the settings of institutions through which religious worlds and relationalities are made. There are also broader social and political reasons for the growing body of work on children and religion, with the "return of religion" to public prominence stimulating wider interest in religion across social scientific disciplines such as geography and sociology, which throughout much of the twentieth century tended to marginalize the study of religion. While these social scientific disciplines have explored how race, class, ethnicity, and gender have shaped children's lives and the understandings of childhood held by children and adults, religion has all too often been a lacuna, which has only in recent years become a growing focus of attention over the period that religion has, like childhood, become a more prominent feature of academic agenda. Much of this growing literature has, however, been somewhat fragmented across disciplines. Furthermore, many contemporary debates about religion and childhood are not new but are related to wider questions about the distinctiveness of childhood and its religious dimensions in historical perspective—how the ways in which we think about what childhood is have been inflected by the genealogies of particular religious modes of thought. Our aim in this Reader is therefore to bring together readings from across these disciplines, and different traditions, times, and places, to help establish key origins, questions, and resources for the study of religion and childhood, and to encourage possibilities for future conversations and studies beyond the themes and contexts we have included here.

Outline of the volume

The texts included in this volume are intended to provide an overview of some of the main debates and intellectual developments within the study of religion and childhood, and also of some of the new areas of study that are beginning to open up. We have selected some extracts from significant work previously published elsewhere as well as commissioning complementary new material. The Reader does not by any means exhaust all the key texts in this field and we hope that the references and bibliography will be useful for further reading beyond what is included here. Nevertheless, we hope that this volume will offer a useful orientation to this field not only for students but to postgraduate researchers and established scholars who want to explore some key ideas in the study of religion and childhood. We would have liked to have included many other texts and voices, and we are conscious that the volume is more heavily weighted toward the Abrahamic religions and toward contributions from US and European contexts. Here we found our choices shaped by the literature available: while keen to make the volume as global as possible, the majority of work that has been done to date (both in contemporary studies and in historical perspectives) has tended to focus on childhood in relation to Christianity in European and North American settings specifically, shaped through the history of the disciplinary trajectories outlined previously. As the field continues to expand, we hope to see a growing number of studies beyond these settings. While there is an extensive body of work in childhood studies on the lives of "street children" in cities in the Global South, for example, future research might attend to the significance of religion in these children's lives and in the moral aspirations of adults engaging with them, such as in narratives of "rescuing" such children. Furthermore, while some of the chapters here explore the significance of religion in the lives of children of migrants in Europe, the global intensification of migration over recent years—in which religion often plays a prominent part—and the experiences of children in relation to this could be seen as an important area for future studies.

In selecting the readings here, we wanted to avoid replicating valuable work that has already been done by other publications. There are valuable resources that discuss how Christianity was implicated historically in forms of institutional abuse, for example, Trafzer, Keller, and Sisquoc's edited collection on American Indian residential schools *Boarding School Blues: Revisiting American Indian Educational Experiences* (2006) and Gordon Lynch's work on child migration programmes in *Remembering Child Migration: Faith, Nation-Building and the Wounds of Charity* (2016). There are also excellent recent resources on the significance of childhood in colonial aspirations, ambitions, and projects, such as Shurlee Swain and Margot Hillel's (2010) *Child, Nation, Race and Empire: Child Rescue Discourse, England, Canada and Australia, 1850–1915;*

Sarah Emily Duff's (2015) *Changing Childhoods in the Cape Colony: Dutch Reformed Church Evangelicalism and Colonial Childhood 1860–1895)*; Karen Vallgårda's (2015) *Imperial Childhoods and Christian Mission: Education and Emotions in South India and Denmark*; and Hugh Morrison and Mary Clare Martin's forthcoming *Creating Religious Childhoods: Children, Young People and Christianity in Anglo-World and British Colonial Contexts, 1800–1950*. Emily Manktelow's (2013) *Missionary Families: Race, Gender and Generation on the Spiritual Frontier* also explores this terrain, providing insight into how at the colonial frontier, originally, the idea was "that the Christian family would be an educative and helpful influence on the natives, and as the European children grew up they also would take part in missionary labour, and be all the better qualified for the work from their intimate knowledge of native life"; however, "this was a fond imagination [and]…like so many others, it fared badly under the rough trial of experience" (Lovett, cited in Manktelow 2013: 1). For exploring methodological, practical, conceptual, ethical, and legal issues surrounding conducting research with children, Ridgely's edited *The Study of Children in Religions: A Methods Handbook* (2011) offers an invaluable resource. Amanda van Eck Duymaer van Twist's *Perfect Children: Growing Up on the Religious Fringe* (2015) explores the place of children in new religious movements and on the "religious fringes" of society, while Jean La Fontaine's edited *The Devil's Children: From Spirit Possession to Witchcraft: New Allegations That Affect Children* (2009) draws together a range of contributions addressing how children are affected—in some cases leading to serious abuse—by allegations of spirit possession and witchcraft. Within theology and religious studies, there are a number of volumes offering an overview of different faith perspectives' teachings and key texts on childhood. The 2009 publications *Children and Childhood in World Religions* and *Children and Childhood in American Religions* each provide an important collection of readings about how different world faiths and American religions view children and parents' responsibilities, while Marcia Bunge's edited *Child in Christian Thought* (2001) highlights a range of Christian theological perspectives on childhood.

In selecting resources for this Reader, our aim has been to move beyond focusing mainly on religious teachings and perspectives on childhood to explore the social construction of childhood, the lived realities of children's religion, and the meanings childhood has for adults in relation to them across a variety of contexts and scales. The central questions we hope to address are:

- What role does religion play in the social construction of childhood? How do religious genealogies of thought still continue to pervade contemporary understandings in both religious and non-religious contexts?

- How does religion shape and how is it shaped by children's experiences and adults' hopes and expectations for children?

- How can we understand the agency of children in relation to religion? To what extent is children's agency enabled or constrained by particular forms of religion, and what does this mean across local, national, and global scales?

- How does religion shape and how is it shaped by particular understandings of education and citizenship?

- What role do media and everyday embodied practice play in shaping children's relations to religion?

- What ethical issues arise from children's involvement or non-involvement in religion?

To present answers to these and other questions, the Reader is structured around five central themes, which form the different parts of the book.

The first part asks "what is a child?" The readings in this part of the book focus on the role that religion plays in defining what a child is and shaping ideas of children's natures as, for example, sinful or innocent. While we cannot hope to exhaust this question through the chapters here—and it is a theme that pervades the book—the readings in this section provide insight into how adults have portrayed what children are in ways that have often denied them agency, for example, in dominant psychological approaches, which have themselves shaped the history of the study of childhood. The readings in this part also reveal how our thinking about what a child is opens up broader social and ethical questions surrounding how we think about what a person is, while also offering perspectives on what a child is from contrasting faith perspectives, including Hinduism, Buddhism, the New Age movement, and evangelical Christianity.

The second part examines changing ideas and spaces of childhood piety, opening up the question of where children's religion is, and how it is located within the spaces of religious institutions, within the home and within family life. Here we gain historical insight into how Reformed Christianity located the home as the heart of faith, a perspective that we still see pervading much more recent scholarship on how the family might be seen as a kind of "secular sacred" and in changing notions of parental responsibilities toward children. While the new social studies of childhood have mostly been little interested in family life, understanding children's lived religion means exploring its location in everyday spaces of home and the family. The chapters in this part also open up the question of what it means to form a person, and the modes of relationality involved in this. As well as the setting of the home, different understandings of the formation of children are also addressed here in relation to the spaces of religious institutions.

Our third part continues addressing the different spaces of children's lives through turning to questions of the relationship between religion, education, and citizenship. Contemporary debates about education and religion often hinge on a sense that religion is somehow opposed to Enlightened modernity. If to be an educated person means to become autonomous and self-determining, religion is often seen as at odds with this, encouraging a sense of submission to a higher authority. The chapters in this part encourage critical reflection on these understandings, beginning with Kant's writings on education, since his Enlightenment principles of the development of rational autonomy, morality, and freedom can be seen as pioneering liberal ideals of education that still permeate many contemporary conceptions of education. As well as these contested understandings of the relation between religion and education, chapters in this part also consider the everyday realities of how children negotiate the relation between the religious and the secular in educational spaces, and their forms of civic sociality. As wider public debates on religion and education can tend toward polarization, often predicated on underlying assumptions that religious groups' involvement in education encourages social segregation or forms of indoctrination, the readings in this part encourage more nuanced understanding of the complex interrelations between religion, education, forms of knowledge, and the secular, through attending to how these are formed and experienced in the everyday lives of children across the spaces of schools and educational institutions, and the moral landscapes associated with these.

Part four moves on to consider the media and materialities of childhood and religion. The turn toward what has become known as "lived religion" has drawn attention to the importance of studying practice, objects, and media in everyday religious lives beyond the focus on religious texts, teachings, and institutions that has historically dominated Religious Studies. This has opened up a growing body of work exploring the intersections of religion, media, materiality, and childhood. The authors in this part demonstrate the importance of attending to the significance of media such as children's literature and radio broadcasts in adults' desires to form children, and the often contested values at stake in these efforts. We also see how toys and forms of play offer insight into adults' desires to form children as particular kinds of subjects. This body of work provides an important challenge to the still common assumption that religion is concerned primarily with cognitive beliefs—as we have seen in relation to psychological approaches to children and religion—or is an interior spiritual life that is somehow removed from the habits and practices of the body and material objects. Instead, this section draws our attention to how children's religion is always mediated— that is, how it is always dependent on particular media and culture that constitute the reality of lived religion.

Our final part addresses the question of children's agency and the ways in which it is constrained or enabled in relation to religion. We see this in global perspective across a range of settings, from the United Nations Convention on the Rights of the Child to local perspectives on child labour in North East Brazil. This part also raises the issue of how we remember historic forms of child abuse, with Lynch's chapter exploring how concepts from the study of religion might provide deeper insight into the complex moral questions surrounding public responses to historic abuse and trauma. The sex abuse scandal in the Roman Catholic Church—the subject of two chapters in this part of the book—may be an extreme example, but it raises important questions that extend beyond this particular crisis to how we think about children's agency more broadly. As Orsi puts it in his chapter, we need to "find ways of making children more authentically and autonomously present in the contemporary Christian context and … [to] protect their autonomy rather than putting in place safeguards that only serve to locate children ever more completely under absolute adult authority and protection" (Orsi, this volume).

Taken together, our aim is for the volume to provide an overview of the field that draws out the significance of religion in social and cultural constructions of childhood and the complex forms of interrelationality involved in shaping the experiences and meanings of childhood, both for adults and for children in relation to them. Given the spatial, temporal, material, and moral complexities of these processes, conversations on these themes are still very much ongoing, and we hope and expect the positions that are advanced here to be refined and challenged further over coming years. In bringing together these readings, we have tried to crystallize some key themes and issues for debate in ways that might stimulate further conversations, while hopefully drawing new students and scholars into this important area. Our hope is that what might follow from this process is not the further development of a sub-discipline of the study of religion and childhood, as if childhood is a niche area to be covered by expert sub-specialists. As Priscilla Alderson puts it, "childhood, like adulthood, is not a discrete specialist topic to be flattened, sliced and squeezed into a distinct sub-sociology. Instead, children and adults exist and interact across practically all social concerns, and are understood through multidisciplinary research" (2016). Attending to the lives and experiences of children, the meanings of childhood, and the hopes and concerns of adults in relation to children, in all their complexities, has the potential to shift our perception and deepen understanding not just of children and childhood but of the everyday social realities we all inhabit.

Notes

1 For example, Prout and James (1997), James et al. (1998).
2 This was prefigured by Chris Jenks's earlier edited *The Sociology of Childhood* (1982) and his later *Childhood* (1996).

References

Alderson, Priscilla (2016), "The Missing Third that Skews Sociology," *Discover Society*, 29. Available online http://discoversociety.org/2016/02/02/the-missing-third-that-skews-sociology/ (accessed May 4, 2016).

Ariès, Philippe (1962), *Centuries of Childhood*, London: Jonathan Cape.

Arweck, Elisabeth and Nesbitt, Eleanor (2011), "Religious Education in the Experience of Young People from Mixed-faith Families," *British Journal of Religious Education* 33 (1): 31–45.

Bales, Susan Ridgely (2005), *When I Was a Child: Children's Interpretations of First Communion*, Chapel Hill: University of North Carolina Press.

Benedict, Ruth (1935), *Patterns of Culture*, London: Routledge and Kegan Paul.

Browning, Don S. and Bunge, Marcia J. (eds) (2009), *Children and Childhood in World Religions: Primary Sources and Texts*, New Brunswick, NJ: Rutgers University Press.

Browning, Don S. and Miller-McLemore, Bonnie J. (eds) (2009), *Children and Childhood in American Religions*, New Brunswick, NJ: Rutgers University Press.

Bunge, Marcia J. (ed.) (2001), *The Child in Christian Thought*, Grand Rapids, MI: William B. Eerdmans Publishing.

Castañeda, Claudia (2002), *Figurations: Child, Bodies, Worlds*, Durham, NC: Duke University Press.

Coles, Robert (1990), *The Spiritual Life of Children*, Boston: Houghton Mifflin.

Duff, Sarah Emily (2015), *Changing Childhoods in the Cape Colony: Dutch Reformed Church Evangelicalism and Colonial Childhood, 1860–1895*, London: Palgrave Macmillan.

Goldman, R. (1964), *Religious Thinking from Childhood to Adolescence*, London: Routledge and Kegan Paul.

Hemming, Peter (2015), *Religion in the Primary School: Ethos, Diversity, Citizenship*, Abingdon: Routledge.

James, Allison and Prout, Alan (1997a), "Introduction," in Allison James and Alan Prout (eds), *Constructing and Reconstructing Childhood: Contemporary Issues in the Sociological Study of Childhood*, second edition, 1–6, London: Falmer.

James, Allison and Prout, Alan (1997b), "Re-presenting Childhood," in Allison James and Alan Prout (eds), *Constructing and Reconstructing Childhood: Contemporary Issues in the Sociological Study of Childhood*, second edition, 230–250, London: Falmer.

James, A., Jenks, C., and Prout, A. (1998), *Theorizing Childhood*, Cambridge: Polity Press.

Jenks, C. (ed.) (1982), *The Sociology of Childhood: Essential Readings*, Aldershot: Gregg Revivals.

Jenks. C. (1996), *Childhood*, New York: Routledge.

La Fontaine, Jean (ed.) (2009), *The Devil's Children: From Spirit Possession to Witchcraft: New Allegations That Affect Children*, Farnham: Ashgate.

Lynch, Gordon (2012), *The Sacred: A Cultural Sociological Approach*, Oxford: Oxford University Press.

Lynch, Gordon (2016), *Remembering Child Migration: Faith, Nation-Building and the Wounds of Charity*, London: Bloomsbury Academic.

McDannell, Colleen (2011), "Scrambling the Sacred and the Profane," in Gordon Lynch, Jolyon Mitchell and Anna Strhan (eds), *Religion, Media and Culture: A Reader*, 135–146. London: Routledge.

Madge, Nicola, Hemming, Peter J., and Stenson, Kevin (2014), *Youth on Religion: The Development, Negotiation and Impact of Faith and Non-faith Identity*, London: Routledge.

Manktelow, Emily (2013), *Missionary Families: Race, Gender and Generation on the Spiritual Frontier*, Manchester: Manchester University Press.

Mintz, Steven (2006), *Huck's Raft: A History of American Childhood*, Boston: Harvard University Press.

Mead, Margaret (1928), *Coming of Age in Samoa*, Harmondsworh: Penguin.

Orsi, Robert A. (2005), "Material Children," in *Between Heaven and Earth: The Religious Worlds People Make and the Scholars Who Study Them*, 73–109, Princeton: Princeton University Press.

Oswell, David (2016), "Re-aligning Children's Agency and Re-socialising Children in Childhood Studies," in Florian Esser, Mieke Baader, Tanja Betz and Beatrice Hungerland (eds), *Reconceptualising Agency and Childhood: New Perspectives in Childhood Studies*, London: Routledge.

Palmer, Susan J. and Hardman, Charlotte E. (eds) (1999), *Children in New Religions*, New Brunswick, NJ: Rutgers University Press.

Prout, Alan (2005), *The Future of Childhood*, London: RoutledgeFalmer.

Prout, Alan and James, Allison (1997), "A New Paradigm for the Sociology of Childhood," in Allison James and Alan Prout (eds) *Constructing and Reconstructing Childhood:*

Contemporary Issues in the Sociological Study of Childhood, second edition, 7–33, London: Falmer.

Qvortrup, J. (1985), "Placing Children in the Division of Labour," in P. Close and R. Collins (eds), *Family and Economy in Modern Society*, London: Macmillan.

Ridgely, Susan B. (2011), "Introduction," in Susan B. Ridgely (ed.), *The Study of Children in Religions: A Methods Handbook*, 1–15, New York: New York University Press.

Smith, Christian, with Denton, Melinda Lundquist (2005), *Soul-Searching: The Religious and Spiritual Lives of American Teenagers*, New York: Oxford University Press.

Swain, Shurlee and Hillel, Margot (2010), *Child, Nation, Race and Empire: Child Rescue Discourse, England, Canada and Australia, 1850–1915*, Manchester: Manchester University Press.

Trafzer, Clifford E., Keller, Jean A. and Sisquoc, Lorene (2006), *Boarding School Blues: Revisiting American Indian Educational Experiences*, Lincoln, NE: University of Nebraska Press.

Turmel, André (2008), *A Historical Sociology of Childhood: Developmental Thinking, Categorization and Graphic Visualization*, Cambridge: Cambridge University Press.

Uprichard, Emma (2008), "Children as 'Being and Becomings': Children, Childhood and Temporality," *Children and Society* 22: 303–313.

Vallgårda, Karen (2015), *Imperial Childhoods and Christian Mission: Education and Emotions in South India and Denmark*, London: Palgrave Macmillan.

Van Eck Duymaer van Twist, Amanda (2015), *Perfect Children: Growing Up on the Religious Fringe*, New York: Oxford University Press.

Wood, Diana (ed.) (1994), *The Church and Childhood*, Oxford: Blackwell.

Wuthnow, Robert (1999), *Growing Up Religious: Christians and Jews and Their Journeys of Faith*, Boston: Beacon.

Zelizer, Viviana (1994), *Pricing the Priceless Child: The Changing Social Value of Children*, Princeton, NJ: Princeton University Press.

PART ONE

What Is Childhood? Theoretical Perspectives

Introduction

Compared with other civilizations, pediatric healthcare was well developed in China from a very early period. In *A Tender Voyage: Children and Childhood in Late Imperial China*, Ping-chen Hsiung (2005) describes how medieval medical texts contain sections devoted especially to the subject of children's health care. Prior to that even, the seventh-century text *On the Origins and Symptoms of Diseases* allocates a section for children's problems, while the eighth-century *Prescriptions Worth a Thousand* also has a section on childhood at the beginning of the book. These two texts cover matters of newborn care, including cutting the umbilical cord, mouth wiping, bathing, feeding, and clothing, and express medical views on common children's illnesses, their origins, treatments, and symptoms (2005: 33). Hsiung interprets this concern for children's health as revealing the high cultural value attached to children in medieval China. Furthermore, in a surprising echo of the division of Western understandings of childhood between the Romantic and Puritan conceptions, she identifies within the Confucian tradition both a neo-Confucian conceptualization of childhood that stresses discipline, control and punishment and the Wang-ming emphasis on awakening the child through education and self-reflection (Wells 2015: 11).

Hsiung's work draws our attention to how particular religious and cultural traditions present different articulations of what a child is, which are implicated in specific practices and ideas about caring for children and in particular understandings of children's value. This idea of childhood as a contingent social and cultural construction was first brought to the foreground of academic agenda through the work of the historian Philippe Ariès, who provocatively argued that "in medieval society, the idea of childhood did not exist," and that it was only in the modern period that ideas of treating children differently from adults emerged (1962: 128). While Hsiung's work and that of other historians has challenged this thesis and questioned its historical accuracy, Ariès's work nevertheless remains significant for the way in which it both stimulated further research on childhood—within history and permeating beyond that to a range of disciplines—and drew particular attention to the social, cultural, and historical dimensions shaping the formation of understandings of childhood.

The readings in this part address how we can see different understandings of what a child is across times, spaces, and methodological apparatuses. We begin with the theological perspective offered by Augustine, whose ideas of different stages of childhood development—from infancy through to early and later childhood—and whose presentation of children's innate sinfulness have proved enormously influential in not only Christian thought but in broader Western frameworks of analysis that bear the historical traces of their Christian heritage, including in the radical rejection of this conception of childhood as we will see later in the volume in the readings by Locke and Rousseau. The idea of childhood innocence is taken up in the following two readings. In Chapter 2, Ariès considers the development of a "religion for children" in Western Christianity, with the development of the solemn celebration of First Communion for example, and how this was related to emerging ideas of childhood innocence from the seventeenth century onwards. Chapter 3 is taken from James Kincaid's *Erotic Innocence* (1998), a groundbreaking work on America's contemporary preoccupation with stories of children's sexual abuse. In this work, Kincaid argued that conceptualizations of childhood innocence "empty" the child of their agency so that adults are able to project their own symbolic desires and demands onto children. Criticizing notions of children's innate innocence as a condition to be protected, Kincaid presents it is a cultural myth that is enforced upon children, ultimately causing them harm.

The following four chapters present insights into what a child is from the perspectives of Hinduism, Buddhism, evangelical Christianity, and the new age movement. Drawing on her research with Hindu children, Nesbitt's chapter offers an overview of and introduction to some key concepts in the study of Hindu understandings of childhood. Sasson's chapter explores contrasting understandings of childhood within Buddhist literature through comparing stories in the Vessantara Jātaka and the Mūgapakkha Jātaka, demonstrating the particular agency accorded to children in the latter and challenging assumptions that Buddhist textual traditions display little interest in children. Strhan's chapter, based on ethnographic fieldwork with two evangelical churches in London, examines how contemporary discourses on parenting and church life in these settings reveal two very different perspectives on what a child is, with conservative evangelical ideals expressing notions of children's innate sinfulness and the need for children's obedience to their parents contrasting with a charismatic evangelical emphasis on the need children's freedom and spontaneity. Within the New Age Movement, there are also widely differing perceptions of childhood. Singler's chapter explores the Indigo Children concept as an example of a New Age perspective, showing how the concept can be seen as an attempted resolution of conflicting contemporary cultural understandings of what a child is.

There has often been—and continues to be—a tendency in how people talk about children and religion to treat children as passive subjects, accepting what they are told and taught by adults. In contemporary debates, this attitude underlies both Richard Dawkins' fears about the religious indoctrination of children (2006) and the opposite fears of some religious people that each generation is becoming progressively more nonreligious, or of "many children passively accepting the values of consumer culture" (Scourfield et al. 2013: 19). The dominant concepts used in the study of children and religion, often drawing from developmental understandings of childhood, have often themselves tended to underplay ideas of children as having agency of their own. The final two chapters in this part turn to the question of how psychological approaches to religion and childhood contributed to these dominant understandings of childhood as a developmental phrase, oriented toward the future attainment of adult rationality. Goldman's chapter provides an example of how psychologists during the 1960s conceptualized the religious and spiritual development of children, while Carrette provides a critical overview of different psychological approaches to understanding religion and childhood.

References

Ariès, Philippe (1962), *Centuries of Childhood*, translated by Robert Baldick, New York: Random House.

Dawkins, Richard (2006), *The God Delusion*, New York: Bantam Books.

Hsiung, Ping-chen (2005), *A Tender Voyage: Children and Childhood in Late Imperial China*, Stanford: Stanford University Press.

Kincaid, James (1998), *Erotic Innocence: The Culture of Child Molesting*, Durham, NC: Duke University Press.

Scourfield, Jonathan, Gilliat-Ray, Sophie, Khan, Asma, and Otri, Sameh (2013), *Muslim Childhood: Religious Nurture in a European Context*, Oxford: Oxford University Press.

Wells, Karen (2015), *Childhood in a Global Perspective*, second edition, Cambridge: Polity Press.

1

From Infancy to Childhood

Augustine of Hippo (397–398)

The reflections of the Christian theologian Augustine of Hippo (354–430) on childhood have had a significant influence on Western Christian understandings of children's natures as essentially sinful. In his Confessions, *as he tried to understand his own nature in childhood, Augustine presented children as revealing an innate human sinfulness and jealousy, and rejected notions of childhood innocence. In this excerpt, he describes infancy and childhood as different stages of life, with childhood emerging with the acquisition of language.*

Afterwards I began to smile; first in sleep, then waking: for so it was told me of myself, and I believed it; for we see the like in other infants, though of myself I remember it not. Thus, little by little, I became conscious where I was; and to have a wish to express my wishes to those who could content them, and I could not; for the wishes were within me, and they without; nor could they by any sense of theirs enter within my spirit. So I flung about at random limbs and voice, making the few signs I could, and such as I could, like, though in truth very little like, what I wished. And when I was not presently obeyed (my wishes being hurtful or unintelligible), then I was indignant with my elders for not submitting to me, with those owing me no service, for not serving me; and avenged myself on them by tears. Such have I learnt infants to be from observing them; and that I was myself such, they, all unconscious, have shown me better than my nurses who knew it …

Who reminds me of the sins of my infancy? For in Your sight none is pure from sin, not even the infant whose life is but a day upon the earth. Who reminds me? Does not each little infant, in whom I see what of myself I remember not? What then was my sin? Was it that I hung upon the breast and cried? For should I now so do for food suitable to my age, justly should I be laughed at and reproved. What I then did was worthy reproof; but since I could not understand reproof, custom and reason forbade me to be reproved. For those habits, when grown, we root out and cast away. Now no man, though he prunes, wittingly casts away what is good. Or was it then good, even for a while, to cry for what, if given, would hurt? Bitterly to resent, that persons free, and its own elders, yea, the very authors of its birth, served it not? That many besides, wiser than it, obeyed not the not nod of its good pleasure? To do its best to strike and hurt, because commands were not obeyed, which had been obeyed to its hurt? The weakness then of infant limbs, not its will, is its innocence. Myself have seen and known even a baby envious; it could not speak, yet it turned pale and looked bitterly on its foster-brother. Who knows not this? Mothers and nurses tell You that they allay these things by I know not what remedies. Is that too innocence, when the fountain of milk is flowing in rich abundance, not to ensure one to share it, though in extremest need, and whose very life as yet depends thereon? We bear gently with all this, not as being no or slight evils, but because they will disappear as years increase; for, though tolerated now, the very same tempers are utterly intolerable when found in riper years …

Passing hence from infancy, I came to boyhood, or rather it came to me, displacing infancy. Nor did that depart – (for whither went it?) – and yet it was no more. For I was no longer a speechless infant, but a speaking boy. This I remember; and have since observed how I learned to speak. It was not that my elders taught me words (as, soon after, other learning) in any set method; but I, longing by cries and broken accents and various motions of my limbs to express my thoughts, that so I might have my will, and yet unable to express all I willed, or to whom I willed, did myself, by the understanding which You, my God, gave me, practise the sounds in my memory. When they named anything, and as they spoke turned towards it, I saw and remembered that they called what they would point out by the name they uttered. And that they meant this thing and no other was plain from the motion of their body, the natural language, as it were, of all nations, expressed by the countenance, glances of the eye, gestures of the limbs, and tones of the voice, indicating the affections of the mind, as it pursues, possesses, rejects or shuns. And thus by constantly hearing words, as they occurred in various sentences, I collected gradually for what they stood, and having broken in my mouth to these signs, I thereby gave utterance to my will. Thus I exchanged with those about me these current signs of our wills, and so launched deeper into the stormy intercourse of human life, yet depending on parental authority and the beck of elders.

O God, my God, what miseries and mockeries did I now experience when obedience to my teachers was proposed to me, as proper in a boy, in order that in this world I might prosper, and excel in tongue-science, which should serve to the 'praise of men' and to deceitful riches. Next I was put to school to get learning, in which I (poor wretch) knew not what use there was; and yet, if idle in learning, I was beaten. For this was judged right by our forefathers; and many, passing the same course before us, framed for us weary paths, through which we were fain to pass; multiplying toil and grief upon the sons of Adam. But Lord, we found that men called upon You, and we learnt from them to think of You (according to our powers) as of some great One, who, though hidden from our senses, could hear and help us. For so I began, as a boy, to pray to You, my aid and refuge; and broke the fetters of my tongue to call on You, praying You, though small, yet with no small earnestness, that I might not be beaten at school. And when You heard me not (not thereby giving me over to folly), my elders, yea my very parents, who yet wished me no ill, mocked my stripes, my then great and grievous ill.

2

A Religion for Children

Phillipe Ariès (1962)

*A*riès's Centuries of Childhood, *originally published in French in 1960, begins from the provocative argument that the category of childhood as a distinct phase of life did not exist before the Middle Ages. While many historians have subsequently criticized these claims as going beyond the available evidence, his work has been of enormous significance in the study of childhood, encouraging attention to the ways in which childhood is socially constructed as a historical process. This excerpt considers the development of a 'religion for children', and how this was related to emerging ideas of childhood innocence.*

The moral and pedagogic literature of the seventeenth century frequently quotes those passages in the Gospel in which Jesus speaks of children. In *L'Honneste garçon*: 'Since the Lord of Lords summons little children to Him, I cannot see that any of His subjects has the right to reject them.' The prayer which Jacqueline Pascal inserts in her regulations for the children of Port-Royal paraphrases expressions used by Christ: 'Be like new-born children…unless you become like children, you will not enter the Kingdom of Heaven.' And the end of this prayer recalls an episode in the Gospel which was to obtain new favour in the seventeenth century: 'Lord, permit us to be among those children whom you summon to you, whom you allow to approach you, and from whose mouths you draw your praises'.

The scene in question, in which Jesus asks little children to be allowed to come to Him, was not absolutely unknown in the iconography of former times; we have already had occasion to mention that Ottonian miniature in which children are depicted as adults, but on a smaller scale, gathered around Christ. Pictures of this scene are also to be found in the moralizing Bibles of the thirteenth century, but they are fairly rare and are treated as commonplace illustrations, devoid of any real fervour or significance. On the other hand, from the end of the sixteenth century on, this scene recurs frequently, especially in engraving, and it is obvious that it corresponds to a new and special form of devotion. This can be seen from a study of a fine print by Stradan, whose engravings, as is well known, were an inspiration to the artists of his time. The subject is given by the caption: '*Jesus parvulis oblatis imposuit manus et benedixit eis*'. Jesus is seated. A woman is presenting her children – naked *putti* – to Him; other women and children are waiting their turn. It is significant that the child here is accompanied by his mother; in the medieval pictures, which were in closer conformity to the letter of the text, a text which did not appeal sufficiently to the artists' imagination to prompt them to embellish it, the children were alone with Christ. Here the child is not separated from his family: an indication of the fresh importance assumed by the family in the general sensibility. A Dutch painting of 1620 shows the same scene. Christ is squatting on the ground, in the middle of a crowd of children pressing round Him. Some are in their mothers' arms. Others, who are naked, are playing or fighting (the theme of *putti* fighting was a common one at the time), or crying and shouting. The bigger children are more reserved, and have their hands folded in prayer. Christ's expression is smiling and attentive: that mixture of tenderness and amusements which grown-ups of modern times, and the nineteenth century in particular, assume when speaking to children. He is holding one hand above one of the little heads, and is raising the other to bless another child running towards Him. This scene became extremely popular: the engraving was probably given to children as a devotional picture, just as they would later be given First Communion pictures …

Henceforth there was a religion for children, and one new devotion was to all intents and purposes reserved for them: that of the guardian angel. 'I would add', we read in *L'Honneste garçon*, 'that although all men are accompanied by these blessed spirits which minister to them in order to help make themselves fit to receive the inheritance of salvation, it seems that Jesus Christ granted only to children the privilege of having guardian angels. It is not that we do not share this privilege; but manhood derives it from childhood.' For their part, he explains, the angels prefer the 'suppleness' of children to the 'rebellious character of men'. And Fleury in his 1686 treatise on studies maintains that 'the Gospel forbids us to despise children for the excellent reason that they have blessed angels to guard them. The soul guided by an angel, and depicted in the form of a child or a youth, became a familiar feature of religious iconography in the sixteenth and seventeenth centuries. There are countless examples, for instance a Dominiquin in which a little child in a flared skirt is being defended by an angel, a rather effeminate boy of thirteen or fourteen, against the Devil, a middle-aged man who is lying in wait for him. The angel is holding his shield between the child and the middle-aged man, providing an unexpected illustration of this sentence in *L'Honneste garçon*: 'God possesses the first age, but the Devil possesses in many persons the best parts of old age as well as of the age which the Apostle calls accomplished …'

The theme of the guardian angel and the soul-child was used in the decoration of baptismal fonts. I have come across an example in a baroque church in the south of

Germany, the church of the Cross at Donauwörth. The lid of the font is surmounted by a globe with the serpent wound around it. On the globe, the angel, a somewhat effeminate young man, is guiding the soul-child. This depiction is not simply a symbolic representation of the soul in the traditional form of the child (incidentally, it is a curiously medieval idea to use the child as the symbol of the soul), but an illustration of a devotion peculiar to childhood and derived from the sacrament of the baptism: the guardian angel.

The period of the sixteenth and seventeenth centuries was also that of the child paragons.... Guillaume Ruffin... used to visit the sick and he gave alms to the poor. In 1674 he had nearly finished his first year in the philosophy class (there were two at that time) when he fell ill. The Virgin appeared to him twice. He was told in advance of the date of his death, 'the day of the feast of my good Mother', the feast of the Assumption. While reading this text I found myself unable to banish a recollection of my own childhood, in a Jesuit college where some of the boys undertook a campaign for the canonisation of a little pupil who had died some years before in the odour of sanctity, at least so his family maintained. It was quite easy to attain sanctity in a short schoolboy's life, and that without any exceptional prodigies or particular precocity: on the contrary, by means of the mere application of the childish virtues, by the mere preservation of one's initial innocence ...

Apart from the lives of little saints, schoolchildren were given as subjects of edification accounts of the childhood years of full-grown saints – or else of their remorse at their remorse at their misspent youth. In the annals of the Jesuit college of Aix for 1634 we read: 'Our young people did not fail to have their sermons twice a week in Lent. It was Père de Barry, the Rector, who addressed the aforesaid exhortations to them, taking as his subject the heroic deeds of the saints in their youth'. The previous Lent, in 1633, 'he had taken as his subject St Augustine's regrets for his youth'.

In the Middle Ages there were no religious festivals of childhood, apart from the great seasonal festivals which were often pagan rather than Christian. From the fifteenth century on, as we have already seen, artists depicted certain episodes, such as the Presentation of the Virgin and particularly the Circumcision, in the midst of a throng of children, many more than were usually present in the crowds of the Middle Ages or the Renaissance. But these Old Testament festivals, for all that they had become festivals of childhood in religious iconography, could no longer play this role in religious life, especially in the refined religious life of seventeenth-century France. First Communion gradually became the great religious festival of childhood, which it still is today, even where the Christian observance is no longer practised regularly. First Communion has also taken the place of the old folklore festivals. Perhaps it owes its continuation, in spite of the de-Christianisation of the modern world, to the fact that it is the child's individual festival, celebrated collectively in church but more particularly in private, within the family: the most collective festivals are those which have disappeared most rapidly.

The increasingly solemn celebration of First Communion was due in the first place to the greater attention given, especially at Port-Royal, to the necessary conditions for the proper reception of the Eucharist. It seems probable that previously children took communion without any special preparation, much as they started going to Mass, and probably quite early in life, judging by the general precocity of manners and the mingling of children and adults in everyday life. Jacqueline Pascal, in her regulations for the children of Port-Royal, stresses the necessity of carefully gauging the moral and spiritual capacity of children before allowing them to take communion, and of preparing them for it a long time ahead: 'Young children, and especially those who are mischievous, frivolous or wedded to some considerable defect, must not be allowed to take communion. They must be made to wait until God has effected some change in them, and it is wise to wait a long time, a year for instance or at least six months, to see if their actions are followed up. For I have never regretted making children wait: on the contrary, this has always served to advance in virtue those who were already well disposed and to bring about a recognition of their unreadiness in those who were not. *One cannot take too many precautions where First Communion is concerned*: for often all the rest depend on that first one ...'.

By the eighteenth century, First Communion had become an organised ceremony in the convents and colleges. Colonel Gérard recalls for us in his memoirs his recollections of a difficult First Communion. He was born in 1766, one of six children in a poor family. Left an orphan, he worked as a servant from the age of ten until the curate of his parish, taking an interest in him, sent him to the Abbey of Saint-Avit where he had become assistant chaplain. The first chaplain was a Jesuit who took a dislike to the boy. He must have been about fifteen when he was 'admitted' – this was the current expression – to the First Communion: '*It had been decided that I should make my First Communion at the same time as several boarders*. The day before, I was playing with the farm dog when M. de N., the Jesuit, happened to pass by. "Have you forgotten", he exclaimed, "that it is tomorrow you are due to receive Our Lord's Body and Blood?" The Abbess sent for me and informed me that I would not be taking part in the *ceremony* next day ... Three months after doing penance ... I made my First Communion. After my second, I was ordered to take communion every Sunday and Holy Day.'

First Communion had become the ceremony which it has remained. As early as the middle of the eighteenth century it was customary to commemorate the occasion with an inscription on a devotional picture. At Versailles in 1931 an engraving was exhibited showing St Francis of Assisi. On the back was written: 'To certify the First Communion made by François Bernard, on April 26th, 1767, Low Sunday, in the parish of Saint-Sèbastien of Marly, Barail, parish priest of Saint-Sèbastien.' This was a certificate inspired by the official documents of the Catholic Church ...

All that remained to be done was to add to the solemnity of the occasion by prescribing a special costume, and this was done in the nineteenth century.

The First Communion ceremony was the most visible manifestation of the idea of childhood between the seventeenth and the late nineteenth century: it celebrated at one and the same time the two contradictory aspects of that idea, the innocence of childhood on the one hand and on the other its rational appreciation of the sacred mysteries.

3

Erotic Innocence

James Kincaid (1998)

James Kincaid is Professor Emeritus of English at the University of Southern California and Adjunct Professor of English at University of Pittsburgh. His work focuses on the eroticization on children in contemporary America. In this excerpt, Kincaid asks his readers what they themselves, and modern society, stand to gain by defining children as innocent and pure on the one hand and savage and sinful on the other. As much as adults might gain, he argues, children are quite certainly losing. In tracing out this argument, Kincaid attends to depictions of children in popular culture and casual conversations.

Our culture has enthusiastically sexualized the child while denying just as enthusiastically that it was doing any such thing. We have become so engaged with tales of childhood eroticism (molestation, incest, abduction, pornography) that we have come to take for granted the irrepressible allure of children. We allow so much power to the child's sexual appeal that we no longer question whether adults are drawn to children. We may be skeptical of the therapy industry and its ability to manufacture so easily people with recovered memories of childhood molestation; we may regard the attacks on the clergy with suspicion; we may think many of the day-care centre trials are witch hunts; we may have doubts about rings of Satan-worshipping child killers; we may know that very few children are abducted by trench-coated strangers – but one thing remains indubitable, and we are all taught to know and believe it: adults by the millions find children so enticing that they will risk anything to have sex with them. What makes such an idea plausible?

It would hardly be an overstatement to say that the subject of the child's sexuality and erotic appeal, along with our evasion of what we have done by bestowing those gifts, now structures our culture. It would not be an overstatement to say the way we are handling the subject is ripping apart our young people. I do not deny that we are also talking sincerely about detection and danger. We worry about the poor, hurt children. But we also worry about maintaining the particular erotic vision of children that is putting them at risk in the first place.

Is the erotic appeal of children really such a mystery to us? Is paedophilia really so 'unspeakable'? Why is it that the figures given for abused children keep climbing without arousing suspicion? Why is it that we now include in our pool of likely child molesters not just misfit middle-aged males but distinguished grandparents, gymnastic coaches, priests, women, teenagers, and, most recently, children themselves. While we maintain the monstrous and perverse criminality of the act, we also move to make it universal and inevitable.

We have made children lovable, which is fine, but we have also failed to make it clear to ourselves just what that means. What is our loving to consist of? And what is it in the child that we are to desire to love? What are the forms of the desirable in our culture?

We see children as, among other things, sweet, innocent, vacant, smooth-skinned, spontaneous, and mischievous. We construct the desirable as, among other things, sweet, innocent, vacant, smooth-skinned, spontaneous, and mischievous. There's more to how we see the child, and more to how we construct what is sexually desirable – but not much more. To the extent that we learn to see 'the child' and 'the erotic' as coincident, we are in trouble. So are the children.

How did we get ourselves into such a fix? One way to put it is that the development of the modern child and modern ideas on sexuality grew up over the last two centuries hand-in-hand, and they have remained close friends.

The Romantic idealisation of the child – 'Mighty Prophet, Seer Blessed!' – was meant as a poetic figure, a metaphor, but it soon developed a quite literal, material base. For the Romantic poets, the child packaged a whole host of qualities that could be made into a poetics and a politics: the child was everything the sophisticated adult was not. The child was gifted with spontaneity, imaginative quickness, and a closeness to God; but that's as far as its positive attributes went. More prominent were the negatives, the things not there. The child was figured as *free of* adult corruptions; *not yet burdened with* the weight of responsibility, mortality, and sexuality; *liberated from* 'the light of common day'.

This new thing, the modern child, was deployed as a political and philosophical agent, a weapon to assault what had been taken virtues: adulthood, sophistication, rational moderation, judicious adjustment to the ways of the world. The child was used to deny these virtues, to eliminate them and substitute in their place a set of inversions: innocence, purity, emptiness. Childhood, to a large extent, came to be in our culture a coordinate set of *have nots*, of negations: the child was the one who *did not have*. Its liberty was a negative attribute, however much prized, as was its innocence and purity. What is purity, anyhow? …

As for innocence: at one point a theological trope, in the nineteenth century it became more and more firmly attached to this world and to this world's sexuality. It was, further, a characteristic that outran any simple physical manifestation: innocence became a fulcrum for the post-Romantic ambiguous construction of sexuality and sexual behavior. On the one hand, innocence was valued deeply and guarded by criminal statutes (albeit often bendable ones); on the other hand, innocence was a consumer product, an article to possess, as a promise to the righteous and the reward to the dutiful. It came to you in heaven or in marriage, a prize. We were trained to adore and covet it, to preserve and despoil it, to speak of it in hushed tones and in bawdy songs.

Freud (or the usual way he is read and allowed to operate) did little to disrupt this historical pattern. In sexualising the infant and then making sexuality merely 'latent' in the slightly older child, Freud, by his now-you-see-it-now-you-don't, smoothed the way for our contemporary crisis. By conceiving of infancy in terms of stark sexual drives, Freud put the essential connection so directly as almost to threaten it: If we posit openly that children are activated by sexual energy, the evasive screens necessary for eroticizing them disappear; that is, it is necessary that they be 'innocent and pure' if they are to be alluring and also give adults the sentimental stories of denial and projection we find indispensable. But Freud carefully protected our main story by driving under cover the sexuality he had just implanted, thereby giving us the cake without calories: the child is both sexual and pure. Freud upset no apple-carts; he provided a useful and dangerous way of telling one story and living another. The latent child, empty of the sexuality by which he had earlier been defined, is haunted by an absence, by an amputation that may seem to leave the child incomplete, unnatural.

4

The Hindu Tradition and Childhood: An Overview

Eleanor Nesbitt

*E*leanor Nesbitt is Professor Emeritus in the Centre for Education Studies at the University of Warwick, UK. She is a specialist in the religious socialization of children of Christian, Hindu, and Sikh backgrounds. In this chapter, she introduces some key themes in the study of the Hindu tradition and childhood.

Introduction

Hindu children have been part of my life since 1974 when I set off to teach in a school in North India. Since then I have carried out fieldwork among Hindu families and young people, and—as a result of my marriage to a Hindu—I am part of Hindu family and community life. My research focused especially on ways in which Hindu children and young people are nurtured in their family's cultural and religious tradition, the changes that are underway and the many aspects of their individual identity formation (Jackson and Nesbitt 1993; Nesbitt 2010). This included the impact of religious education in school in alerting children to the fact that they were Hindu (Jackson and Nesbitt 1993: 162). Just by asking a child about his or her religion we affect the way that the child feels about it. In general, young Hindus feel enthusiastic about being Hindu (Jackson and Nesbitt 1993: 32). To quote one Gujarati girl: "It's nice. I enjoy going to *mandir* [temple] and praying and I just like being one."

This chapter introduces pointers to exploring childhood(s) in a faith community that stretches back several millennia and which currently numbers over one billion individuals, with India alone being home to over 966 million Hindus according to the 2011 census. Hindus are ethnically, culturally, and linguistically very diverse. So, information about the experience of some young Hindus must not be generalized to all young Hindus and we all need to be receptive to individual life stories rather than stereotyping millions of people on the basis of a little knowledge.

Diversity and commonality

To take just one example of ethnic diversity, children in Tamil Nadu will be celebrating Pongal in January on the day when Punjabi parents of newborn sons are celebrating Lohri, carrying the infant around a winter bonfire for protection from harm. This diversity is further compounded by a family's current location: young Punjabi and Gujarati Hindus living in Toronto or Harrow will experience childhood differently from their cousins in Amritsar (Punjab) and Ahmedabad (Gujarat) respectively. Of course, socioeconomic standing is a major factor in determining the sort of childhood that people have and Hindus are no exception—children's experience in India's poorest families differs markedly from the experience of their wealthiest contemporaries.

Hindu society, the context for Hindus' childhoods, is woven from strands of many types. Among these are not only socioeconomic status and ethnicity but also *sampradaya*. *Sampradaya*s are the spiritual groupings, many of which originated centuries ago, with which families identify. They provide a framework and focus for their devotional activity and for their lives more generally. A child may be brought up as a strict vegetarian, as exhorted by, say, the Swaminarayan and Pushtimargi *sampradaya*s (whose followers are from Gujarat) or the International Society for Krishna Consciousness (ISKCON) (with its international following) (see Nesbitt 2010: 21–34 for a discussion of the complex relationship between being Hindu and valuing the principle of vegetarianism). Also, children will hear and learn *sampradaya*-specific prayers, in some cases—especially in the diaspora—because of attending supplementary classes organized by a *sampradaya*.

Despite the diversity, there are many commonalities and "family likenesses" between different Hindu communities' experience and world views. One young British Hindu Punjabi man related a discussion in Manchester with two fellow Hindu students—a Gujarati from Kenya and an "Indian Malaysian" (Nesbitt 2010: 113). They discovered that although they had grown up in ethnically and geographically distinct communities, each of them would start answering an examination paper by writing a small *om* (ancient Hindu symbol) on the paper. This symbol had been a part of their experience as young Hindus.

Young Hindus, whatever their background, tend to be encouraged by their families to do as well as they can academically and to aim for well-paid employment—preferably in professions such as law and medicine. They are also brought up in the expectation of marrying appropriately and having children. Children living outside India gain a sense of connection with India, even if the family has its strongest links with Nepal, Mauritius, Trinidad, Surinam, Kenya or some other place of Hindu settlement.

Hindu children's experience combines continuity with antiquity (like the *om* sign which the Hindu students mentioned) and continual change. The sacred syllable *om* figures as far back as the Vedas (whose oral form probably long predates the written scripture, which itself may be over 2000 years old). At the same time, Hindu children and their parents (like families in other communities) are also likely to turn to the Internet, often as their first port of call, for answers to their questions about their religious heritage. The Internet and the rise in social media constitute the biggest transformation of Hindu childhood in the twenty-first century.

Hindus sometimes refer to their religious tradition as *sanatana dharma*, the eternal *dharma*. *Dharma* denotes cosmic right ordering and so includes an individual's duty, that is the behavior appropriate to one's gender, age, and social position. According to the key concept of *varnashrama-dharma*, everyone's *dharma* depends upon two key factors: hereditary status (*varna*) and stage of life (*ashrama*). So, caste still plays its part: in rural India at least children's prospects are deeply affected by it and, everywhere, Hindu families' self-identification as members of, say, the goldsmith or tailor *jati* (caste) or the *kshatriya* or *brahman varna* (class) persists, regardless of members' actual occupations.

Turning from *varna* to *ashrama*, individuals progress from one stage of life— each with its own expectations—to another: after infancy a child's role is to learn in preparation for adult life, whereas the *grihasthi* (householder) stage means bearing family responsibilities, including bringing up one's children, and the final two stages mark gradual withdrawal from family duties.

Gender

In all societies, a boy's childhood differs from a girl's, and this is evident (see below) in some continuing gender-specific traditional roles in Hindu *samskaras* (life-cycle rites) and festivals. However, gender has much graver implications: India's 2011 census shows that the Hindu population's gender ratio is 931 females: 1000 males, a ratio lower than that in all other faith communities apart from Sikhs. This reflects a continuing "son preference" resulting in some families opting for the ante-natal sex selection that is possible with medical technology: many female foetuses are aborted. When women do give birth to a daughter (especially if they have already borne daughters but not sons), in many cases they are not congratulated and the birth is not celebrated (e.g. by distributing traditional sweets) as a boy's would be. Daughters begin to realize the preferential treatment shown to boys. Gender expectations and son preference, though challenged by feminists and by modernity itself, do have a basis in Hindu scripture as well as an economic rationale. Thus, a parent's funeral *samskara* and afterlife prospects require a son's performance of certain rites. Traditionally, too, care for aging parents falls to the son and daughter-in-law. This perception persists despite a changing social reality. A daughter's birth still brings anxieties for many parents about finding a dowry for her and about ensuring that family honor is not compromised by her actual or perceived conduct after puberty. This website (accessed on September 11, 2015) lists reasons why a son is preferred and a daughter is often unwanted: http://www.hinduwebsite.com/hinduism/h_children.asp

Nonetheless, in many Hindu families, in India as well as outside, daughters too are cherished and, indeed, welcomed as incarnating the goddess. They are encouraged—like their brothers—to study, while generally being brought up knowing that they will be gifted at marriage to another family, unlike their brothers. Also, changes are underway in many families. Among both Sikhs and Hindus in Punjab there are moves to celebrate Lohri for a daughter's birth as well as a son's. Moreover, reformers use dance and song to spread the message that female foeticide must end.

While processes of social change are accelerating, some child-related practices and attitudes can nevertheless best be understood if one explores centuries-old approaches to children and their socialization. Accordingly, this chapter acknowledges the significance of sacred myth for Hindu childhood and suggests the usefulness of the concept of *samskara* (see below) in appreciating what it means to grow up in a Hindu family.

Sacred myth

Krishna is one of the best-loved Hindu deities, an incarnation of God Vishnu. The name "Bal Krishna" means infant Krishna. Searching online for images of Bal Krishna, you will see a chubby, smiling baby or young child, often with a bluish skin. In popular stories (drawn from the *Srimad Bhagavatam*), Krishna plays pranks, stealing freshly churned butter and breaking the earthenware pots that women are carrying. For centuries, Hindus' love for the divine Krishna as a mischievous little boy has translated into a relaxed and indulgent attitude to infants.

However, initial indulgence gives way to elders' stricter control of adolescents and young adults (Kakar 1981). Despite recent decades of social change, in many Hindu families, parental influence on young people's career path and marriage partner continues to be stronger than in most non-Hindu societies. Moreover, most children and young people are (in common with non-Hindus of South Asian background) brought up in contact with many more relatives and often with relatively little regard for personal space and private time.

Samskara: Early influences and involvement in life-cycle rites

Samskara is a word in Hindus' ancient language Sanskrit (in Hindi and related modern languages it is *sanskar*). Its root meaning is polishing or refining. Through *samskara*s a new human being is conditioned and processed or, we might say, humanized or civilized. Children are thought to be born with *samskaras*, or deep impressions, from previous births and are then deeply influenced (conditioned) by their families' attitudes and expectations. They are also "processed" by a succession of *samskaras*, in the further sense of rites of passage, such as *namakarana* (naming).

A baby's name is often chosen by a senior relative, in many cases after consulting an astrologer. Traditionally, the astrologer draws up the child's birth chart and indicates the appropriate initial letter for his or her forename. Many parents also search online for names. Of recent decades some children have been given non-Hindu names such as Nikita or Aisha, but many Hindu names are traditional, conveying good qualities, the name of a god or goddess, or a flower or other natural phenomenon. Examples for girls include: Jyoti (light), Asha (hope), Pushpa (flower). Boys' names include: Ravi (sun), Vijay (victory), Deepak (lamp).

Another *samskara* is *chūḍakarana* (*mundan* in Hindi), a ceremonial head-shaving (almost solely) for boys. In this rite an infant boy's hitherto uncut hair is completely shaved off. The infant is bathed and dressed in a new outfit and his hair may be disposed of in an Indian river—not simply thrown away.

Many Hindus' earliest memories of a *samskara* in the sense of a life-cycle rite are of marriages, which involve customary rituals over several days. As preparations intensify and excited anticipation mounts, children observe and internalize assumptions about expected roles within the family—such as the part played by the bride's maternal uncle. For instance, before a Punjabi Hindu wedding, the bride's *mama* (mother's brother) gives her the red and white marriage bangles (*churian*). Similarly, at a Punjabi boy's *mundan*, it is his mother's brother who provides his outfit. Children absorb the necessity of getting married, the importance of gift exchange at the time of a marriage, and the expected emotions—for example, the jubilation of the bridegroom's friends and relatives on their way to the wedding and the weeping of the bride's family when she leaves with her husband after the wedding. Photographs and videos of weddings reinforce this informal learning. Moreover, a child may have a specific part to play—a boy as *sarbala* (the companion to the bridegroom in Punjabi weddings) and—in Gujarati families—a designated girl, carrying on her head a decorated pot holding a coconut, may welcome the bridegroom into the wedding hall.

Funerals, another *samskara*, may nowadays also involve children: at the funeral of a grandparent it has become usual, in the UK at least, for grandchildren to read a poem or some other tribute during the crematorium service. They are aware of the period of mourning during which acquaintances come to sit in the house and talk about the deceased.

Textbooks often mention another life-cycle rite, the *upanayana*, also referred to as the *yagnopavita* (sacred thread ceremony). However, it is only boys—and, unlike the *mundan* ceremony, only a small minority of boys at that—who are invested with the *janeu* (sacred thread). For centuries, boys of Brahmin (priestly) caste have had a *yagnopavita*, marking the start of their years as a student, learning from a spiritual master, a guru. Nowadays, this *samskara* persists more strongly in some communities (e.g. high-caste Gujaratis) than others (e.g. Punjabis). The rite no longer marks any such real-life transition, happening as it does at any point between the ages of about seven and fifteen. It involves more than investiture with the thread—the young man's head may be shaved and he is, later in the rite, equipped with a staff and small bundle, as if for a journey.

As the vast majority of Hindus live in India, and most of those living elsewhere are of Indian ancestry, published accounts of Hindu life-cycle rites generally focus on Indian communities, rather than Nepalese or Balinese Hindus. For many Nepalese Hindu girls, an important rite is marriage to the sun god. In Bali (Indonesia), where about 90 percent of the population are Hindus, a new-born baby is believed to represent the soul of an ancestor and is regarded as god for the first forty-two days. Balinese Hindu customs perpetuate pre-Hindu indigenous rites, which include ceremonial filing of a young person's six upper canines, marking the start of puberty.

Calendar

Just as the lifespan is punctuated by *samskara*s, so the year runs to a rhythm of annual festivals. While all Hindus of Indic background, whatever their family's level of observance, are likely to be aware of Divali and possibly other major festivals, some young Hindus will also be aware of weekly and monthly patterns of devotional observance and one or other relative's—usually a woman's—associated abstinence from certain foods.

Divali, on the darkest night of the lunar month of Kartik (approximately October), is fun because of its fireworks. It marks a climax in a period of celebrations: approximately twenty-eight days earlier, Hindus from Gujarat commence a succession of nine evenings (Norta) of exuberant all-generation circle dancing (*garba*) and stick dancing (*ras dandian*). Girls wear new outfits. In North Indian states such as Uttar Pradesh, these are the days of Navaratri, when the story of Rama and Sita, the Ramlila, is enacted, with children playing the part of monkeys in the army of Rama's devoted supporter, the monkey-headed god, Hanuman. In Bengal, this is the period of Durga Puja, when children see ever more spectacular temporary shrines to the goddess erected in the streets. Bengalis celebrate Durga's victory over evil, in the shape of the buffalo-headed demon. Norta/ Navaratri reaches a climax on day ten (Dassehra/ Vijayadashami) when gigantic, fire-work-stuffed effigies of the demon king, Ravana, explode in public celebrations in northern states such as Uttar Pradesh and Punjab, and in north Indian Hindu communities outside India. Holi, a spring festival, is an opportunity for children to throw themselves into the excitement of dousing everyone around in brilliant colors and being plastered in colors by others. The anarchic free for all is underpinned with stories—especially of the evil queen Holika and her virtuous nephew, Prahlad.

Festivals are not only integral to the transmission of traditional dances, stories, and emotion to a new generation but children also learn about relationship roles. For example, the August festival of Raksha Bandhan (on the full moon day of the lunar month of Shravan) reinforces the relationship between brothers and sisters and illustrates the understanding that cousins are on a par with siblings. The festival is celebrated by Hindus, of all ages, all over India and overseas. Sisters tie a decorative thread (a *rakhi*) around their brothers' and cousin-brothers' right wrists (or post it to them). In return, brothers give their sisters a gift.

Concepts and values

Of course generalizing about Hindu families is risky but it is fair to say that respect—for parents and other elders, for teachers, guests, the gods and for family tradition—is a key value that children learn. Respect is expressed in Indian languages in ways which do not translate easily into English. Even in diaspora communities some Hindu children learn to greet older relatives by stooping as if to touch their feet. They also learn to refer to aunts and uncles and other relatives by terms such as (in Hindi) "*mamaji*" (respected brother of my mother) or "*chachaji*" (respected younger brother of my father).

Related to respect is hospitality: whether expected or unexpected, guests are to be welcomed and honored. This is verbalized as "The guest is God." Children are involved in serving guests with plenty of tasty food. Like all children young Hindus pick up customary norms concerning food, like lifting food to the mouth with one's right hand, not putting a licked spoon into food that others will be eating, and receiving *prashad* (blessed food) with cupped hands.

Worship

Prashad is food such as fruit, nuts, sweets that has been offered in worship and is then shared among worshippers. *Puja* (the worship of God) is an honoring of God as one's guest who is offered water, clothing, and food. Domestic shrines and public temples are both called *mandir* and children are nurtured into the appropriate postures and gestures. For instance, infants in many families are encouraged to press both palms together, with fingers pointing upwards, while saying "*Jay*," as a greeting to the deities in the shrine. An adult may hold an infant up so that he or she can ring the bell hanging in the temple. Children become used to the sounds of worship, the scent of incense sticks, the taste of the sweets, nuts and fruits that the temple priest distributes. They may discover the calming, reassuring effect of reciting sacred words while fingering a *mala* (rosary), bead by bead.

Supplementary classes

Most Hindus learn their family roles and any ritual observances by copying older relatives of the same sex. Especially in the diaspora, some parents are concerned that their children are far more influenced by the dominant non-Hindu culture and so they send them to supplementary classes, usually at the weekend. Classes are run under the auspices of temples and *sampradayas* (Pocock 1976; Brear 1992) and teach the basics of an Indian language (Tamil, Hindi, or Gujarati, for example) and/or how to recite Sanskrit prayers and perform drama (e.g. on a festival theme). Some children attend classes in classical Indian dance forms such as *bharat natyam*, or learn to play the harmonium (the usual accompaniment for devotional singing), the tabla (hand drums), or (less frequently) the sitar.

Continuity and change

To an unprecedented extent, the Internet is mediating aspects of Hindu tradition to children and their parents. Once elders were the family's resource of information and guidance (on worship, traditional stories, festival foods, and so on). Now children access answers to their questions online. Whether or not parents nurture their children in an explicitly devotional environment, Hindus grow up identifying as Hindu and associating this identity with considerable religious freedom and a respect for other communities while seeking to respect their elders' expectations of them.

In conclusion

Hindu childhood is a vast subject: this chapter has pointed to some aspects of children's experience (such as life-cycle rites and values) and emphasized the need for alert sensitivity to both diversity and change. What is indisputable is the importance of increasing our understanding of the experience of children in the world's third-largest faith community.

References

Brear, D. (1992), "Transmission of a Swaminarayan Hindu Sacred Scripture in the British East Midlands," in R.B. Williams (ed.), *A Sacred Thread: Modern Transmission of Hindu Tradition in India and Abroad*, 209–227, Chambersburg, PA: Anima.

Jackson, R. and Nesbitt, E. (1993), *Hindu Children in Britain*, Stoke on Trent: Trentham.

Kakar, Sudhir (1981), *The Inner World: A Psychoanalytic Study of Childhood and Society in India*, second edition, Delhi: Oxford University Press.

Nesbitt, Eleanor (2010), *Intercultural Education: Ethnographic and Religious Approaches*, Eastbourne: Sussex Academic Press.

Pocock, David (1976), "Preservation of the Religious Life: Hindu Immigrants in England," *Contributions to Indian Sociology* 10 (2): 341–365.

5

Children as Stepping Stones, Children as Heroes: Contrasting Two Buddhist Narratives

Vanessa R. Sasson

Vanessa Sasson is Professor of Religious Studies at Marianopolis College, Canada. She is also a Research Fellow at the University of the Free State, South Africa. Trained as a scholar of comparative religion, her work has increasingly focused on Buddhist studies, with an emphasis on hagiography, gender, and children and childhoods. She is the editor of Little Buddhas: Children and Childhoods in Buddhist Texts and Traditions *(Oxford University Press, 2013). In this chapter, she compares two different constructions of childhood within Buddhist textual traditions.*

One of the most famous narratives in the Buddhist tradition is, without a doubt, the Vessantara Jātaka.[1] It is dramatic, heart-wrenching, and layered with meaning. Children in Buddhist countries the world over grow up learning this story in school, sermons are regularly given on it, there are musicals inspired by it and ritual readings performed of it, and there is a wealth of literature and art associated with it—from the earliest period of Buddhist art to the present day. The Vessantara Jātaka is, in other words, a staple in Buddhist story-telling.

Less well known is the Mūgapakkha Jātaka. It belongs to the same collection of stories in the Pali Canon and carries significant weight in the literature as a result, but compared to the Vessantara Jātaka, it is marginal. Both of these texts present their readers with dramatic stories in which children play pivotal roles. The roles the children play are, moreover, extremes of each other. As we shall see, in the Vessantara Jātaka, children can be read as obstacles on the path to awakening, whereas in the Mūgapakkha Jātaka, a child displays extraordinary agency that turns an entire kingdom on its head. By comparing these two texts, I hope to challenge simplistic assumptions where children in Buddhist literature are concerned and demonstrate that things are always more complicated than they might at first seem.

Vessantara Jātaka

The Vessantara Jātaka belongs to the Jātaka collection of the Pali Canon. It closes the Buddha's past life stories, being the 547th. It is also the longest Jātaka in the collection, running almost 60 pages in the English edition of the Pali Text Society and 786 verses (the shortest Jātaka, by contrast, is just a few lines long).

The Vessantara Jātaka is understood as being the Buddha's penultimate life; after this one, he is reborn as the Prince Siddhattha and eventually becomes the Buddha, never to be reborn again. Its status in the collection of past life stories is therefore particularly significant in this regard. He is as close to human perfection as it is possible to be. One would therefore not be wrong in expecting a great deal from his character in this narrative.

The Vessantara Jātaka is special for another reason: in the vast collection of more than 500 stories, the final ten stories have come to be interpreted as perfection narratives. It is not clear when this interpretation of the final ten tales developed,[2] but regardless, it is clear that for much of Buddhist history, the final ten stories have been understood to reflect the final steps of perfection taken by the Bodhisatta (the Buddha in a past life) before his last rebirth. Each of these ten stories is understood to reflect a different perfected virtue. In the case of the Vessantara Jātaka, the perfected virtue is associated with generosity.

The skeleton of the story goes as follows: A long time ago, a queen gives birth to a son (who we quickly learn is the Bodhisatta). The newborn, soon to be named Vessantara, emerges from the womb with his hand stretched out and asks, "Mother, I wish to make some gift; is there anything?" (485). The mother does not seem concerned with the fact that her newborn is speaking. She finds a purse of gold and drops it into his tiny hand. When Vessantara is about four years old, the king gives his son a necklace worth a hundred thousand pieces of money. Vessantara gives the necklace away to his nurses and refuses to take it back when they try to return it (486). When the nurses explain the situation to the king, he consents that what was given "was well given" and he has another necklace made for his son. This too Vessantara gives away.

By the time he is eight years old, the young Vessantara realizes that his desire to give is so powerful, he would pluck out his own eyes if someone asked for them, and he would cut off all of his flesh should someone need it. The depth of this realization causes the universe to quake and tremble, for this is not a passing whim.

The story moves forward. The prince marries and has children, and he travels throughout his kingdom on a special white elephant that his subjects believe brings their kingdom good luck. Unfortunately, a neighboring kingdom is struggling with drought and although the king has spent seven days praying for rain, nothing comes of it. He realizes, however, that wherever Vessantara travels with his magical white elephant, rain falls behind him. He sends his brahmins to ask for the elephant as a gift. Since Prince Vessantara is incapable of refusing a request, he gives the precious, rain-delivering magical elephant to the neighboring community. His subjects watch in dismay as their greatest treasure is taken away.

It is now clear that a prince with so much at his disposal cannot be so generous. Vessantara is risking the safety of his kingdom by practicing generosity to such an inordinate degree, so the king decides to expel his son from the kingdom before things go too far. The prince accepts his banishment and soon he, his wife and two children prepare for their new life of exile in the forest. He distributes a tremendous gift "of the seven hundreds" before his departure (giving seven hundred slaves, seven hundred pieces of gold, etc.). He then climbs into the chariot with his family and distributes even more alms to the passersby as he drives away.

Vessantara and his wife Maddī create a new life for themselves in the forest. She spends her days in the woods gathering fruit while he remains behind with the children and life settles into a pleasant routine. They have nothing to give and thus have nothing to lose. Or so it seems.

One day, an elderly man named Jūjaka comes looking for Vessantara in the forest. Jūjaka's wife refuses to fetch water from the well (there is a back-story here, but for the purposes of this chapter, I will move forward), so he is looking for slaves to do the work in her place. Jūjaka hopes that Vessantara's children might be able to play that part.

The night before Jūjaka reaches Vessantara's hut, Maddī has a terrifying nightmare in which a man grabs her by the hair, drags her out of her hut, throws her down on the ground and amidst her shrieks, tears out her two eyes, cuts off her two arms, cuts open her chest, tears out her heart dripping with blood and carries it away (540). When she wakes up, she runs to her husband and asks him to interpret the nightmare. As soon as Vessantara hears it, he understands the meaning and thinks to himself, "the perfection of my giving … is to be fulfilled: this day comes a suitor to ask for my children" (540).

The story does not pause at this point, but keeps moving as though the Bodhisatta's reaction is perfectly normal. He realizes, as a result of her dream, that a man will come to ask for his children and his response is enthusiastic, because he will finally be able to perfect his generosity. He understands, moreover, that this act will be experienced by his wife as torture—as though her eyes are torn out and her heart is ripped from her body. Instead of telling her the truth, he lies to her and suggests that she is probably just suffering from indigestion.

Jūjaka arrives the next day while Maddī is out collecting fruits, and just as predicted, he asks for the children. Vessantara "is delighted" (543) to hear the request and accepts. Presumably, readers are horrified by the Bodhisatta's behavior, and perhaps some of the authors felt the same way, for right after agreeing to give his children away, the story changes tone and the Bodhisatta (somewhat paradoxically) suggests a series of possible alternative arrangements (such as going to see his father the king and asking for riches that will provide Jūjaka with all the resources he could possibly need instead), but Jūjaka adamantly refuses. Jūjaka wants the children and he wants to take them away immediately.

The authors turn their attention to the children, who are described as having been listening to the exchange. When they realize that they are about to be taken away, they run and hide in a lotus pond, but when they hear their father calling, they cannot ignore him and they come out.

The text then provides a heart-wrenching struggle during which the father insists on giving his children away and the children beg him to reconsider. They clutch at his legs and plead with desperation, but Vessantara is determined to perfect his generosity. He explains to his own children, "don't you know that I have gladly given you away? So do that my desire may attain fulfillment" (546). He then goes so far as to put a price on each child's head, determining what each one would be worth should either of them try to buy their freedom back from Jūjaka, "as one puts a price on cattle" (546). The segment concludes with the following description:

> When the Great Being had made the gift, he was joyful, thinking how good a gift he had made, as he stood looking upon the children. And Jūjaka went into the jungle, and bit off a creeper and with it he bound the boy's right hand to the girl's left, and drove them away beating them with the ends of the creeper. (548)

The story does not end here. It continues for many more pages, providing a very complex emotional struggle in which the Bodhisatta navigates through a wide range of complicated emotions. He feels rage, regret, joy, and sadness as he works his way through the experience of having given his children away. In the end, however, he decides not to take back what was given and rejoices in the perfection of his virtue. I will not go into further detail,[3] but will stop here and reflect on the role the children are playing in this narrative.

According to the Pali rendition, Vessantara was determined to give all that he had from the moment of his birth. He came out of the womb asking to give and he spent the rest of his life continuing in that direction. He gave and gave, and everyone around him gladly took. Indeed, I would argue that his generosity is contrasted by the greed of those benefiting from his generosity. When he departs for the forest with his family in a chariot, for example, some of his subjects (who missed the distribution of alms) race after him to ask for his chariot. Vessantara, of course, agrees and the family makes the rest of their long and arduous journey on foot. Vessantara's generosity is thus set against the backdrop of ordinary human greed. This contrast is most obvious when it comes to Jūjaka, who insists on taking the children and refuses any alternative arrangement Vessantara proposes.

There is no question that the children function as stepping stones on the Bodhisatta's path toward perfection. He needs to give them away if generosity is to be perfected, and the narrative is explicit about the fact that giving them is not done easily. Although the Bodhisatta is initially described as joyful when he realizes that the time has come for him to do this, after the giving has happened he is tortured and even considers racing after Jūjaka to kill him. The Bodhisatta did not struggle when he gave away his chariot or made the gift of the seven-hundreds, but when his children are given, he sinks into turmoil.

What makes this story so compelling, however, is that the children are not voiceless, static characters. On the contrary, their feelings are acknowledged by the writers. They cry and plead and are afraid. They are also loyal and well-behaved children, for they cannot resist their father's command. Although they are bartered like cattle—a parallel the authors willingly draw—the children in this text are represented in the fullness of their child-like human selves.

The father is likewise fully developed as a character. Although he pursues his goal relentlessly, he is not cold and calculating about it. He loves his children and is tormented by the loss (or the giving) of them. It is to his legs that they cling. The authors of the Vessantara Jātaka see the humanity of all of these characters and they make them all visible to us. It is precisely in the seeing of the characters—particularly the children—that the tragedy unveils itself. The children are bartered like cattle, but the emotions elicited as a result prove that the children are not cattle at all.

Mūgapakkha Jātaka

I would like to contrast this very famous story with another Jātaka that belongs to the same collection. It is the first of the ten perfection narratives (the Vessantara was the last of the ten), and it is known as the Mūgapakkha Jātaka. It is not as well-known as the Vessantara Jātaka, despite its place in the textual collection. It presents children in a very different light. Whereas children are used as stepping stones in the Vessantara Jātaka, in the Mūgapakkha Jātaka, it is the child who has all the power.

The story begins with a king who cannot conceive a child of his own. He has 16,000 wives, but none of them produces an heir until finally the queen becomes pregnant. Upon hearing the good news, "paternal affection arose [in the king], and piercing through his skin reached to the marrow in his bones; joy sprang up within him and his heart became refreshed" (2). The king's ministers are likewise thrilled, for as they explain, "we were before helpless, now we have help, we have obtained a lord" (2). The attachment to this child is profound for a number of reasons, only some of which are political.

When the child is born, he is named Temiya and he is brought to the astrologers who do not foresee any obstacles on his path to the throne. But one day, something happens when he is just one month old. Temiya is brought to his father. The king embraces his son, places him on his hip and plays with him while he attends to matters of state. Four robbers await their sentence. The king declares that one will be sentenced "to receive a thousand strokes from whips barbed with thorns, another to be imprisoned in chains, a third to be smitten with a spear, the fourth to be impaled" (3).

Little Temiya, who is (I am compelled to repeat) only one month old, hears these sentences and is terrified because he realizes that his father will go to hell as a result of the sentences he has pronounced. The next day, after he has been placed on a soft bed underneath an umbrella, the infant reflects on the previous day's events and remembers that in his past life, he too was a king, but as a result of his actions, he spent the next 80,000 years in a hell realm. He realizes that if he becomes king again, he will be forced to act ruthlessly and that this will once again land him in hell. His tiny body becomes pale and faded "like a lotus crushed by the hand" (4) and he wonders if there is a way to escape the path that lies ahead.

At that moment, the goddess that resided in the umbrella above him appears and proposes the following: "pretend to be a cripple, although not really one; though not deaf, pretend to be deaf, and though not dumb, pretend to be dumb. Putting on these characteristics, shew [sic] no sign of intelligence" (4).

The infant (who is just one month old) realizes the brilliance of this strategy, and from that moment onwards, freezes himself into absolute stillness. He pretends to be deaf, dumb, and crippled, despite the fact that until then, he functioned like a normal one-month-old baby. He maintains this discipline for the next sixteen years.

His family and entourage of nurses are confused by his behavior. Other babies in the kingdom would cry for milk, but no matter how long the nurses waited, Temiya would not cry for milk. Even if they withheld milk for an entire day, he "stung by fear of hell, even though thirsty, would not cry for milk" (5).

The nurses study his body and can not understand why he has stopped responding. His hands and feet look normal; he does not have the body of a cripple. His jaw is not the jaw of someone incapable of speaking, but no matter how thoroughly they examine him, they cannot find an explanation for his sudden change in behavior.

Eventually, when he is older, they decide to try to force him into responding. They invite the other children of the kingdom and bring out a feast of sweet foods. The other children pounce on the delicacies, but Temiya did not move, reminding himself "eat the cakes and dainties if you wish for hell" (5).

They try with other foods, but nothing evokes a response. Then they try to frighten him. They make a house with many doors and cover it with palm leaves and they place him, along with the other children, in the middle of it and then they set the house on fire. The other children run out of it shrieking, but Temiya says to himself that "it was better than the torture in hell and remained motionless as if perfectly apathetic, and when the fire came near him they took him away" (6).

Over and over again, people try to awaken the child into some form of reaction, but nothing stirs him. They try to entertain him, they blow conch shells into his ears, try to startle him with sudden bursts of light in the darkness, and abandon him to his own filth, but never once does the boy react. He remains perfectly silent and perfectly still for sixteen years.

Eventually, the king has had enough and decides to put an end to this useless boy who will obviously never take the throne. The queen begs for a reprieve, but he only grants her seven days, during which time she begs her son to respond: "O my child, prince Temiya, on thy account for sixteen years I have wept and taken no sleep and my eyes are parched up, and my heart is pierced with sorrow; I know that thou art not really a cripple or deaf and dumb;—do not make me utterly destitute" (10).

But even his mother's plea does not break Temiya's resolve and after seven days the king orders his son's execution. A chariot driver is commissioned to drive him to a charnel ground, dig a hole, throw him into it, and break his head with a shovel.

The chariot driver does as he is commanded. When he reaches the charnel ground, he turns his back on Temiya and begins to dig. At that moment, as Temiya faces execution, he finally moves. He stretches his body out for the first time since he was one month old and tests his strength by lifting the chariot and flinging it over his head. The chariot driver turns around and is shocked by what he sees. Temiya then explains to him that he was never crippled, deaf, or dumb, but that he was acting the part so as to be liberated from the role of kingship that would otherwise have been required of him. Now that he has been condemned, he is finally free to live the life of an ascetic.

The chariot driver is so impressed with Temiya that he vows to follow him into a life of asceticism. When the king and queen learn what has happened, they are so impressed by the Bodhisatta's resolve that they choose to join him in his ascetic practice and they renounce the throne. The subjects, upon hearing this news, eventually do the same too, following the royal couple into the religious life. By the end of the story, nothing remains of that once thriving kingdom.

The contrast

These two Jātaka stories present children playing very different roles. In the Vessantara Jātaka, as we have seen, children are likened to cattle. Prices are placed on their heads. They are slaves exchanged for the perfection of generosity. The children cry and plead, but the father insists on moving forward with the transaction. He even asks his children to accept the trade, asking them to do as he wills so that he might "attain fulfillment." It is a heart-breaking narrative focused on generosity and yet selfish beyond comprehension.

It is no surprise that Buddhism has been consistently interpreted as having little interest in children when stories such as the Vessantara Jātaka take such a prominent place. Given the popularity and centrality of this epic narrative, combined with the story of the Buddha in his last life abandoning his newborn son so as to pursue his quest for awakening, Buddhism is bound to seem devastatingly anti-family as a result.

But reading the tradition exclusively in this light is limiting. Although the children in the Vessantara Jātaka have little say in the situation, Temiya—as a child—has extraordinary agency and power. In the Mūgapakkha Jātaka, a newborn contemplates, considers, analyzes, and takes action. He has unparalleled determination as he chooses to act crippled, deaf, and dumb for sixteen years in order to achieve his goal. The child in this story is never compared to cattle and there is no price tag on his head. From the perspective of this Jātaka, Buddhism can be interpreted as a tradition that places great value on children and their potential capacities.

One might argue that Temiya is granted such agency in the text because he is not an ordinary child. He is the Buddha in a past life, so his precocious nature is particular to his status in the tradition. To some extent, this may be the case, but one must also consider the fact that Buddhist literature features other children with similar precocious qualities who are not necessarily Buddhas-to-be.[4] The Bodhisatta is not the only character to receive such praise. Indeed, I would argue that Buddhist literature often demonstrates a confidence in children that I have not seen elsewhere. The notion that children are capable of making extraordinary decisions, of pursuing extraordinary paths and of having extraordinary insight, demonstrates a valuing of children that is not sufficiently appreciated.

Even in the case of the Vessantara Jātaka, children are not ignored by the authors. The children are not dismissed as pawns in a greater narrative. The children are fully developed characters with their own agency and strong voices. In the Mūgapakkha Jātaka, the son is loved and cherished. The king is described as feeling the joy of fatherhood in the marrow of his bones. He and his family members do everything in their power to bring Temiya out of his self-imposed stillness. These are not anti-children texts, but on the contrary, Ithey are narratives that brim with love and appreciation. They honor children's potential, recognize their capacities, and record what children have to say.

Notes

1   For an English translation, see Cowell (1990). Shortly after this piece was written, a new translation of the last ten Jātakas came out. Unfortunately, I did not have the opportunity to use it here, but it is worth citing for future reference: Appleton, Naomi and Sarah Shaw, trans. (2015). *The Ten Great Birth Stories of the Buddha: The Mahānipāta of the Jātakatthavaṇṇanā*. 2 volumes. Chiang Mai: Silkworm.

2   For a discussion on this theme, see Appleton (2010), in particular pages 98-103.

3   For one of the most insightful readings of this complex narrative, see Steven Collins' (1998) chapter on the Vessantara Jataka in his book.

4   The most obvious example in this regard is the complex *tulku* phenomenon from the Himalayan tradition. For descriptions of other precocious children in the literature, see Wilson (2013) and Levering (2013).

References

Appleton, Naomi (2010), *Jataka Stories in Theravada Buddhism: Narrating the Boddhisatta Path*, Surrey: Ashgate.

Collins, Steven (1998), *Nirvana and Other Buddhist Felicities*, Cambridge: Cambridge University Press.

Cowell, E.B. (ed.) (1990), *Jataka Stories*, Oxford: Pali Text Society.

Levering, Miriam (2013), "The Precocious Child in Chinese Buddhism," in V.R. Sasson (ed.), *Little Buddhas: Children and Childhoods in Buddhist Texts and Traditions*, New York: Oxford University Press.

Wilson, Liz (2013), "Mother as a Character Coach: Maternal Agency in the Birth of Sīvali," in Liz Wilson (ed.), *Family in Buddhism*, 169–186. New York: SUNY.

6

Children in Contemporary British Evangelicalism

Anna Strhan

Anna Strhan is a Lecturer in Religious Studies at the University of Kent. In this chapter, drawing on ethnographic research conducted for a three-year early career research fellowship, she explores different understandings of childhood in British evangelical Christianity.

Introduction

How do evangelicals in Britain understand the nature and significance of childhood? How does that relate to wider cultural changes shaping perceptions of the personhood and agency of children? And how does this shape their sense of the relation between their faith and wider British society? In this chapter, I address these questions through describing how childhood is being constructed today in two different evangelical churches, and consider how these different positionings of childhood reflect wider differences in how evangelicals respond to processes of individualization. I draw on two eighteen-month periods of ethnographic fieldwork, one conducted with a conservative evangelical church I call 'St John's', and the other with a charismatic evangelical church, which I call 'St George's', both in central London. St John's is a large conservative evangelical church, with a congregation that is predominantly white, affluent, and middle-class, and the church is an influential representative of the conservative evangelical wing of the Church of England. The congregational demographic here is marked by a high proportion of students, graduates in their twenties and early thirties, and married couples and young families with children. St George's has a strong sense of its identity as a charismatic church – this is emphasized more than its being evangelical, for example, on its website. The membership of St George's, like St John's, is young compared with broader age demographics in the Church of England. While the majority of children at St John's are from affluent white families, some of whom often travel some distance to come to the church on Sundays, St George's has a significant proportion of its children from the local area whose families are from East, West, and South African, Afro-Caribbean, and Chinese backgrounds.

Although both churches are Anglican and evangelical, their cultures and their conceptions of the self are, in many respects, markedly different. In *Religion and Modern Society*, Bryan Turner argues that American fundamentalism can be seen as 'a struggle between two conceptions of the self – the Kantian ascetic and disciplined self, and the expressive-affective mobile self. The first is the direct descendent of Protestant asceticism and the second is a distortion of the expressive self of the conversionist sects of the eighteenth and nineteenth centuries' (2011: 81). I do not wish to suggest that either St John's or St George's could or should be seen as fundamentalist (although it is worth noting that this *is* often how conservative evangelicalism is simplistically stereotyped). However, characterizing their respective cultures with broad brush strokes, St John's can be seen as – at least in what they say – privileging the ascetic, disciplined self, who relates to God through knowledge and reason rather than emotion, while St George's emphasizes the expressive-affective self who knows God through effervescent forms of embodied experience and is found in a love relationship with the divine. These two ways of conceiving the self shape their ideals for their work with children.

In what follows, I describe the ideas of childhood that are articulated in how these two different churches seek to form children as Christians. I examine how children respond to these processes, and consider the meanings that childhood has for adults within the churches in relation to their different kinds of engagement with children and the understandings of the relationship between personhood, agency and modernity this opens up.

Evangelical Anglicans and the Democratization of the Family

Unsurprisingly for a church that locates its institutional identity squarely within the history of Reformed Christianity, sermons are constructed as the high point of Sunday services at St John's: as David, the rector, said during one service: 'we come now to the heart of our meeting, the reason why we're here, to hear God speak to us. It is, you might say, the high point, to hear God's Word as it is read to us and explained'. One Sunday during my fieldwork, David preached a sermon about Ephesians 6: 1–9, a passage in which the author writes that children are to obey their parents 'in the Lord', and slaves are exhorted to obey their earthly masters 'with respect and fear, and with sincerity of heart' (NIV). David began by stating that 'marriage is a hot topic and a subject that's increasingly in the public eye', and then said that in Ephesians, Paul states that God's aim is for churches to be 'display cabinets ... of what it looks like to have relationships rightly ordered under the rule of the Lord Jesus Christ ... family life is designed to be part of God's display cabinet', and therefore because of this, it should be something that all members of the church 'have a stake in', whether or not they themselves have children. He situated this emphasis on the sacrality of the family as becoming more widely at odds with wider social norms, stating: 'increasingly in a culture that departs from the teaching of Jesus, one should expect what goes on here on a Sunday morning to be a radical countercultural example, old and young, different backgrounds ... meeting together in rightly ordered relationships and radiating what it looks like to belong to the Lord Jesus Christ.'

David then said that the first principle for family relationships that Paul expresses in this passage is that 'children are to obey their parents', and he expanded: 'Paul has in mind a hierarchy of relationships, where God-given authority in the human family is to be recognized and respected. So God rules, he's delegated his authority to the head of the family. And then the father, and the mother under the headship of the man, are in authority over the children, who are to obey'. He described this hierarchical ordering of familial relationships as a working out of 'the redeemed community, restored order, with the anarchy of Genesis Three now, under Christ, put back in its proper place and overturned'. He continued: 'Parents, we need to realize that whether we warm to the idea or not ..., and whatever our culture might say, God has given us a position of authority within the home. It is ours, by virtue of our parenthood, and children are to recognize it.' He described the term 'obedience' in this passage as stronger than the idea of mere 'submission', and he emphasized that 'children are to obey their parents in everything'. He then gave examples such as this idea of obedience precluding 'things like answering back, or obedience only when threatened or bribed. Parents should not have to explain or discuss or worse still argue through every decision with their children: children are to learn to do as they're told, as part of their Christian witness.'

David situated this emphasis on children's obedience to their parents and male headship as increasingly at odds with a broader cultural turn towards the autonomy of the child. He said, 'I'm aware that this cuts right across the trend of much of our culture, which at its worst extreme has enthroned a child's individual rights above that of their God-given duty to their parents.' He then predicted that this direction towards recognizing the autonomy of children would lead to disorder: 'So we should anticipate ... that as a culture drifts away from Christ and refuses to recognize the rule of God, we would expect over time, ... that anarchy will develop within the home, whether middle-class, celebrity, or low-income. Within the Christian home, under the loving, gracious, gentle rule of Christ, modeled by a sacrificial selfless loving leadership of a father, we should expect to see order restored.' He then stated that it was fathers' responsibility in particular to bring their children up 'in the discipline and instruction of the Lord'. In continuity with the conservative evangelical conceptualization of the centrality of knowledge rather than emotion as marking the sense of relationship with God, David emphasized this upbringing as characterized in terms of teaching and knowledge first and foremost, saying: 'there is an imperative on instruction ... Instruction is literally "to put into the mind", that's what the word means, a putting into the mind.' He expanded on what fathers' duties were in terms of regularly reading the Bible with their children, making space for the routine of 'family prayer time', and 'taking an interest in your children.' He then briefly addressed mothers in the congregation and said: 'Mothers, the best thing you can do for your children is to submit to your husband. How is your child ever going to learn the meaning of the word authority if all the time you are undermining the authority that God has put in the place in the home?'

A recent parenting manual by two conservative evangelical ministers, Tim Chester and Ed Moll, articulated this same emphasis on children's obedience to their parents' authority, drawing out further the theological significance of this: 'Let your child realize they're not the centre of the world. ... Parents are to model God's good, liberating, just rule in the way they bring up their children. We're to show that it is good to live under authority' (Chester and Moll 2009: 13). They situated this model of obedience to parents as enabling an orientation of obedience to God: 'Don't let your child rule the home. If they do, you'll be teaching them that they are king in their lives. They're not. It won't prepare them for wider social interaction. And it won't prepare them to meet the true King' (2009: 13)

David's sermon repeatedly emphasized that this thinking about childhood is countercultural. This is part of a broader narrative articulated by conservative evangelical Anglicans of their becoming increasingly countercultural in a de-Christianizing British social context. As David said in another sermon, 'As this country careers away from its Christian heritage, we will increasingly be considered immoral, bigoted, out-of-date'. David's words suggest an understanding of a secular temporal logic of progression that situates conservative evangelical teachings on issues such as sexuality, family life, and other religions as in particular tension with universalizing modern norms, and this sense of an increasing cultural distance between conservative evangelicals and wider society was something that many members of the church also articulated to me. Issues related to sexuality most frequently command attention in relation to conservative evangelicals' tensions with liberals. Yet it is also possible to see this articulation of how they seek to form children as obedient religious subjects, figuring obedience to the father as a model of obedience to a divine Father, as indexing tensions between their teachings and ideals of progressive freedoms, which also extend to children. In 'Democratization of the Family' (1997), Ulrich Beck describes how Western modernization has increasingly provided children with their own freedoms and rights to lives of their own. In this, he describes this as part of a democratization of family life, and argues that this is bound up with the broader process of individualization. This was also an emphasis in Anthony Giddens' work during the same period, in which Giddens developed a revivified and idealized notion of the family, and located it as a 'basic institution of civil society' (1998: 89). Giddens argued that: 'The family is becoming democratized, in ways which track processes of public democracy; and such democratization suggests how family life might combine individual choice and social solidarity' (1998: 93). This process of democratization in the context of the family 'implies equality, mutual respect, autonomy, decision-making through communication and freedom from violence' (1998: 93). Giddens's conception of the democratization of the family here emphasized, as David Oswell notes, ideals of 'emotional and sexual equality, mutual rights and responsibilities, co-parenting, lifelong parental contracts, negotiated authority over children, obligations of children to parents and social integration' (Oswell 2013: 103).

In his 1984 book, *The Minimal Self*, Christopher Lasch argued that these changing modes of familial relationality were rooted in much longer term social changes that drew authority away from parents, and from the father in particular. He argued that 'a combination of philanthropists, educators, and social reformers' began to side with 'the weaker members of the family against patriarchal authority. They played off the housewife against her husband and tried to make women the arbiters of domestic morality [and] championed the rights of children, condemning the arbitrary power parents allegedly exercised over their offspring and questioning their competence as well' (Lasch 1984: 185). Thus, Lasch argues, 'children gained a certain independence from both parents, not only because other authorities asserted their jurisdiction over childhood but because parents lost confidence in the old rules of child-rearing and hesitated to assert their own claims in the face of professional expertise' (1984: 185–6). At the same time, he argues that the advertising industry in the twentieth century further weakened parental authority through glorifying youth: 'Advertising … insisted that parents owed their children the best of everything while insisting that they had only a rudimentary understanding of children's needs' (1984: 186). While, as Oswell argues, this conceptualization of the democratization of the family is based on a problematic 'transposition of a model of sovereignty from the domain of the state' (2009: 148), there is nevertheless a clear tension to be seen in how conservative evangelicals speak about family life between this broader cultural dynamic moving towards the progressive autonomy of children, and their own more conservative ideals of childhood submission and obedience. This then contributes to members of St John's perceiving their faith as becoming increasingly at odds with broader modern secular norms of subjectivity and personhood as bound up primarily with autonomy and self-determination.

However, despite this narrative of a drift away from a Christian cultural heritage towards an individualizing secular modernity, I found that the everyday concerns of most parents' at St John's about their children did *not* focus on questions of (male) authority, or around the issues such as sex education that conservative organizations like Anglican Mainstream present as a key battleground where childhood is under threat from a hostile increasingly non-religious British society. Indeed, some of the mothers I spoke to at St John's described Anglican Mainstream's campaigns around these issues as perhaps 'unhelpfully scaremongering' and did not want to promote them in the church. The more usual everyday anxieties parents expressed about their children were about such things as which schools to send their children to, how their children were doing at school, and the effects of the media on their children's attention spans or sense of self-worth, for example, criticizing the excessive commodification of childhood and advertising aimed at children, expressed in terms pretty similar to those that might be used by *Guardian*-reading middle-class parents, whether religious or not.

Although I did not hear anyone at St John's challenge the official church teaching on children's obedience and male headship, in practice, observing their interactions and conversations with their children, their children appeared to have relative autonomy within the home. While parents did seek to instill disciplines such as Bible-reading through practices such as shared family reading at meal times or regular bedtime Bible stories and prayer, such practices would not be enforced by the time the children were of secondary school age. Therefore, although members of St John's held to the ideal of paternal authority in what they said about their family relationships, they also described the everyday practicalities of family life in terms of democratic relationships that afforded children autonomy and voice. The question of authority was not necessarily therefore a zero-sum game: children might be able here to both have a voice, to be able to speak for themselves and to have autonomy in the context of their everyday home lives, and it would also be possible for their parents to have authority as well. As Oswell argues, 'to speak as a child is not [necessarily] to usurp the power of the father. Political voice is not a matter of subtraction' (2009: 149).

Yet in the physical space of the church in Sunday services, children occupied a somewhat liminal place in relation to their being seen as capable of having a full Christian personhood or not. Children leave the services for their own Sunday school groups approximately fifteen minutes into the service, and other than in infant baptisms, they were not a visible part of church services. They were therefore always absent for the sermon, 'the high-point of the service', in David's words. This liminality was also seen in infant baptisms. The church practised infant baptisms in Sunday morning services, while also offering adult baptisms for those who preferred this. These baptisms followed the Church of England liturgy and were usually attended by the family's friends and wider family dressed in their smart Sunday best. Yet, they were performed not at the traditional stone font which was located near the entrance of the church, but using a blue ceramic bowl of water on a table in front of the congregation. Ministers would typically introduce the baptism by stating to the congregation that the child would not be a Christian until they had made their own choice to accept Jesus, and emphasize that there was nothing 'magical' happening through the physical act of pouring water on the baby's head.

At the same time, however, the resources and techniques that the church's children's ministers used in their work with children in their Sunday school meetings were very much modeled on their approach to forming adults as religious subjects (Strhan 2015). The children's ministers aimed, for example, for the children to be able to attain knowledge and understanding of theological doctrines such as sacrificial atonement, the resurrection and redemption. The worksheets that they used with children employed a language of 'us' to imply that the children *were* understood to be included as and to understand themselves as Christians in these narratives. The ideals of adult religious subjectivity at St John's located biblical literacy and the desire to from a 'personal relationship with Jesus' as central, and these ideals were to a certain extent also available to middle-class literate children who were able to engage with the techniques of self-formation that the adults also used. This was so, despite the somewhat ambivalent positioning of children's religious personhood in the space of church services.

Charismatic evangelicals, childhood and emotional intimacy

While at St John's an articulated desire for order, coherence, and an ethic of obedience, which was perceived as increasingly countercultural, played an important part in shaping what was said about the contemporary significance of childhood, the story at St George's was very different. In contrast with the emphasis on order and hierarchy at St John's, members and leaders at St George's emphasized messiness and spontaneity as central features of the church's institutional identity. At St John's, desire for a hierarchical order shaped how individuals came to understand 'rightly ordered' relationships both with God and with each other. At St George's, the emphasis was instead primarily on the ideal of 'intimacy' with God, and an experience of him as a friend. This ideal shapes how the church leaders and children's workers seek to form children as religious subjects who experience a sense of intimate friendship with Jesus. Their particular emphasis on messiness and spontaneity was reflected in the fact that Katie, the church's lead children's worker, said she was happy if the Sunday 'kids' church' did not follow her plans for sessions, and interpreted this as a sign that what was happening in the meeting was being 'led by the Holy Spirit', which she said was 'great'.

Children were more visibly prominent in Sunday services at St George's than they were at St John's. At the start of services, children ran around the main space of the church freely (including the stage and pulpit), and this everyday form of energetic exuberance was something the church leadership saw as significant. In prayers before one Sunday service, for example, one of the church leaders prayed, thanking God that the children have freedom in the space of the church, to 'run around, be free, and play, which is becoming increasingly countercultural'. After this time of the children running around before the service gets underway, one of the ministers then came to the stage to welcome the congregation to mark the start of the service, and said that they would then have a time of 'worship for everyone', and invited 'smaller members of the congregation and their parents to come to the front'. The congregation then sang children's songs that reinforced the idea of Jesus as being their 'mate' through lyrics and actions focusing on the idea of Jesus loving them and being their friend, and which stated their love for Jesus. One, for example, was the song 'God's love is Big', by Simon Parry, the lyrics of which state 'God's love is fab and He's my mate / God's love surrounds me everyday / and I love to sing and say / God loves me WEHAY!'[1] The children stood prominently on the stage with the musicians and in the space in front of the stage for the songs with their parents, and danced and performed actions to accompany the music, often including a song that required them to 'zoom zoom zoom around the room room room'. After this, they headed out to their children's groups while the adults remained in the church for the rest of the service. The vicar of St George's at times described this period of 'worship for everyone' as 'the high point' of services, contrasting with David's description of the sermon at St. John's as 'the high point' of services. The contrast in these two 'high points' says much about their distinctiveness as cultures from each other – the messiness and freedom given to the children to run around the church noisily, jumping about on stage while singing and doing actions, in contrast with the serious-minded adults seated at St John's to listen to the minister addressing them for this 'high point' of the service, in the absence of children.

A more democratized notion of church life was institutionalized at St George's than at St John's, as Katie frequently told the children that the church is *their* church and *their* space just as much as the adults', and she asked them about what they would like to be doing in their 'kids' church' meetings, taking up their suggestions and encouraging them to lead activities. The children were involved in forms of hospitality together with the adults, for example, serving croissants and bacon rolls to people before the Sunday service. The children I interviewed said that this made them feel like they were valued within the church.

The leaders at St George's placed a strong emphasis on emotion and feelings, and this affected how they thought about the formation of children, expressing a desire for the 'kids' church' to be a space where the children could express their emotions and form emotional attachments to each other and God. This was also reflected in how they thought about relationships within family life. While male leaders at St John's emphasized parental duties in terms of discipline and instruction, St George's ran parenting classes that used attachment therapy. These stressed the centrality of the child's emotional needs for the parent to provide a secure emotional base for children to explore the world, and aimed to enable the parent 'to understand the emotional world of their child.'

Yet, while the children's workers sought to form the children as subjects with a sense of intimate relationship with Jesus and a desire to share Jesus with others, the children were not passive in this, and they sometimes resisted the worker's desires. In a session focused on encouraging evangelism, for example, one eleven-year-old girl was asked to talk to the other – younger – children about a time she had set up church in her living room for a non-Christian friend. The other children were then asked to write the names of friends they would like to invite to church inside some photocopied picture frames and to decorate the frames. Some of the children did this. One boy, Luke, wrote the name of a friend, and wrote by the side 'Joe would be a good person to invite to this church, because he is unkind to me'. This perhaps suggests he saw the act of inviting a friend to church not in terms of the evangelism his leaders articulate, but as having the potential to change his friend's behavior. Some other children wrote 'no-one', and others wrote nothing at all, and just coloured in their picture frames. When I asked one of them about this, he said, 'most of my friends live in Islington; it would be too far to invite them'. Other children more intentionally subverted the activity, writing things like 'Mr Banana', 'Mr Orange', or 'Mrs Chicken'.

Their actions here could be interpreted in terms of Michel de Certeau's (1984) differentiation between 'strategies' and 'tactics.' These are two different modes of acting, in which 'strategies' are actions linked with and available to those with institutional power, whereas 'tactics' name modes of practice available to those without such power, that seek to reverse and alter its operation. Although there was an emphasis on children's autonomy and freedom at St George's, adults still largely controlled children's resources and time and there remained a construction of two camps, the stronger and the weaker, so that 'the generational division is mapped onto a division between space and time, strategy and tactics, power and resistance' (Oswell 2013: 59). Their drawings can thus be seen as a form of 'tactical interstitial agency,' (2013: 59) in which children were able to improvise and make their own places through the structures and resources that were at hand to them in the 'borderland condition' they inhabit, in which they were 'able to be mobile and grab opportunities the moment they arise' (Honwana, cited in 2013: 59). They might also be interpreted as modeling precisely the expressive freedom that their parents and the church leaders hope for. When I chatted to parents at St George's, they talked about their hopes that their children would be free to explore things and the world for themselves and they said that while they wanted to provide security and stability for them (using the kind of language that the parenting courses use), they were also explicit about not wanting to impose their own views on them.

Conclusion

Beck writes: 'To the extent that the future cannot be understood and mastered from the background, the power of youth grows' (1997: 165). It is perhaps in part because of an increased cultural sense of uncertainty and anxiety about the future that debates about religion and secularity in contemporary Western societies have become particularly intense when these concern children, as children uniquely offer 'embodied access to the inchoate possibilities of [a] culture's future' (Orsi 2005: 78). These temporal orientations towards the future are also to do with how the past and lost potentialities are experienced and constructed in particular ways. For conservative evangelicals at St John's, their particular desires for the formation of children were bound up not only with practical worries and concerns about their children's religious lives as individuals, but also with their perceptions of a Christian culture passing into the chaos of a lost potentiality, as they experienced a sense of becoming 'out of step' with narratives of progressive universalizing freedom. There was also a tinge of a nostalgic construction of a Christian past in how charismatics at St George's talked about their work with children, as they described the toddlers' groups and after school clubs they run, for example, as a means through which local families would 'come back' to church, and such services were also extremely popular with local families who otherwise have no connection with the church, with a very long waiting list for the toddlers group, for example. Playing alongside this narrative of children's work as a mode of evangelism and families 'returning' to church, the language of 'hope' was also a frequent refrain. This was articulated in terms of the church's work with children and families making a practical difference to improve these children's lives, and although they use the secular language of 'service delivery' and 'provision' to describe these, they also use the language of this being a 'gift' to others in 'backstage performances' (Goffman 1959) such as praying with each other about this work. For the adults in both evangelical churches, children can therefore be seen as indexing both the future and the past of their faith. Exploring these articulations of childhood is significant in opening up not only questions about the place and experiences of children within these cultures, but also the different textures of evangelicals' engagements with and sense of place within wider British society, and how ideas of the past and the future are imagined and represented.

Note

1 From https://www.youtube.com/watch?v=-IFSTnFMN0g (accessed 21 April 2016).

References

Beck, Ulrich (1997), 'Democratization of the Family', *Childhood*, 4(2): 151–168.

Chester, Tim and Ed Moll (2009), *Gospel-Centred Family: Becoming the Parents God Wants You to Be*, Epson: The Good Book Company.

De Certeau, Michel (1984), *The Practice of Everyday Life*, trans. Steven Rendell, Berkeley: University of California Press.

Giddens, Anthony (1998), *The Third Way: The Renewal of Social Democracy*. Cambridge: Polity Press.

Goffman, Erving (1959), *The Presentation of Self in Everyday Life*, New York: Anchor Books.

Lasch, Christopher (1984), *The Minimal Self: Psychic Survival in Troubles Times*, New York: W.W. Norton and Company.

Orsi, Robert A. (2005), *Between Heaven and Earth: The Religious Worlds People Make and the Scholars Who Study Them*, Princeton: Princeton University Press.

Oswell, David (2009), 'Infancy and Experience: Voice, Politics and Bare Life', *European Journal of Society Theory*, 12(1): 135–154.

Oswell, David (2013), *The Agency of Children: From Family to Global Human Rights*, Cambridge: Cambridge University Press.

Strhan, Anna (2015), *Aliens and Strangers? The Struggle for Coherence in the Everyday Lives of Evangelicals*, Oxford: Oxford University Press.

Turner, Bryan S. (2011), Religion and Modern Society: Citizenship, Secularisation and the State, Cambridge: Cambridge University Press.

7

The New Age Movement and the Definition of the Child

Beth Singler

*B*eth Singler is a Research Associate at the Faraday Institute for Science and Religion at the University of Cambridge, where she explores popular and religious re-imaginings of science and technology – specifically Artificial Intelligence and robotics. Her recently completed PhD thesis is the first in-depth ethnography of the 'Indigo Children'. In this chapter, she explores the Indigo Children concept within the New Age Movement.

Introduction

'The Coming has gone wrong', Charles W. Leadbeater told his colleagues in the Theosophical Society (Lutyens 1975: 277–279, 315). His protégé, and the Society's chosen 'World Teacher', Jiddu Krishnamurti, had turned against the hierarchical models of Theosophy developed by Leadbeater, and the Society's founder, Madame Blavatsky. Leadbeater had discovered Krishnamurti in the Spring of 1909, finding himself amazed by the fourteen year old boy's aura as he played on the Society's beach in Chennai (Madras). An aura 'without a particle of selfishness in it', he told his colleagues (Lutyens 1975: 22). Some years later, after long term separation from his family, isolation in foreign countries, the difficulties of being regarded as a guru when still a child, and the death of his brother, Krishnamurti came to oppose Leadbeater's and Blavatsky's claims to privileged personal intercession with the spiritually superior beings known as the Mahatmas, or Masters. Instead, he stated that individuals should find their own way to enlightenment. Krishnamurti withdrew from teaching, and

Theosophy, which had been a 'major force in the British Empire', began to decline (Washington 1996: 282)

The Theosophical Society was however highly influential on the later development of what is commonly called the 'New Age movement', and the story of Krishnamurti's election as their promised World Teacher illustrates some of the roots of the New Age movement's contemporary conception of the child. These include a belief in children's greater purity, the perceived nature and importance of their auras, the value of children's insights, and children's perceived role in bringing about the new age. However, while Krishnamurti's 'rebellion' followed his election, in a particular manifestation of New Age thought about the 'child', election is in fact *indicated* by rebellion. This chapter will explore the Indigo Children concept from the New Age Movement to argue that these spiritually evolved, psychic, and sometimes difficult, children represent an attempt at the unification of utopian ideals with real world problems. A unification that previous idealizations of children as messianic did not manage, as in the case of Krishnamurti and Theosophy. This chapter will argue that even when the Indigo Child category is retrospectively applied by adults to themselves this reinforces its role as an attempted resolution of a contemporary crisis in the definition of the child. Drawing on ethnographic research, both on and offline, this chapter will provide a resource grounded in evidence for those wanting to explore the issues around childhood in the New Age Movement.

The New Age Movement

Before describing this understanding of the child in the New Age movement in more depth, we must first address how the New Age movement itself has been characterized in academic discourse. Initially, attention was focused on the millenarian and utopian hopes expressed in the idea that there is going to be a 'new age' of human higher consciousness. However, in the 1990s New Age scholars began to highlight the diminishing use of the term 'new age' in the milieu: a term that had appeared to be so significant in key Theosophical texts, such as Alice Bailey's prophetic writings where it appeared in two hundred and eighty five passages, appeared to be falling out of favour (Sutcliffe 2003: 49). In response to this shift in the emic lexicon, some academics proposed that there had been a 'crisis' in the New Age movement's epistemological frameworks, and they linked this decline to problems of verification. For example, they drew attention to an apparent exile of techniques such as crystal healing to a hinterland of un-falsifiable effects, where they were only put to esoteric uses that 'accommodated and blocked further criticism from those knowledgeable of current science' (Melton 2014: 210). The early millenarian hopes expressed in the writings of Theosophists like Bailey, and embodied in the child Master Krishnamurti, were seen to have been passed over in favour of a New Age defined in terms of the personal experience, the latter espoused in Krishnamurti's adulthood, and described by academics as a 'primal experience of transformation' (Melton, Clark and Kelly 1991: 3). However, I argue that the Indigo Child provides a synthesis of these two conceptions of the New Age movement. It highlights the continuation of millenarian hopes and predictions, scientific rhetoric, and the elevation of the 'pure' child in the milieu still commonly referred to as the New Age movement.

The Indigo Child

The first to describe the Indigo Child was Nancy Ann Tappe, in a 1982 book called *Understanding Your Life Thru Color*. Tappe, who passed away in 2012 during the course of my ethnographic fieldwork among the Indigos,[1] was subsequently followed in exploring the concept by other New Age authors such as Doreen Virtue, James Twyman, and Lee Carroll and Jan Tober. Much like Leadbeater, Tappe described herself as being able to see the auras of others. But instead of finding just one pure boy playing in the sea in India, she wrote about starting to see numerous young children being born with a new 'life colour', or colour of aura. These colours defined their mission on Earth, in this incarnation, and Indigo is commonly related to psychic abilities in this milieu. Other psychics and spirit mediums adopted Tappe's definition of the Indigo Child, adding new iterations such as the Crystal Child, and expounding on a list of characteristics that she had provided; in which the rebelliousness of the Indigo Child indicated their true nature:

- They are very intelligent, and very oriented toward their purpose on earth.
- They come into the world with a feeling of royalty (and often act like it).
- They have a feeling of deserving to be here.
- They often tell the parents 'who they are'.
- They may seem antisocial unless they are with their own kind. If there are no others of like consciousness around them, they often turn inward, feeling like no other human understand them. School can be very difficult for them socially.
- They will not respond to 'guilt' discipline ('Wait till your father gets home and finds out what you did').
- They are not shy in letting you know what they need.
- They often have lots of energy.

(Tappe, in Carroll and Tober 1999, 6–17)

Spirit channellers Lee Carroll and Jan Tober explained that they had written their first book on the Indigo Children as a response to what they saw as a new 'kind of problem for the parent' (Carroll and Tober 1999: xi–xii). It is perhaps not surprising then that the few academic attempts that there have been to theorize this New Age phenomena have picked up on this 'problem', and argued that the Indigo Child concept is a particular response to problematic changes in children. A key example is Sarah

Whedon's 2009 paper, which draws on Bruce Lincoln (1989) to propose that the Indigo Child is a re-inscription of value after good children have turned bad. Specifically, she argues that it is a response to the exponential increase in diagnoses of ADD and ADHD, together with incidents of youth violence, specifically mass shootings exemplified by the tragedy at Columbine High School in Colorado.

Locating the Indigo Child in relation to societal changes is valuable, and certainly connections can be drawn with public conceptions of ADD, ADHD, and autism, as well as with forms of bio-medical conspiricism (Singler 2015). Moreover, Indigo authors directly connected the Indigo Children to the High School shooters, who are 'are Indigo – wise humanity in small bodies, being forced into a paradigm that is absolutely devastating to some of them. If they're full of rage, you can blame the restrictive situations they were put in' (Carroll and Tober 1999: 233). Rebellion against the society that they are here to change is considered a key motivation of the Indigo Children.

However, Whedon does not note the perennialism of re-interpretations of the 'child' within wider society, of which the Indigo Child is merely a more recent development. Chris Jenks proposes that historically the child has been conceived of in either 'Dionysian' or 'Apollonian' terms (Jenks 1996). Apollo is the Greek god of logic and laws, and the parental account of such children presents these 'infants [as] angelic, innocent and untainted by the world which they have recently entered. They have a natural goodness and a clarity of vision that we might "idolize" or even worship as the source of all that is best in human nature' (Jenks 1996: 73). Leadbeater's vision of the pure Krishnamurti playing in the sea might have been informed by such a view, combined with a particular romantic orientalism that the Theosophical Society certainly supported at this time in their relationship with sacred India.[2] Conversely, the Dionysian view of the child has focused on what is seen as an inherent tendency in the child towards evil, historically described in relation to particular theologies. For example, in the seventeenth century evangelical Hannah More (1745–1833), founder in 1789 of the Sunday School Movement, considered children to be 'beings who bring into the world a corrupt nature and evil dispositions' (Robertson 1976: 421).

If we recognize that the category of the child has never been stable, we can understand the Indigo Child as the result of particular reactions to this other being that comes through us but is not us, to paraphrase the poet Kahlil Gibran on children (Gibran: 1923). Or, as Andrew Solomon explains in *Far From the Tree: Parents, Children and the Search for Identity*:

> There is no such thing as reproduction. When two people decide to have a baby, they engage in an act of production, and the widespread use of the word reproduction for this activity, with its implication that two people are but braiding themselves together, is at best a euphemism to comfort prospective parents before they get in over their heads … Parenthood abruptly catapults us into a permanent relationship with a stranger and the more alien the stranger, the stronger the whiff of negativity.
>
> (Solomon 2014: 1)

In exploring the Indigo Child through ethnographic methods, I found myself in fact more often in contact with adults who described themselves, or their children, as Indigo, than with actual children. Those who had adopted the term as adults commonly had a list of 'symptoms' that they could match to the lists of characteristics provided by the Indigo authors. These symptoms included past experiences, and retrospective reassessment of their childhood was extremely common, with references to not fitting in, hating school, or feeling like an 'alien' among their peers (sometimes literally in some interpretations of the Indigo Child concept). We can see this as another example of the instability of the category of the child: the child that we have been also varies in interpretations.

Parents also had a list of characteristics, or problems, for this 'stranger', as Solomon described the 'child'. Through online research they would discover the lists of Indigo traits, and then begin to recognize, or be told, that their child's problems were in fact symptoms of being an Indigo Child. As one mother wrote on *Indigosociety.com*, a popular forum for Indigo Children:

[My son] has always struggled with school, and now his struggle has intensified. He feels that any institutional setting is a form of government control. He thinks he can't survive in this society, because getting a job will mean he is earning money which is part of the government system. He can't imagine a job he would enjoy doing, and would prefer to just help people, and spread love [...] I would greatly appreciate any perspectives and advice you kind souls might be willing to offer.

Being a New Age Parent

In order to understand these parents' developing perceptions of their children as Indigo I also sought to grasp the wider New Age understanding of being a parent. For example, during fieldwork I employed a Free-listing survey at three Mind Body and Soul Fayres in the UK (Peterborough, Kings Lynn, and Crystal Palace in London). Free-listing is a word association method where participants are asked to write their unrestricted responses to key words or terms. It is a qualitative method that attempts to map out the emic 'cultural domain', an 'organized set of words, concepts, or sentences, all on the same level of contrast, that jointly refer to a single conceptual sphere' (Weller and Romney, 1988:9). In this fieldwork I presented four terms to respondents: 'New Age', 'Indigo Child', 'Parenting' and 'Spiritual'.

Across all three fieldsites the most popular response to 'Parenting', was 'love', including variations such as 'unconditional love', 'lovely', 'loving', 'loving our children', and 'mother love'. We might expect love to be intrinsically connected with parenting, based upon the wider contemporary characterization of this relationship. In this specific case we might also note that love is a key modality in the New Age movement, as Wouter Hanegraaff explains, 'There is wide agreement in New Age sources that 'love' is the supreme answer to negativity. We saw that it is the solvent of "fear", and of all the negative patterns associated with it' (Hanegraaff 1996: 297). Returning to Solomon's refutation of our common understanding of reproduction, above, the relationship with the small stranger that is the child also has potential for fear: fear of the unknown, and of the uncontrollable. This fear of the child has long been employed in horror fictions, a prime example being *The Midwich Cuckoos* by John Wyndham (1957), which also expresses the psychic child narrative trope that the Indigo Child can be seen to interplay with historically. Among Indigo Children adherents real world monstrous actions by children were frightening, but they were also explained in terms of the individual's response to corrupting and restrictive society, as in the case of the American highschool shootings that we have seen described by Whedon as a social catalyst for the concept itself (Tappe 1999: 9).

More pertinent to this chapter were the words that indicated the role that the respondents believed parents should take. These included both words related to rules and boundaries, as well as words promoting children's freedom to develop naturally: 'instilling values', 'learning', 'nurture', 'protect', 'provide', 'safety', 'teacher', 'mother', 'guardian', 'father', 'consciously guiding children', 'empowering', 'being examples of what they want to imbue into their children', 'allowing children to be themselves', 'protect', 'lessons for life', 'discipline', and 'listen to your kids'. This delicate balance between rules and freedom is also being worked out through the Indigo literature, as New Age authors attempt to provide guidance to the parents of Indigo Children by recommending particular child-centred pedagogical approaches, especially those espoused by Montessiori and Waldorf (Steiner) Schools. These are schools where 'the holistic curriculum, under the direction of a specially prepared teacher, allows the child to experience the joy of learning, time to enjoy the process and ensure the development of self-esteem, and provides the experiences from which children create their knowledge' (American Montessori School material, Carroll and Tober 1999: 98).

Interestingly, the number of words related to the role of parents was greater than the number related to holistic or spiritual motifs in this milieu. In total, the latter were: 'mystic', 'forever', 'organic', 'teaching a young soul', 'teaching traditions', 'soul', 'beliefs', and 'forever'. The last response may relate to theories around reincarnation in the New Age movement; Courtney Bender notes in her ethnography of New Agers in Cambridge Massachusetts that 'discourse about past lives evoked connections (and marked moral claims) to others lives' (Bender 2010: 139). In the case of the Indigo Children, parents might bear in mind that their rebellious child may have specifically chosen them as their parents in this life (Day and Gale 2004), providing another example and form of election.

The Free-listing results also included negative terms such as 'difficult!', 'stressful', as well as words and phrases that emphasized the work involved in parenting: 'it could be a challenge', 'hard work', '24 hours', 'challenging (physical and mental)', 'hardest job in the world', 'work', 'tough', 'stress'. As I had become a parent during the course of my fieldwork among the Indigo Children I could recognize some of these sentiments, and it is important to highlight the wider experience of parenting in the West, one that is not necessarily coloured by holistic or spiritual ideas, even among New Agers. An experience that has been described in terms of an 'intensification' by sociologists considering parenting in the UK and USA; a feeling that parents are increasingly 'trapped by a series of impossible expectations for their work' as parents (Lofton 2016).

Conclusion

The Indigo Child concept is a way into understanding the New Age apprehension of what a child 'is'. The key aspect is the rewriting of rebellion, difficulties, or natures normally diagnosed medically, into symptoms of this election. Moreover, this particular narrative is reflective of a longer standing troubled encounter between the parent and the child throughout history, as one tries to make sense of the other. That the Indigo Child is presented as a new revelation of truth by New Age authors only serves to highlight that movement's ahistoricism and rhetoric of perennialism. Further, the 'rebellious messiah' may serve contemporary discourses resulting from the current relationship between parent and a precious child, but it is not entirely created by them. Had Krishnamurti rebelled in this era, his model for enlightenment would perhaps have had more affinity with our society than with the Theosophical Society and Leadbeater's more rigid hierarchical frameworks.

Notes

1 Fieldwork was located both online (through observation of websites, blogs, forums, and social media) and offline (through interviews and participant observation at talks, events, and 'Mind Body and Soul Fayres'). This took place roughly between April 2013 and November 2015; 'roughly' as online fieldwork is difficult to bound temporally.

2 We must also note that Leadbeater had been accused of the sexual abuse of young boys, which lead to his resignation from the Society in 1906. He was never convicted and later re-joined the Society in 1908, before meeting Krishnamurti.

References

Bender, C. (2010), *The New Metaphysicals: Spirituality and the American Religious Imagination*, Chicago, USA: The University of Chicago Press.

Carroll, L. and Tober, J. (1999), *The Indigo Children: The New Kids Have Arrived*, Carlsbad, California: Hay House Publishing.

Day, P. and Gale, S. (2004), *Edgar Cayce on the Indigo Children: Understanding Psychic Children*, republished as *Psychic Children: A Sign of Our Expanding Awareness*, Virginia Beach, VA, USA: A.R.E. Press.

Gibran, K. (1923), *The Prophet*, London: W. Heinemann.

Hanegraaff, W.J. (1996), *New Age Religion and Western Culture: Esotericism in the Mirror of Secular Thought* (Studies in the History of Religions), Leiden, New York: E.J. Brill.

Jenks, C. (1996), *Childhood*, London: Routledge.

Lincoln, B. (1989), *Discourse and the Construction of Society: Comparative Studies of Myth, Ritual, and Classification*, Oxford: Oxford University Press.

Lofton, K. (2016), 'Religion and the Authority in American Parenting', in *Journal of the American Academy of Religion*, 2016: 1–36.

Lutyens, M. (1975), *Krishnamurti: The Years of Awakening*, London: J. Murray.

Melton, J.G. (2014), 'Revisionism in the New Age Movement: The Case of Healing With Crystals', in E. Barker (ed.), *Revisionism and Diversification in New Religious Movements*, 201–212, Farnham, UK: Ashgate.

Melton, J.G., Clark, J. and Kelly, A. (1991), *New Age Almanac*, New York: Visible Ink.

Robertson, P. (1976), 'Home as a Nest: Middle Class Childhood in Nineteenth-Century Europe', in L. De Mause (ed.), *The History of Childhood*, 407–431, London: Souvenir Press.

Singler, B. (2015), 'Big, Bad Pharma: New Age Biomedical Conspiracy Narratives and Their Expression in the Concept of the Indigo Child', *Nova Religio*, November 2015: 17–29.

Solomon, A. (2014), *Far From the Tree: Parents, Children and the Search for Identity*, London, UK: Vintage.

Sutcliffe, S. (2003), 'Category Formation and the History of "New Age"', *Culture and Religion: An Interdisciplinary Journal* 4 (1): 5–29.

Tappe, N.A. (1999), 'Introduction to the Indigos', in Carroll, L. and Tober, J. (eds) *The Indigo Children: The New Kids Have Arrived*, Carlsbad, California: Hay House Publishing, 6–18.

Washington, P. (1996), *Madame Blavatsky's Baboon: History of the Mystics, Mediums and Misfits Who Brought Spiritualism to America*, London, UK: Secker & Warburg.

Weller, S. and Romney, A. (1988), *Systematic Data Collection* (Qualitative Research Methods), California, USA: Sage Publications.

Whedon, S. (2009), 'The Wisdom of Indigo Children: An Emphatic Restatement of the Value of American Children', *Nova Religio: The Journal of Alternative and Emergent Religions* 12 (3): 60–76.

Wyndham, J. (1957), *The Midwich Cuckoos*, London, UK: Michael Joseph.

8

Thinking and Its Application to Religion

Ronald Goldman (1964)

*R*onald Goldman's work in the psychology of religion in the 1960s applied Jean Piaget's theories of stages of childhood cognition to thinking about religion and childhood. In Religious Thinking from Childhood to Adolescence (Routledge and Kegan Paul, 1964), he proposed a stage model of the development of religious thinking in childhood in which children grasp progressively more complex and abstract religious ideas at different stages of development. In this excerpt, Goldman discusses Piaget's ideas, and how these relate to children's religious development.

Little application of the processes of thinking has been made to religion. It is evident at once, however, that the crudities and confusions of much that is seen in children's religious concepts can be accounted for in terms of pre-operational limitations, and even by the later limits set by concretisation of data. G. Jahoda (1951) quoting Piaget, remarks that 'thought is very largely sense tied, hence the high level abstractions abounding in religion are well above the mental horizon of the small child'. D. Ainsworth's work (1961) on parables is also appropriate to mention here. Taking a group of six to ten year olds she points out the difficulties caused by parables due to their demand for propositional thinking. 'It is likely', she concludes, 'that until nine or ten years of age, any story heard by a child will probably be interpreted literally, and that the details of the text and incidents of the story will be of paramount importance to the child.' This is interesting corroboration of Lodwick's and Peel's findings. J.G. Kenwrick (1949) using Spearman's concepts of education of relations and correlates as criteria, reports that with eleven and twelve year olds the power to recognise the relevance of an idea to new situations is greatly limited. He discovered a high percentage of failure in understanding the relevance of such widely accepted parables as the Good Samaritan. M. E. Hebron (1957) finds that the majority of 'C' stream pupils in Secondary Modern schools reach their twelfth year of mental age during the third year of their secondary school course. This age is commonly recognised, she reports, through the work of Piaget 'as the level of mental maturity necessary for generalisation with some degree of abstraction'. This must therefore considerably limit their grasp of religious ideas. Much earlier Beiswanger (1930) found that of 63 Old Testament stories recommended for children six to nine years of age very few could be understood and little religious value could be discovered by children before nine years. These and other researchers infer that that the limits are not only the limits of experience, but are limits of process or structured thought. For children before 10 years old or later maturational development has not arrived at the point where the complexity of thinking demanded by religion can be coped with at a satisfactory intellectual level.

Many of those who suggest the possibility of religious developmental stages have little or no experimental data upon which to base their assumptions. Theodor Reik (1955) for example, draws from his psychoanalytic experience and discusses three stages in a child's developing view of prayer. He talks of the stage of magic – 'My will be done'; the stage between magic and religion – 'My will be done, because I am God'; and the stage of religion – 'My will be done, if it be God's will.'

Another is P. E. Johnson (1957) who uses theological terms, borrowed principally from Martin Buber, and posits four stages of religious thinking in terms of relationships. These are the relationships of I-Me, I-It, I-We, and I-Thou. The first is the relationship of the Mind to the Body, and shows the beginnings of self-identity. The second is the relationship of the self to the environment of things. The third relationship is that of self to group life, and finally the relationship matures into the self confronted by God. Johnson envisages the child's spiritual growth as a series of concentric circles or relationships each one encompassing the previous ones.

The only clearly defined series of religious stages based upon sound research appears to be that of E. Harms (1944). Because he felt the intellectual content of religion to be only a small ingredient of religious experience he devised non-verbal methods for exploring religion in the child. Taking a large sample of children from three years up to early adolescence he asked the children to imagine God or the 'the highest being they thought to exist'. He then asked them to draw or paint what they imagined. In criticism of this method we could cite J. E. Johnson (1961) who found six year olds very reticent in drawing pictures of God. The children taken by Harms were further asked to write any comments on the back of the picture, or with younger children, their spoken comments were written for them by the teacher. In the 3–6 year group 800 children's pictures were evaluated; from 7–12 years a similar number; and more than 4,000 were assessed for those above 12 years of age. No attempt was made to evaluate the results in terms of the religious background or the ability of the children and we have no information of the sampling taken other than that they were children from both private and state schools in the United States.

From his analysis Harms claimed to discern a threefold structure of development:

Stage 1. (3–6 years) The fairy tale stage of religion.
Stage 2. (7–12 years) The realistic stage.
Stage 3. (12+ years) The individualistic stage.

The first stage showed greater uniformity than later stages, portraying God as a king, as a 'Daddy of all children', living in a house resting on clouds, or as a cloud in the form of an animal floating in the sky with GOD written upon it. All these pictures are commented on in fairy tale language and as fantasised experience. God is in the same category as dragons and giants, all are regarded as equally valid, and God is only different in so far as he is greater and bigger and held accordingly in greater awe by the child. At the realistic stage, approximating roughly to our Junior age range, Harms claims that the greater emotional stability of these years is reflected in the pictures. The child is more able to adapt himself to institutional religion and he is much more realistic in his portrayal. Symbols appear and God as a father, even with angels or saints, is not shown in mystical fashion but as a human figure in real life. Children in the individualistic stage in adolescence show a wide variety of interpretations from the conventional to the creative and mystical.

In discussing the implication for religious education, Harms suggests that religious teaching for the younger child is too rational in attempting to make him 'understand' God. Adults are often misled by the apparently profound questions asked in infancy and childhood. Rational and instructional ideas should be delayed because 'the entire religious development of the child has a much slower tempo than the development of any other field of his experience'. This, we would assume, is a natural accompaniment of recognising religious experience as secondary and dependent upon the development of many other concepts before religious concepts can develop …

Gesell and Ilg (1946) in their studies of the child from five to ten years summarise interesting reactions. The five year old, they suggest, is innocent of causal and logical relationships and his views are strongly tinged with animisms. Clouds move because God pushes them; when God blows it is windy. At six years Gesell and Ilg report that the child more easily grasps the idea of God as the creator of the world, of animals and of beautiful things. Prayers become important and a certain awe enters into worship. The seven year olds they report as becoming more sceptical and are leaving behind a naïve view of God. Such questions arise as 'Can you see heaven?', 'Does God live in a house?', 'How can God be everywhere, and see everywhere?' These observations, however, like many from the Yale Clinic of Child Development are rather generalised and appear to present too simplified a picture in terms of a given year age group.

There are many related researches in which religion is not the direct subject for investigation, but where views on God are involved. Anthony's (1940) study of the child's discovery of death reflects fear of God 'who has taken away' a pet or parent, and reveals concepts related to the child's slow discovery of the impermanence of life …

Finally, Piaget (1929) yields extremely stimulating material in his investigations into how the child thinks of the natural world. His work on physical causality (1930) is interesting and shows the function of animism in children's religious development. In the former work, however, Piaget examines what he terms 'Artificialism' in the life of the child. Artificialism he defines as the child's tendency to 'regard things as the product of human creation'. By human he means both the idea of God seen as a powerful man, and power of human beings, to whom the child attributes divine qualities.

Piaget suggests that the child explains the origin of the sun and moon, clouds, the sky, storms and rivers, in roughly three stages. First, origins are attributed to human or divine agency, as for example, when the six year old sees the sun originating in God, who lit a fire in the sky with a match. This, Piaget terms 'mythological artificialism', extending roughly from four to seven years of age. Then comes an intermediate stage when a natural explanation is joined with an artificial solution as, for example, when the child suggests the sun and moon are due to the condensation of clouds, but these clouds originate from God or from the smoke from men's houses. This is the stage, about seven to ten years, referred to as 'technical artificialism'. Finally, there is the stage where human and divine activity are seen as having no connection with these origins and they are conceived in purely natural terms, which a child may reach some time after approximately ten years of age. In a concluding chapter on the meaning and origins of child artificialism, Piaget discusses the role of religious education as a stimulant to the child's interest in artificial solutions. He suggests that artificialism is a natural stage in the child's view of the world. 'We have been struck by the fact that the majority of children only bring in God against their will, as it were, and not until they can find nothing else to bring forward. The religious instruction imparted to the children between the ages of four and seven years often appears as something foreign to the child's natural thought.' He concludes, 'The child's real religion, at any rate during the first years, is quite definitely anything but the over-elaborated religion with which he is plied'. If I understand Piaget aright, he suggests that the child naturally sees the origin of things as due to man or God, because both are seen by the child as interchangeable, both being all-powerful and all-knowing. As, however, man's limitations are seen in the increasing fallibility of parents, and his operational thinking begins to grow as he looks at the physical world, artificialist reasons gradually lose their cogency. At last artificialism is renounced altogether as improbable and unsatisfactory. At the same time physical cause and effect is recognised with the beginnings of formal operational thinking. Piaget does not suggest this, but it is a permissible addendum to say that during this final logical-scientific stage the child may return to an artificialism of a higher and refined nature with God posited as a first cause, and as an immanent divine law within a universe acting according to preconceived scientific laws …

Because religion is fundamentally a pattern of belief, and not an intellectual formula, the emotional aspect of religious thinking is of great importance. Whilst theoretically it is quite possible to have well developed concepts about certain subjects in which we disbelieve, in practise it is rarely possible, since negative emotional behaviour interferes with our thinking. The influence of racial prejudice, attitudes to the other sex, beliefs about the authority of the Bible, for example, may lead quite intelligent persons to the most astonishing conclusions, in defiance of a great deal of evidence against their point of view. Further, the amount of intellectual effort we are prepared to expend on a subject will depend upon the level of our interest or motivation in relation to that subject. This is not merely a quantitative matter but also a qualitative one, and may account for the many varied levels of insight on any one subject seen in a single one year age group in school …

The major problem posed by research is that about the time when more abstract thinking becomes possible, and so more religious insights can be seen, many adolescents appear to lose interest in religion or develop more negative attitudes to religion. This appears to be less of a problem with brighter and girl pupils. It is a problem to which we shall return in our concluding chapter.

References

Ainsworth, D. (1961), *A Study of Some Aspects of the Growth of Religious Understanding of Children Aged Between 5 and 11 Years*, Unpublished DipEd dissertation, University of Manchester.

Anthony, S. (1940), *The Child's Discovery of Death*. London: Kegan Paul, Trench and Trubner.

Beiswanger, G.W. (1930), 'The Character Value of the Old Testament Stories.' *University of Iowa Studies in Character* 3 (3): 63f.

Gesell, A., and Ilg, F.L. (1946), *The Child from Five to Ten*, London: Hamish Hamilton.

Harms, E. (1944), 'The Development of Religious Experience in Children.' *American Journal of Sociology* 50 (2): 112–122.

Hebron, M.E. (1957), 'The Research into the Teaching of Religious Knowledge.' *Studies in Education*, University of Hull.

Jahoda, G. (1951), 'Development of Unfavourable Attitudes Towards Religion.' *British Psychology Society Quarterly Bulletin* 2.

Johnson, P.E. (1957), *Personality and Religion*, New York: Abingdon Press.

Johnson, P.E. (1961), 'An Enquiry into Some of the Religious Ideas of 6 Year Old Children', Unpublished DipEd dissertation, University of Birmingham.

Kenwrick, J.G. (1949), *The Training of the Religious Sentiment*, Unpublished PhD thesis, University of London.

Piaget, J. (1929), *The Child's Conception of the World*, London: Routledge and Kegan Paul.

Piaget, J. (1930), *The Child's Conception of Causality*, London: Routledge and Kegan Paul.

Reik, T. (1955), 'From Spell to Prayer.' *Psychoanalysis* 3: 4.

9

Religious Minds: The Psychology of Religion and Childhood

Jeremy Carrette

Jeremy Carrette is Professor of Philosophy, Religion and Culture at the University of Kent, UK. His work examines interdisciplinary aspects of the study of religion focusing on questions of epistemology, power, and the politics of knowledge, and he has published widely on the psychology of religion. In this chapter, he provides a critical overview of psychological attempts to understand religion and childhood.

From its foundations in the late nineteenth century to the developments of neuroscience in the twenty-first century, the field of the psychology of religion has always been concerned with issues of childhood. However, behind this history is a complex set of contested assumptions and confessional biases about the nature of religion and children's minds. It reveals how theoretical modeling in psychology interplays with ideas of religion and biology in every age. The complexity of this interaction reveals how thinking about children is always, in part, related to competing ideas in the domains of philosophy, physiology, and politics (power and organizational structures). As a consequence, how childhood is understood in science is never something we can separate from the philosophical ideas we have of the child and notions of religion. These questions bridge both science and the humanities; a factor that sustains the tensions between the diverse theories of the psychology of religion. As the methods and approaches in psychology have been, and continue to be, so diverse, the truth about childhood in psychology is always related to a belief and commitment to a theory of knowledge about childhood. From the first questionnaire methods and psychoanalytical case histories to more recent cognitive modeling, the ways of knowing are shaped by a commitment to the method. Nonetheless, as the fashions of various psychological theories—the beliefs behind the study of belief—come and go, the shared fascination and questions behind the research remain a continual motivation. How do we know and understand the religious mind of the child? How do children acquire religious knowledge? What are the cognitive processes involved in the child's religious thinking? What is the relationship between human development and the child's religious feelings? What are the biological roots of the child's beliefs? And, how do we map the stages of life in relation to childhood and religion? These questions underline the quest of researchers since the foundations of the psychology of religion.

Foundations of childhood and religion

The earliest studies of childhood in the psychology of religion were shaped by ideals of Protestant religious education in the work of Granville Stanley Hall (1844–1924) and Edwin Starbuck (1866–1947) in the 1880s and 1890s. Their work explored issues within moral education, conversion, and adolescence (Hall 1882, 1904; Starbuck 1899, 1909). There is a mixed response from contemporary psychologists to the legacy of these early studies, ranging from concerns about the blurring of science and religious instruction to a positive recognition of the foundational models for later developmental psychology and the understanding of religion (see Arnett 2006; White 1992). Importantly, what they sought to establish was measurement of childhood and religious ideas with the establishment of some of the first questionnaires for understanding children. They revealed developmental frames in religious understanding and provided recognition that moral education required appreciation of the developmental stages of the child. The focus largely rested on the nature of adolescence as a point of conversion due to the social and physiological change. While these early attempts to measure childhood and religion set the ground for later developmental theories, it was psychoanalysis that dominated the early part of the twentieth century in terms of theories of religion and childhood.

While Sigmund Freud (1856–1939), the founder of psychoanalysis, discussed the child and religion, his work was principally concerned with adults and their memories of childhood. He did nonetheless theorize that religion arose out of childhood wishes and desires. In his 1927 study *The Future of an Illusion*, he developed the German theologian Ludwig Feuerbach's idea—from *The Essence of Christianity* (1841)—that God was a projection of human characteristics, which provided psychological comfort in a uncertain world. It was, as Freud argues, our vulnerability in the world that required a divine protector: "As we already know, the terrifying impression of helplessness in childhood aroused the need for protection—for protection through love—which was provided by the father; and the recognition that this helplessness lasts throughout life made it necessary to cling to the existence of the father, but this time a more powerful one" (Freud 1927: 212). In his later study *Civilization and Its Discontents* (1930), he speculated in response to a suggestion by the French writer Romain Rolland (1866–1944) that religion might be connected with an "oceanic feeling," the "feeling of an indissoluble bond of being one with the external world" (Freud 1927: 252). Freud only briefly entertained the idea before he squashed the possibility. As he asserted: "The origin of the religious attitude can be traced back in clear outlines as far as the feeling of infantile helplessness. There may be something further behind that, but for the present it is wrapped in obscurity" (Freud 1927: 260).

While Freud's theories were largely based on patriarchal ideas of religion and the father, later psychoanalytical theory, following the work of Melanie Klein and Anna Freud (known as Object Relations), explored links with very early (pre-oedipal) development before Freud's infamous Oedipal phase. These ideas were more positive in terms of linking the "oceanic feeling" to early nurturing bonds between mother and child. This early maternal–infant matrix was developed by feminist psychologist of religion Diane Jonte-Pace (1987), who showed how early feelings of unification, nourishment, and renewal could be linked to ideas, images, and emotions in relation to the goddess.

The construction of images in relation to religion and childhood was a key part of object relations in the work of the British pediatrician and psychoanalyst Donald Winnicott (1896–1971). In developing ideas of the relational basis of mother and child, he showed how religious symbols rested on the separation of mother and child in the emergence of transitional objects (such as the teddy bear). In his 1971 work *Playing and Reality*, he explored the transitional object as "the intermediate area of experiencing, to which inner reality and external life both contribute" and linked this to the emergence of religious symbols (Winnicott 1971: 3). Paul Pruyser (1974) developed these ideas extensively in relation to religion and sought to show how fantasy, play, and reality are important parts of religious and cultural development. According to Jim Jones (1997), Winnicott is important in underlying the place of the imagination in the child's religious experience and in refusing the dichotomization of the subjective and objective world in understanding religion.

Another psychological model that expanded and revised Freudian theory was put forward by Erik Erikson in his 1950 study *Childhood and Society* (see Erikson 1950). He constructed a life-cycle model of development from childhood to old age in the creation of eight stages of life. This model saw childhood as determined by a series of competing tensions: basic trust-mistrust (0–1 years), autonomy-shame (1–3 years), initiative-guilt (3–6 years), industry-inferiority (6–12 years), identity-confusion (12–19 years), and going on to map three further phases in adult life: intimacy-isolation (early adulthood), generativity-stagnation (adulthood) and integrity-despair (old age). This model was specifically developed in relation to religious faith by James Fowler (1981) in his work *Stages of Faith*, showing how psychological theories provided resources for pastoral development as much as psychological insight.

Not surprisingly, the assumptions within these theories were subject to critical scrutiny. In her groundbreaking critique of developmental psychology, Carol Gilligan (1982) showed the bias of psychological modeling based on the male subject. Following the same critical perspective, Jane Flax (1990) revealed the hidden social processes behind gendered models within object relations theory. As she clearly stated: "Object relations theory lacks a critical, sustained account of gender formation and its costs to self and culture as a whole" (Flax 1990: 120).

Theories of child development and religion: Jean Piaget and Ronald Goldman

Despite the development of psychoanalytical theories of childhood and religion, it was the work of the Swiss psychologist Jean Piaget (1896–1980) that was to dominate much of the thinking about childhood and religion in the twentieth century, with his stages of childhood cognition. Piaget's work outlined the stages of cognitive understanding in the child from motor and sensory understanding to abstract thinking (Piaget [1923] 2002). Piaget developed three distinct periods of development: the period of sensorimotor activity (birth to 24 months), the period of operational thought (2–11 years)—with pre-operational thinking, intuitive thinking and concrete thinking—and, finally, the period of formal operations (11 years onwards). In the 1960s, Ronald Goldman (1964, 1965) applied Piaget's ideas to religious education through a series of experiments to test children's understanding of religious stories. He sought to demonstrate that Piaget was correct in his assessment by showing how children grasp progressively more complex religious ideas at different developmental stages. Using a series of picture and story tests on a range of children from 6 to 16 years old, Goldman distinguished between different types of religious thinking according to Piaget's stages of development. For example, using the story of Moses and the burning bush (Exodus 3: 1–6) in "The Picture and Story Religious Thinking Test," the responses to the question "why was Moses afraid to look at God?" reflected different stages of thinking: "God had a funny face" (intuitive religious thinking), "Because God had a beard and Moses doesn't like beards" (intermediate religious thinking), "Moses thought God would chase him out of the holy ground, because Moses hadn't taken off his shoes/hadn't been going to church" (concrete "operational" thinking), "Perhaps he had done evil things" (intermediate concrete-abstract religious thinking), and "God is holy and the world is sinful" (abstract religious thinking) (Goldman 1964: 51–67, 247–59). Goldman mapped the implications of these findings to religious education in his later work *Readiness for Religion*, but this practical application was never sufficiently critical. Later commentators have questioned the uncritical use of Piaget, the problems of Goldman's method and the liberal Protestant bias within the material (see Slee 1990; Kay 1996). The persistence of Goldman's work for many decades showed how ideas of childhood and religious thinking were constrained as much by British educational curricula as the limitations of psychological theory. It unraveled within a multicultural and pluralistic context. Goldman's work, nonetheless, was a milestone in attempting to recognize that childhood and religious understanding (as with other forms of understanding) were developmentally linked.

Part of the challenge to Goldman arose from the increasing recognition that Piaget's work was also problematic. In 1978, Margaret Donaldson produced an incisive work entitled *Children's Minds* in which she showed how slight modifications to Piaget's tests revealed different abilities within the child (Donaldson 2006). This can be seen in relation to her discussion of Piaget and a similar test of children's understanding by Martin Hughes, which revealed that children could understand more when given a human interest narrative to the questions rather than being presented with abstract questions, that is the child is given a story in which to understand the ideas. Donaldson revealed that the method and approach of Piaget limited the results. Another critical challenge came from Carol Gilligan (1982), who questioned Piaget and other developmental psychologists from the perspective of a feminist understanding of development, arguing Piaget understood moral development according to the bias of a male rational subject, which needed to be challenged on the basis of a gendered relational understanding of morality. As she argues, there is a need to "expand" development from a feminine voice (1982: 4).

These critical perspectives for understanding developmental psychology were powerfully brought together in Erica Burman's study *Deconstructing Developmental Psychology* (1994). Here Piaget's work was shown to be built on a series of unexamined theoretical presuppositions about the child and knowledge. Burman sought to show how it assumed a "genetic epistemology," that the child is framed as an "abstracted epistemic knower," that there was no account of cultural context, no appreciation of the "colonial and gendered nuances" operating in Piaget's work (1994: 151–62). Burman's study was showing how philosophical and cultural assumptions inform the ideas about the child in psychology and opened a new critical psychology for developmental thinking. This critical understanding of child development led both Robert Coles (1990) and John Morss (1996) to challenge the very notion of "development" in childhood studies. Morss (1996), through a discursive understanding of childhood, wanted to establish recognition of the social and political processes behind ideas of child development. It was, as Morss shows following Ben Bradley, William James who rejected the "genetic fallacy" for understanding ourselves (1996: 151).

Cognitive science and belief

Despite the illuminating perspectives from critical psychology, new developments in cognitive-neuroscience in the later part of the twentieth century and early twenty-first century provided opportunity for new models of childhood and religion, many of which continued to reinstate the same forms of bias and theoretical assumptions. They did, however, underline the importance of evolution for making sense of childhood and belief and sought to correlate the "natural" capacities of cognition with forms of religious thinking. Cognitive and evolutionary psychologists, for example, have attempted to show the innate cognitive capacity of children to develop religious thinking, arguing that the structure of the child's mind is "programmed" for religion. Building on the cognitive work of Piaget, cognitive psychologists sought to establish which forms of cognitive processes were supportive of religious belief.

Following the work of Pascal Boyer (2001) on the cognitive and evolutionary nature of belief, Justin Barrett (2012), in his study *Born Believers*, seeks to underline the naturalness of religious belief in children. He argues that belief in supernatural agents emerges through the child's capacity to distinguish natural objects and agents in the world. According to the evolutionary model of survival, children are sensitive to agency, even if these agencies are not visible. As Barrett suggests, "we naturally develop the ability to think about unseen agents" (2012: 32). These natural capacities may be "overridden by other factors," but belief in God, according to Barrett's work, is part of the "default assumptions" of the mind (2012: 80, 126).

These cognitive theories raise as many questions about the nature of religious language as they do about cognition and evolution (see Bennett and Hacker 2003). The theoretical assumptions hidden within cognitive science about the nature of cognition were too heavily based on computer modeling and neglect of environmental factors, as well as having unsophisticated ideas of religion at the heart of their studies (see Carrette 2007). While important in identifying cognitive capacities emerging in evolutionary processes and child development, the lack of critical thinking about their own methods and assumptions continued to plague their insights and value.

Conclusion: The enigma of childhood, psychology, and religion

This brief critical overview has sought to show that the various psychological attempts to understand religion and childhood reveal the underlying problems that psychologists have in linking theories of mind to theories of religion. What rests at the basis of all these models, as I have stated, is a tension between biology, philosophy, and culture (including the very nature of language). The problem of finding a scientific basis of childhood and religion is the lack of agreement about the nature of the very object of study, the idea of the child, and the idea of religion. As Graham Richards (1996: 131) points out, diverse images of childhood operate in all cultures: "All cultures produce such images to guide and justify child-rearing and educational practices, and in European cultures some have served, often covertly, to underpin Psychological work" (1966: 131). There is, as Richards illustrates, no agreement on images of childhood, only a plurality of theories. And yet, despite the lack of consensus, the question of the child and the nature of religious experience remains vital to our identity as human beings.

References

Arnett, J.J. (2006), "G. Stanley Hall's *Adolescence*: Brilliance and Nonsense," *History of Psychology* 9 (3): 186–197.

Barrett, J. (2012), *Born Believers: The Science of Children's Religious Belief*, New York: Free Press.

Bennett, M.R. and Hacker, P.M.S. (2003), *Philosophical Foundations of Neuroscience*, Oxford: Blackwell.

Boyer, P. (2001), *Religion Explained: The Human Instincts that Fashion Gods, Spirits and Ancestors*, New York: Basic Books.

Burman, E. (1994), *Deconstructing Developmental Psychology*, London: Routledge.

Carrette, J. (2007), *Religion and Critical Psychology: Religious Experience in the Knowledge Economy*, London: Routledge.

Coles, R. (1990), *The Spiritual Life of Children*, Boston, MA: Houghton Mifflin.

Donaldson, M. (2006), *Children's Minds*, London: Harper Perennial.

Erikson, E. (1950), *Childhood and Society*, New York: W.W.Norton & Co.

Fowler, J.W. (1981), *Stages of Faith: The Psychology of Development and the Quest for Meaning*, New York: Harper Collins.

Flax, J. (1990), *Thinking Fragments: Psychoanalysis, Feminism and Postmodernism in the Contemporary West*, Berkeley, CA: University of California Press.

Freud, S. (1927), "The Future of an Illusion," in *Civilization, Society and Religion*, vol. 12, The Pelican Freud Library, London: Penguin, 1985, 183–241.

Gilligan, C. (1982), *In A Different Voice: Psychological Theory and Women's Development*, Cambridge: Harvard University Press.

Goldman, R. (1964), *Religious Thinking from Childhood to Adolescence*, London: Routledge and Kegan Paul.

Goldman, R. (1965), *Readiness for Religion: A Basis for Developmental Religious Education*, London: Routledge and Kegan Paul.

Hall, G.S. (1882), "The Moral and Religious Training of Children," *The Princeton Review* 1: 26–48.

Hall, G.S. (1904), *Adolescence: Its Psychology and Its Relations to Physiology, Anthropology, Sociology, Sex, Crime, Religion, and Education*, 2 vols, New York: D. Appleton.

Jones, J. (1997), "Playing and Believing: The Uses of D.W. Winnicott in the Psychology of Religion," in J.L. Jacobs and D. Capps (eds), *Religion, Society and Psychoanalysis*, Boulder, CO: Westview, 106–126.

Jonte-Pace, D. (1987), "Object Relations Theory, Mothering, and Religion: Towards a Feminist Psychology of Religion," *Horizons* 14 (2): 310–327.

Kay, W.K. (1996), "Bringing Child Psychology to Religious Curricula: The Cautionary Tale of Goldman and Piaget," *Educational Review* 48 (3): 205–216.

Morss, J.R. (1996), *Growing Critical: Alternatives to Developmental Psychology*. London: Routledge.

Piaget, J. [1923] (2002), *The Language and Thought of the Child*, London: Routledge.

Pruyser, P.W. (1974), *Between Belief and Unbelief*, New York: Harper & Row.

Richards, G. (1996), *Putting Psychology in its Place*, London: Routledge.

Slee, N. (1990), "Getting Away from Goldman: Changing Perspectives on the Development of Religious Thinking," *The Modern Churchman* 32 (1): 1–9.

Starbuck, E.D. (1899) *The Psychology of Religion: An Empirical Study of the Growth of Religious Consciousness*. New York: Walter Scott Publishing.

Starbuck, E.D. (1909), "The Child-Mind and Child-Religion," *The Biblical World* 33 (1): 8–22.

White, S.H. (1992), "G. Stanley Hall: From Philosophy to Developmental Psychology," *Developmental Psychology* 28 (1): 25–34.

Winnicott, D. [1971] (2005), *Playing and Reality* London: Routledge.

PART TWO

Changing Ideas and Spaces of Childhood Piety: The Secularization, Resacralization, and Reinvention of Childhood

Introduction

Many Christian and Jewish parents and teachers have been reassured by the biblical passage (Proverbs 22:6): "Train the children in the right way and when they are old they will not stray." The Vedas have stories about how one learns to live a good life in childhood, while the Qur'an has similar surahs on ensuring children pray salat into adulthood. These verses emphasize the importance of childhood as the time during which one builds the foundation that will determine if one remains faithful to one's religion. Moreover, these statements about education, the bible verse in particular, imply that children perform as adults instruct.

Parents, however, frequently find their children wander from the path before them, particularly when that path is littered with tasks to be accomplished, verses to be memorized, and facts to be learned. Presbyterian minister, Jonathan Edwards' jeremiads, such as "A Faithful Narrative of the Surprising Work of God" (1737), offer an early examination of the fallen morality of youth who strayed from the intense convictions of their parents. Here Edwards offered an early public expression of how easily young people can deviate from their parents' teachings for something more interesting, more tempting: "Licentiousness for some years prevailed among the youth of the town; there were many of them very much addicted to night-walking, and frequenting the tavern, and lewd practices, wherein some, by their example, exceedingly corrupted others" (Edwards 1832: 34). In Edwards' example, the young people were set back on the righteous path by an act of God's Grace.

Worried parents and religious leaders, however, often have done more than just rely on God or the gods, as Edwards highlights; they have turned frequently to experts in religious parenting and pedagogy to help them figure out exactly how one "trains" children "in the right way." After all, the future of the tradition hangs in the balance. Edwards, for instance, was concerned not only for the souls of the youths in the taverns but also for what would happen to his tradition if there were no young people left who cared enough to pray the proper prayers and rear their children as God intended. His tradition, the tradition he believed to be the right one according to God, would disappear. This fate seemed both possible and unthinkable to Edwards. Many parents and religious leaders before and since have found the fates of the familial or communal traditions in a similarly precarious position, resting on the choices of the young. Adults cannot control children and adolescents as easily as the verse from Proverbs makes it seem.

Through sermons or prescriptive literature, ministers, priests, imams, and rabbis have been trying to help parents enact the precepts of their sacred texts in their everyday life with their children. Using these prescriptions and participating in religious education, parents learn to act in accordance with their tradition as they assist their children, serving to align the whole family more closely with their community's ideal. The chapters that follow explore the variety of different approaches religious educators have used to attempt to ensure that children will build a foundation that keep them within their faith. As they focus on creating ideal religious childhoods, they also provide insight into how children received and responded to these adult efforts.

Since children can easily reject or ignore adult lessons, religious educators worked to develop forms of religious education that were both engaging and informative. The chapters that follow explore how religious educators and the children they educated sought to form systems of learning that would ensure that each tradition lived on through the next generation.

Four historical excerpts by Richard Baxter, John Locke, Friedrich Froebel, and George Hamilton Archibald ground this part with a broad discussion of (religious) education. Baxter begins the part with his advice to Christian parents on how to educate their children to fulfill their divinely ordained roles as children and as Christian boys and girls. Like Baxter, Locke also understood that there was a clear distinction between children and adults; however, he applied that knowledge to build his own philosophy of education. In this chapter, he describes the role for adults, not as disciplinarians, but as models for children. Children, he argues, need nurture over discipline because they are still developing their rationality. Froebel deepens these distinctions as he applies them to how children learn about God in both formal and informal ways. The piece from George Hamilton Archibald then exemplifies how to put many of Froebel's methods into practice as he uses a child-centered approach to critique major theories about children and about education.

The next three chapters, by Sofia Cavalletti, Jerome Berryman, and John Hull, explore how religious educators expand and delineate various educational models to keep children engaged and committed to their religious tradition. Cavalletti offers an example of her Catechesis of the Good Shepherd in which she applies Montessori educational techniques to discussions of God with Catholic Children. Berryman's Godly Play approach to religious education also offers a child-centered approach teaching based upon storytelling and open-ended questions. Hull's excerpt also highlights the uses of open-ended conversations in his discussions about how children view God. Through these conversations, Hull nuances Piaget's developmental stages, stages that have guided and constrained many religious education curricula.

While these excerpts focus on techniques and philosophies for developing children's understandings of God and faith, the next three pieces examine how adults and children work together to develop, teach, and continue their traditions. The chapter by Scourfield, Gilliat-Ray, Khan, and Otri explores how Muslim families and communities effectively keep their children from leaving the tradition. Marianne Holm Pedersen analyzes how in Danish Muslim families, children and youth learn about being Muslim from their parents, peers, and significant others, and investigates what religiosity means to children of different gender and age. Ridgely asks similar questions to Pedersen, but returns the conversation back to the classroom to discover how children and adults work together to create their traditions. Together this part demonstrates how children appropriate elements of their religion that give meaning to them in different social contexts.

Reference

Edwards, Jonathan (1832), *A Faithful Narrative of the Surprising Work of God in the Conversino of Many Hundred Souls in South Hampton, Massachusetts*, New York: Dunning & Spaulding.

10

The Domestic Context of Child Rearing in Reformed Christianity

Richard Baxter
(from the published edition, 1825)

The Puritan divine, Richard Baxter (1616–1691) understood the Godly family to be one in which each member—mother, father, child—fulfilled distinct roles, in particular, that children should conform to the biblical injunction to 'honour one's father and mother'. This extract demonstrates how Baxter defined familial roles and the responsibilities parents and children had towards one another in the Christian household. These texts have been widely cited since, and remain in the circulated discourse of Christians across the world.

The special duties of children and youth towards God

Though I put your duties to your parents first, because it is first learned, yet your duty to God immediately is your greatest and most necessary duty. Learn these following precepts well.

Direct I

Learn to understand the covenant and vow which in your baptism you made with God the Father, the Son, and the Holy Ghost, your Creator, Redeemer, and Regenerator: and when you well understand it, renew that covenant with God in your own persons, and absolutely deliver up yourselves to God, as your Creator, Redeemer and Sanctifier, your Owner, your Ruler, and your Father and felicity. Baptism is not an idle ceremony, but the solemn entering into covenant with God, in which you receive the greatest mercies, and bind yourselves to the greatest duties. It is but the entering into that way which you must walk in all your lives, and avowing that to God which you must be still performing. And though your parents had authority to promise for you, it is you that must perform it; for it was you that they obliged. If you ask by what authority they obliged you in covenant to God, I answer, by the authority which God hath given them in nature, and in Scripture; as they oblige you to be subjects of the kind, or as they enter your names into any covenant, by lease or other covenant; and if you grudge at it, and refuse your own consent when you come to age, you lose the benefits. If you think they did you wrong, you may be out of covenant when you will, if you will renounce the kingdom of heaven. But it is much wiser to be thankful to God, that your parents were the means of so great a blessing to you, and to do that again more expressly by yourselves which they did for you; and openly with thankfulness to own the covenant in which you are engaged, and live in the performance and in the comforts of it all your days.

Direct II

Remember that you are entering into the way to everlasting life, and not into a place of happiness or continuance, Presently therefore set your hearts on heaven, and make it the design of all your lives, to live in heaven with Christ for ever. Oh happy you, if God betimes will thoroughly teach you to know what it is that must make you happy; and if at your first setting out, your end be right, and your faces be heavenward! Remember that as soon as you begin to live, you are hasting towards the end of your lives: even as a candle as soon as it beginneth to burn, and the hour-glass as soon as it is turned, is wasting, and hasting to its end; so as soon as you begin to live, your lives are in a consumption, and posting towards your final hour. As a runner, as soon as he beginneth his race, is hasting to the end of it; so are your lives, even in your youngest time. It is another kind of life that you must live for ever, than this trifling, pitiful, fleshy life. Prepare therefore speedily for that which God sent you hither to prepare for. O happy you, if you begin betimes, and go on with cheerful resolution to the end! It is blessed wisdom to be wise betimes, and to know the worth of time in childhood, before any of it be wasted and lost upon the fooleries of the world. Then you may grow wise indeed, and be treasuring up understanding, and growing up in a sweet acquaintance with the Lord, when others are going backwards, and daily making work for sad repentance or final desperation. Eccl. Xxi. 1: 'Remember now thy Creator in the days of thy youth, while the evil days come not, nor the years draw nigh, when thou shalt say, (of all things here below) I have no pleasure in them'.

Direct III

Remember that you have corrupted natures to be cured, and that Christ is the Physician that must cure them; and the Spirit of Christ must dwell within you, and make you holy, and give you a new heart and nature, which shall love God and heaven above all the honour and pleasures of the world: rest not therefore till you find that you are born anew, and that the Holy Ghost hath made you holy, and quickened your hearts with the love of God, and of your dear Redeemer. The old nature loveth the things of this world, and the pleasures of this flesh; but the new nature loveth the Lord that made you, and redeemed and renewed you, and the endless joys of the world to come, and that holy life which is the way thereto.

Direct IV

Take heed of loving the pleasures of the flesh, in over-much eating, or drinking, or play. Set not your hearts upon your belly or your sport; let your meat, and sleep, and play be moderate. Meddle not with cards or dice, or any bewitching or riotous sports: play not for money, lest it stir up covetous desires, and tempt you to be over-eager in it, and to lie, and wrangle, and fall out with others. Use neither food nor sports which are not for your health; a greedy appetite enticeth children to devour raw fruits, and to rob their neighbours' orchards, and at once to undo both soul and body. And an excessive love of play doth cause them to run among bad companions, and lose their time, and destroy the love of their books, and their duty, and their parents themselves, and all that is good. You must eat, and sleep, and play for health, and not for useless, hurtful pleasure.

Direct V

Subdue your own wills and desires to the will of God and your superiors, and be not eagerly set upon any thing which God or your parents do deny you. Be not like those self-willed, fleshy children, that are importunate for any thing which their fancy or appetite would have, and cry or are discontent if they have it not. Say not that I must have this or that, but be contented with any thing which is the will of God and your superiors. It is the greatest misery and danger in the world, to have all your own wills, and to be given up to your hearts' desire.

Direct VI

Take heed of a custom of foolish, filthy railing, lying, or any other sinful words. You think it is a small matter, but God thinketh not so; it is not a jesting matter to sin against the God that made you: it is fools that make a sport with sin ... One lie, one curse, one oath, one ribald, or railing, or deriding word, is worse than all the pain that ever your flesh endured.

Direct VII

Take heed of such company and play fellows, as would entice and tempt you to any of these sins, and choose such company as will help you in the fear of God. And if others mock at you, care no more for it, than for the shaking of a leaf, or the barking of a dog. Take heed of lewd and wicked company, as ever you care for the saving of your souls. If you hear them rail, or lie, or swear, or talk filthily, be not ashamed to tell them, that God forbiddeth you to keep company with such as they ...

Direct VIII

Take heed of pride and covetousness. Desire not to be fine, nor to get all to yourselves; but be humble, and meek, and love one another, and be as glad that others are pleased as yourselves.

Direct IX

Love the word of God, and all good books which would make you wiser and better; and read not play-books, nor tale-books, nor love-books, nor any idle stories. When idle children are at play and fooleries, let it be your pleasure to read and learn the mysteries of your salvation.

Direct X

Remember that you keep holy the Lord's day. Spend not any of it in play or idleness: reverence the ministers of Christ, and mark what they teach you, and remember it is a message from God about the saving of your souls. Ask your parents when you come home, to help your understandings and memories in any thing which you understood not or forgot. Love all the holy exercises of the Lord's day, and let them be pleasanter to you than your meat or play.

Direct XI

Be as careful to practise all, as to hear and read it. Remember all is but to make you holy, to love God, and obey him: take heed of sinning against your knowledge, and against the warnings that are given you.

Direct XII

When you grow up, by the direction of your parents choose such a trade or calling, as alloweth you the greatest helps for heaven, and hath the fewest hindrances, and in which you may be most serviceable to God before you die. If you will but practise these few directions, (which your own hearts must say have no harm in any of them,) what happy persons will you be for ever!

11

On Discipline, Praise and Parental Authority

John Locke (1693)

Many historians of the late modern period agree that from the late seventeenth century onwards, new ideas of childhood began to emerge. John Locke's Some Thoughts Concerning Education, *published in 1693, was highly influential in this regard, attacking ideas of childhood sinfulness and proposing an idea of children as* tabula rasa *and recognizing the individuality of children. It was translated into most written European languages in the eighteenth century, and has been a significant influence on educational theory since. In this excerpt from Part 3, Locke discusses the place of discipline and praise in childrearing.*

Those therefore that intend ever to govern their children, should begin it whilst they are very little, and look that they perfectly comply with the will of their parents. Would you have your son obedient to you when past a child; be sure then to establish the authority of a father as soon as he is capable of submission, and can understand in whose power he is. If you would have him stand in awe of you, imprint it in his infancy; and as he approaches more to a man, admit him nearer to your familiarity; so shall you have him your obedient subject (as is fit) whilst he is a child, and your affectionate friend when he is a man. For methinks they mightily misplace the treatment due to their children, who are indulgent and familiar when they are little, but severe to them, and keep them at a distance, when they are grown up: for liberty and indulgence can do no good to children; their want of judgment makes them stand in need of restraint and discipline; and on the contrary, imperiousness and severity is but an ill way of treating men, who have reason of their own to guide them; unless you have a mind to make your children, when grown up, weary of you, and secretly to say within themselves, When will you die, father?

I imagine every one will judge it reasonable, that their children, when little, should look upon their parents as their lords, their absolute governors, and as such stand in awe of them; and that when they come to riper years, they should look on them as their best, as their only sure friends, and as such love and reverence them. The way I have mention'd, if I mistake not, is the only one to obtain this. We must look upon our children, when grown up, to be like ourselves, with the same passions, the same desires. We would be thought rational creatures, and have our freedom; we love not to be uneasy under constant rebukes and brow-beatings, nor can we bear severe humours and great distance in those we converse with. Whoever has such treatment when he is a man, will look out other company, other friends, other conversation, with whom he can be at ease. If therefore a strict hand be kept over children from the beginning, they will in that age be tractable, and quietly submit to it, as never having known any other: and if, as they grow up to the use of reason, the rigour of government be, as they deserve it, gently relax'd, the father's brow more smooth'd to them, and the distance by degrees abated, his former restraints will increase their love, when they find it was only a kindness to them, and a care to make them capable to deserve the favour of their parents, and the esteem of everybody else.

Thus much for the settling your authority over your children in general. Fear and awe ought to give you the first power over their minds, and love and friendship in riper years to hold it: for the time must come, when they will be past the rod and correction; and then, if the love of you make them not obedient and dutiful, if the love of virtue and reputation keep them not in laudable courses, I ask, what hold will you have upon them to turn them to it? Indeed, fear of having a scanty portion if they displease you, may make them slaves to your estate, but they will be nevertheless ill and wicked in private; and that restraint will not last always. Every man must some time or other be trusted to himself and his own conduct; and he that is a good, a virtuous, and able man, must be made so within. And therefore what he is to receive from education, what is to sway and influence his life, must be something put into him betimes; habits woven into the very principles of his nature, and not a counterfeit carriage, and dissembled outside, put on by fear, only to avoid the present anger of a father who perhaps may disinherit him.

This being laid down in general, as the course that ought to be taken, 'tis fit we now come to consider the parts of the discipline to be us'd, a little more particularly. I have spoken so much of carrying a strict hand over children, that perhaps I shall be suspected of not considering enough, what is due to their tender age and constitutions. But that opinion will vanish, when you have heard me a little farther: for I am very apt to think, that great severity of punishment does but very little good, nay, great harm in education; and I believe it will be found that, caeteris paribus, those children who have been most chastis'd, seldom make the best men. All that I have hitherto contended for, is, that whatsoever rigor is necessary, it is more to be us'd, the younger children are; and having by a due application wrought its effect, it is to be relax'd, and chang'd into a milder sort of government.

A compliance and suppleness of their wills, being by a steady hand introduc'd by parents, before children have memories to retain the beginnings of it, will seem natural to them, and work afterwards in them as if it were so, preventing all occasions of struggling or repining. The only care is, that it be begun early, and inflexibly kept to 'till awe and respect be grown familiar, and there appears not the least reluctancy in the submission, and ready obedience of their minds. When this reverence is once thus established, (which it must be early, or else it will cost pains and blows to recover it, and the more the longer it is deferr'd) 'tis by it, still mix'd with as much indulgence as they make not an ill use of, and not by beating, chiding, or other servile punishments, they are for the future to be govern'd as they grow up to more understanding.

That this is so, will be easily allow'd, when it is but consider'd, what is to be aim'd at in an ingenuous education; and upon what it turns.

1. He that has not a mastery over his inclinations, he that knows not how to resist the importunity of present pleasure or pain, for the sake of what reason tells him is fit to be done, wants the true principle of virtue and industry, and is in danger never to be good for anything. This temper therefore, so contrary to unguided nature, is to be got betimes; and this habit, as the true foundation of future ability and happiness, is to be wrought into the mind as early as may be, even from the first dawnings of knowledge or apprehension in children, and so to be confirm'd in them, by all the care and ways imaginable, by those who have the oversight of their education.

2. On the other side, if the mind be curb'd, and humbled too much in children; if their spirits be abas'd and broken much, by too strict an hand over them, they lose all their vigour and industry, and are in a worse state than the former. For extravagant young fellows, that have liveliness and spirit, come sometimes to be set right, and so make able and great men; but dejected minds, timorous and tame, and low spirits, are hardly ever to be rais'd, and very seldom attain to any thing. To avoid the danger that is on either hand, is the great art; and he that has found a way how to keep up a child's spirit easy, active, and free, and yet at the same time to restrain him from many things he has a mind to, and to draw him to things that are uneasy to him; he, I say, that knows how to reconcile these seeming contradictions, has, in my opinion, got the true secret of education ...

Beating them, and all other sorts of slavish and corporal punishments, are not the discipline fit to be used in the education of those we would have wise, good, and ingenuous men; and therefore very rarely to be apply'd, and that only in great occasions, and cases of extremity. On the other side, to flatter children by rewards of things that are pleasant to them, is as carefully to be avoided. He that will give to his son apples or sugar-plumbs, or what else of this kind he is most delighted with, to make him learn his book, does but authorize his love of pleasure, and cocker up that dangerous propensity, which he ought by all means to subdue and stifle in him ...

First, children (earlier perhaps than we think) are very sensible of praise and commendation. They find a pleasure in being esteem'd and valu'd, especially by their parents and those whom they depend on. If therefore the father caress and commend them when they do well, shew a cold and neglectful countenance to them upon doing ill, and this accompany'd by a like carriage of the mother and all others that are about them, it will, in a little time, make them sensible of the difference; and this, if constantly observ'd, I doubt not but will of itself work more than threats or blows, which lose their force when once grown common, and are of no use when shame does not attend them; and therefore are to be forborne, and never to be us'd, but in the case hereafter-mention'd, when it is brought to extremity …

And here give me leave to take notice of one thing I think a fault in the ordinary method of education; and that is, the charging of children's memories, upon all occasions, with rules and precepts, which they often do not understand, and constantly as soon forget as given. It be some action you would have done, or done otherwise, whenever they forget, or do it awkwardly, make them do it over and over again, 'till they are perfect … [B]y repeating the same action 'till it be grown habitual in them, the performance will not depend on memory or reflection, the concomitant of prudence and age, and not of childhood, but will be natural in them. Thus bowing to a gentleman, when he salutes him, and looking in his face, when he speaks to him, is by constant use as natural to a well-bred man, as breathing; it requires no thought, no reflection. Having this way cured in your child any fault, it is cured forever: and thus one by one you may weed them out all, and plant what habits you please.

I have seen parents so heap rules on their children, that it was impossible for the poor little ones to remember a tenth part of them, much less to observe them … Make but few laws, but see they be well observ'd when once made.

12

The Basis of Religious Education

Friedrich Froebel (1885)

*F*riedrich Froebel (1782–1852) was a teacher and educationalist, who recognized the unique needs and abilities of children, and developed kindergarten and educational toys for young children. This extract, drawn from his Education of Man, is his articulation of the ontological and epistemological basis for religious education. Here Froebel stresses the myriad ways in which children learn about God, beyond the confines of formal schooling, in particular through their play and experiences of nature.

If child and parents have grown up in a union of life and mind, this union will certainly not only remain undiminished, through the whole time of boyhood, and yet longer, if new obstructing and disturbing causes do not come in between to separate them, but will become so much the more confirmed and vivified as the boy advances in age.

The question here is not of that hollow indefinite union of feeling which, as it were, makes one of two bodies, such as is found between parents and child; but of that union of active minds and clear spirits which shows life in its effects and phenomena as a whole. This union of active minds and clear spirits, not the union which is perhaps at most only outward community of life, is the firm basis and foundation of genuine religiousness. The inner life, the clear representation of the inner spiritual life of man, is common to the union of spirit between parents and child, between parents and boy …

Children are early awakened to and taught concerning a mass of externalities which they cannot understand, just because this mass is strange and external to them, and they remain unroused in reference to many inner things, untaught concerning so many, in fact almost all, inner things which yet they might understand within themselves. So children are early introduced into the strange outer life, and, on the other hand, are estranged from the inner life; for which reason their inner life is so hollow and withered …

Definite religious teaching should rather present, demonstrate to the boy in his own life and the life of all, and make perceptible in all development in Nature and humanity, the saying that he who truly desires the pure representation of humanity with earnestness, effort, and devotion, must necessarily live in outward oppression, in outward pain and need, in outward care and sorrow, in outward want and trouble and poverty; for the demand of that effort is, that the inner spiritual true life should reveal, manifest, and represent itself …

That they may have a vivid recognition and conception of this, let the boys view the requirements and limitations, the phenomena, of the development of a tree, in comparison with the necessary requirements and limitations, the phenomena, of the spiritual development of the man.

Each stage of development attained, though so beautiful and symmetrical in its place, must vanish and pass away, must be absolutely destroyed, if a higher stage of development and improvement is to appear: the protecting warning scales must fall off, if the young twig, the fragrant blossom, is to unfold, although the tender twig, the delicate blossom, may be and often is exposed to the still inclement spring weather. The fragrant blossom must fall off to give place to a fruit at first insignificant, sour and bitter. The delicious red-cheeked fruit so refreshing to man must fall and decay, so that the young plant and tree may germinate in youthful freshness …

The recognition of each thing, of each being, of its destination and properties, proceeds everywhere most precisely and clearly from the local references and relations of objects in which the things stand, and expresses itself most loudly and clearly in such references and relations; therefore the boy and scholar is necessarily brought to the clearest insight into the nature of objects, of Nature, and of the outside world in general, when the things are brought before him, and recognised by him, in the natural connection in which they stand.

Further: the relations and proportions of objects, and their significations, are naturally the plainest and clearest to the boy where he sees himself most impressively and constantly surrounded by them and their effects; where, perhaps, the cause of their existence lies in himself, or at least proceeds from and relates to him.

These are the objects most closely surrounding him, – the objects in the room, in the house, in the garden, the yard, the village (the city), the meadow, the field, the wood, the plain. From the room, his nearest surrounding, this arranged and arranging contemplation of Nature and the outside world proceeds, passing from what is near and familiar to what is farther off and unfamiliar; and, on account of this order, this summing-up and dividing now appears as an actual school-subject.

The course of teaching is as follows. The instruction again begins with the pointing-out of the object, which has before been recognised as necessary. Thus, for example, pointing to the table:

'What is that?'… and so on.
Now the summing-up question,
'What do you see here in the room?'
'The table, the chair, the bench, the widow, the door, the flower-pot', and so on.

The teacher writes down upon the slate the objects named by one or more children, and then repeats in concert with the scholars. The teacher further questions:

'Do the tables and chairs stand in the same relation to the room as the window and door?'

'What is outside of the village, and surrounds it?' ...

'Can arbours, hedges, vineyards, and the like be called pure works of man?'

'Such objects as arbours, vineyards, fields, meadows, and improved fruit-trees, are called *works of Nature and man ...*'

'Do the objects of Nature come nearer to or farther from people according to the place in which they live? Is there any difference in the way of living, the behaviour, the utterances and qualities, of these objects of Nature, according to whether they are nearer to or farther from people?'

'Yes.'

'No.'

'Why yes? Why no?'

The objects of Nature which are nearer to men, and more subject to their influence, are weaker, more sensitive, needing more care. Care more tractable, etc.; they are generally more *tame*; the objects of Nature which are remote from man, and less subject to his influences, are more *rough*, are *wild ...*

Thus, after a great circuit and many windings, the scholar has returned to the house and the family-room from which he started at the beginning of the contemplation of the outside world and of Nature; he has returned to the middle point of all earthly human impulses and efforts... He has found in his different relations to the things of the outside world; he has found – himself.

13

The Modern Sunday School

George Hamilton Archibald (1926)

*G*eorge Hamilton Archibald (1858–1938) played a key role in reforming and professionalizing Sunday Schools in Canada. His work with Sunday Schools became a model used by churches worldwide. He argued for a child-centred approach to religious education. This extract typifies Archibald's approach, drawing upon Froebel and with an emphasis on child-centred learning.

And what shall we say of play, its place, its power, and its possibilities in the functioning of the life of the child and youth in the Sunday school? Day-school education is recognising its value. Sunday schools and churches are following their lead, though, truth to tell, somewhat reluctantly. The significance of play as a recreation has long been recognised, but play as a unique, useful, and efficient ally in religious education is a different thing. Great teachers work *with* nature, and recognise play not only as a recreation but as an educational method, with roots as deep as instinct is deep. The tendency to express oneself in play is nearly as old as heredity. As hunger and thirst express a physiological necessity, so play is the expression of a psychological necessity, and its authoritative demand must be heeded …

But let us look deeper into the meaning of play, for it has a wide significance. As long ago as the seventeenth century the poet Schiller wrote: 'Deep meaning oft lies hid in childish play.' Poets are seers. They glimpse into the dim and distant future and blaze the trail for the scientists. Except by the seer the value of play was not appreciated in the olden days, and it is only beginning to be realised in the twentieth century. The love of play is something comparable to the love of a story …

Play is a racial inheritance. That is why it offers such an irresistible appeal to all grades of unfolding life. Play is more than mere idleness. No adult was ever more busy in his life's work than when in childhood he was absorbed in play. It is safe to assert that the best player makes the best prophet. The child who plays needs a director; the child who does not play needs a doctor.

So we ask again, Why does play make such a powerful appeal to the child? A number of theories have been advanced; they are worth considering ...

The surplus energy theory

It was Schiller in the beginning of the eighteenth century who first propounded the theory of Surplus Energy....The argument was, that children, who do not need to expend their nervous energy in the useful activities pursued by their parents, consume surplus energy in playing – that is, they play merely because they must do something to give expression to their rapidly-growing muscular system.

For a long time this was the accepted theory. It is, of course, obviously insufficient to say that play is due only to overflowing energy. A child will often play when he is practically exhausted. Neither is it true to say that the normal state of a child is that of resting or working, and that only when he gets superabundance of energy does he play.

Moreover, this theory does not give any help in understanding the *kind* of play that children indulge in. Why is 'make-believe' and 'let's pretend' so full of enchantment to child life? Nor does the theory explain the motive behind the difference in children's play at different ages or during differing stages of their development.

The recapitulation theory

The recapitulation theory of play may be stated as follows: Children play because of the nervous mechanism inherited from their forefathers....The theory is that the child recapitulates the race – that is, the individual lives over again the history of his ancestors.... In play, when the will is set free from the compulsive habitudes, the mind and body lean to the old racial activities which operate through reflexes and instincts, the nervous mechanism of which is born fully developed.

The catharsis theory

Psychoanalysis teaches us that if we do not give expression to instinctive emotions, even though they are primitive and in themselves anti-social, we imperil our physical, mental and moral health ...

These old impulses must not be disregarded. They cannot be laid aside at will or repressed into the subconscious; if they do, they will take their revenge and affect the physical as well as the mental and moral health of the individual ... the chief aim should be to sublimate, that is, to turn the use of the instinct to a higher purpose, but we must first recognise the immense purgative value of harmless expression, especially (but not only) to adolescents. Of all the gifts Nature has bestowed upon immaturity none is perhaps comparable in value to that of play.

...

The catharsis theory of play is...the most attractive and satisfying answer to the question, Why do children play? The theory might almost have been called the vaccination theory. Play vaccinates the child just as the vaccine lymph inoculates against a more serious and harmful form of the complaint.

Now all this helps us to understand why the child so much loves to play. We talk about learning by doing; we must learn to talk about purifying by playing. The Church is only beginning to recognise the power and possibilities of play in purging the soul of some of its uncouth biological inheritance.

...

But the old instincts may also be sublimated, that is, diverted into other channels 'satisfying to the individual and useful to the community.' The child's impulse of construction can be turned into building something that is useful; curiosity directed into scientific search; the fighting impulses can be sublimated into combating error, and wrong, and sin; later, the sex impulses into creative handicrafts, art, music, gardening, nursing, teaching...

The release theory

The release theory gives light on the play of man, adult man, but does not generally assist in the answer to the question. Why do *children* play? Men play as a release from habituated work, but to children all play is work.

...

In these days if industrial life, when men are compelled to lead a life of close confinement indoors to some habituated employment, the nerves are kept at high tension and the strain is severe. Whether our calling keeps us in the office, the shop, the factory, or the schoolroom, release is essential to good health, and this release must be a complete change from the shut-in employment. More than this, if it is to be genuinely refreshing it must revert to the exercise of the old activities of the race. We may be assured that if his cannot be done it will take an unhealthy form, and find satisfaction in prize-fighting and other unworthy occupations

14

The Religious Potential of the Child

Sofia Cavalletti (1983)

*S*ofia Cavalletti (1917–2011) believed that children have an innate spirituality and a deep desire to know God for themselves. To facilitate this knowing, she brought Montessori methods into religious education, urging churches to create atria where children can engage directly with the objects of their faith. In her Catechesis of the Good Shepherd, she emphasizes that this engagement in not play, but important work being done by children so that they may know God better. This excerpt highlights the opinions and responses of the children who worked with Cavalletti to develop the atria where they could have a hands-on encounter with the sacred.

Before beginning any discussion about the religious education of children, we should ask ourselves a basic question: Is it justifiable to give religious education to children?

Nowadays we are very careful, and with good reason, not to impose our own personal choices on others. In initiating children into some form of religious life, are we not perhaps offering them something that may be most valuable to us, but without which the child would be just as happy, the absence of which would in no way affect the child's life or his harmonious development? Or worse still, are we not perhaps complicating the child's life with inessential superstructures that weigh him down with a burden that does not correspond to his needs?

We must search for the answers to these fundamental questions within the child himself. The adult cannot and should not reply on a theoretical plane. The response should arise only from an attentive and impartial observation of the child, so that it is the child himself who tells us if he does or does not want to be helped to discover God and the transcendent reality. It must be the child who tells us if the religious experience is or is not constitutive of his personality. An interpersonal relationship is always a mystery; it is more so when it involves a relationship with God; when the relationship is between God and the child the mystery is greater still. Nevertheless, it has been possible at times to penetrate fleetingly the secret of this relationship; some documents have been collected that attest to a spontaneous *religiosita* (religiousness) in the child.

The child's attraction to God

Evidently we are dealing with transient moments, and we wonder what degree of awareness the child himself has of them. This does not prevent them from constituting true facts of life, which sometimes ferment for a long while within the depths of the child's spirit without his being conscious of it. Read, for instance, the experience written by the famous French novelist Julien Green:

> In the course of these dim years, I can remember a minute of intense delight, such as I have never experienced since. Should such things be told, or should they be kept secret? There came a moment in this room when, looking up at the windowpane, I saw the dark sky and a few stars shining in it. What words can be used to express what is beyond speech? That minute was perhaps the most important one of my life and I do not know what to say about it. I was alone in the unlighted room and, my eyes raised toward the sky, I had what I can only call an outburst of love. I have loved on this earth, but never as I did during that short time, and I did not know whom I loved. Yet I knew that he was there and that, seeing me, he loved me too. How did the thought dawn on me? I do not know. I was certain that someone was there and talked to me without words. Having said this, I have said everything. Why must I write that no human speech has ever given me what I felt then for a moment just long enough to count up to ten, at a time when I was incapable of putting together a few intelligible words and did not even realize that I existed? Why must I write that I forgot that minute for years, that the stream of days and nights all but wiped it out of my consciousness? If only I had preserved it in times of trial! Why is it given back to me now? What does it mean?

Another similar moment of intense delight is narrated in the unpublished writings of M. C.:

> I was standing in front of an open window one summer evening. A little below the windowsill a roof sloped down, behind which still other rooftops descended, so that the window opened out toward a very wide space. On the nearest roof a cricket sang at intervals in the darkness. I distinctly remember the sharp crack, interrupted and then renewed, that the cricket's sound made in the silence of the night. Yet I remember just as well (and, even more, if I recollect myself, I feel once again) that that perception opened me toward a feeling, or better, to a general state of consciousness which, in a graduated way, but with extreme rapidity

and extraordinary power, led me from this perception to a kind of immaterial and universal revelation.

First of all I had the feeling of space, or more precisely, I had the sensation that an unlimited vastness was thrown open before me, and for an instant perhaps I was dismayed before that immensity. Yet, just an instant later, all my hesitation disappeared, swept away by an impetus which arose from the depths of my being, and which urged me ahead and led me to go toward that space, almost as if it were opened solely so that I would expand within it. And this was the first moment that I can distinguish in that swift progression which I experienced at that time.

The next moment, which followed in an imperceptible fraction of time, was distinct from the preceding one because I became aware that an irresistible ardour had been enflamed within me in that moment. I was wholly moved; warm, tender, full of fervour; I overflowed with affection. That movement was, more intimately in me, a violent transport of all my affectivity. From tenderness to avidity, that movement was pervaded by all that I later knew under the name of love. That moment remains present to me, in fact, as one in which a powerful seduction inundated me and enveloped me, and to which I re-acted by accepting it and, even more, by wanting it. That movement in space, which I had experienced a moment before for the first time consciously, returned to my mind at that point like an embrace, to which I had been opened up passionately from within the depths of myself, toward an unimaginable thing which revealed itself to me.

And then the third moment came with a continuity which, I would say, was more perfect than what I had experienced up to that point, following the change of my consciousness. Of itself, and truly all by itself, that embrace that I was experiencing was transformed in my heart into an absolute plentitude of joy. An astonishing joy, a kind of enthusiasm of joy, invaded me. I was all aflame in the luminosity of a happiness so intense and complete that I was immobilized by that feeling, in a state that remains in my memory as one of perfect satisfaction and absolute union. And that is how my experience of that event of living concluded that evening.

I am certain that my experience unfolded in the way I have said: from an expansion in space, an act of love, and happiness. It unfolded through a rising spiral, ascending in that way, and drew me, but not more than I felt inclined toward and had decided to follow. I do not know exactly how old I was when that event happened in my life; I think I must have been five years old, maybe six, or perhaps four. The event of that evening is, however, the first memory that I have been able to discover in myself. As much as I have tried, I have not found anything in my memory that precedes it. So I think I am able to date that evening as the birth of my consciousness. I can also say that, even if that event seemed strange to me later on and compelled me to reflect and try to understand it, at the time however it passed over me as something very natural. I am convinced that, in that moment of my life, I was oriented forever toward existence, and that the whole life of my consciousness depends upon it. Still, the event of that moment did not upset my childlike state. I continued to live my childhood in a completely normal way. It was certainly wonderful, what I had known, and yet it was as if that wonder had been at that time something altogether natural.

These are documents of a relationship with God that goes beyond the intellectual plane; it is founded on a deep, existential level. The experience just described is remarkable in its complexity, the nature of which is affective, cognitive, and moral: the certitude of a presence, a presence of love that attracts with a great force of 'seduction', but not more than the child was 'inclined toward and had decided to follow'; therefore a presence that does not impose but appears to await a response.

Linda related an experience that has some similarities...it is an experience she remembers having happened at the beginning of her life – certainly before the age of six. One day she noticed a butterfly in flight and she felt drawn to it; she followed it and suddenly 'everything seemed to open up around me'. It appeared that she was able to see everything more clearly, and she 'felt filled with joy and warmth throughout my whole body' in a way she had never experienced before. The sensation was so strong that the little girl burst into tears of joy, ran to her mother, and said: 'Mommy, I know God'. Only much later, in thinking over that event, did Linda associate it with love; at the time it was something 'very new and different, for which I had no reference points'. It was something that the child did not perceive with her mind; what she had said afterwards to her mother 'was not an explanation, it was an exclamation'.

All three examples deal with religious experiences lived in the first years of life, which oriented the lives of those who lived them, and which pose the problem of the existence of the religious fact in the child prior to any promptings that are cultural in character...As we said earlier, we are dealing with ephemeral moments, like a flash of light that shines vibrantly and then fades away. However, they let us glimpse in some way the mysterious reality present within the child; they manifest the child's potentiality and richness, the nature of which we are not successful in defining clearly ...

Charlotte (three and a half years old) was staying at her aunt's house. When she saw her aunt preparing to leave she asked her where she was going; the aunt replied that she was going to Mass and the child declared: 'I am coming too!'. And so it continued for days, without the slightest urging on anyone's part. One day another child came to play with Charlotte and she told her aunt that she would not be going to Mass with her. Then a moment later she was back again saying: 'Stefano can wait, first I'm coming with you'.

Anne Marie van der Meer also noted something interesting about her young son Pieterke. Before she and her husband converted, they took a trip to Italy with their five-year-old son; later she reminisced with her husband:

Weren't you struck by the way Pieterke, who was only five years old, followed the services in the churches we visited in Italy? Think of the ceremonies in the cathedral of Siena and in the Roman basilicas: they were never too long for him and he did not want to leave. For such a restless boy the opposite would have been natural and understandable! He thought the celebrations were magnificent. I don't think I have ever told you what he asked me as soon as we returned to Uccle from our trip to Italy: 'Mother,' he said to me one day, 'why don't we ever go to church as we did in Italy?'

Still during the time before her conversion, Anne Marie van der Meer, at her friend's insistence, told her son that they would pray the Our Father together at night. 'The child was strangely happy at those words', she noticed... 'when I forgot the prayer on the evenings we were giving a reception, Pieterke never failed to remind me to say the Our Father with him. I recited it every night. Meanwhile, even though I was praying this way, we were not believers. But the child was happy'.

Another noteworthy example is contained in the letter sent to a parish priest in Moscow regarding a little girl whose age was unspecified but who obviously had to have been quite young:

... having rushed into my room and seen the icons, the little girl began asking me questions; ... with eyes wide open she fastened her gaze on the faces of Jesus and the Mother of God, which she was seeing for the first time in her life. Although with effort, I explained to the child, who is a young cousin of mine, the meaning of what had struck her in a way she could understand. But my worries proved to be superfluous. 'You know,' she said to me, 'I knew He existed and I have always talked with Him before going to sleep; I knew He was everywhere and that He sees me when I get into mischief, only sometimes I was afraid of Him. How can I speak with Him?'

　Moved by the child's words, I taught her the sign of the cross, and I experienced an extraordinary feeling watching those small hands making the sign of the cross on her slender little body... 'And now can I kiss Him,' she continued to my great surprise, 'but not on His face or cheek, not the way I kiss Mommy? Because He is greater than my mother, He is better than my mother. He sees everything and He doesn't scold me. He is better than everyone, and He loves me. Give me the icon please, I want to see it always. I'll put it beside my bed, and the icon of His mother too. Give it to me as a gift!'

　When her mother arrived the child said: 'Mommy, quick, come here. Kiss Him. He loves you too. At last I've seen His face, but I've known Him for a long time.' Before her mother's embarrassed silence the child continued: 'Mommy, why don't you say anything? Mommy, tell me about Him; I need to hear about Him.' But the icon was taken away from little Irina. Her mother described the child's reaction: 'She cries, she asks to hang it above her bed, saying: 'I want to see Him, I need to talk to Him'.

The child's attraction toward the religious reality also leads him to become involved in conflict, and to overcome negative environmental conditions. How many children from atheistic families the author has seen who thirst to come close to God! Massimo (six years old) was a difficult child. One day it was necessary to tell him:

'If you continue to make such a disturbance I will not be able to let you come again'; Massimo's changed facial expression showed how deeply the warning had struck him. From that day he made no further disturbances.

For children who live in atheistic environments, contact with the religious reality represents, quantitatively, an infinitesimal part of their lives. Why does it have such a hold on them? Why, among all the influences in their lives, do those of a religious nature – even if sporadic and limited – find a special responsiveness in children? Often there appears to be a disproportion between what children receive in the area of religion and what they express. The above-mentioned examples refer to children of different ages, belonging to diversified environments, and thus they demonstrate a diffused attraction in the child toward God …

The child's mysterious knowledge

In the religious sphere, it is a fact that children know things no one has told them. An impressive example, recounted earlier, is that of the little girl who recognized God as maker of the world. Listening to her father's explanation, she felt in some sense betrayed by his words without having the ability to defend herself; it was enough for her father to pronounce the word 'God' for the girl to realize what she had been searching for and she clasped it with infinite joy. I would like to say here what I have had occasion to speak of elsewhere: Many years ago I was presenting Baptism to a group of children from four to six years of age, and I was unsure whether or not to speak of the meaning of the imposition of the hands, thinking that it was too difficult for children of that age to understand. But in any event I wanted to try: I put a ring in my hand and two or three times I extended my arm, opened my hand, and let the ring fall out, explaining that this is what I would do if I wanted to give them a gift. Then I repeated the gesture without the ring, saying: 'At Baptism, the priest makes this gesture over the child; but you do not see anything fall. Then why does he do it?'. The children replied in chorus, as if the question were completely superfluous: 'Because he is giving us the Holy Spirit'. Two theology students were present; I could see they were startled. Where do the children get such knowledge? I do not know how to respond; what is certain is that they knew.

15

Godly Play

Jerome Berryman (1991)

The American Episcopalian religious educator, Jerome Berryman, devised 'Godly Play' as an approach for use with children in church contexts. This approach has proven internationally popular, and has been extended and adapted for use in day schools of a religious character.

Godly play attempts to create a situation where wonder, community, an awareness of existential limits, religious language, the creative process, and the structure of the Holy Eucharist work together to enable the child to enter religious language in order to make meaning and find direction with God in life and death …

We will proceed by asking three questions. How does the organisation of space in the classroom teach? How does the time spent in the classroom teach? How do the people in the classroom teach when they are not speaking?

Teaching with space

When we walk into a room, the colours, the arrangement of the furniture, the light, the odours, the noise, the taste on the tip of the tongue, the shape of the room, and other perceptions combine to 'speak' to us. We notice how the room is cared for. Is it clean and orderly? Are things torn or broken? We notice much more than we can make an inventory of, but what this all adds up to is the sum of the values that are embedded in the room. This is why the church has always been careful with the environment in which we teach the art of using the language by which we worship.

The environment is at work communicating even when we are not attending to its communication. Children are even more vulnerable to this communication than we adults are. At some level they notice whether the room is clean, orderly and in good repair. This communicates to them whether the people in charge of the room really care about the place they have entered. That in turn suggests to the children whether they will be cared for there or not.

Children cannot focus very well on the learning task when the room about them is always changing. They need a steady, stable environment to deal best with the changes of learning. They need an orderly background against which to discover something new … The focal point of the room shows Christ as the centre … this anchors the room's meaning. Another anchor for the room's meaning is the ream of adults … *where* these people are in the room has a great deal to do with the meaning they communicate. This is in addition to *how* they do what they do.

The storyteller sits in front of the altar shelf. This person embodies the story, parable, and liturgical action. The meaning that is incarnate in the person who sits by the door is as important but different. It has to do with welcoming and saying good-bye. It helps to draw the line at the door between ordinary language and experience and the language and experience being shown and used in the classroom.

The storyteller organises the circle and brings focus to the embodiment of the art. The door person welcomes the children, helps them get ready, helps with the art responses, helps prepare the classroom for the feast, and helps with the goodbyes. Neither person can do his or her job without the other …

The circle itself is a space of great importance. The circle of children indirectly includes the teachers, but these adults must also take a leadership role. The door person remains by the door unless there is an emergency in the circle. The role of the presenter is not to take possession of the lesson but to go to the shelf and bring the lesson to the circle for that community – the children and the adult presenter …

The presenter puts the lesson in the middle of the circle. The presenter shows how to 'enter' the lesson rather than telling the children how to think about it or what answer it should be reduced to. This shows respect for each member of the circle and an awareness of each one's own journey … it is like a small church …

The sacred story lessons sit on their own trays, which help organise them in a sensorimotor way. The trays, of course, also give the child the means to carry the whole set of materials to the rug, the desert box, or wherever the lesson will be worked with … . An example of a sacred story material is the lesson for the Exodus. The tray includes a basket to hold the People of God. There are also two blue pieces of felt rolled up. The principle employed is that 'less is more'.

To see what the child does, imagine a young girl. She goes to get out a rug from the rug box, takes it over to where the desert box is, and places it underneath the box … the desert box is a clear, shallow plastic box with a lid that contains sand … . When the box is pulled out from its special shelf section and is resting on the rug, the children can pull the rug to the place where they want to work … the struggle with the weight of the sand makes this really 'big work'.

Next, our little girl goes to the sacred story shelves and gets the tray for the Exodus. She puts the people in the desert and moves them through the story as the presenter has shown in a lesson in the circle or as she has seen another child do who has already had the lesson. The rule is that the children can work with any material in the classroom, provided they have had the lesson first.

The rule makes it clear that the materials are not for free play. The freedom comes in the response to the sacred story, parable or liturgical material. If the children were allowed to change the material's use, then there would be nothing left for them to use from religious language to make meaning with …

The girl working with the lesson of the Exodus in the desert box puts away her work before the lesson is considered finished. The parts of the lesson go back on the tray with care and respect. The tray is carried with two hands to its place on the top shelf of the sacred story shelves. The desert box is dragged back to its place and the plastic box is slid back onto the lower shelf.

16

God Talk with Young Children

John Hull (1991)

John Hull was a leading religious educator of the late twentieth century. He was most influential in reforming Religious Education in schools in the British context, especially in the 1970s and 80s, was the longstanding editor of the British Journal of Religious Education, and co-founder of the International Seminar on Religious Education and Values. In the following extract Hull focuses upon religious formation in the domestic setting, as illustrated by conversations with his own children.

Several concerns have led to this study of children's conversations about God. There is, first of all, a problem in the religious education of young children in county schools. There is often a tendency to concentrate upon preliminaries and a reluctance to teach children about the central issues of religion. The result is that many children are not acquiring the vocabulary which will enable them to talk about God and the issues of human life which God-talk entails. This is a loss not only to the religious education of the children but to their general social, personal and cultural development.

There are many factors in this reluctance to teach children how to talk about God, but one central issue is the fact that many teachers believe that young children are incapable of such conversation, My experience, and that of my colleagues providing teacher education in Birmingham University, is that when teachers do encourage young children to talk about God the results are fascinating and delightful. A rich vein of human experience and spiritual sensitivity can be opened up, and teachers often find that they are not only teaching their children but learning from them.

Many teachers have a concern that such conversations about God might be thought to nurture the faith of young children in God, and thus not only do the work which the churches, mosques and synagogues should do, but even perhaps indoctrinate children. While this confusion of the role of the religious community and the county school is always possible, and would be a mistake if it occurred, it should not be taken for granted that conversation about God cannot fulfil an educational purpose. The emphasis should not be on teaching children correct or orthodox doctrine about God. This is clearly a matter for the religious communities. Rather the emphasis should be on enriching children's vocabulary and, through conversation, developing images and concepts which will enable children to grapple, at their own level, with the issues and experiences involved in God-talk. To talk about something or someone is not to assume that the thing or person in question exists, but it does affirm the richness and significance of the idea. The conversational world of many young children is already far too restricted, in spite and perhaps because of the endless pressure from television and other aspects of the media and the commodity culture. The introduction in school of conversational skills about God should be thought of as offering children a spiritual resource.

Having said this, it is important to emphasise that the conversations reported in this booklet did not take place in school but at home. They often express shared assumptions, values and beliefs which are normal for the intimacy of family life, but could not necessarily be assumed in school, nor would an assumption be educationally proper. Allowance should be made for this domestic context when considering the educational appropriateness of these conversational techniques....

A second concern is for the nurture of children in the Christian faith through their families and churches. Not enough has been done to apply contemporary discussions in the social sciences to this area. Many Christian families seem to be stuck fast in the pietistic stereotypes of family life from the past. Others have given up entirely, and leave their children to the tender mercies of the peer group, the media and the school, hoping perhaps that a viable Christian education will be provided by the local church. Others create a Christian family lifestyle centred round identity with the poor and marginalised, but do not always enable children to interpret this lifestyle in the light of explicit Christian language and symbol. The art of theological conversation with young children is undeveloped, and this goes for much of the Christian education in churches as well as homes. God will be real to children brought up in homes and churches where the reality of God through peace and justice issues is made clear, but this requires language about God as well as commitment to peace and justice issues....

The intellectual background of this study is provided by three main streams of the social sciences. First, there is the tradition of cognitive stage development associated with Jean Piaget. The often repeated claim that young children are capable of much more than would be expected on Piagetian grounds does not mean that the work of Piaget and his successors has no contribution to make. Piaget emphasised again and again that the socio-genetic unfolding of intelligence, although preserving the same succession of stages, is greatly influenced by the culture, including family and educational background. It may well be that children in modern European cities, for example, are passing through the cognitive stages more rapidly than was the case several decades ago or is now the case in more remote areas. It is also necessary to say that some of those who reject this tradition do not appear to be well informed about its current developments. The work of Ronald Goldman in applying the Piagetian stages to religious thinking in the early 1960s remains of lasting significance, but needs to be supplemented by the work of the American school associated with James Fowler and the Swiss school of Fritz Oser. These offer far more flexible, rich and imaginative interpretations of the relationship between cognitive stage development and religion than was possible thirty years ago.

The second stream of intellectual tradition is provided by psychoanalysis. There is still a prejudice on the part of many Christian educators and Christian parents against the use of psychoanalysis in undertaking religious upbringing. Much of this suspicion springs from the fact that Sigmund Freud himself was so hostile to religion. In the past two decades, however, several aspects of psychoanalytic research have enabled us to see religious development in new ways, and these have an important bearing not only upon the religious lives of adults but upon the lives of children in religious families.

The third intellectual strand is provided by hermeneutics, the art of interpretation, Our understanding of the relationship between readers and books has changed very much in recent years, and these developments in interpretation have an important bearing upon how children are to be taught the Bible, how they are to learn prayers, hear stories and join in conversation. Hermeneutics also influences the way that we ourselves interpret children's conversations, and this is why the discussions which follow each conversation are described as interpretations. They are intended to be creative and suggestive rather than definitive and dogmatic. These conversations are often extremely subtle and could be interpreted in the light of many other frames of reference. What is offered here is, at any rate, an attempt to point one way forward .... .

Where is God?

If the abstract thinker is capable of abstract theological thought, is not the concrete thinker equally capable of concrete theological thought? Concrete theology can be just as faithful and a lot more vivid than abstract theology. Here is another example. Once again, the subject is 'Where is God?':

First Child (aged 3):   He's in a little cottage in the sky .... .
Second Child (aged 6):   No, God is everywhere. God is here (stabbing finger at tablecloth) and he's on this crumb (laughing).
Third Child (aged 8):   It means he's in our hearts and in our thoughts and in everything.

Interpretation

The youngest child is thinking in intuitive ways i.e. pre-concrete. There is a literal acceptance of an image expressed in matter-of-fact spatial language. At the same time, the reality described is special (tone of voice) and far away (in the sky, up and up). The second is borderline intuitive/concrete. This six-year-old knows that the literal image is not right, or is not considered adequate by some adults, and has heard the expression, 'God is everywhere', from adults or other children.

The child continues, however, to interpret it in concrete terms. 'Everywhere' means here and here and there all put together. The child also realises that this attempt to move into a generalised everywhere by means of multiplying specific is somehow not quite right, because it leads to a ludicrous result which is both funny and slightly daring: 'He's on this crumb'. Children in this situation will often continue 'Look! I'm squashing God' or 'I've eaten him!' (laughing).

The eight-year-old is borderline concrete/abstract. The child knows that 'everywhere' in reference to God does not mean a mere cumulation of many specific places but refers to a sort of human universality of emotion and thought, i.e. God is in our hearts and in our thoughts. The child has moved from physical to psychological categories: he has humanised God by speaking of God as dwelling within that which is distinctively and universally human.

You may say 'but even the older child could not have been thinking this and could not have said it in those words'. Of course, I agree, but my point is that the third child, although concrete, is flexible and creative and is a genuine theology. What it is saying does not have to be translated into abstract terms to be understood. Its truth lies in itself. This child did not mean that God was in his head the way a pea is in a pod. This would have been simply another example of a specific location. The fact that the child uses the plural and concludes the sentence by referring again to the concept 'everywhere' suggest that the child has broken through specific location into some kind of affirmation of a universal but internal relationship. What is said certainly does not lack meaning, and that is true of all three of these children. They are all speaking meaningfully of God at their own levels.

Germs and God

Let us take on final example of children's concrete thinking about the abstract concepts of God.

First Child (aged 6):   Are germs everywhere?

Parent: Yes, I suppose germs are just about everywhere. They're certainly everywhere in this house?

First Child: Then germs are like God (*triumphantly*) because God's everywhere. Look (*jabbing at tablecloth*) there's a germ and there's God (*laughs*).

Parent: Yes, that's how God is like germs. How is God not like germs?

Second Child (aged 8):   Germs are many but God is one.

Interpretation

This is another interesting example of the difference between the child who interprets the omnipresence of God in terms of multiplicity of locations and the child who grasps the idea that the omnipresence of God is qualitatively different. Germs, like air and atoms, may be widely, even generally, distributed, but the omnipresence of God is arrived at not through multiplying specific locations but through contrasting location with that which in principle is not located.

The reply of the older child has such a balanced style, such an archaic inversion ('germs are many') that one cannot help wondering whether it has simply been modelled on the formula 'God is one' which has been learned, of course, and is not the child's own creation. However, it is difficult to believe that the words were a mere verbalism, uttered from memory without understanding, because the reference to the germs and God was surely a novel feature of this single conversation, and not something the child would have been taught about at school or church. The fact that the child was able to make conversational use of the acquired formula 'God is one' and to contrast it with the manyness of the germs seems to me to go beyond the limits of concrete thought.

At the same time, although the younger child cannot spot the difference between germs and God, which requires a judgement of quality, the quantitative similarity is well within this younger child's grasp. Moreover, the younger child spots this similarity for herself. Nobody suggests it to her. There is thus evidence of a theological concept and a biological concept (both rather abstract ideas) being related in an amusing and creative way. Once again, there is a concrete theology at work here.

Let us summarise. The concrete thinker is often flexible, creative and versatile. Even the pre-concrete child, the intuitive thinker, can leap from one association to another in a way which often yields adequate and satisfying insights both to child and parent. There is a theological process at work during every pattern of reflection, there is a theology appropriate to the concrete thinker just as there is one available to the abstract thinker. We should not only be challenging children, so that their readiness for abstract thinking will be enhanced, but we should be encouraging them to think imaginatively within their immediate experience and in concrete terms.

17

Learning to Be a Muslim

Jonathan Scourfield, Sophie Gilliat-Ray, Asma Khan and Sameh Otri

In their recent major qualitative study of British Muslims' everyday religious socialization of children, Jonathan Scourfield, Sophie Gilliat-Ray, Asma Khan, and Sameh Otri explore why British Muslims are more likely to pass on their faith to the next generation than Christians. This chapter presents four key theoretical perspectives that help to explain this relatively strong inter-generational transmission of Islam.

Analysis of data from the UK Home Office Citizenship Survey (HOCS) (Scourfield et al. 2012) shows that Muslims are much more likely to pass on religion across generations than Christians and also slightly more likely than people from other religious groups. In this short chapter we briefly review four theoretical perspectives which help to explain this trend. All have emerged from our qualitative research with parents and children aged 12 and under in 60 Muslim families in Cardiff (Scourfield et al. 2013). These perspectives are: firstly, theories about the universal cognitive processes that can be seen in religious transmission; secondly, an emphasis on embodiment and the development of *habitus*; thirdly the social significance for religious transmission of being in an identifiable and sometimes beleaguered minority; and fourthly the role of religious organizations in passing on religion.

Cognitive transmission

'Soft' social science has recently met the hard sciences in the merging of anthropological research with the cognitive science of religion. The idea here is that local manifestations of religious belief and practice are built on cognitive structures that are universal. Several different theories have been advanced within the field of the cognitive science of religion and it is beyond the scope of this short chapter to properly review them all. Useful reviews are provided by Barrett (2007, 2011). Instead, we focus on just one theory within the field that might have some purchase in explaining the especially successful transmission of Islam. This is Whitehouse's (2002, 2004) idea of modes of religiosity.

Whitehouse is an anthropologist who has embraced the cognitive science approach. He identifies two modes of religious belief and practice into which religions can be categorized and which relate to different kinds of memory capacity. The imagistic mode involves intense and relatively rare events of high emotion. In contrast, the doctrinal mode involves frequent repetition of teaching and ritual. As Whitehouse explains, 'ritual action tends to be highly routinized, facilitating the storage of elaborate and conceptually complex religious teachings in semantic memory, but also activating implicit memory in the performance of most rituals' (2004: 65–66).

Mainstream Sunni Islam, with its five daily prayers and repeated recitation of the Qur'an, falls squarely into the doctrinal mode (Shankland, 2004). Although many other religious traditions also fall into the doctrinal mode – mainstream Catholic and Anglican Christians, for example – our research shows the intensity with which Muslim children learn about Islam, in contrast to the approach of much Christian teaching. Most children attend Qur'an classes at least once a week and often at least three times a week (typically after school, e.g. 5–7 pm).

Even more routine is the repetition of Islamic phrases at key points throughout the day for some children. Frequent repetition of ritual, from a very young age in some cases, allows bodily practices to be stored in implicit memory. Frequent repetition of religious teachings at home, in formal classes and through informal social interaction with Muslim friends and wider family members allows for the storage of these messages in semantic memory. This may be happening despite the language barrier for most learners of the Qur'an being read in classical Arabic, in which they lack fluency. These processes of transmission arguably apply to any Muslim children who are brought up in their faith. They do rely on parents teaching children at least some messages about Islam and usually on supplementary education. In addition to these cognitive processes, Shia Muslims typically have a religious experience in the imagistic mode if they mark Muharram, the martyrdom of Ali, which is a highly emotional event.

Islam is not uniquely placed in the doctrinal mode of course and this mode alone cannot explain why inter-generational transmission seems to be relatively successful. Many anthropologists have asserted strongly the need to understand the specific context of any religion being studied. In the words of Berliner and Sarró, '"Acquiring religion" is not merely a cold-blooded technical process of cognitive downloading. It takes place in a specific interactive social and cultural environment, and one must, therefore, also examine it as a "dimension of social practice"' (Berliner and Sarró, 2007: 10).

It is not enough to consider cognitive processes alone and neither do advocates of a cognitive science of religion claim that it is enough. Some Christian churches also have worship which is firmly in the doctrinal mode but may not be holding on to their children and young people as successfully. Cognitive science explanations, although coming first in our list of perspectives, are far from being our primary theoretical reference point. Additional theoretical contributions from social science are needed to more fully understand the relative strength of Islamic nurture. However, accepting a role for cognitive transmission means acknowledging that humans are not a blank slate at birth. As Pinker (2003) argues, blank slate theory has become an under-pinning assumption, tacit or not, of much social science. It effectively denies any cognitive architecture which humans bring to their social existence. Cognitive science theories of religion acknowledge that there may be some universal processes involved in becoming religious as well as context-specific ones.

Embodiment and *habitus*

Another crucial process for the passing on of religiosity to children is micro-level socialization, both within the family and in interaction with peers. A key sociological concept here is '*habitus*'. The term refers to our deeply rooted social inclinations, such as our values, tastes and bodily style. The term was used by Aristotle and Mauss (Mahmood, 2012 [2001]; Mellor and Shilling, 2010), but the best-known use in the social sciences is that of Bourdieu (1984). Bourdieu does not regard these inclinations as being consciously learned or developed through imitation. They are socially structured and are the means by which social conditions become naturalized. Mahmood (2012 [2001]) has used the idea of *habitus* in relation to Islamic practice. She takes issue with Bourdieu on the basis of his 'lack of attention to the pedagogical process by which a habitus is learned' (p130). We regard the concept of *habitus* as a very useful one for understanding how religion is learned, provided that a pedagogical dimension is included, as in the work of Mahmood.

Other scholars have also applied the idea of *habitus* to Islam. Winchester (2008) uses the concept of 'moral *habitus*' in relation to research with American Muslim converts. He argues that becoming a good Muslim is not just a process of taking on certain moral attitudes but embodied religious practice is also crucial. He writes that moral selfhood and practice mutually constitute and influence each other, rather than there being a unidirectional process. Embodied practices such as fasting, ritual prayer and wearing an appropriate form of dress, help to produce the moral dispositions of a good Muslim 'such as mindfulness, humility, discernment, moderation and modesty' (Winchester, 2008: 1755).

Oestergaard (2009) also applies the theory of *habitus* to Muslim converts, writing about the role of ritual and embodiment in converts proving themselves to be 'real' Muslims when some are suspicious of them. There are also echoes here of what Mellor and Shilling (2010) call 'body pedagogics' in religious socialization and what Orsi (2004, 74) terms the 'corporalization of the sacred'. All this adds up to the internalization of religious learning via a mutually constitutive relationship between morality and bodily practices.

From the first moments of life, a Muslim child is marked as Muslim by having the *adhaan* (call to prayer), and perhaps also *iqamah* (second call to prayer), spoken into her ear. This happened in almost all the families in our study. The child will probably be given a name which marks her as Muslim. As she grows up she will probably be expected to identify first and foremost as Muslim, before any national or ethnic identification. It is likely she will grow up in a home where religion is made material (Orsi, 2004) to some degree or other, for example with few or no images of people displayed but instead verses from the Qur'an and images of famous mosques up on the walls. In many family homes there will be frequent repetition of ritual and religious teachings. As other researchers working on Muslim *habitus* have noted, there is interaction between the repetition of embodied ritual and the development of moral deportment. Each reinforces the other.

Learning ritual prayer (*salat*), even if it the ritual is not strictly observed five times a day in families, is a core aspect of the embodied learning of Muslim *habitus*. As Mellor and Shilling (2010) note, *salat* constitutes a physical enactment of submission to Allah (the meaning of the term 'Islam'). There is a pedagogical process – you learn by participation – but this is not being thrown in the deep end. It is gradual socialization into particular ways of thinking and doing. And the doing is very much embodied. If a great deal of children's time and space features other Muslims, because of parents' own social networks and their control of children's, as well as attendance at supplementary education classes and mosques, then socialization into a religious *habitus* is quite likely to be successful.

Minority defence

In making sense of how children learn to be Muslims in a Western country, it is essential to keep in mind the social significance of being in a minority. The UK Muslim population is marked out from the non-Muslim population in several ways. Most Muslims are from a visible ethnic minority. Most have experience of migration, if not in their own lives then in the lives of parents or grandparents. Migration tends to be from countries of origin which are more religious than the host country (Voas and Fleischmann, 2012). The UK Muslim population is socially and economically disadvantaged (and especially Bangladeshis and Pakistanis) (Hussain, 2008).

The formation of minority identities is a complex process, with identity being both ascribed by others (and by the State) and also achieved by subjects. It can also be contingent and fluid. To some extent, collective identities are up for negotiation, but only within the limits of what is externally ascribed (Song, 2003). Despite the rise in primary identification with Islam rather than ethnicity amongst adults, we found some evidence of overlap between ethnicity and religious identity for Muslim children who have had less exposure to adult identity debates and may have a taken-for-granted Muslim identity on the basis of ethnicity.

Religion may remain stronger in the context of minority ethnic status than in the rest of the population as it has other work to do – helping to preserve the distinctive culture of an ethnic group which is outnumbered (Bruce, 1996) and perhaps helping to maintain social bonds in the face of discrimination and deprivation. There can be pride in minority status; what we might call a resistance identity (Castells, 1997). The idea of resistance identity may be especially pertinent in a post 9/11 climate where the identity Muslim has become politicized.

There was ample evidence in our study of the reinforcement of religious identity and practice through social networks which are dominated by the same minority culture. Most parents showed preference for Muslim (and usually same-ethnicity) social networks for their children, including wider family members and bonding social capital much more in evidence than bridging. Field's (2011) summary of opinion polling shows that a significant minority of young Muslim adults espouse 'apartism' and think integration into British society had gone too far. This ideological stance is not the opinion of the Muslims majority (however see Phillips, 2006), and for most people it is more likely that the company of other Muslims and especially those from the same ethnic and linguistic background is just more comfortable and more familiar, as well as providing a guarantee (in theory) of a suitable moral framework for children.

Time spent with people from the same ethnic background is not straightforwardly a choice for Muslims. Employment patterns in Cardiff are certainly racialized, and this may also be true for the housing market. In practice, attendance at most mosques is dominated by a single ethnic group. This in turn can reinforce the identification of religion with ethnicity, a phenomenon we saw in data from some of the children – a conflation of ethnic origin and religious identity which whilst not being about minority *defence* as such, certainly is a feature of being in a social minority. This conflation is particularly to be found in childhood, as amongst adults there is now a dominant discourse of separating ethnic culture from pure Islam; something the children in our study were generally not aware of.

Finally there is the issue of religion being strengthened as a response to hardship and discrimination. Hypothetically this might ring true and it might also mark Muslims out somewhat from other ethno-religious minorities in the UK. Firstly this is because the Muslim population is especially deprived, and indeed more so than Hindus and Sikhs (Mercia Group, 2006). Secondly, a Muslim identity has become highly politicized, since the Rushdie Affair to an extent and then even more so since 9/11. Voas and Fleischmann (2012) note that some scholars have speculated about this process, i.e. Islam being strengthened as a reaction to discrimination, but evidence is currently lacking. On the basis of our qualitative study we would suggest there is indeed *some* evidence for this phenomenon but it is not over-whelming. There was some talk of needing to defend the reputation of Islam. There were some glimmers of resistance identity. There were also some examples of hostility experienced since 9/11 but in fact there were fewer of these examples than might have been expected. Parents were asked what it was like being in a minority in Cardiff and the vast majority were very positive about their experience of living in the city as Muslims. Several made positive comparisons with living in a Muslim country.

The role of religious organizations

The final theoretical perspective that we argue is necessary to aid understanding of religious nurture in Muslim families is the role of religious organizations. Almost all parents with children old enough arranged for them to attend some kind of formal learning, usually to read the Qur'an and sometimes too to learn Islamic Studies. These classes are of central importance to religious nurture. There is a combined influence of mosques which organize classes, well-known local teachers who take small groups in their own homes or the homes of their students and the Islamic media such as TV channels and websites which are increasingly available to parents for religious nurture.

It is worth stating that we are not dealing here with large bureaucracies and complex hierarchies. There are no UK-wide organizations which have any particular influence on religious nurture. Field notes that opinion polls confirm 'the fragmentation and relative irrelevance to grass-roots Muslims' of British Islam's national leadership (2011: 163). Rather there are mosques and other Islamic institutions set up by local social networks, but building on wider traditions of epistemological authority. Despite the recent tendency to deculturation – that is, younger adult Muslims' distancing from the ethnic culture of their parents – described by Roy (2004), there was evidence of continuing respect for historical threads of Islamic authority, in the form of local scholars and respected local teachers and also sometimes in the form of nationally- or internationally-recognized *shaykhs*.

Supplementary schools are strongly connected to other Muslim organizations so are part of a nexus of Islamic institutions. They facilitate participation in a Muslim community, so children who attend Islamic education classes not only learn about the Qur'an and the foundations of Islam, but they are also socialized to be members of a faith community; one which in most cases is made of people from the same ethnic background. Religious organizations therefore have an important role to play in the development of Muslim *habitus* and the reinforcing of minority identity.

There are tentative comparisons to be made with the roles of religious organizations in other faiths; tentative because ours was not a comparative qualitative study. Data from the HOCS Young People's Survey suggest that attendance at 'out-of-school clubs' in religious organizations is more prevalent amongst 11–15 year old Muslims than in other religious groups. It is not too clear whether, in making this survey response, Muslim children are referring to supplementary religious education classes. The data might under-estimate the attendance at such classes if respondents did not regard them as 'out-of-school clubs'. The same methodological limitations apply to the other faith groups, however. It is therefore reasonably valid to compare religious groups and the differences between them should be taken seriously.

One difference between religions is that whereas Islam is in a phase of global resurgence (Sutton and Vertigans 2005), Christianity is experiencing decline, at least in the UK (Crockett and Voas 2006). Although we lack comparative data, it is likely that regimes of religious teaching in most churches are relatively 'light touch' compared to those organized by mosques and Muslim families. Certainly there has been a historical move away from disciplinarian teaching in the Catholic Church, see for example, Orsi (2004) on the United States. The material on the religious nurture of Hindu and Sikh children in Nesbitt's (2004) book, although referring occasionally to supplementary education, does not give the impression of classes taking places several times a week as is the case for close to half of the Muslim families in our study.

One theory of organizations which has been applied to religion is that of resource dependency (Scheitle and Dougherty, 2008). This might suggest that the non-negotiable truth claim of Islam (there is one God and Muhammad is his Messenger) makes individuals more dependent on the religious organization than would be the case in those belief systems without a taken-for-granted core of universally accepted truths. This might suggest that the tendency towards theological and textual conservatism, wherein the Qur'an and *hadith* are literally applicable in 2012, rather than being historically contextualized, might reinforce people's affiliations to Islamic organizations.

References

Barrett, J. (2007), 'Cognitive science of religion: What is it and why is it?', in *Religion Compass* 1. Available online: DOI: 10.1111/j.1749-8171.2007.00042.x

Barrett, J. (2011), 'Cognitive science of religion: looking back, looking forward', in *Journal for the Scientific Study of Religion* 50(2): 229–239.

Berliner, D. and Sarró, R. (2007), 'On learning religion. An introduction', in D. Berliner and R. Sarró (eds), *Learning Religion: Anthropological approaches*, New York: Berghahn.

Bourdieu, P. (1984), *Distinction. A social critique of the judgement of taste*, New York.

Bruce, S. (1996), *Religion in the Modern World: From cathedrals to cults*, Oxford: Oxford University Press.

Castells, M. (1997), *The Power of Identity*, Oxford: Blackwell.

Crockett, A. and Voas, D. (2006), Generations of decline: Religious change in 20th century Britain, in *Journal for the Scientific Study of Religion* 45(4): 567–584.

Field, C.D. (2011), 'Young British Muslims since 9/11: A composite attitudinal profile', in *Religion, State and Society* 39(2/3): 159–175.

Hussain, S. (2008), *Muslims on the Map: A national survey of social trends in Britain*, London: I B Tauris.

Mahmood, S. (2012 [2001]), 'Rehearsed spontaneity and the conventionality of ritual: Disciplines of salat', in J. Kreinath (ed.), *The Anthropology of Islam Reader*, Abingdon: Routledge, 121–141.

Mellor, P. and Shilling, C. (2010), 'Body pedagogics and the religious *habitus*: A new direction for the sociological study of religion', in *Religion* 40: 27–38.

Mercia Group (2006), *Review of the Evidence Base on Faith Communities*, London: Office of the Deputy Prime Minister.

Oestergaard, K. (2009), 'The process of becoming Muslim: Ritualization and embodiment', in *Journal of Ritual Studies* 23(1): 1–14.

Orsi, R. (2004), *Between Heaven and Earth. The religious worlds people make and the scholars who study them*, Princeton: Princeton University Press.

Phillips, D. (2006), 'Parallel lives? Challenging discourses of British Muslim self-segregation', in *Environment and Planning D: Society and Space* 24(1): 25–40.

Pinker, S. (2003), *The Blank Slate. The Modern Denial of Human Nature*, London, Penguin.

Roy, O. (2004), *Globalized Islam: The Search for a New Ummah*, New York: Columbia University Press.

Scheitle, C.P. and Dougherty, K.D. (2008), 'The sociology of religious organizations', in *Sociology Compass* 2/3: 981–999.

Scourfield, J., Gilliat-Ray, S., Otri, S. and Khan, A. (2013), *Muslim Childhood: Religious Nurture in a European Context*, Oxford: Oxford University Press.

Scourfield, J., Taylor, C., Moore, G. and Gilliat-Ray, S. (2012), 'The intergenerational transmission of Islam: Evidence from the Citizenship Survey', in *Sociology* 46(1): 91–108.

Shankland, D. (2004), 'Modes of religiosity and the legacy of Ernest Gellner', in H. Whitehouse and J. Laidlaw (eds) *Ritual and Memory: Toward a comparative anthropology of religion*, Walnut Creek, CA: Alta Mira.

Song. M. (2003), *Choosing Ethnic Identity*, Cambridge: Polity.

Sutton, P.W. and Vertigans, S. (2005), *Resurgent Islam: A sociological approach*, Cambridge: Polity.

Voas, D. and Fleischmann, F. (2012), 'Islam moves West: Religious change in the first and second generations', in *Annual Review of Sociology* 38: 525–545.

Whitehouse, H. (2002), 'Modes of religiosity: Towards a cognitive explanation of the sociopolitical dynamics of religion', in *Method and Theory in the Study of Religion* 14: 293–315.

Whitehouse, H. (2004), *Modes of Religiosity: A cognitive theory of religious transmission*, Walnut Creek, CA: Alta Mira.

Winchester, D. (2008), 'Embodying the faith: Religious practice and the making of a Muslim moral *habitus*', in *Social Forces* 86(4): 1753–1780.

18

Becoming Muslim in a Danish Provincial Town

Marianne Holm Pedersen

*M*arianne Holm Pedersen is a senior researcher at the Danish Folklore Archives, The Royal Library, in Denmark. Her research focuses on belonging and placemaking, family and generational relations, religious socialization, and ritual performance and everyday life, primarily among Arab migrants in Denmark. Her publications include Iraqi women in Denmark: Ritual performance and belonging in everyday life (Manchester University Press, 2014). In this chapter, she explores how being a Muslim is passed on in families in a provincial town in Denmark.

Introduction

During a research project on the passing on of religion within Muslim families in a Danish provincial town, I interviewed 13-year old Zainab and her younger brother, Musa. Juice and cookies were on the table, and we were sitting nicely relaxed in two large leather couches in the living room. With their mother next to us, we talked about different kinds of Islamic practice in everyday life:

Marianne: Do you sometimes pray?
Musa: Sometimes we try to say the prayer and stuff like that. But no so often.
Zainab: With our dad. And maybe I'll say some prayers inside myself. That's also part of our everyday lives, for instance after dinner we say *al-hamdulillah*. It's one of those things. And I was thinking that I'll soon start praying. I'm just waiting for something to cover myself with. Because my dad said that if I start praying, then maybe the others will pray too. And maybe my mom will also start to pray, if I begin.

At Zainab's last remark her mother pulled a face with embarrassment. She was not happy to admit that she did not regularly pray the obligatory five daily prayers.

Apart from showing that the parents performed Islam in different ways, this example highlights the role of children in the religious life of the family. Zainab and her father agree that she should begin praying on a regular basis, not only for her own sake, but also to make a positive influence on the rest of the family. The example illustrates that all family members take part in giving meaning to what it means to be religious in this particular family, even if they do not have the same degree of influence. As Susan B. Ridgely has pointed out, it is 'in the interplay between the generations that both children and adults shape their religious traditions by developing a modifying ritual and theology to fit their particular needs' (2012: 240).

In this chapter I will explore how being a Muslim is passed on within ethnic minorities in a Danish provincial town through considering the case of Zainab's family as a starting point for reflection. More specifically, I will discuss processes of informal socialization within the family and how children navigate these. While studies of religious socialization often consider children as passive receivers of knowledge (Ridgely 2012: 242), and studies of the learning of religion among children and young people often prioritize institutional contexts, I will argue for including a perspective on both parents and children in examining how religion is passed on from one generation to the next. The chapter is based on data from fieldwork among Muslim parents, children and young people in the region of western Zealand, Denmark.[1]

Religious socialization across time and space

Teaching children about religion is often considered particularly difficult in the context of migration, where immigrants with a different religion than the majority need to reinvent their religious practices in a new social setting (Pedersen 2014, Levitt 2001, Schiffauer 1988). If, for instance, Muslim children are to become practicing believers in a non-Muslim society it requires special attention, among other things because the acquisition of religious practices and values is not necessarily backed up by religious education or regular religious festivals in the majority society. Yet, passing religious beliefs and practices on to the next generation always involves a 'crisis of transmission', because new generations are never just copies of preceding ones (Hervieu-Léger 1998: 214). The transmission of religion hence highlights how religious practices and interpretations necessarily undergo change over time.

The process of continuity and change is exemplified in the case of Muslim parents in the Danish province. When they figure out how to pass on Islam or how to respond to a particular situation in Danish society, they are reinterpreting their own religion and defining how it gives meaning to them to live as Muslims in Denmark. While there appears to be a certain shared 'curriculum' of Islamic knowledge that parents want their children to learn – central Islamic practices (praying, reading Quran, and fasting) and issues of morality – there were significant differences in the interpretation of Islam among families, for instance regarding the importance of practice versus moral behavior, and the question of how one should live as a Muslim in a non-Muslim society. Such differences were closely connected with the parents' own learning trajectories: how they have been taught about Islam, how they have acquired religious practices, and the role that Islam has played throughout their life courses. In order to understand how children learn about religion, it is thus relevant to examine how the parents themselves have acquired it. Likewise, when studying continuity and change across generations it is not necessarily interesting to see whether a religious practice is transmitted and acquired in a right or wrong way, but rather the processes through which religion changes or stays the same over time (Hervieu-Léger 1998).

In order to examine the transmission and formation of socio-religious identities, the French sociologist Daniele Hervieu-Léger has suggested exploring religious 'trajectories of identification' (1998: 218). Hervieu-Léger identifies four dimensions of identification. These are, first, the communal dimension, which defines the boundary of the group and relates to the formal and practical definitions of belonging; second, the ethical dimension, which concerns acceptance of the values associated with a religious tradition; third, the cultural dimension, which involves the material, symbolic and practical heritage of a particular religious tradition; and finally the emotional dimension, which concerns the emotional experience associated with identification (1998: 219ff).

Trajectories of learning in the family

If we take a look at Zainab's case, we can see how the different trajectories of identification are developed within the family setting. Zainab's parents have arranged private lessons in Islam for the children once a week. Yet, it is only to an extent that the children learn by explicit teaching, because passing Islam on also takes place naturally as part of everyday life within the family. For example, through reading, watching television or listening to narratives about the prophets and their deeds or about Muslims elsewhere, children become included in a larger, historical community of practice. Ethics are transmitted through the continued conversation about norms and morality. The cultural dimension is acquired by observing and imitating what their parents do in daily life. As Zainab mentioned, mealtime may serve as occasions for socialization when parents start the meal by saying *bismillah* or ending with *al-hamdulillah* (Ochs and Shohet 2006). Routines like removing the shoes before entering the house in order to keep the floor clean for prayers, are not taught explicitly, but simply appropriated as family practice. In this way, before the children explicitly learn the doctrines of religion, Islam becomes embodied through various practices and techniques of the self. The process taking place resembles the general process of upbringing in which parents, throughout childhood, are 'continuously attempting to direct their children's awareness to the moral dimensions of particular social situations in which they are engaged' (Ochs and Kremer-Sadlik 2007: 6).

It is an important point that when the family develops a shared repertoire, the children are not only included in a general Muslim community, but also very specifically into the community of the family. As many studies of kinship have pointed out, the family is not a given, but needs to be continuously constructed (Carsten 2000). By sharing practices and including children in the same religious community as themselves, parents make children into family members (Pedersen 2011: 134). This is not a one-way process. Religious identification also functions as a process by which children themselves create their relations to the family. This was illustrated in young girls' stories about wanting to be like their mothers in deciding to wear the hijab, or in a young man's pleasure at joining his father for the Friday prayer. Religious practices are thus also family practices. Older children often influenced younger ones, and discussions of religious practice could be an important aspect of sibling relations. All in all, my interviews with the younger generation pointed to the great importance of social relations in the learning of religion (Day 2009). By connecting the concrete family community with a more abstract Muslim community, a sense of belonging – the emotional dimension mentioned by Hervieu-Léger – was developed during childhood.

Contrary to the common expectation that immigrant parents are reproducing a religious upbringing from their place of origin, the religious upbringing of many Muslim parents in Denmark is strongly influenced by the experience of living in a minority setting (Pedersen 2011). Zainab's father, for instance, did not have much knowledge about Islam before he moved to Denmark. There he started attending a mosque, and Muslim practices became a large part of his life. He wants to pass Islam on to his children because he believes it is the right path, but his emphasis on a religious upbringing is increased by, on the one hand, a felt need to teach his children how they live as Muslims in a non-Muslim society, and on the other hand, a wish to prevent them from becoming 'radical Muslims' or buying into interpretations of Islam with which he does not agree. He tells:

> We talk a lot when we sit at the table. For me it is an important point to pass on to the children. Because I don't *in any way* want that they enter the extremist world at some point. If they don't have knowledge, if they just think well, my parents are Muslims, but I'm just following a different way. Because of their skin colour, because of their area, because of their background, the places they go, who they are, they risk falling into the wrong hands or into the wrong...places that may lead them to something else. So for me, at least I know that they have the principal [knowledge], the basis, they have the real thing. [...] It's part of our upbringing.

This example highlights that the religious socialization of children in the home is constructed in relation to the current societal context and the parents' current stage of life where religion is important to them. It also shows how Zainab's father is considering some of the threats to the children's future when bringing up the children.

The desire to secure them a good future becomes part of the reason for why Islam and the proper interpretation of it need to be passed on (Pedersen 2011: 132).

Navigating as a Muslim child in a Danish context

In what ways do children then acquire what their parents try to pass on? If passing religion on means children learning exact dogma and acquiring precise knowledge, parents were not always completely successful. Across the spectrum of families, more or less all the young people I interviewed said that in some respects they lack detailed knowledge of their religious practices, they do not understand what they read in the Quran, and that they often have problems understanding what is said in the mosque. Instead, their way of acquiring religion was more a matter of creating a relationship to God and incorporating a sense of being Muslim into their day-to-day lives. In this way, they developed a 'potential religiosity' that could be more or less important to them in different situations and at different times of their lives (Østberg 1998: 6).

While parents tend to be concerned about the differences between norms and values taught within and outside the home, studies have argued that moving between different social arenas does not necessarily cause a problem for the children. Rather, they move between social contexts that together constitute different arenas of the same lifeworld (Østberg 1998: 233, Stene 2004: 352). This, however, does not imply that children did not have to make moral navigations in terms of how they should or should not behave as Muslims. Here age made a difference. Older youth had to make decisions in relation to very 'politized' issues such as whether or not to drink alcohol, participate in parties and have boyfriends or girlfriends, and younger children navigated in relation to practices such as swearing, fighting, eating candy, and other aspects of everyday life that were important to them. In order to illustrate children's different strategies of navigating practices outside the family home, let me end with two examples from Zainab's life.

During my conversation with Zainab and Musa, we talked about the recent 'scissor and paste day' at their school where each class meets in early December to craft Christmas decorations for the class room:

Marianne: And what did you do at the 'scissors and paste day'?
Musa: We didn't go that day, I mean, we just had the day off.
Zainab: Well, I was there … it's because it's very rare that our class we just sit and have a good time [*hygger*], it's very very rare. So it would be, maybe a little bit a pity, if I didn't join. Not because I want to make Christmas things, I just made snow men and stuff like that, that didn't have anything to do with Christmas. But there was, you know, *hygge* [it was cosy], and there was *æbleskiver* [Christmas doughnuts], and those things you usually do. And it's very seldom that we just have a good time together in class, so it would be too bad if I couldn't stay there. So I was allowed to just go that day.

The fact that Musa did not go to school on the particular day represents the family's official stance: Although the parents considered their religion a private affair that was not relevant to life outside the home, they found it important that their children did not participate in activities which in their interpretation were incompatible with being Muslim. Among other things, this meant that in school the kids were exempted from the teaching of a religion class ('Knowledge of Christianity') and they did not participate in any activities related to Christmas. However, to Zainab being part of her school class was in this case more important than staying away for religious reasons. She managed to convince her parents to let her go, emphasizing the importance of *hygge* over the occasion of Christmas. Whereas her brother Musa considered the Christmas gathering as related to a religious occasion, Zainab interpreted it as is more common in Denmark, namely as a social occasion related to an annual Danish tradition.

While Zainab convinced her parents to let her participate in the 'scissors and paste day', there were other times when she prioritized loyalty towards family practice. Like Christmas, Zainab's parents were skeptical towards the celebration of birthdays. This meant that the children only rarely participated in the birthday parties of their friends, an otherwise very widespread activity among young children. This was an issue of contention with the children's teacher who supposedly felt sorry for Zainab and worried that she would feel excluded. In our conversations Zainab appeared to be more in line with her parents who emphasized that she had other good experiences to appreciate and who considered the teacher's comments as an inappropriate interference in the private life of the family. However, Zainab was very aware of the attitudes of her teacher and class mates which led her to develop tactics to avoid others thinking 'that my parents are mean'. This implied that she would tell other children beforehand not to invite her to a party or birthday, because she would not be available on the date in question anyway.

These two examples show how Zainab moves between being 'visible' and 'invisible' as Muslim in the school context (Stene 2004: 38). Her approach to her religious identity seems to be very pragmatic (Ridgely 2011: 13). Sometimes she downplays her Muslim identity and practice, and other times she prioritizes this, both as a matter of behaving according to Muslim norms and as a strong commitment to her parents. Learning to navigate also implies her becoming skilful in avoiding awkward situations. In this way, the relationship between the family and representatives of the school (e.g. the teacher) influences her trajectory of identification and her understanding of her own position in this social space.

Conclusion

Teaching children about Islam is both to pass religion on and to reproduce the family as institution. Focusing on both parents and children when studying the process of passing religion on sheds light on trajectories of learning both within a life course and across generations, and it shows the role of family relations in the learning of religion. Religious socialization takes place in both explicit and tacit ways, and what the children learn is not necessarily what the parents intend to teach them. Parents may focus on passing on particular religious practices, dogma and traditions, but the embodied knowledge that children acquire is much broader than the specific practices. Like adults, children appropriate elements of their religion that give meaning to them in different social contexts. When children make sense of being Muslim, they also make sense of their relations to others, and they position themselves in the context of a non-Muslim majority society.

Note

1 Excerpts from this chapter have previously been published in the article 'Islam in the family. The religious socialization of children in a Danish provincial town', in M. Sedgwick (ed.), *Making European Muslims. Religious Socialization Among Young Muslims in Scandinavia and Western Europe*, London and New York: Routledge.

References

Carsten, J. (ed.) (2000), *Cultures of relatedness: new approaches to the study of kinship*, Cambridge: Cambridge University Press.

Day, A. (2009), 'Believing in belonging: an ethnography of young people's constructions of belief', *Culture and Religion* 10(3): 262–278.

Hervieu-Léger, D. (1998), 'The transmission and formation of socioreligious identities in modernity: an analytical essay on the trajectories of identification', *International Sociology* 13(2): 213–228.

Levitt, P. (2001), *The transnational villagers*, Berkeley: University of California Press.

Ochs, E. and T. Kremer-Sadlik (2007), 'Introduction: morality as family practice', *Discourse & Society* 18(1): 5–10.

Ochs, E. and M. Shohet (2006), 'The cultural structuring of mealtime socialization', *New Directions for Child and Adolescent Development* 111: 35–49.

Østberg, S. (1998), *Pakistani children in Oslo: Islamic nurture in a secular context*, Ph.D. thesis, University of Warwick.

Pedersen, M.H. (2011), '"You want your children to become like you": the transmission of religious practices among Iraqi families in Copenhagen', in M. Rytter and K.F. Olwig (eds), *Mobile bodies, mobile souls: family, religion and migration in a global world*, Aarhus: Aarhus University Press.

Pedersen, M.H. (2014), *Iraqi women in Denmark: ritual performance and belonging in everyday life*, Manchester: Manchester University Press.

Ridgely, S. (2012), 'Children and religion', *Social Compass* 6(4): 236–248.

Ridgely, S. (ed.) (2011), *The study of children in religions: a methods handbook*, New York: New York University Press.

Schiffauer, W. (1988), 'Migration and religiousness', in T. Gerholm and Y. G. Litman (eds), *The new Islamic presence in Europe*, London: Mansell.

Stene, N.P. (2004), *Engler i platåsko. Religiøs socialisering av koptisk-ortodokse barn i London*, Dr.art.thesis, University of Oslo.

19

Faith Co-Creation in US Catholic Churches: How First Communicants and Faith Formation Teachers Shape Catholic Identity

Susan B. Ridgely

Susan B. Ridgely is an Associate Professor of Religious Studies at the University of Wisconsin, Madison, US. In this chapter, she shifts away from the common concerns of religious educators about transmission of the faith to questions of how children craft a useful tradition for themselves in concert with the adults around them.

On December 10, 2000, twenty-two Catholic Euro-American and children whose families recently emigrated from Central America met for their first religious education class since their First Reconciliation. On the pink carpet in the front of their classroom, their teacher, Mrs. Fabuel, told the class: "You did a great job. Even though you were nervous and shaking when you went in you all came out smiling." Then she moves to discuss the different Christmas symbols and their connection to Christianity. "The star is Jesus, the light of the world; the evergreen is Jesus' undying love for us; and the candy cane is the shepherd's staff." Here eight-year-old Michael jumps in to demonstrate what he's learned adding, "the red stuff is Jesus's blood." As the class continues, Mrs. Fabuel tells the children that their homework is to write a Christmas card to the parish's shut-ins. As she explains what "shut-in" means, Annie raises her hand to add, "My uncle is in a wheel chair." The teacher tries to placate her and gloss over this difficult subject by responding, "He'll get better soon." Annie corrects Mrs. Fabuel: "No, he broke his back and he'll be in a wheelchair for the rest of his life."

Fifteen years later, these children were adults, my own child was the age they were then, and I was an associate professor, not a graduate student. In the intervening years I had been developing my skills as a child-centered researcher all built on the time spent with these children and others like them, attending classes and Masses, seeking to understand how they interpreted their preparation for and experience of First Communion.

Returning to my fieldnotes from these events with more distance and theoretical tools evinced nuances that I had not noticed before, nuances that both enhance and explain my original thesis. When I originally re-read my fieldnotes in 2003, as I wrote my book on children and First Communion, I saw only two distinct categories: the adults as teachers and the children as active creators. My attention centered on how children used the various building blocks the adults offered to construct their Catholic tradition. The adult-authored foundations and the children's interpretations seemed like distinct entities. At the time, Religious Studies scholar Paul Numrich's concept of parallel congregations resonated with my data, which showed that the children's interpretations of the event differed significantly from the adults.[1]

I drew my evidence for this argument from a four-year-long ethnographic project with seven-, eight-, and nine-year-old Catholics at Blessed Sacrament Catholic Church, a split Anglo and Latino parish in Burlington, North Carolina, as well as their counterparts in the 1997 First Communion class at Holy Cross Catholic Church, an African American parish in Durham, North Carolina, as they prepared for and celebrated their First Communion. In interviews, rehearsals, and classroom exercises, I watched as the children and the adults who supported them co-created a Catholic identity founded in action—from the sign of the cross to a hug during the "kiss of peace" to a first communion gift—that cemented their place in the Church.

From the children's perspective, they were under adult supervision and also at the adult's side during Mass; and yet they still understood themselves to be separate from and even invisible to the parish before First Communion. Emphasizing the children's feelings of difference through this image of parallel parishes, parishes that exist right next to each other but never actually meet, gave me a framework that highlighted how the children's religious practices were much more than just pantomimes of adults' more authentic and intentional actions. My work had revealed that the children's own practices and theologies were deeply significant to their Catholic children's culture, to their own parish interests. For instance, the children understood that practicing the sign of the cross was ritual action, not preparation for it: through this repetitive motion the children demonstrated their connection to their Church and love for their families who would come to see them receive the sacrament in May. Focusing on the children's community revealed much that had been ignored or dismissed by priests, parents, and academics. However, it also obscured the fact that the adults crafted the "building blocks" they offered the children in the midst of, and in response to, that children's culture. The guiding assumptions of this chapter, then, are that children are active participants in their religious traditions and that the traditions in which they practice constantly transform to meet the current needs of their practitioners. With this in mind, the chapter examines the importance of critical self-reflection on one's research by demonstrating the new interpretations I developed by returning to my fieldnotes. In my case, the intervening years had seen the development of the Childhood Studies Group in the American Academy of Religion and a growing body of work on children's agency in their religious traditions. With the new approaches to child-centered research available to me, I found myself attending to the annoying, interrupting, and dismissed actions of these young people that all the adults around me ignored.

Bringing Childhood Studies to Religion Studies: The Case for Co-Creation

Historian Robert Orsi has noted:

> Children signal the vulnerability and contingency of a particular religious world, and of religion itself, and in exchanges between adults and children about sacred matters the religious world is in play. On no other occasions except perhaps in times of physical pain and loss is the fictive quality of religion- the fact that religious worlds are made and sustained by humans—so intently and unavoidable apprehended as when adults attempt to realize the meaningfulness of their religious worlds in their children. (Orsi, 2005)

In his work, Orsi offers great insights into adult efforts to instantiate religion in children and how these efforts do more than transfer Catholicism from one generation to the next—they serve to create it. In a series of papers and chapters beginning in 2003, Boyatzis supported Orsi's argument, using child-centered methodology to examine parent–child conversations about Christianity and the participation of children in the creation of a family's religious stories and traditions (Boyatzis, 2004, 2006; Boyatzis and Janicki, 2003). In diverging from traditional studies of socialization, which almost exclusively positioned adults as the teachers and children as the receivers, he takes a more dialogical approach to understanding each person's influence on the discussion.[2] His work has begun to push against developmental psychology's reliance on stage theories by emphasizing agency of children in these discussions and highlighting the uniqueness of the spirituality of each child and each family. By including children's perspectives in his analysis, Boyatzis lays bare moments of destruction and re-creation. As Boyatzis, others, and myself have begun to explore young people's religious worlds apart from questions of spiritual development and religious socialization, they have started to expose more of the instability of religious traditions.

Using these theories and others from the sociology of childhood, I have tried to push back on the common notion that these children are "the next generation of Catholics," or "Catholics in the making," rather than Catholics in their own right. I understand them as one of many current cohorts of Catholics that intertwine with other generations, such as Vatican II Catholics, African American Catholics, Latino Catholics, disabled Catholics, Euro-American Catholics, all who have their own unique understanding of the Church. Placing children alongside adults in this research can be daunting since when it comes to children, adult concern for the future often eclipses whatever is happening in the present both in religious education (RE) classrooms and in scholarly studies. This unexplainable pull toward viewing children as "the next generation," rather than as current participants, leaves many unanswered and undiscovered questions about children as religious actors. By positioning children as placeholders, it also obscures children's influence, leaving adults firmly in control of defining and transmitting their tradition, even when parents, RE teachers, and other adults openly wrestle with children's efforts to pushback and negotiate with the adult interpretation. Congregations position young people as future, rather than current, practitioners of their traditions even as they actively engage in Sunday school and services, even if it is just to protest their forced presence in these places. As Ms Fabuel said during our interview the following week: "Every year you have the kids that you remember their names ... just because of the way they act in class you always can put that name with that face. The ones (names) I can't remember ... they're always the good kids." In remembering these children's names, she and other teachers, priests, and parents remember the lessons that held their attention and often seek to adjust other lessons to captivate them. In so doing, they emphasize, elide, and eliminate the aspects of their tradition they will pass on to their student. Through this process of adults and young people coming together in conversation and physical expressions of enthusiasm and complaint, they engage in an often unseen processes of co-creation.

Overt and covert creation: Real presence comes to the classroom

From the perspective of co-creation, Michael demonstrating that he can apply his knowledge of First Communion to the candy cane or Annie's efforts to include her families' struggle into the more generic category of "those in need" become meaningful moments of engagement. Since these moments were not overtly acknowledged by the teacher or elaborated on by the children, the moments seemed to be forgotten. However, hearing the children, like Allison, express their sadness, loneliness, and pain each week influenced Ms. Fabuel to teach the children that Jesus was always with them in a tangible way; he did not reserve his real presence solely for the consecrated host. Almost every week, she asked the children to stand and give themselves a "bear hug." When the communicants grew especially rowdy, Ms. Fabuel stopped talking, raised her hands over her head to make a half circle, and said, "What is this?" "A circle," the class answered almost in unison. "What does it represent?" she continued. "Jesus," they answered even louder. On some days, this response marked the first time in the lesson when all the children (even those inclined to wander around the room or hit their neighbor) attended to what Ms. Fabuel was saying and doing. "And when you bring it down...." "Jesus is giving you a bear hug!" the children would shout before she could finish the question. Then Mrs. Fabuel asked, "Why is it a circle?" "Because Jesus' love is never ending," the children quickly replied. She would follow this response with, "Why is that important?" The crowd usually yelled a wide variety of answers. Each week I listened to these responses, trying to distinguish one child's answer from that of another. In the end, a Latino boy's statement seemed to encapsulate the majority of his classmates' sentiments: "Because it tells us that Jesus is there when we're lonely." Ms. Fabuel did this exercise so often, she said, because she wanted the children to realize that "Jesus loves them always. That's why we have the big circle and the big hug, so that whenever they do feel alone and feel like they need help...they can get it just by closing their eyes and feeling Jesus' presence around them." The students found this exercise so memorable that even those communicants who only attended Faith Formation classes sporadically included it in our conversations. Christy, an endearing seven-year-old Latina who usually attended class once every two to three weeks, explained, "God is always with us, that's why I don't have to be afraid of thunder anymore," as she performed a modified "hug" from Jesus.

When I first analyzed this interaction, I concluded, "through this lesson the children were taught, and came to understand, that God was not a distant historical or spiritual figure, but was always ready to show each of them his love by giving them a big bear hug" (Bales, 2005). Going back through my notes, however, demonstrated that this was not a teacher-driven lesson. Rather students' statements and prayer served as the catalyst for its design, which is perhaps why it was so very popular. Without even realizing it, Ms. Fabuel explained the process of co-creation when she described designing this lesson in response to the sorrows the children shared with her. "That concept [of the hug] really got to them because these little kids have a lot of trauma in their lives that we are not aware of here. This gives them the opportunity to really know that somebody is caring and loving." In creating this lesson, Ms. Fabuel attempted to speak directly to the children's needs rather than to address the key points of doctrine outlined in their First Communion text. As their first reconciliation and first Eucharist begin to meld with the many others they have since received, this exercise remained in the children's imagination, an exercise that presented them with a characterization of Jesus that shared more similarities with their protestant neighbors than it did with the one held by their co-religionists in other age cohorts.

Father Barry, at Holy Cross Catholic Church, tried a child-centered approach to teaching the children about the abstract concept of transubstantiation, a concept that instructors at the Blessed Sacrament taught mainly through memorization. Fr. Barry, however, understood that immersing children in roleplay activities would help them to learn how the bread and the wine in communion became Jesus' body and blood when he blessed them. So with the children's needs in mind he developed an exercise that began with a reenactment of the Last Supper and ended with an effort to offer them a tangible sense of Jesus being physically present in the Eucharist in churches all over the world. Like so many efforts to engage children, this one included toys and a story to help make the mysteries of the Church more concrete. When Fr. Barry saw my fieldnotes for the exercise, however, he edited them in thick green marker and asked that they not be included in any published work. While it is difficult to see exactly how the lesson worked from the material above, which was approved for publication, the priest's efforts to use child-friendly methods demonstrate these young people's influence on how and, by turn, what is taught to Catholic children. Although this lesson did not seem to deviate from official Catholic doctrine any more than Ms. Fabuel's, the exchange afterward demonstrated that in seeking to connect with the children this moment of co-creation had gone too far for the priest. Yet, it was a lesson that the children would carry with them. Although I was asked to remove much of the interaction from my notes, the children were never given supplemental instructions that might bring this highly effective lesson—which also involved allowing the children to wear his stoles, look in the tabernacle, and learn about all the symbols of the mass—in line with Church teachings.

Later, when I talked with the children they frequently mentioned the various colors of the priest's stoles and, like Michael from Blessed Sacrament, delighted in their understanding of the material culture of the church. Further, these children clearly understood transubstantiation. Eight-year-old Katie, for instance, followed Fr. Barry's script when she explained, "the first we took the practice one, the first one we took it wasn't really real it was the practice one ... it didn't taste very good." This comment perhaps came directly from the priest's own assessment when he told the class on the day of their church tour that the host they were receiving "was not the real thing and that it would not have much taste." By contrast, the consecrated host, the host that was "made," as Katie described it, "Good, it tasted very good. I liked the taste." The intersection of Katie's interpretation and Fr. Barry's instructions within this child-centered exercise emphasizes a moment of co-construction in which Holiness can be discerned through the taste buds.

The first time I read these notes, concentrating on the parallel nature of the adult/child interaction, I failed to see this moment of co-creation. Here thoughts of the children's needs covertly led to the construction of a child-friendly lesson, which in turn helped to facilitate the development of a "theology of taste" among Katie and her classmates. This embodied theology simultaneously expressed the children knowledge of church teaching, while it undermined the traditional Catholic teaching that the physical substance of the host remained the same before and after consecration.

Unfortunately in the case of the First Communion tour at Holy Cross and the December 10th class at Blessed Sacrament, my inattention to adult/child interactions that went beyond simply conveying or receiving information meant that I did not follow children's attempted contributions to individual lessons or overall themes in later interviews or casual conversation. Returning to my notes I have been able to reconstruct some of these moments, to inform future researchers of the importance of these moments when the parallel congregations of children and adults meet either directly or indirectly to create a new interpretation, action, or theology. Attending closely to interactions when children spontaneously rebellion, disrupt, and laugh might reveal that it these instances of seeming interruption are actually moments of construction.

Notes

1 I borrow the term "parallel congregations" from Numrich (1996: xxii).
2 For more on the dialogical approach, see also Christensen (2004).

References

Bales, Susan Ridgely (2005), *When I Was a Child: Children's Interpretations of First Communion*, Chapel Hill, NC: University of North Carolina Press.

Boyatzis, Chris (2004), "The Co-construction of Spiritual Meaning in Parent-Child Communication," in Daniel Radcliff (ed.), *Children's Spirituality: Christian Perspectives, Research, and Applications*, 182–200. Eugene, OR: Wipf & Stock Publishers.

Boyatzis, Chris (ed.) (2006), "Unraveling the Dynamics of Religion in the Family and Parent-Child Relationships," Special Issue, *International Journal for the Psychology of Religion* 16 (4).

Boyatzis, Chris and D. Janicki (2003), "Parent-Child Communication about Religion: Survey and Diary Data on Unilateral Transmission and Bi-Directional Reciprocity Styles," *Review of Religious Research* 44: 252–270.

Christensen, Pia (2004), "Children's Participation in Ethnographic Research: Issues of Power and Representation," *Children and Society: The International Journal of Childhood and Children's Services* 18: 165–176.

Numrich, Paul David (1996), *Old Wisdom in the New World: Americanization in Two Immigrant Theravada Buddhist Temples*, Knoxville: University of Tennessee Press.

Orsi, Robert (2005), *Between Heaven and Earth: The Religious Worlds People Make and the Scholars Who Study Them*, Princeton: Princeton University Press.

PART THREE

Religion, Education, and Citizenship

Introduction

Aside from proselytization, religions rely on forms of socialization and education to secure their future. In this context, religious education takes on a preeminent importance, and threats to restrict it are often taken to be attacks upon religious freedom. However, religious education means more than one thing (Parker et al. 2016). Firstly, and as already explored in Part Two, religious education in its most basic form could be adult–child interactions in the domestic context. Secondly, and also considered in Part Two, religious education may occur in a more organized and collective sense, but associated with the life of a religious community. The character of religious education in these settings is directed toward informing, nurturing, and sustaining religious understanding, identity, and belief. Moreover, these forms of religious education may be aligned with regular attendance at a place or worship, as well as participation in the rituals and festivals of the religion, so that the child becomes religiously enculturated. The term "confessional" is sometimes used to describe religious education in these first two senses. Religious education of this character may also occur within religious schools, whether independent or government-funded, though the legitimacy of "faith" schools is often called into question on the basis of their being indoctrinatory, or that they normalize children's experience of religion in ways which mitigate their integration into religiously plural societies. Thirdly, with the advent of the modern state and funded education systems, religious education, where this occurs as part of formal schooling, may take on a different and functional character in relation to its purpose in building a sense of collective or national identity, or in terms of particular ideas of citizenship formation. This form of religious education in particular is likely also to be defined by a curriculum of some kind, which delineates what should be taught at each age or phase of a child's education. Of course, these different ways of conceiving of religious education may intermingle or get confused, making discussion of the issues around them somewhat fraught. This confusion of meaning becomes exacerbated when related terms (e.g. religious instruction, or religious studies) are used to describe what is being done without making clear the different purposes for it. What is more, moral education, as an aspect of religious education, moves from being adherence to the norms of a religious tradition (as in sense one and two of religious education here) to obedience to the norms of a state or society (in sense three).

These differing understandings of religious education position children in relation to the religious in contrasting ways. Where the first sense of religious education is intended, children in this domestic context are seen as subject to their parent's or community's religion and identity. The second understanding of religious education positions children as "vessels" of religious knowledge, with an expectation of social or moral conformity to the norms of a particular religious tradition (whether they in fact conform is an interesting question, which is illuminated by the readings below). The third sense of religious education positions children in a more objective way in relation to religion, while imparting a sense of civic duty upon them in relation to the religious.

Each contrasting understanding of religious education is worthy of investigation, historically, and in the contemporary world. Many of the readings in this part, building on the readings in Part Two, illustrate these different understandings, and the justification given for them. The extract from the Enlightenment thinker, Immanuel Kant, grounds moral education not in the religious per se, but in the balance between obedience to maxims with freedom of moral will. Good character, he argues, is formed in the growth toward moral autonomy, not simply in obedience to externally applied disciplines and rules. Similarly, the atmosphere into which babies are born and children are reared is explored by Rousseau in the extract from his Émile. Moral character is formed in the home, in the relationship between parents and children; indeed, Rousseau asserts that "the charms of the home are the best antidote to vice." The first thing a child must learn in their Jewish religious education is that they are different, and that they must expect persecution, points out Rabbi Green in an historical piece entitled *Religious Training Among the Jews*. Jews learned early on the importance of children and their religious education to the people's continuity. Through their religious education, Jewish children learn a sense of history and the character of belonging.

The nature and character of Islamic religious education in Nigeria, and how this is experienced and resisted by the young *almajirai*, is brought to life by Hannah Hoechner's chapter. Her contribution offers an antidote to simplistic understandings of Islamic education, in particular demonstrating ways in which the instrumental character of certain forms of religious education is resisted by children. That children are not passive recipients of religious education is also underlined in the following chapter based upon research in a Qur'anic school in Senegal undertaken by Anneke Newman. How children receive, imbibe, adapt to, or resist the religious education offered or imposed is illuminated here, and invites further investigation concerning children's agency in their religious education.

The next three chapters explore the extent to which religious education is both a vehicle of values and a mediator of forms of citizenship. Friedrich Schweitzer examines the case for religious education as a right enshrined in the United Nation's Convention on Children's Rights (1989), arguing that the potential implications of this have yet to be fully realized. In their chapter, Stephen Parker and Rob Freathy describe how fears about children's lack of religious knowledge would lead to the further erosion of Britain's standing as a "Christian society" led to a groundswell of support, across the years of the Second World War, for compulsory religious education in schools. Sian Roberts' contribution indicates how religious communities themselves sometimes construct modes of religious and moral education which run counter to the dominant norms of wider society, in this case styling a form of pacifism as fashionable and appealing to children amidst a wider militaristic culture amongst youth. Her piece also underscores that religious education is also sometimes gendered. The final chapter in this part, by Sally Anderson, explores ongoing debates about faith-based schooling in contemporary societies, drawing on fieldwork carried out in a small Jewish private school in Denmark.

Reference

Parker, S.G., Freathy, R.J.K., and Doney, J. (2016), "The Professionalisation of Non-denominational Religious Education in England: Politics, Organisation and Knowledge," *Journal of Beliefs and Values* 37 (2): 201–238.

20

Education, Discipline, and Freedom

Immanuel Kant (1803)

*T*he philosopher Immanuel Kant's (1724–1804) Enlightenment principles of the development of rational autonomy, morality and freedom can be seen as pioneering liberal ideals of education that still pervade contemporary understandings of education. In this excerpt from his lectures on education, Kant outlines his understanding that moral education should not be grounded in ideas of obedience to God, and reflects on the interrelation between ideas of childhood submission and freedom.

Man may be either broken in, trained and mechanically taught, or he may be really enlightened. Horses and dogs are broken in; and man, too, may be broken in. It is, however, not enough that children should be merely broken in; for it is of greater importance that they shall learn to *think*. By learning to think, man comes to act according to fixed principles and not at random. Thus we see that a real education implies a great deal. But as a rule, in our private education *the fourth and most important point is still too much neglected*, children being for the most part educated in such a way that moral training is left to the Church. And yet how important it is that children should learn from their youth up to detest vice; – not merely on the ground that God has forbidden it, but because vice is detestable in itself. If children do not learn this early, they are very likely to think that, if only God had not forbidden it, there would be no harm in practising wickedness, and that it would otherwise be allowed, and that therefore He would probably make an exception now and then. But God is the most holy being, and wills only what is good, and desires that we may love virtue for its own sake, and not merely because He requires it.

We live in an age of discipline, culture and refinement, but we are still a long way off from the age of moral training. According to the present conditions of mankind, one might say that the prosperity of the state grows side by side with the misery of the people. Indeed, it is still a question whether we should not be happier in an uncivilised condition, where all the culture of the present time would find no place, than we are in the present state of society; for how can man be made happy, unless he is first made wise and good? And until this is made our first aim the amount of evil will not be lessened....

How long, then, should education *last*? Till the youth has reached that period of his life when nature has ordained that he shall be capable of guiding his own conduct; when the instinct of sex has developed in him, and he can become a father himself, and have to educate his own children. This period is generally reached about the sixteenth year....

In the first period of childhood the child must learn submission and positive obedience. In the next stage he should be allowed to think for himself, and to enjoy a certain amount of freedom, although still obliged to follow certain rules. In the first period there is a mechanical, in the second a moral constraint....

One of the greatest problems of education is how to unite submission to the necessary *restraint* with the child's capability of exercising his *free will* – for restraint is necessary. How am I to develop the sense of freedom in spite of the restraint? I am to accustom my pupil to endure a restraint of his freedom, and at the same time I am to guide him to use his freedom aright. Without this all education is merely mechanical, and the child, when his education is over, will never be able to make a proper use of his freedom. He should be made to feel early the opposition of society, that he may learn how difficult it is to support himself, to endure privation, and to acquire those things which are necessary to make him independent....

Moral culture must be based upon 'maxims', not upon discipline; the one prevents evil habits, the other trains the mind to think. We must see, then, that the child should accustom himself to act in accordance with 'maxims', and not from certain ever-changing springs of action. Through discipline we form certain habits, moreover, the force of which becomes lessened in the course of the years. The child should learn to act according to 'maxims', the reasonableness of which he is able to see for himself....

Supposing a child tells a lie, for instance, he ought not to be punished, but treated with contempt, and told that he will not be believed in the future, and the like. If you punish a child for being naughty, and reward him for being good, he will do right merely for the sake of the reward; and when he goes out into the world and finds that goodness is not always rewarded, nor wickedness always punished, he will grow into a man who only thinks about how he may get on in the world, and does right or wrong according as he finds either of advantage to himself.

'*Maxims*' ought to originate in the human being as such. In moral training we should seek early to infuse into children ideas as to what is right and wrong. If we wish to establish morality, we must abolish punishment. Morality is something so sacred and sublime that we must not degrade it by placing it in the same rank as discipline. The first endeavour in moral character is the formation of character. Character consists in readiness to act in accordance with 'maxims'....

If we wish to *form the characters* of children, it is of the greatest importance to point out to them a certain plan, and certain rules, in everything; and these must be strictly adhered to. For instance, they must have set times for sleep, for work, and for pleasure; and these times must be neither shortened nor lengthened. With indifferent matters children must be allowed to choose for themselves, but having once made a rule they must always follow it. We must, however, form in children the character of a child, and not the character of a citizen ....

Obedience is an essential feature in the character of a child, especially of a school boy or girl. This obedience is twofold, including absolute obedience to his master's commands, and obedience to what he feels to be good and reasonable will. Obedience may be the result of compulsion; it is then *absolute*: or it may arise out of confidence; it is then obedience of the second kind. This *voluntary* obedience is very important, but the former is also very necessary, for it prepares the child for the fulfilment of laws that he will have to obey later, as a citizen, even though he may not like them ....

The child must form friendships with other children, and not be always by himself. Some teachers, it is true, are opposed to these friendships in schools, but this is a great mistake. Children ought to prepare themselves for the sweetest enjoyment of life ....

Children ought to be open-hearted and cheerful in their looks as the sun. A joyful heart alone is able to find its happiness in the good. A religion which makes people gloomy is a false religion; for we should serve God with a joyful heart, and not of constraint.

Children should sometimes be released from the narrow constraint of school, otherwise their natural joyousness will soon be quenched. When the child is set free he soon recovers his natural elasticity. Those games in which children, enjoying perfect freedom, are ever trying to outdo one another, will serve this purpose best, and they will soon make their minds bright and cheerful again.

Many people imagine that the years of their youth are the pleasantest and best of their lives; but it is not really so. They are the most troublesome; for we are then under strict discipline, can seldom choose our own friends, and still more seldom can we have our freedom ....

Children should only be taught those things which are suited to their age. Many parents are pleased with the precocity of their offspring; but as a rule, nothing will come of such children. A child should be clever, but only as a child. He should not ape the manners of his elders. For a child to provide himself with moral sentences proper to manhood is to go quite beyond his province and to become merely an imitator. He ought to have merely the understanding of a child, and not seek to display it too early. A precocious child will never become a man of insight and clear understanding. It is just as much out of place for a child to follow all the fashions of his time, to curl his hair, wear ruffles, and even carry a snuff-box. He will thus acquire affected manners not becoming to a child. Polite society is a burden to him, and he entirely lacks a man's heart. For that very reason we must set ourselves early to fight against all signs of vanity in a child; or, rather, we must give him no occasion to become vain. This easily happens by people prattling before children, telling them how beautiful they are, and how well this or that dress becomes them, and promising them some finery or other as a reward. Finery is not suitable for children. They must accept their neat and simple clothes as necessaries merely.

21

The New-born Child

Jean-Jacques Rousseau (1762)

Jean-Jacque Rousseau's seminal philosophical romance, Émile, had a profound influence on a range of educational reformers from the eighteenth century onwards, with his emphasis on children's essential innocence and innate goodness contributing to the development of ideas of 'natural education' and of protecting children from the effects of institutionalized social orders. In this excerpt, Rousseau outlines his ideas for the treatment of new-born children.

God makes all things good; man meddles with them and they become evil….We are born weak, we need strength; helpless, we need aid; foolish, we need reason. All that we lack at birth, all that we need when we come to a man's estate, is the gift of education. This education comes to us from nature, from men, or from things. The inner growth of our organs and faculties is the education of nature, the use we learn to make of this growth is the education of men, what we gain by our experience of our surroundings is the education of things….

We are born sensitive and from our birth onwards we are affected in various ways by our environment. As soon as we become conscious of our sensations we tend to seek or shun the things that cause them, at first because they are pleasant or unpleasant, then because they suit us or not, and at last because of judgements formed by means of the ideas of happiness and goodness which reason gives us. These tendencies gain strength and permanence with the growth of reason, but hindered by our habits they are more or less warped by our prejudices. Before this change they are what I call Nature within us. Everything should therefore be brought into harmony with these natural tendencies….

The new-born child requires to stir and stretch his limbs to free them from the stiffness resulting from being curled up so long. His limbs are stretched indeed, but he is not allowed to move them. Even the head is confined by a cap. One would think they were afraid the child should look as if it were alive.

Thus the internal impulses which should lead to growth find an insurmountable obstacle in the way of the necessary movements. The child exhausts his strength in vain struggles, or he gains strength very slowly. He was freer and less constrained in the womb; he has gained nothing by birth.

The inaction, the constraint to which the child's limbs are subjected can only check the circulation of the blood and humours; it can only hinder the child's growth in size and strength, and injure its constitution. Where these absurd precautions are absent, all the men are tall, strong, and well-made. Where children are swaddled, the country swarms with the hump-backed, the lame, the bow-legged, the rickety, and every kind of deformity. In our fear lest the body should become deformed by free movement, we hasten to deform it by putting it in a press. We make our children helpless lest they should hurt themselves.

Is not such a cruel bondage certain to affect both health and temper? Their first feeling is one of pain and suffering; they find every necessary movement hampered; more miserable than a galley slave, in vain they struggle, they become angry, they cry. Their first words you say are tears. That is so. From birth you are always checking them, your first gifts are fetters, your first treatment, torture. Their voice alone is free; why should they not raise it in complaint? They cry because you are hurting them; if you were swaddled you would cry louder still.

What is the origin of this senseless and unnatural custom? Since mothers have despised their first duty and refused to nurse their own children, they have had to be entrusted to hired nurses. Finding themselves the mothers of a stranger's children, without the ties of nature, they have merely tried to save themselves trouble. A child unswaddled would need constant watching; well swaddled it is cast into a corner and its cries are unheeded. So long as the nurse's negligence escapes notice, so long as the nursling does not break its arms or legs, what matter if it dies or becomes a weakling for life ....

These gentle mothers, having rid themselves of their babies, devote themselves gaily to the pleasures of the town. Do they know how their children are being treated in the villages? If the nurse is at all busy, the child is hung up on a nail like a bundle of clothes and is left crucified while the nurse goes leisurely about her business. Children have been found in this position purple in the face, their tightly bandaged chest forbade the circulation of the blood, and it went to the head; so the sufferer was considered very quiet because he had not strength to cry. How long a child might survive under such conditions I do not know, but it could not be long. That, I fancy, is one of the chief advantages of swaddling clothes.

It is maintained that unswaddled infants would assume faulty positions and make movements which might injure the proper development of their limbs. That is one of the empty arguments of our false wisdom was has never been confirmed by experience. Out of all the crowds of children who grow up with their full use of their limbs among nations wiser than ourselves, you never find one who hurts himself or maims himself; their movements are too feeble to be dangerous, and when they assume an injurious position, pain warns them to change it....

Not content with having ceased to suckle their children, women no longer wish to do it; with the natural result – motherhood becomes a burden, means are found to avoid it.... But when mothers deign to nurse their own children, then will be a reform in morals; natural feeling will revive in every heart; there will be no lack of citizens for the state; this first step by itself will restore mutual affection. The charms of home are the best antidote to vice. The noisy play of children, which we thought so trying, becomes a delight; mother and father rely more on each and grow dearer to one another; the marriage tie is strengthened. In the cheerful home life the mother finds her sweetest duties and the father his pleasantest recreation. Thus the cure of this one evil would work a wide-spread reformation; nature would regain her rights. When women become good mothers, men will be good husbands and fathers.

22

The Religious Training of Children Among the Jews

Rabbi A.A. Green (1905)

In a volume on the Child and Religion, *published in 1905, a chapter appears on 'The Religious Training of Children Among the Jews'. The background to this volume is somewhat obscure, and its interfaith authorship is somewhat surprising. This extract from the chapter by Rabbi Green demonstrates the idea of the importance of children's religious education to the perpetuation of traditions.*

In no denomination does the religious training of children take a higher place than among the Jews. It goes without saying that every religious denomination must of necessity depend for its stability upon the care expended in the direction of child-training. It would perhaps be too much to say that more attention has been expended in this direction by Jews than by other religionists, but it is no exaggeration to assert that Judaism has been, through a variety of circumstances, more dependent for the religion of its men and women upon the religion of its children than any other denomination of equal standing.

The reason for this is twofold. Firstly Judaism is a religion which teems with ceremonial and is hedged around with various ritual observances, and a manifold disability of restriction, all of which are characteristic of observant Judaism, assert themselves very early in domestic training, and depend for their continuance in grown-up life entirely upon their intelligibility to the child, upon the place they assume in his sacred associations and in the loyalty implanted in his young mind and heart.

The second distinctive element is found in the fact that Judaism has for so many centuries stood before the world as a religion of general nonconformity. Allegiance to its principles has been in some instances a matter of martyrdom, and in all cases a question of self-sacrifice and an appreciable amount of disability. One of the most important features in the training of a Jewish child inevitably and unconsciously takes the shape of preparation for this disability, of explanation that his denomination is in a distinct minority, of anticipation of the restrictions it imposes, and of furnishing an armoury sufficiently strong to be proof against the temptation to waver in allegiance to a creed which is appreciably unpopular.

One of the first things that a Jewish child learns is that the term 'Jew' is one of opprobrium in so many places. If he does not learn it from his unthinking Christian school-fellows, or from the brutality of the streets where it still survives, it dawns upon him as he reads his history, and, as a general rule, his brave young heart is already prepared, at a time when other children know nothing of such problems, to meet with and to combat misunderstanding and injustice.

Judaism, however, had not to wait until modern times for the exaltation as a religious duty of the care for the upbringing of the child. Already, in the first throes of the birth of the nationality, the spirit of Judaism foreshadowed the interest of the child in the first ordinance prescribed by Moses to the newly-formed people – viz. that of the Passover. 'And it will come to pass when your children ask you, "What is the meaning of this?"' Nothing was to take anything like a high place in Jewish ceremony unless accompanied by the awakening of the interest of the children and the satisfying of that interest when aroused. Modern Jewish ceremony is still loyal to this initial prescription of the faith for the whole of the Passover home celebration. The most important and the most impressive of all Jewish domestic ceremonies hinges upon the questions of the children, and the place of highest importance in the ceremony is that of the youngest of the children who may be present. Nowhere, perhaps, does the duty of child-education assert itself with greater eminence, or with more simple impressiveness, than in the classic words occurring in that Bible passage which forms, one might say, the Magna Charta of the Jewish Creed: 'And these words, which I command thee this day, shall be upon thine heart: and thou shalt teach them diligently unto thy children, and shall talk of them when thou sittest in thine house, and when thou walkest by the way, and when thou liest down, and when thou risest up' (Deut. Vi 6, 7). There never has been any misconception as to the meaning of these words, there being nothing more clear throughout the Rabbinical writings than the complete comprehension that when the Bible says: 'And *thou* shalt teach them unto *thy* children', it means that the duty of religious training belongs to the parent, cannot be delegated to strangers, however competent, and is the highest privilege of responsibility of fatherhood and motherhood.

One of the sources of the strength of the Jewish position in this respect has always been the complete accord existing between parents and teachers. The Talmud, that wonderful record of all Jewish feeling, is as full of the duty to teachers as it is of the duty to parents. 'Let the fear of your teacher be like the fear of Heaven', say the Rabbis, and it is, perhaps, not so much to the intellectuality of the Jew as it is to the recognition of the Jewish parent that the teacher of his children is his *alter ego* that we have to look for an explanation of the remarkable successes of Jewish children in the public schools. The Talmud says: 'There is no poverty except ignorance', and there is sufficient of the true Jewish spirit in this aphorism to makes Jews proud and to cause others to ponder.

It will be easily understood that the sense of history is very strong in the Jew and is awakened very early in the training of his child. Ordinary boys and girls learn the history of their country; but while the Jewish child learns the history of England, learns it as his own, and takes pride in it accordingly, he learns the Bible as his own history, and its influence as such is an enormous lever in his religious education. Waterloo and Trafalgar, Harfleur and Agincourt, Cressy and Poitiers, make the ordinary English child swell with pride; but their effect is slight indeed compared with the spirit with which the Jewish child reads of the passage of the Red Sea, of the journeyings in the wilderness, and of the battles of David, and knows that there flows within his own veins the blood of those who made his nation great and distinguished when Greece and Rome were struggling into existence, and when the great powers of the modern world were undreamed of by civilised men.

23

"People will think you are nobody": How Qur'anic Students in Nigeria Struggle for Respect and Knowledge

Hannah Hoechner

Hannah Hoechner is a postdoctoral research fellow of the Research Fund Flanders at the University of Antwerp, and a teaching fellow in Anthropology at the Université Libre de Bruxelles. Her doctoral research was an ethnography of "traditional" Qur'anic schooling in northern Nigeria, and she is currently researching the involvement of the diaspora within the religious education sector in Senegal. As part of her work in northern Nigeria, she produced a participatory docu-drama with young Qur'anic students, showing their experiences and perspectives (online at: https://www.youtube.com/watch?v=A-SDeFX5rfl).

> *Nowadays, if you have only the Qur'anic studies, there are places that when you go there, people will think you are nobody.*
>
> (IBRAHIM, QUR'ANIC STUDENT IN KANO, CA. 24 YEARS)

In a climate of fear about Muslim radicalization and militancy, institutions of Islamic learning have attracted overwhelmingly negative attention. Influential think tanks and publishing houses such as the *Brookings Institution* and *Foreign Policy* have labeled them "terrorist training schools" (Singer 2001) and "universities of jihad" (Haqqani 2002). Within policy circles, they spark concern as presumed obstacles to universal basic education, apparently displacing children from the public education system and jeopardizing their opportunities to acquire economically useful skills (e.g. Adetayo and Alechenu 2012). Their teaching pedagogy has been equated to rote learning and indoctrination, which presumably stifles children's creativity and leaves no room for independent or critical thinking (e.g. Looney 2003).

In West Africa, boys and young men of rural origin who live with an Islamic scholar in town to learn the Qur'an have attracted a lot of—overwhelmingly negative—attention in the context of attempts to universalize primary education, growing concerns about child welfare, and fears of Muslim militancy. Given their mostly precarious living conditions, children's rights NGOs consider them "street children" and "quasi-orphans" (e.g. COCFOCAN n.d.). In Nigeria, with its track record of interreligious and sectarian violence, "traditional" Qur'anic students are believed to be likely foot soldiers of violence and easy recruits for radical groups like *Boko Haram* (e.g. Soyinka 2012), even though to date no systematic evidence backs up such claims.

Unfortunately, sensationalist accounts as those described here are rarely matched with adequate empirical scrutiny of the actual practices within Islamic schools. Despite anxieties about the values and attitudes young people studying in such schools presumably acquire, the literature is largely silent about their experiences and perspectives. This is a problem because it means that some of the pressing difficulties of young people in Islamic schools go unnoticed. In this chapter, I will discuss two of the challenges "traditional" Qur'anic school students in northern Nigeria face that haven't received much attention to date: their struggle for dignity in an environment where they are frequently scorned and disparaged, and their struggle to come to terms with exclusion from modern forms of knowledge—which are today widely valued within society.

The material in this chapter stems from thirteen months of fieldwork carried out in Kano State in northern Nigeria between 2009 and 2011. In addition to data from observation and interviews, my data also include material from "participatory" research, for example, discussions of the photographs that young *almajirai* took with disposable cameras, and "radio interviews" they conducted among each other with my tape recorder. In addition, I draw on data from the production process of a "participatory" documentary film/docu-drama (online at: https://www.youtube.com/watch?v=A-SDeFX5rfl), which I organized during my research about the perspectives of *almajirai* on their lives and the challenges they face. The nine participating youths were aged between 15 and 20 years, and came from three different Qur'anic schools in Kano in which I had previously taught English.

The next section traces the historical decline of the once prestigious Qur'anic education system to the social and economic margins of society. I then show how the *almajirai* come to terms with their marginal position within society and the frequent abuse they are exposed to. Taking recourse to explicitly moral and religious conceptions of what it means to be an *almajiri* helps them maintain a positive outlook on themselves in the face of denigration. While the *almajirai* struggle to defend their own education system against critics, they nonetheless try to subvert the boundaries to the acquisition of knowledge it imposes on them.

The *almajiri* system: Decline of a once prestigious institution

The *almajirai* are boys and young men from primary-school age to their early twenties who come to urban areas to study the Qur'an, often in deprived circumstances. They are enrolled in "residential colleges" beyond the state's purview and regulatory interventions. Many schools lack physical infrastructure beyond a canopied forecourt where the teaching takes place, compelling their students to cohabit other spaces like mosques or neighbors' entrance halls. The *almajirai* learn to read, write, and recite the Holy Qur'an. Modern/secular or Islamic subjects other than the Qur'an do not form part of their curriculum. During the lesson-free time, the *almajirai* earn their livelihood.

Lacking alternative means of subsistence, many young students beg daily for food and money, a task rendered arduous by widespread contempt for *almajirai*. Many *almajirai* complain of being chased away, or given leftovers on the brink of spoiling. Students may also find employment as domestic workers, particularly in middle-/upper-class households. Yet, payment for such work is often minimal, and treatment is sometimes abusive.

The "traditional" Qur'anic school system is widespread in Muslim West Africa and used mostly by poor rural families. Such families often have few alternative educational choices, as the modern schooling accessible to them tends to be both poor in quality and financially burdensome (Baba 2011). The system is also valued for the Qur'anic knowledge, character training, and life skills it is believed to impart (Ware 2014 on Senegal). Children are handed over to the teacher (*malam*), who receives no salary but lives off the support given by the local community, the alms received in exchange for his spiritual services, the contributions of his students, and supplementary income-generating activities. While many students return home at least once a year (for the major holidays or to help their parents farm), others do not see their parents for years.

Since modern education was introduced in Nigeria under British colonial rule, the prestige and political influence of "traditional" Qur'anic scholars have gradually diminished. Economic decline since the 1980s affected the *almajirai* as it reduced both their income opportunities and the ability of others in society to support them through alms (Lubeck 1985). The emergence of reform-oriented Islamic movements in Nigeria marginalized the *almajiri* system further (Kane 2003). Increasingly, it attracted criticism as a Hausa cultural accretion to Islam. Many object to the *almajirai's* practice of begging, which, in their view, Islam permits only in acute emergencies. Prestige and status increasingly derive from mastering the "modern"/reformed forms of knowledge associated with "high culture" Islam. Such knowledge is taught for example in *Islamiyya* schools, which have become popular with many northern Nigerian Muslims. Whereas "traditional" Qur'anic schools focus almost exclusively on Qur'anic memorization and recitation, *Islamiyya* schools teach the Qur'an as well as other Islamic subjects, including *Fiqh*, *Hadith*, and Arabic.

Two factors were of particular importance for the daily experiences of the *almajirai* I worked with: their exclusion from forms of knowledge that the people in their environment valued (and that they themselves deemed important for their own economic and social advancement), and the repeated confrontation with critical and even openly hostile attitudes. I will explore these in turn below.

Reclaiming respect

The *almajirai* I worked with were painfully aware of negative opinions about them and frequently voiced their distress about being insulted, chased away, and physically assaulted while begging, and denied even a minimum of respect as human beings. Bashir[1] (12 years old) felt they were treated as even less than animals, for no reason other than being *almajirai*: "Some of them don't think *almajirai* are human. To some, a dog is better than an *almajiri*....They think he is an animal, that a donkey is even better than an *almajiri*."

In this context, the *almajirai* sought to maintain a positive outlook on themselves by refuting negative descriptions of their education system and by putting forward instead a narrative of a devoted search for religious knowledge. One boy (15 years), for example, explained that: "especially now that there is *boko* [modern school], if you come for *almajiri* education, some people think it's because you don't have food in your house, that's why you come out to beg. But it's not like that; it's because you're searching for knowledge."

Mann writes about refugee children in Dar es Salaam that it is their "efforts to maintain their morals and notions of what is 'good' and 'correct' behaviour" that keep them feeling strong (2012: 194). Similarly, the *almajirai* managed to mitigate the detrimental effects of widespread stigma and exclusion on their self-esteem by conceiving of themselves in specifically moral ways, in contrast to the negative representations of them. They had very clear-cut ideas about what it meant to be an *almajiri*, and what sort of conduct one could legitimately expect from those living as *almajirai*.

Older *almajirai* would often reprimand younger ones for not behaving as an *almajiri* should. When Abubakar (10 years old), for instance, began singing into my tape-recorder and fooling around, his older brother Bashir (12 years old) told him that he, as an *almajiri*, should not be singing like that. While they did "take time off" from following the principles they had adopted for themselves (e.g. in order to play football on a lesson-free Thursday outside the purview of the teacher who disapproved of their play, or to visit the public TV parlor whose attendance their teacher frowned upon), the *almajirai* put an enormous emphasis on "behaving well." They pointed out that rough play and football were inappropriate, particularly for *almajirai*, and that children should rather focus on their studies. Even though they were aware of their own "trespasses," knowing that they knew how to behave well and possessed the "moral knowledge" society often claimed they lacked helped them maintain dignity in the face of negative attitudes. When conducting group interviews with younger *almajirai*, I sometimes encouraged them to enact particular situations so as to make it easier for them to convey their experiences. The following "instruction" Naziru (15 years old) gives as teacher to "his" students in a role-play about begging reveals the link between behaving well and coping with societal rejection: "Please, if you go out to beg, I want you to always pull yourself together, because some people use to say, *almajirai* are not well-behaved, that they like playing rough play."

Interestingly, within the sheltered atmosphere of our training for our participatory film-making project, the *almajirai* also acknowledged deviations from "ideal *almajiri* behaviour." However, when it came to deciding on the public messages to be included in the film, they unanimously wished to portray themselves as particularly moral people, as evidenced for example by their statements in the end credits of the film: "Through this film, I want to show people who think *almajirai* are hoodlums, that this is not true" and "I want those who think *almajirai* are bad people, to know that they aren't."

These statements signal, I think, how closely the *almajirai*'s concerns with morality are related to their wish not to be looked down upon.

Another of the *almajirai*'s tactics to preserve their dignity was to construct themselves as particularly pious. Mann writes about young refugees in Tanzania that they cope with rejection by "assert[ing] their cultural superiority over that of their hosts" (2012: 194). Similarly, the *almajirai* in my research criticized those denying them support and respect for being malign and lacking faith and religious knowledge. One *almajiri* (15 years old) argued that *almajirai* in urban areas are treated worse than in rural areas because "most of the village people are [Qur'anic] teachers, they know the Qur'an and its importance very well. In Kano, some of them are illiterate. They only have the *boko* [modern] studies."

Bashir (18 years old) and Nura (ca. 19) equated supporting *almajirai* with having strong faith—and a failure to do so with a lack thereof:

Bashir: In Nigeria, how many *almajirai* do the rich take responsibility for?
Nura: Actually, the rich in Nigeria, not all of them have faith [*imani*]. Out of a hundred, you can only get one per cent that have faith.

The young *almajirai* thus struggled to portray themselves as morally upright and religiously devoted searchers for sacred knowledge, criticizing those looking down on them or refusing to support them. While defending their education system against critics, in a context where modern forms of knowledge are widely valued, however, the *almajirai* simultaneously strived to subvert the boundaries to the acquisition of knowledge that this system imposes on them.

Access to modern Islamic (*Islamiyya*) and secular knowledge

As I have mentioned before, the *almajirai* do not learn modern, secular subjects in their schools. Nonetheless, most of the *almajirai* I met throughout my research saw modern education in a very positive light, and were convinced of its importance for an economically successful life—to which they aspired. They deemed modern education important in order "to progress," because it would "help [them] on earth," and because, in the words of Ibrahim whom I cited at the beginning of this chapter, "if you have only the Qur'anic studies, there are places that when you go there, people will think you are nobody."

Of the *almajirai* participating in the film project, several approached me for support in their aspiration to acquire, or further their secular education. They also daydreamed about university admission (in case I became a university lecturer in Nigeria and could help them secure admission) and even a doctoral degree. Several of those who had attended primary school for a number of years expressed regret about their parents' decision to interrupt this education to enroll them as *almajirai*.

Many of the *almajirai*, aware that they were missing out on something they deemed important, consoled themselves with the thought that they would be able to pursue modern education sometime in the future. One *almajiri* (whose parents were strictly opposed to anything Western) resolved the tension between his need (and wish) to obey his parents and his sense of frustration about being denied a valued opportunity to learn, by reinterpreting his obedience toward his parents as a service to God, and as such easier to render:

> If your parents took you to Qur'anic school, and you refuse to study and say you only prefer *boko* [modern studies], what will you tell Allah in heaven?…. After I complete my school, I can go to *boko*, because my parents will not give their consent for me to go to *boko* now. I have to obey them, because it is said that "whoever obeys his parents, obeys Allah" … we still have hope that we will go to *boko*. We will not lose hope.

Despite his "resolution" to obey his parents, the boy eagerly took up my offer to teach him English on his lesson-free days.

Most *almajirai* thus regretted not having access to modern/secular education. Yet, the *almajirai*'s exclusion extends beyond modern/secular knowledge to modern forms of Islamic knowledge as it is taught in *Islamiyya* schools. As outlined above, the memorization of the Qur'an is largely the only explicitly taught content of the *almajiri* system. *Almajirai* are therefore frequently reproached with failing to acquire the necessary knowledge to practice their religion, a criticism insiders of the system are aware of. One Qur'anic teacher for instance commented to me that many people say about the *almajirai* that they "know how to read [the Qur'an] (*karatu*) but not how to worship (*ibada*)." *Islamiyya* schools, modernized Islamic schools, on the other hand, teach such "applied" knowledge.

What is more, with the spread of *Islamiyya* schools that readily give access to both translations of, and Islamic subjects other than, the Qur'an, competition for the spiritual capital, prestige, and economic benefits available to the religiously learned, for instance employment as Islamic teacher, or payments in exchange for prayers/

recitation, has grown. It is hardly surprising that in this context, the *almajirai* want to achieve Islamic knowledge apart from the memorization of the Qur'an, a wish the young people I got to know well during my research expressed repeatedly. They even went so far as to express clear dissent from their teachers:

Naziru (ca. 15 years):   If they brought the Hadith[2] teachers now, would your teachers agree to them staying and teaching [the students]?

Habibu (ca. 11 years):   We are not of the same opinion as our teachers, but we want the Hadith teachers.

Denied formal access to *Islamiyya* knowledge, the young *almajirai* I got to know sought to acquire religious knowledge excluded from their curriculum "clandestinely." Some students secretly enrolled in an *Islamiyya* school in the neighborhood, but had to drop out after their teacher found out. The *almajirai* learned the meaning of the text they memorized from the Qur'anic exegesis at the Friday mosque, from books they owned which contained both Arabic verses and Hausa translations (which the boys who had received some modern education could decipher), from the radio, from preachers on the street or in the market, and by guessing from similarities between Arabic and Hausa. This way, they sought knowledge they did not formally have access to.

Conclusion

This chapter has argued for the value of conducting empirical research directly with young people enrolled in institutions of Islamic learning. Such research can bring to the fore voices that are usually drowned out by the noisier pitch of sensationalist accounts of Islamic schools as "terrorist training schools" and "universities of jihad." However, listening to what young Qur'anic school students have to say about their own lives can offer surprising insights into their concerns and difficulties. In this chapter, I have focussed on two of the challenges "traditional" Qur'anic students in northern Nigeria face.

Being looked down upon affects the young students deeply. In this context, the *almajirai* seek to regain respect by emphasizing their moral and religious worth. Understanding how young religious students deal with denigration is particularly important in a global context where Islamic school students are frequently disparaged, for example as "cannon fodder" for religious radicalization and violence. A second aspect I focussed on in this chapter is the *almajirai*'s frustration with being excluded from forms of knowledge valued widely in society. Full-time enrollment in a "traditional" Qur'anic school is often considered an act of rejection of modern knowledge. The material presented here calls for a more nuanced analysis that takes into account potential differences in opinion between parents and children, as well as the structural constraints making it difficult for the children of poor parents to access secular education of meaningful quality.

Notes

1 All names have been changed to protect the informants' identity.
2 Teachings of the Prophet Muhammad.

References

Adetayo, O. and Alechenu, J. (2012), "Growing Almajiri Population Dangerous to National Devt—Jonathan," *The Punch*, April 11.

Baba, N.M. (2011), "Islamic Schools, the Ulama, and the State in the Educational Development of Northern Nigeria," *Bulletin de L'APAD*, 33. Available online: http://apad. revues.org/4092 (accessed August 9, 2016).

COCFOCAN (n.d.), "Coalition of Community Based Organizations Focused on Child Almajiri in Nigeria," in *The Child-Almajiri* (leaflet), Kano: Nigeria.

Haqqani, H. (2002), "Islam's Medieval Outposts," *Foreign Policy* 133: 58–64.

Kane, O. (2003), *Muslim Modernity in Postcolonial Nigeria: A Study of the Society for the Removal of Innovation and Reinstatement of Tradition*, Boston, MA: Brill.

Looney, R. (2003), "Reforming Pakistan's Educational System: The Challenge of the Madrassas," *The Journal of Social, Political, and Economic Studies* 28 (3): 257–274.

Lubeck, P. (1985), "Islamic Protest under Semi-Industrial Capitalism: 'Yan Tatsine Explained'," *Africa* 55 (4): 369–389.

Mann, G. (2012), "On Being Despised: Growing Up a Congolese Refugee in Dar es Salaam," in J. Boyden and M. Bourdillon (eds), *Childhood Poverty: Multidisciplinary Approaches*, 185–199, Basingstoke: Palgrave Macmillan.

Singer, P.W. (2001), *Pakistan's Madrassahs: Ensuring a System of Education Not Jihad*, Analysis Paper No. 14, The Brookings Institution.

Soyinka, W. (2012), "Wole Soyinka on Nigeria's Anti-Christian Terror Sect Boko Haram," *Newsweek Magazine*, January 16. Available online: http://europe.newsweek.com/ wole-soyinka-nigerias-anti-christian-terror-sect-boko-haram-64153?rm=eu (accessed August 9, 2016) .

Ware, R. (2014), *The Walking Qur'an. Islamic Education, Embodied Knowledge, and History in West Africa*, Chapel Hill: University of North Carolina Press.

24

Passive Victims or Actively Shaping Their Religious Education? Qur'anic School Students in Senegal

Anneke Newman

*A*nneke Newman has recently completed her PhD in Social Anthropology at the University of Sussex, UK. Her research interests focus on the anthropology of development, education, West Africa, and Islam. In this chapter, she addresses the experiences and voices of students at Qur'anic schools in Senegal.

For eight months from 2010 to 2012, I lived in a commune in northern Senegal, investigating how inhabitants negotiated between secular state and Islamic schools. One of the children I knew was thirteen-year-old Moussa. Halfway through the academic year his sister told me that, unbeknown to his family, Moussa had dropped out of the final grade of primary school. He explained to me confidentially that he had been attending the local Qur'anic school instead: "I just prefer to learn the Qur'an. That's all I want to do. And it's easy!" A few months later, Moussa's uncle found out, and debate ensued within his extended family over what to do. His uncles, aunts, and grandparents felt that he should finish primary school. However, his parents understood his commitment to learning the Qur'an. Moussa's mother had misgivings about allowing him to continue at the local Qur'anic school, feeling he would be distracted by his friends. Finally, she used her income from commerce to send Moussa to a boarding Qur'anic school in the capital of Dakar. After three years this became too expensive and he moved to another school not far from his home village.

Two key facts emerge from Moussa's story. First, he played an active role in shaping his religious education trajectory, even in opposition to adults around him.

Second, he deliberately chose the Qur'anic school over the accessible secular state school. Moussa's story is not exceptional, yet it challenges widespread assumptions in academic and other literature about students' negative experiences of Qur'anic schools in West Africa, and their supposed passivity in educational decisions. This chapter describes the Qur'anic schools in Senegal, and critiques these assumptions about them. To overcome presumptions of students' passivity, I propose a theoretical framework to aid our understanding of their active involvement in shaping their religious education trajectories relevant to both academics and policy-makers.

Qur'anic schools in Senegal

Ninety-six percent of Senegal's population of fourteen million are Muslims. Although Qur'anic schools, locally known as *daaras*, and their students are not quantified (MEN 2009), the majority of children attend at some point, if only as day students to learn basic verses. *Daaras* are run by Muslim clerics, date from the eleventh century, and are dedicated primarily to moral education and Qur'anic memorization, from basic verses for daily prayers to the entire text. Within classical Islamic pedagogy, memorization was privileged before literal comprehension, although students did pick up literacy over the years, as only those who had proven their moral character had the right to interpret the sacred text. *Daaras* were located in rural areas and students, known as *talibés*, usually lived with the cleric for several years. Tuition was paid for by parents' gifts, students' working the clerics' fields, and begging locally for food. Students endured hardship to encourage the ability to withstand difficult life conditions. They experienced strict discipline, intended to motivate learning and instil respect for the Qur'anic text. Students were mainly boys, as conditions were considered inappropriate for girls.

Rural *daaras* close to this model still exist today. In addition, clerics have diversified the *daaras'* form and content since the colonial period. They created day schools teaching part-time alongside state school timetables, or full-time boarding *daaras*, in return for payment. These schools also admitted girls. Some clerics devoted more time to French or Arabic literacy, and secular and further religious subjects. Following droughts in the 1970s, some impoverished clerics moved from rural areas to cities and some became dependent on students' begging for cash.

"Passive victims of ignorant and neglectful parents": Assumptions about Qur'anic schools and *talibés*

Portrayals of *daaras* within much academic and other literature in international development are predominantly negative. Since the colonial period, Qur'anic schools across the Islamic world have been criticized by outsiders who do not understand the cultural and spiritual values underlying hardship, work, begging, and Qur'anic memorization before literacy (Starrett 1998; Loimeier 2009; Ware 2014). In Senegal, these representations spread to the indigenous elite and intensified following ratification of the UN Convention on the Rights of the Child in 1989. The 1990s saw UNICEF and partner NGOs push for *daara* reform under the framework of child rights (Perry 2004; Ware 2004).

Policy toward *daaras* has since shifted to reflect critiques that they do not provide "quality" basic education according to dominant definitions enshrined within the Millennium Development Goal (MDG) framework. It is assumed that *daaras* confer fewer economic benefits than secular state schools given low attention to literacy and numeracy. The Senegalese Ministry of Education's *Strategic Plan for Development of the Daara* presents such a negative portrayal, stating that "the majority of daaras are (...) in total destitution" (MEN 2009: 5) in an "archaic state" and "situation of marginalization, exclusion and oblivion" (2009: 9). Supposedly "the daara sector undermines the very future of thousands of children each year" (2009: 3). To meet universal primary enrollment demanded by the MDGs, in 2002 the government introduced reforms including a proposed *daara* curriculum replacing much Qur'anic memorization with the existing primary school syllabus (Villalón and Bodian 2012).

Assumptions about the low quality of *daaras* are typically accompanied by presumptions that parental choice of such schools is due to irrationality, ignorance, or lack of alternatives. For example, an influential report on *talibés* in Senegal by Human Rights Watch (HRW) states: "parents' treatment of the children they choose to send hundreds of kilometers away to marabouts [a local term for Muslim clerics] ranges from neglect to knowing complicity in abuse." It asserts that "pressed financially, some parents send their children ostensibly to learn the Quran, but also to alleviate household expenditures" (HRW 2010: 85).

These assumptions reflect a historical tendency in Western thought to analyze preference for faith-based schools through the lens of secularization theories. Secularization theorists portrayed religious belief as a figment of the imagination of pre-modern or "primitive" irrational minds, which would eventually disappear or take on more "rationalized" forms (Stark and Finke 2000). Although scholars now reject secularization theories, the idea that religion is irrational has persisted insidiously within sociology. For instance, Socialization Theory argues that individuals are socialized into religious belief and make decisions reflecting this internalized logic even if it harms them (Furseth and Repstad 2006). Alternatively, Deprivation Theory (Glock and Stark 1965) attributes religious behavior to constraints of material or social poverty. These theories are still prevalent, and fail to do justice to the possibility that faith-based schools may offer something of value to parents (and indeed students) which secular schools do not.

Alongside these presumptions about parents, portrayals of *talibés* reveal widespread assumptions of students' passivity in decisions determining their attendance at *daaras*. While some reports document *talibés'* experiences, they rarely acknowledge that they have decision-making influence or that they might choose or prefer the *daara* over alternatives. Dominant discourses within MDG policies frame all children not attending state-recognized schools as "marginalized" or "excluded," thus denying the possibility that this could be a conscious choice. Organizations such as Anti-Slavery International (Delap 2009) assume that all begging undertaken in Qur'anic schools is forced labor. They use the definition coined by the International Labour Organization (ILO) of "work or service which is exacted from any person under the menace of any penalty and for which the said person has not offered himself voluntarily" (ILO 1930: Article 2). Again, assuming that all *talibé* begging is forced denies them any agency.

Intrinsic and extrinsic motivations: Theorizing pursuit of faith-based schooling

Social scientists have criticized many elements of these dominant assumptions about Qur'anic schools. They impose Western norms about ideal childhood which oppose that children work or live away from their parents; fail to understand the cultural and pedagogical justifications for hardship, working for the cleric, begging, and memorizing the Qur'an before learning literacy; generalize from the worst examples of urban *daaras* (Ware 2004, 2014; Perry 2004; Thorsen 2012)[1]; and subscribe to a secular and rationalist definition of "quality education" which does not coincide with popular epistemologies, priorities, or economic realities (Newman 2016).

However, my critique here focuses on the assumption that *talibés* are passive victims who cannot choose their education, and who would never prefer Qur'anic schools if alternatives were available. While children and young people clearly have limited power to challenge their parents' decisions or overcome adverse economic circumstances, my doctoral thesis (Newman 2016: especially chapters 4 and 7) demonstrates that young Senegalese people (especially from late childhood or early adolescence) can actively shape their education, and choose in favor of Qur'anic schools.

The question remains, what theoretical concepts can we employ to understand the complexity of children and young people's agency in shaping their religious education? In her recent book, *The Rational Believer: Choices and Decisions in the Madrasas of Pakistan*, Masooda Bano (2012) demonstrates that understanding of education preferences among parents and young people is possible through paying attention to both intrinsic and extrinsic motivations underpinning behavior. Intrinsic motivation entails doing something for inherent satisfaction, such as well-being or self-esteem. Extrinsic motivation is undertaking an activity for a separable outcome, including livelihood opportunities, marriage prospects, networks, and authority or status.

The intrinsic–extrinsic distinction was developed within psychology, and its application to education and religion has been critiqued for being simplistic, individualistic, and imposing value judgments on behavior. Bano overcomes these challenges by using the distinction as informed by recent debates in New Institutional

Economics. This field assumes that people are rational, but draws on social sciences to recognize the diverse things that people pursue beyond narrowly economic goods, and the limits of decision-making processes due to power inequalities. This approach also entails using sensitive interview techniques to illicit people's own explanations for their actions. Thus, Bano explains that individual education preferences reflect subjective combinations of intrinsic and extrinsic motivations, and historical and group trends. Educational trajectories reflect the practical outcomes of people's agency in trying to achieve their preferences faced with structural and social constraints. Intrinsic motivations are more likely to persist if they coincide with extrinsic returns, and people re-adjust their preferences in light of experience.

Bano's analysis of Pakistan concerns parents' educational decisions for their offspring, and the experiences of young adults. In general, few studies of Islamic education consider the involvement of children or adolescents in shaping their trajectories. However, my discussions with *talibés* in Senegal clearly revealed that intrinsic and extrinsic motivations underpinned their engagement with different school options. My findings therefore show that Bano's framework is equally useful for understanding children and young people's agency in shaping their faith-based education trajectories.

The story of Souleymane demonstrates this process. Souleymane's father felt that he would have more economic opportunities if he attended the local state school and learned the Qur'an during the holidays. However, once Souleymane was fifteen and in third grade of secondary school, he had become bored and disillusioned. He wished to attend a full-time boarding *daara* in Dakar, where he could complete Qur'anic memorization within 3–4 years. Souleymane's positive evaluation of the *daara* reflected the intense intrinsic pleasure he derived from reciting the Qur'an. Souleymane had experienced hardship, beatings, and isolation from his family in an urban boarding *daara* when he was twelve. Nonetheless, he accepted these conditions as a necessary part of his desired trajectory. Souleymane also sought a *daara* education for its significant spiritual benefits:

> The Qur'an contains all the rules and the stories of the Prophets, what is and isn't forbidden. If you learn it, angels will come and pray for you. And the Qur'an contains secrets. All illnesses, problems and catastrophes can be cured with the Qur'an. Even if you stay in your room and just pray and learn the Qur'an, you will have all you need in life.

The high value Souleymane accorded to memorization reflects the fact that the Qur'an is considered to possess a sacred essence called *baraka*, which translates as blessing or divine grace. *Baraka* cleanses the soul, protects the recipient from temptation, enables them to be a better Muslim, and confers benefits in the afterlife. It can be amassed through Qur'anic recitation regardless of whether the text is literally understood. It can also be transmitted to a student from a cleric in return for their labor, a reason for the popularity of rural *daaras*.

Souleymane's intrinsic motivations coincided with extrinsic incentives, as possession of *baraka* is seen to confer material success in the current world. Souleymane's decision was also informed by aspirations to status linked to his family's social position, as he said: "You can't say you're the son of a cleric if you haven't studied the Qur'an! The other sons of clerics in the village have completed it, why not me?!" His comments reflect how, for centuries, memorizing the Qur'an in northern Senegal has conferred enormous prestige and marriage prospects on males from elite families of Muslim clerics. The possible returns of status also coincided with perceived economic benefits:

> If I memorize the Qur'an, I would go to America and do *dabaade* [performing prayers or making amulets]. One of my uncles does that in the Congo. Or you can be the imam of a mosque, they pay you a salary each month, like my other uncle. If I finished French [state] school I could still go to the USA, but what job could I do?!

Souleymane's evaluation is shaped by the fact that in Senegal, men from clerical families who have memorized the Qur'an have a long history working as clerics, imams, performing prayers for others, and confectioning amulets derived from the Qur'an. Individuals seen to possess *baraka* by virtue of their education or lineage have a competitive advantage in this prayer economy. Today, livelihoods have shifted toward trade and international migration, also dominated by networks of clerical families. In a context of state school graduate employment as low as 5 percent (Barro 2009: 23), given that he had already mastered French literacy, Souleymane perceived that memorizing the Qur'an promised greater economic utility, through religious professions in Senegal or abroad, than further state school diplomas.

The stories of Moussa and Souleymane are corroborated by data which show that students can also choose urban *daaras,* including ones where they beg in the streets on behalf of the cleric. Indeed, one study of *talibés* who migrated from Guinea Bissau to Senegal identified children who ran away from Qur'anic schools, but also ones who wanted to attend in order to study and to travel, and even some who had been forcibly "repatriated" home against their will by NGOs (Einarsdóttir et al. 2010: 41).

The stories of Souleymane, Moussa, and other *talibés* reveal that they are motivated by perceived intrinsic and extrinsic benefits of different educational options, and negotiate to realize their aspirations. Clearly, children and adolescents experience constraints in accessing capital, or opposing the preferences of adult family members. Nonetheless, complementary evidence from Burkina Faso (Thorsen 2006), the Sudan (Katz 2004), and Ghana (Hashim 2004: chapter 6) shows that despite such constraints, children and young people often find ways to influence their education, covertly or overtly.

Nonetheless, this scholarship neglects young people's agency in pursuing religious education. This is therefore a fruitful area of future research that can enhance understanding of the formation of religious subjectivities and patterns of school attendance. In particular, it can inform effective policy toward the maligned Qur'anic schools. Such policy should be underpinned by sensitive qualitative studies which uncover children and young people's aspirations, and the values they attribute to their educational experiences, rather than assuming what is best for them.

Conclusion

Much academic and other literature portrays Qur'anic schools in Senegal negatively, as failing to protect children's rights or provide a "quality" education. It presumes that parents choose Qur'anic schools due to ignorance or poverty, and that students are passive victims of these decisions. However, the stories of *talibés* show that young people can exhibit conscious preference for Qur'anic schools over state schools, and engage in strategies to achieve their educational aspirations even when faced with opposition from adults. Theory which acknowledges that parents' choice of faith-based schools reflects intrinsic and extrinsic motivations, and agency within constraints, is equally applicable to children and young people. Their active pursuit of religious education is an under-explored area of inquiry, useful for understanding religious subjectivities, school attendance patterns and informing sensitive policy concerning faith-based schools.

Note

1 A more recent Human Rights Watch report (2014) does well to stress that urban Qur'anic schools where students beg excessively, and risk abuse and poor health, reflect a small minority of Islamic schools in Senegal. The report still fails, however, to overcome problematic assumptions about parents' and students' reasons for choosing these schools.

References

Bano, Masooda (2012), *The Rational Believer: Choices and Decisions in the Madrasas of Pakistan*, Ithaca, NY and London: Cornell University Press.

Barro, Aboubacar Abdoulaye (2009), *Ecole et Pouvoir Au Sénégal: La Gestion Du Personnel Enseignant Dans Le Primaire*, Dakar: l'Harmattan-Senegal.

Delap, E. (2009), *Begging for Change: Research Findings and Recommendations on Forced Child Begging in Albania/Greece, India and Senegal*, London: Anti-Slavery International.

Einarsdóttir, J., Boiro, Hamadou, Geirsson, Gunnlaugur, and Gunnlaugsson, Geir (2010), *Child Trafficking in Guinea-Bissau. An Explorative Study*, Reykjavik: UNICEF Iceland.

Furseth, Inger and Repstad, Pal (2006), *An Introduction to the Sociology of Religion: Classical and Contemporary Perspectives*, Aldershot: Ashgate Publishing Ltd.

Glock, Charles Y. and Stark, Rodney (1965), *Religion and Society in Tension*. Chicago, IL: Rand McNally.

Hashim, Iman (2004), "Working with Working Children: Child Labour and the Barriers to Education in Rural Northeastern Ghana," PhD thesis, University of Sussex, Department of International Development, Falmer.

Human Rights Watch (2010), *Off the Backs of the Children: Forced Begging and Other Abuses Against Talibés in Senegal*, New York, NY: Human Rights Watch.

Human Rights Watch (2014), *Exploitation in the Name of Education: Uneven Progress in Ending Forced Child Begging in Senegal*, New York, NY: Human Rights Watch.

ILO (1930), *Forced Labour Convention (No. 29): Convention Concerning Forced or Compulsory Labour*, Geneva: International Labour Organization.

Katz, Cindi (2004), *Growing up Global: Economic Restructuring and Children's Everyday Lives*, Minneapolis, MN: University of Minnesota Press.

Loimeier, Roman (2009), *Between Social Skills and Marketable Skills: The Politics of Islamic Education in Twentieth Century Zanzibar*, Leiden: Brill.

MEN (2009), *Plan Stratégique de Développement Des Daara*, Dakar: Ministère de l'Education Nationale (MEN) Sénégal.

Newman, Anneke (2016), "Faith, Identity, Status and Schooling: An Ethnography of Educational Decision-Making in Northern Senegal," Unpublished PhD thesis, University of Sussex, Department of Social Anthropology.

Perry, Donna (2004), "Muslim Child Disciples, Global Civil Society, and Children's Rights in Senegal," *Anthropological Quarterly* 77 (1): 47–86.

Stark, Rodney and Finke, Roger (2000), *Acts of Faith: Explaining the Human Side of Religion*, London & Berkeley, CA: University of California Press.

Starrett, Gregory (1998), *Putting Islam to Work: Education, Politics and Religious Transformation in Egypt*, Berkeley, CA: University of California Press.

Thorsen, Dorte (2006), "Child Migrants in Transit: Strategies to Assert New Identities in Rural Burkina Faso," in C. Christiansen, M. Utas, and H.E. Vigh (eds), *Navigating Youth, Generating Adulthood: Social Becoming in an African Context*, 88–114, Uppsala: Nordiska Afrikansinstituet.

Thorsen, Dorte (2012), *Children Begging for Qur'ānic School Masters: Evidence from West and Central Africa*, Dakar: UNICEF.

Villalón, Leonardo A. and Bodian, Mamadou (2012), *Religion, Demande Sociale, et Réformes Éducatives Au Sénégal*, Miami, Niamey, London: University of Florida, Laboratoire d'Etudes et de Recherches sur les Dynamiques Sociales et le Développement Local, Overseas Development Institute.

Ware, Rudolph Treanor (2004), "Njàngaan: The Daily Regime of Qur'ânic Students in Twentieth-Century Senegal," *The International Journal of African Historical Studies* 37 (3): 515–538.

Ware, Rudolph Treanor (2014), *The Walking Qur'an: Islamic Education, Embodied Knowledge, and History in West Africa*, Chapel Hill, NC: The University of North Carolina Press.

25

Children's Right to Religion in Educational Perspective

Friedrich Schweitzer

*F*riedrich Schweitzer is Professor of Practical Theology at the University of Tubingen, Germany. He has published widely on religious education in differing international settings. In this chapter, he considers children's right to religion from an educational perspective. In particular, he discusses the understanding of this right within the 1989 United Nation's Convention on Children's Rights as well as in other UN documents. Against this backdrop, the author develops specific demands for how this right should become more explicit and clear-cut in legislation.

Introduction

In speaking about children's right to religion, it is important to keep a distinction in mind from the beginning—the distinction between the educational understanding of children's rights and the legal understanding of such rights in terms of written laws and of claims ensuing from them. The educational understanding of children's rights goes beyond the realm of legal claims. It makes use of a special kind of rhetoric that is meant to strengthen the position of the child in education and in society at large. In a broader sense, the reference to children's rights came into use in the early twentieth century, with internationally influential authors such as the Swedish social analyst Ellen Key (1909) or the Polish-Jewish pediatrician and educator Janusz Korzak. It was their aim to establish an awareness of the need to view children as persons who deserve equal respect to adults. The rights they referred to, therefore, included the right to respect or to parental love. While such rights can hardly be adjudicated in court, the educational reference to children's rights was also connected to parallel attempts of finding ways for the legal establishment of children's rights. Consequently, the two understandings of rights in education and in law are different but they are also interrelated, in that both understandings hinge upon new and respectful ways of treating children. Religion and the children's right to religion have played an important role in both respects which is why, in the following, we will first look at how children's rights came to be established during the twentieth century. Historically, the educational discourse paved the way for respective legal developments, while the legal developments, in turn, influenced the educational understanding of children's rights. This is why the present article is in dialogue with the parallel article by Rachel Taylor (in this volume) who writes from a law perspective.

The movement for children's rights and children's right to religion

The movement for establishing children's rights permeates most of the twentieth century. It is telling, however, that it was not until 1989 that the United Nations finally adopted their now famous Convention on Children's Rights.

The Geneva Declaration of the Rights of the Child adopted in 1924 by the League of Nations, one of the precursor bodies of the United Nations, is considered the first official declaration in this field. It was in fact a very brief declaration, including only five points that were meant to oblige individual adults as well as society at large vis-à-vis the needs of children (UN Documents 2015a). The first of its five points states: "The child must be given the means requisite for its normal development, both materially and spiritually."

The 1924 declaration includes a clear reference to children's needs that go beyond the material world. Yet in doing so, the declaration does not refer to "religion" but to "spirituality" or at least to the adjective derived from this noun. In the sense of spirituality then the reference to children's right to religion was clearly present. The meaning of the terms "religion" and "spirituality", as well as the difference between these terms, is a complex question of its own. In the following, I will use the term "religion" in a very broad sense that also encompasses spirituality.

The next major step in the history of official declarations of children's rights can be seen in the United Nations 1959 Declaration of the Rights of the Child (UN Documents 2015b). This declaration is again rather brief. It includes ten principles. Opposed to the Geneva declaration, however, it makes no reference to spirituality or religion. Its second principle appears to be its way of rephrasing the Geneva Declaration's views of children's development and its different dimensions by focusing on the more palpable aspects of the mental and social dimensions: "The right to special protection for the child's physical, mental and social development."

Both declarations from 1924 and 1959 must be seen against the backdrop of the educational discussion on children's rights of the time. It is probably fair to say that especially Korczak's writings that were translated into many different languages and continue to be reprinted (e.g., Korczak 2007) were operative in keeping the issue of children's rights alive at this time. Many of the rights that Korczak demanded for children either included a religious overtone or were directly religious by referring to God (for a current discussion, see Hammarberg 2009).

The United Nation's Convention on Children's Rights (1989) and beyond

Against the background described above the United Nations' 1989 Convention on Children's Rights (UN Document 2015c) can be considered a hallmark and a breakthrough in the history of children's rights as human rights. It was this document through which, for the first time in history, children's rights were given a broad and detailed basis.

The convention directly refers to the relationship between religion and education especially in two places. Interestingly enough, the first reference to religion—in Article 14.1—was the object of many controversies, even to the point of delaying the whole process of passing the Convention (see Dorsch 1994, also see Taylor in this volume). It states that freedom of religion must also apply to children: "States Parties shall respect the right of the child to freedom of thought, conscience and religion."

This was a big step in giving space to children's own decisions. Yet it also raises far-reaching questions. Can children really make use of this right, for example, against their parents' will? Article 14.2 takes up this concern by stating: "States Parties shall respect the rights and duties of the parents and, when applicable, legal guardians and provide direction to the child in the exercise of his or her right in a manner consistent with the evolving capacities of the child."

The freedom granted to children by Article 14.1 could be understood as an expression of extreme educational liberalism. Article 14.2 excludes this interpretation by stating the parents' right to "direction" of the child "in the exercise of his or her right" of the freedom of religion. It is an open question if the interplay between Articles 14.1 and 14.2 should be seen as a successful balance, or if Article 14.2 in fact takes back what Article 14.1 has granted the child (see Taylor in this volume). Yet one must also consider that Article 14.2 limits parents' rights with the reference to the "evolving capacities of the child"—a reference which, naturally, is open to different interpretations and which again indicates how legal and educational or psychological understandings are intertwined. Heiner Bielefeldt, for example, the UN Special Rapporteur on freedom of religion or belief, interprets it in an educational sense by demanding that the self-determination of the child should be respected increasingly in line with the age of the child: "Such direction should be given in a manner consistent with the evolving capacities of the child in order to facilitate a more and more active role of the child in exercising his or her freedom of religion or belief, thus paying respect to the child as a rights holder from early on" (Bielefeldt 2015). Estimates concerning the "evolving capacities of the child" can hardly be based on legal criteria alone but have to draw on respective insights from the field of education.

While I cannot discuss this question here in more detail, it should be clear that viewing children themselves, rather than just their parents, as owning the right of freedom of religion can also be an important step toward strengthening the claim to religious education. Religious education could then be seen as part and expression or a practical consequence of children's freedom of religion (a consideration that is still often omitted in legal interpretations). Yet it is also clear that Article 14 only establishes the parents' rights, in the sense of giving the child "direction." This clause includes protection of parental rights against other social agencies that might want to determine the aims and contents of religious education. Historically, the state and the church or other religious bodies have acted as such agencies, by only allowing for certain kinds of religious education considered orthodox by them.

In terms of religious education, however, the most direct reference to religion and education of the 1989 Convention is found in Article 27.1: "States Parties recognize the right of every child to a standard of living adequate for the child's physical, mental, spiritual, moral and social development."

It is interesting to note that this article which is of central importance from the perspective of education is often not even mentioned in this context by legal interpretations. The legal discussion appears to be most interested in how children can be protected from undue influences while the educational discussion also includes the question of how children's access to programs of (religious and/or spiritual) education can be guaranteed.

Article 27.1 was clearly formulated in continuation to the Geneva Declaration. Opposed to the 1959 UN declaration quoted above, however, it reinserts the reference to "spiritual" development. Article 27.1 explicitly affirms the child's right to "spiritual" development. For this reason, the 1989 Convention has been praised by religious educators for giving religious education a firm legal basis that goes beyond the regulations found in the legislation of individual countries (Hull 1998). This is certainly true to some degree. Yet it should not be overlooked that the focus of Article 27 is not on education but on the "standard of living." Consequently, the reference to religious education of this article is again only indirect.

Education is the main topic of Articles 28 and 29. Article 28.1 states the "right of the child to education": "States Parties recognize the right of the child to education, and with a view to achieving this right progressively and on the basis of equal opportunity." While Article 29 specifies a number of aims of education ("the education of the child shall be directed to ...") and in this manner identifies what should be considered important in education, religious education is not mentioned in Articles 28 and 29. However, the references in these articles can be applied to religious education— depending on its interpretation. For example, Article 29.1 states: "The preparation of the child for responsible life in a free society, in the spirit of understanding, peace, tolerance, equality of sexes, and friendship among all peoples, ethnic, national and religious groups and persons of indigenous origin."

Religious educators would most likely claim that their work is included here, especially concerning the demand for a "spirit of understanding, peace, tolerance, equality of sexes, and friendship among all peoples." Indeed, "religious groups" are mentioned explicitly here—in line with Article 30 addressing the situation of, among others, religious "minorities" and of children belonging to them who should not be prevented to "practice" their "own religion." Yet again it cannot be overlooked that religious education itself is in fact not mentioned.

Summing up, we can say that, from an educational perspective, the 1989 Convention on children's rights clearly goes beyond its precursors in respect to religion and that it gives more reason to consider religious education a human right. Yet it can also not be overlooked that things are not sufficiently clear in the 1989 Convention either, at least not in respect to religious education. From the point of view of religious education, much clearer statements should be included. This is why we need to go beyond the 1989 Convention in order to state children's right to religion and religious education more clearly.

The most far-reaching statement of the UN concerning children's right to religion in terms of religious education was actually passed several years before the 1989 Convention. The United Nations' 1981 Declaration on the Elimination of All Forms of Intolerance and of Discrimination Based on Religion or Belief (UN Document 2015d) comes close to stating children's right to religion in the sense of guaranteeing them access to religious education: "Every child shall enjoy the right to have access to education in the matter of religion or belief in accordance with the wishes of his parents." Obviously, this guarantee expressed in 1981 has not made it into the 1989 Convention.

The fact that the more far-reaching formulation from 1981 was not included later on may have to do with the difficulty of identifying a legal claim that can be based on children's right to religion. In discussing this question in more detail which is only possible within the more concrete context of national legislation, Heinrich de Wall, a German law professor, considers the parents, the state, and religious communities as the three possible addressees of such a claim. According to him, at least within the German legal context, there is no such right in relationship to the parents. Parents are not legally obliged to raise their child religiously (an obligation which would actually contradict the parents' freedom of religion that must also encompass the right to abstain from all religious beliefs and practices). Concerning religious communities the state has no right to regulate their tasks vis-à-vis their members. Consequently, only internal church law can apply in this respect which, in the case of the Roman Catholic Church, indeed includes an obligation for parents to raise their children in the Christian faith (De Wall 2014: 431). Concerning the state as the third possible addressee of respective claims, the principle of freedom of religion and, correspondingly, of state neutrality prevents the state from providing religious education for children. Yet at least within the German system, the state may be required to support parents in their wish to make religious education available within institutions like the school (De Wall 2014: 432). This conclusion from a legal analysis of the German context can be seen in line with the 1981 UN declaration quoted above in that the state would follow the demand to guarantee "access to education in the matter of religion or belief" without taking responsibility for the contents of this education.

In sum then it can be said that the UN Convention from 1989 includes important starting points for both, for an educational understanding of children's right to religion which cannot be the basis for legal claims and for a legal understanding of children's right to religion which would oblige the state to make sure that children (and parents) will have access to programs of religious education of their choice. In both respects, however, the educational as well as the legal understanding, the Convention is not sufficiently outspoken and therefore in need of further elaboration in the future.

Practical consequences

Educators tend to have less interest in legal questions than in practical consequences. This is why it is important to point out such consequences that can actually be found at different levels. First of all, it is important for all contexts of religious education, whether theoretical or practical, to realize that children have rights of their own, in respect to religion no less than in other respects. This realization implies that the religious self-determination of children has to be respected from early on and that it has to be supported and strengthened in its development. Moreover, children's religious rights include entitlements, in a general educational sense vis-à-vis their parents and vis-à-vis the religious communities they may belong to, and possibly also in a legal sense in relationship to the state as a provider of educational programs that should include religious education, even if the state cannot provide such programs independently from parents and religious communities.

Second, stating children's right to religion stands for a corresponding educational awareness of all those who are concerned with nurturing and educating children, whether parents, teachers, social educators, or others. Realizing that children have needs and interests referring to religion can make them aware that their educational responsibilities include religious education. From this point of view, religious education is not a task that can be limited to specialists but it is a crucial dimension of all education.

Third, in terms of educational institutions, guaranteeing children access to religious education means that no educational institution that claims to comprehensively support children in their development ("the whole child," see Erricker 1997) can make do without including the religious dimension. Concretely this means that, for example, kindergartens will have to make sure that religious questions will be addressed although there is no special subject called Religious Education as in schools. In later years, the school subject Religious Education also receives additional support, as a consequence from children's right to religion.

Fourth, children's right to religion should also be developed further in a legal sense. Even the 1989 UN Convention does not include clear provisions for children having access to the religious education they desire. National legislation often seems to be lacking sufficient clarity in this respect as well.

Finally—and in some ways most importantly—basing religious education on children's rights has important implications for the kind of religious education that children should be offered. It would be a contradiction in terms if one wanted to call upon children's rights as the basis of religious education while favoring, for example, an authoritarian approach in practice. Religious education informed by children's rights must be child-oriented and thoroughly sensitive to the needs of children. From early on it needs to respect the children's religious self-determination and must aim at strengthening them in this respect.

Further questions

It is not possible to address all possible questions referring to children's rights and religion in a single article. The focus of this chapter is on foundational questions that are important for the field of education in general. Yet a number of additional questions should at least be mentioned here. Some of them refer to future tasks for research, others to current controversies. Given the increasingly multi-religious situation in many countries, it is increasingly important to be aware of the different religious traditions' views of the child and children's rights as well as of their understanding of religious education. Studies of this kind are available for the Christian tradition (Schweitzer 1992; Bunge 2001) but in writing on other religious traditions, there is a lack of focus on views of children and children's rights (see Tulasiewicz and To 1993). Future studies should also include a clear focus on children's rights in the perspective of different religious traditions, especially concerning children's right to religion.

The 1989 UN Convention also includes an especially controversial clause, in Article 24.3: "States Parties shall take all effective and appropriate measures with a view to abolishing traditional practices prejudicial to the health of children." This clause was introduced in respect to so-called female circumcision—that really is, in my understanding, not a religious ritual but a clear violation of a girl's bodily integrity (see Dorsch 1994: 169). Nowadays, some courts are wondering if this clause could also apply to male circumcision—in order to ban this practice as well (see Landgericht Köln 2012). While this very complex issue cannot be dealt with here in any detail, it is easy to see why, given the religious grounding of male circumcision especially in Judaism and Islam, religious commandments and legal rulings may come into conflict with each other.

Beyond this specific issue there also are a number of controversial questions concerning corporal punishment that—allegedly—is religiously motivated and legitimized, as well as the problem of indoctrinating or proselytizing children especially against their parents' will. Such issues make clear that there also is a need for protecting children against undue influences based on religious motives.

All of these questions indicate that future debates on children's rights—including children's right to religion—should be more aware of the need for interdisciplinary cooperation in this field of discussion and research. To say it again, legal and educational perspectives are clearly intertwined once it comes to assessing the claims associated to such rights. On a worldwide level, children's rights are far from being respected effectively and consistently. This does not only include children's basic survival needs like food and clothing. It also refers to children's religious rights, for example, in situations of forced early marriage that imply a child's conversion to another religion. Compared to the devastating experiences many children of the world are still exposed to, this chapter, with its plea for respecting children's right to religion, may even appear beside the point. Yet it should not be overlooked that, ultimately, children's rights are indivisible. Either children's rights are respected or they are not. If this is true, respecting children necessarily implies respecting their religious rights, no less than other rights. And speaking up for their religious rights will also contribute to the respect children deserve and are entitled to in all other fields and dimensions. Clearly this was the understanding of the pioneers of children's rights like Janusz Korcak and there may still be lessons to be learned from him for the future.

References

Bielefeldt, Heiner (2015), "Children's Right to Freedom of Religion or Belief Must Be Protected." Available online: http://www.un.org/apps/news/story.asp?NewsID=52359 (accessed December 12, 2015).

Bunge, Marcia J. (ed.) (2001), "The Child in "Christian Thought," in Thomas Schlag and Henrik Simojoki (eds), *Mensch—Religion—Bildung. Religionspädagogik in anthropologischen Spannungsfeldern*, 418–432, Gütersloh: Gütersloher.

De Wall, Heinrich (2014), "Das Recht des Kindes auf Religion. Orientierungen aus juristischer Sicht," in Thomas Schlag and Henrik Simojoki (eds), *Mensch—Religion—Bildung. Religionspädagogik in anthropologischen Spannungsfeldern*, 418–432, Gütersloh: Gütersloher.

Dorsch, Gabriele (1994), *Die Konvention der Vereinten Nationen über die Rechte des Kindes*, München: Duncker & Humblot, 1994.

Erricker, Clive (ed.) (1997), *The Education of the Whole Child*, London: Cassell.

Hammarberg, Thomas and Korczak, Janusz (2009), *The Child's Right to Respect Janusz Korczak's Legacy. Lectures on Today's Challenges for Children*, Strasbourg: Council of Europe.

Hull, John M. (1998), "Religious Education and the Spiritual Rights of Children," in John M. Hull (ed.), *Utopian Whispers: Moral, Religious and Spiritual Values in Schools*, 59–62, Norwich: RMEP.

Key, Ellen (1909), *The Century of the Child*, New York & London: G. P. Putnam's Sons.

Korczak, Janusz (2007), *Loving Every Child. Wisdom for Parents*, in Joseph, Sandra (ed.), Chapel Hill: Algonquin.

Landgericht Köln, "1. kleine Strafkammer, Urteil Az. 151 Ns 169/11, 07.05.2012." http://dejure.org/dienste/vernetzung/rechtsprechung?Gericht=LG%20K%F6ln&Datum=07.05.2012&Aktenzeichen=151%20Ns%20169/11 (accessed November 30, 2013).

Schweitzer, Friedrich (1992), *Die Religion des Kindes. Zur Problemgeschichte einer religionspädagogischen Grundfrage*, Gütersloh: Gütersloher.

Tulasiewicz, Witold and To, Cho-Yee (eds) (1993), *World Religions and Educational Practice*, London/New York: Cassell.

UN Documents (2015a), Geneva Declaration of the Rights of the Child. Adopted 26 September, 1924, League of Nations http://www.un-documents.net/gdrc1924.htm (accessed December 8, 2015).

UN Documents (2015b), Declaration of the Rights of the Child, 1959 http://www. humanium.org/en/childrens-rights-history/references-on-child-rights/declaration-rights-child/ (accesssed December 8, 2015).

UN Document (2015c), Convention on the Rights of the Child (November 20, 1989) http://www.humanium.org/en/convention/text/ (accessed December 8, 2015).

UN Document (2015d), Declaration on the Elimination of All Forms of Intolerance and of Discrimination Based on Religion or Belief (1981) http://www.un.org/documents/ga/res/36/a36r055.htm (December 8, 2015).

26

Childhood, Faith, and the Future: Religious Education and "national character" in the Second World War

Stephen G. Parker and Rob Freathy

Stephen Parker and Rob Freathy have published widely on the history of religious education. In this chapter, they explore how ideas of childhood were implicated in the national imaginary during the Second World War. Concerns about the parlous state of children's religious education lent weight to arguments for a reform of the (religious) educational system in England in order to preserve the nation's Christian identity. The chapter concludes by making some remarks about how childhood has been conceived of in relation to religious education and national religious identity in the UK since 1945.

Introduction

Among the incidental results of the evacuation scheme has been the discovery that large numbers of town children are being brought up with no religious knowledge at all [revealing] the grim fact that in a country professedly Christian, and a country which at the moment is staking its all in defence of Christian principles, there is a system of national education which allows the citizens of the future to have a purely heathen upbringing […]. Yet education with religion omitted is no education at all […]. The basis of good citizenship is character, and a man's character depends upon his beliefs. Yet if the war has emphasized the deficiencies of our educational system, something more than wartime expedients will be needed to remedy them. More than before it has become clear that the healthy life of a nation must be based upon spiritual principles….Christianity cannot be imbibed from the air….The highest of all knowledge must be given frankly the highest place in the training of young citizens. It will be of little use to fight, as we are fighting to-day, for the preservation of Christian principles if Christianity is to have no future[1]

Whether British national character is Christian or not has been much debated since the 1960s, an observation to which we shall return in the conclusion of this chapter. However, as Matthew Grimley has shown of the inter-war years, the intimate connection between English/British character and Christianity was widely understood if not accepted, being circulated and reinforced by the arts, the new media of film, and by the radio programmes of the BBC (Grimley 2007).[2] Likewise, that national character had been fundamentally influenced by, in particular, a "common religious heritage," especially a Protestant and Puritan one, found intellectual acceptance amongst authors as divergent as D.H. Lawrence and Prime Minister Stanley Baldwin (Grimley 2007: 895).

The distinctions between British national character and that of other nations' identities became one spoken and written of increasingly through the 1930s and into the Second World War, as nationalism in the political form of Communism, Fascism and Nazism became ominous threats. According to Grimley, it was argued that, in contrast to Germany, the British peoples were united by a common religious heritage which, since Cromwell's Puritan revolt, had been imbued with a sense of liberty and opposition to civil and ecclesiastical control (Grimley 2007: 900–1). Religion rather than race was espoused as the defining factor in the formation of the British national community.

Wartime rhetoric in general reinforced the notion of Britain's standing as a Christian nation (see Parker 2006, 2012; Freathy 2007, 2008). From politician to parish clergy, much was spoken and written of national Christian character, of the war being both a test of this, as well as presenting an opportunity to reaffirm it. Adult citizens were encouraged to attend to the "Big Ben minute," a brief time of prayer before the nine-o'clock news on the BBC's Home Service, and to displays of civil religion such as National Days of Prayer (Parker 2006: 92, 110). Children were not considered exempt to similar calls to prayer, the flagship children's radio show, *Children's Hour*, establishing its own Epilogue, Children's Hour Prayers, in 1940, in addition to a new BBC *Religious Service for Schools* (Parker 2010).

In line with what Gordon Lynch has observed of the sacrality of the Irish Catholic nation in the twentieth century, British (Protestant) Christian character was similarly valorized (Lynch 2012: 66–70). Moreover, the "long childhood," which was becoming the norm across societies with a state-funded education system, including Britain, led increasingly to a view of, what Lynch has called, the "sacrality of the care of children" (2012: 70–3). In this context, children were seen as "vulnerable to poor social conditions and corrupting moral forces," their protection and moral nurture taking on an increasing imperative (2012: 72). The cultural imaginary of British national character and the sense of the sacrality of the care of children combined to create a heightened sense of moral panic when at the outset of the Second World War, in September 1939, some 800,000 children were evacuated from towns and cities to the countryside in anticipation of aerial bombardment. This mass evacuation provided evidence which ran counter to notions of a Christian society, a matter which resulted in anxiety amongst religious educationalists in particular. This galvanized their sense of the importance of a more thoroughgoing Christian education in the future.

Evacuation

Writing of the results of a national inquiry into this evacuation, published in the British journal *Religion in Education* in 1940, Canon Tissington Tatlow, an Anglican cleric, and founding Director of the Institute of Christian Education, summed up the report's alarming findings as this: "No religious influences in the home, no ordered home life nor discipline."[3] The report went on:

> Reference to fish and chips as the staple fare is frequent, also the novelty of knives and forks. The slum child in many cases attends Sunday School, but there are no indications that such attendance is of religious value to him. Three things are constantly mentioned together [...] very little is done for children in the way of home training by parents in the majority of homes; church-going is the exception rather than the rule, and religious teaching is left almost entirely to the school [...] We find very little religious influence of an effective kind in the majority of homes. There is a definite minority in which religion counts; but it is rather pathetic to see the ignorance of many children of the simplest Bible stories [...] a higher proportion of children from working-class than from middle-class homes receive some systematic religious teaching. This is due to the number who attend Sunday school. But the great majority of these children when they leave school at fourteen also leave the Sunday school, and such contact as they have had with the Church comes to an end.[4]

These shocking discoveries were contrasted with the children's responses to life in the bucolic settings of their reception areas, where it was reported they had been taken to church, some for the first time, and liked it. As a result, Tatlow asserted, "dirty little heathens have been turned into decent little Christians in a matter of months."[5]

In the same issue of *Religion in Education* R.B. Henderson, Headmaster of Alleyn's School, Manchester, felt able to conclude that the existence of prayers and a "Divinity" lesson at the beginning of the school day in many schools were having little effect and "nearly the whole of England has gone pagan—pagan elementary schools, pagan secondary schools, and pagan universities."[6] The only remedy as far as he was concerned was a renewed understanding that "all education is religious" and to focus more systematically on making it so.[7]

Tatlow's and Henderson's anxiety about the situation, and their judgment concerning its remedy were echoed in *The Times* leader quoted at length at the head of this chapter. If there was to be a necessary renewal or reaffirmation of Christian national character, and it was thought there clearly there had to be given the appalling physical, moral and spiritual situation children were reportedly growing up in, then greater prominence needed to be given to children's religious education in schools. The reported national scandal of a childhood lived amidst such turpitude was staged in such rhetoric in order to create a sense of moral purpose at home for the war being fought abroad. There was clearly no point in fighting the "heathen" overseas, if only "heathens" were being nurtured at home.

Religion in education

Over the next few months *The Times* leader, and the 400,000 copies of it circulated as pamphlet, elicited much correspondence in the newspaper's letters page, and debate elsewhere (Parker 2012). Likewise, religious educationalists publishing in the pages of *Religion in Education* at the height of the blitz over Britain, in 1940 and 1941, wrote with candour and urgency of the opportunities wartime presented for religious education in the present, and its future place in the school curriculum. Christians in the south of England united, according to the editor of *Religion in Education*, Basil Yeaxlee, to declare that "our case in this war is spiritual, not just political"; he went on "this is the accepted hours in which to claim for the Christian faith its fundamental place in British education."[8] Indeed, F. A. Cockin, Canon of St. Paul's, reflected that "the most encouraging by-products of war conditions' was the interest in the teaching of religion in school."[9] The headmaster of an evacuated school wrote that evacuation to a rural area had presented teachers and children with freedoms and opportunities to engage in activities which laid the foundations of what he deemed to be "real" religious education. Rehearsing plays, engaging in debates, listening to gramophone records, chopping wood, cultivating fields, were cited as "in the deepest sense 'religious', since any real initiative within an individual is a spiritual activity."[10] Another author, a teacher, Arnold Lloyd, wrote of a qualitatively different kind of religious education, and the need for young people to be able to debate ideas in lessons, not just accept what their teachers told them.[11] Because children were in "peril," he argued, then schooling needed to take on a different tenor. It followed that teachers needed to be given the opportunity to develop an understanding of adolescent psychology; schools should offer an assembly in which quiet reflection is possible; and education professionals needed be an example to the young.[12] Moreover, Maxwell Garnett, the internationalist and long-time General Secretary of the League of Nations Union, wrote stridently of the contrast between Nazism and the values of Christian England. Decreeing that "there is no reason why the schools of Christian England should not be seeking to make Christians with the unanimity and fervour that is shown by the schools of Nazi Germany."[13] He contrasted the clear way in which the Nazis pursued the education of their young people with the British education system, within which 83 percent of children received no further religious education beyond aged 14.[14] Total Christian education would provide a bulwark against Totalitarianism.

When in 1941, the Archbishops of Canterbury, York and Wales published a statement calling for Christian education in all schools, their "five points," it must have been scarcely believable that all of these would be achieved. But in the end, on a wave of ostensibly widespread and popular support, which wished to reassert British national character as indisputably Christian, it was precisely these five goals that constituted the religious settlement of the 1944 Education Act. Specifically these were: (i) a daily act of collective worship in all schools; (ii) compulsory religious instruction in all schools; (iii) taught by teachers competent to deliver it; (iv) inspected in line with other subjects; and that (v) religious knowledge should be an optional subject in the teachers' certificate of qualification.[15]

Of course, in all of this few asked children what they thought of religious education. When one educationalist did so, Irene Showell Cooper, the resultant responses were not entirely satisfactory to her. One response from a fourteen year-old in particular piqued her. When asked what she liked and disliked about her scripture lessons the girl replied:

> Personally, I do not think that the teaching of Scripture should be compulsory in schools. If the children or their parents feel a need or desire to study the works in the Bible, a church or chapel is the best place to attend. Here [in church] the Bible is learnt and discussed in the right atmosphere. Scripture cannot be just a study of the Bible—it becomes a set book in which passages must be studied and learnt by heart.[16]

Irene Cooper's rejoinder was: "there is some muddled thinking here, and it is obviously the remark of someone who has been badly taught," but she also concluded that, "actual religion is always needed," and that there is a "necessity for teaching religion all the time."[17] Thus in the 1940s, where one child at least could see the distinctions in what might justifiably be taught in school, home and church, the majority of educationalists writing in *Religion in Education* took the view that, for the sake of the nation's spiritual health and moral character, children should be nurtured in an ethos reflective of Christian values, experience a daily act of worship, and be taught Christian education.

Conclusion

The social imaginary of the interwar and Second World War years asserted British national character to be Christian. This imaginary was mediated in multiple ways, which fed directly into a mass emotional climate supportive of the morality of war and in sustenance of civilian morale. Because of this, moral panic ensued when it was found that the majority of children did not exhibit the necessary morality and religious knowledge which would guarantee a future Christian society. Compulsory Christian education, it was thought, was the essential means by which a more fully Christianized society could be achieved; prominent educationalists, churchmen and politicians agreed upon this. The end result was a long-lasting settlement for religious education forming part of the now iconic 1944 Education Act.

Whatever the veracity of the claim that British national identity is Christian, this national religious imaginary has become much more vocally contested since the 1960s. Moreover, religious education, still perceived as being one vehicle by which national religious identity is formed, has been often been implicated in these debates (Parker and Freathy 2012). In the face of increased religious diversity and secularity the nature and purpose of religious education in Britain has gradually altered to take into account the diversity of perspectives present within society and its schools, but not without a good deal of contestation (Freathy and Parker 2013). Even so, the religious settlement of 1944 remained and remains the basic legal framework within which the subject operates. At times when it has been challenged, national character and identity have been invoked in the face of purported internal and external threats. In a House of Lords debate on "Religious Education in [County] Schools" on November 15, 1967, for example, Lord Butler of Saffron Walden, who had been President of the Board of Education when the 1944 Education Act was passed, called upon parliament to remember the "sentiments and the emotion" of the time of this "religious settlement... in the flush of war... in Church House with the bombs actually raining." To challenge the religious clauses of the Butler Act was presented as tantamount to challenging the cause for which Britain had gone to war.

It is a moot point whether this original settlement was representative of the social reality of the 1940s, or whether it merely reflected a Christian social imaginary of politicians, religious leaders, educationalists and others. Regardless, dissatisfaction with the representativeness and effectiveness of this settlement has grown recently amongst many religious educationalists and stakeholder groups, such that a series of reports in 2015 have called for a wholesale review of this historic settlement.[18] Within these reports children are thought of as deficient in, and therefore requiring, an education which fosters the development of a "religion and belief literacy."[19] In a cultural context fearful of religious extremism, children are seen on the one hand as vulnerable to being led astray by radical religious ideologies, or to an intolerance of particular religious groups, and on the other to be pioneers of a new, fairer and more inclusive society. Whereas in the Second World War Christianity was seen as the bulwark to political extremism, arguably today the values underpinning the Western/British socio-political order (so-called British values) are seen as the bulwark to religious extremism.

Commenting upon the Commission on Religion and Belief in British Public Life Report of 2015, the Chair of the Religious Education Council of England and Wales, Professor Trevor Cooling, has written that:

> Britain is a changing society, becoming more diverse and increasingly plural. In this context, finding ways of nurturing national identity is urgent. We need a positive ongoing national story which reflects this new future.[20]

This begs the questions, what kind of national story; what national religious character should be nurtured (if any)? The history of British religious education points to a British religious identity which is continually in negotiation. Although clearly defining itself as Christian in the interwar years, appealing in particular to a Protestant heritage, the nature of this Christian character was flexible enough to include Christians of a variety of hues, and in practise a Jewish community also. Although this Christian character reasserted itself in debates over national character between the 1960s through to the 1980s, there were gradual moves towards one which was multi-cultural and multi-faith (Feldman 2011; Parker and Freathy 2012).

In this context, religious education takes on a different form and content. A thoroughgoing knowledge and understanding of the Bible and Christian belief has given way to the need for an essential knowledge of a range of different religions and philosophies. These religions and philosophies are taught in schools without prejudice as being equivalent in value and as potentially informative of pupil's personal development, religious literacy, and civic awareness. Even so Christianity is still afforded special status in the religious education curriculum (Parker and Freathy 2012).

Notes

1 *The Times* (1940).
2 The two terms English/British were often elided, but we have opted to use the term British here.
3 Tatlow (1940: 140).
4 Tatlow (1940: 140–1).
5 Tatlow (1940: 144).
6 Henderson (1940: 133).
7 Henderson (1940: 136).
8 Yeaxlee (1941: 2).
9 Cockin (1941: 136).
10 Author Unknown (1940: 76).

11   Lloyd (1941: 26).

12   Lloyd (1941: 27–28).

13   Garnett (1941: 14).

14   Garnett (1941: 15).

15   *Christian Education* (1941).

16   Shewell Cooper (1940: 44).

17   Shewell Cooper (1940: 44).

18   A New Settlement for Religion and Belief in Schools. Available online: http://faithdebates.org.uk/wp-content/uploads/2015/06/A-New-Settlement-for-Religion-and-Belief-in-schools.pdf (accessed December 2015);Collective Worship and Religious Observance in Schools: An Evaluation of Law and Policy in the UK. Available online: http://collectiveschoolworship.com/documents/CollectiveWorshipReligiousObservanceAHRCNetworkReport13November2015.pdf (accessed December 2015);RE for Real. Available online: http://www.gold.ac.uk/media/goldsmiths/169-images/departments/research-units/faiths-unit/REforREal-web-b.pdf (accessed December 2015).Living with Difference. Available online: https://corablivingwithdifference.files.wordpress.com/2015/12/living-with-difference-community-diversity-and-the-common-good.pdf (accessed December 2015).

19   https://corablivingwithdifference.files.wordpress.com/2015/12/living-with-difference-community-diversity-and-the-common-good.pdf [accessed December 2015], p.25.

20   Response to the Woolf Institute on Religion and Belief in Public Life in Britain. Available online: https://blogs.canterbury.ac.uk/expertcomment/response-to-the-woolf-institute-on-religion-and-belief-in-public-life-in-Britain/ (accessed December 2015).

References

Author Unknown (1940), "Opportunities of Religious Education in War-Time," *Religion in Education* 7 (2): 76.

Christian Education: A Call to Action, Statement by the three Archbishops, Canterbury, York and Wales, February 12, 1941.

Cockin, F.A. (1941), "Why Christian Education Matters," *Religion in Education* 8 (4): 136.

Feldman, D. (2011), "Why the British Like Turbans: A History of Multiculturalism in One Country," in David Feldman and J. Lawrence (eds), *Structures and Transformations in Modern British History*, 281–302, Cambridge: Cambridge University Press.

Freathy, R.J.K. (2007), "Ecclesiastical and Religious Factors which Preserved Christian and Traditional forms of Education for Citizenship in English Schools, 1934–1944," *Oxford Review of Education* 33 (3): 367–377.

Freathy, R. (2008), "The Triumph of Religious Education for Citizenship in English Schools 1935–1949," *History of Education* 37 (2): 295–316.

Freathy, R.J.K. and Parker, S.G. (2013), "Secularists, Humanists and Religious Education: Religious Crisis and Curriculum Change, 1963–1975," *History of Education: Journal of the History of Education Society* 42 (2): 222–256.

Garnett, M. (1941), "Nazis or Christians: A Problem of Education," *Religion in Education* 8 (1): 14.

Grimley, M. (2007), "The Religion of Britishness: Puritanism, Providentialism, and 'National Character', 1918–1945," *Journal of British Studies* 46 (4): 884–906.

Henderson, R.B. (1940), "Will the Structure Hold?" *Religion in Education* 7 (3): 133.

Lloyd, A. (1941), "Living Religion in Schools," *Religion in Education* 8 (1): 26.

Lynch, G. (2012), *The Sacred in the Modern World: A Cultural Sociological Approach*, Oxford: Oxford University Press.

Parker, S.G. (2006), *Faith on the Home Front: Aspects of Church Life and Popular Religion in Birmingham, 1939–1945*, Oxford: Peter Lang.

Parker, S.G. (2010), "'Teach them to pray Auntie': Children's Hour Prayers at the BBC, 1940–1961," *History of Education* 39 (5): 659–676.

Parker, S. (2012), "Reinvigorating Christian Britain: The Spiritual Opportunities of the War, National Identity, and the Hope of Religious Education," in S.G. Parker and T. Lawson (eds), *God and War: The Church of England and Armed Conflict in the Twentieth-century*, Aldershot: Ashgate.

Parker, S.G. and Freathy, R.J.K. (2012), "Ethnic Diversity, Christian Hegemony and the Emergence of Multi-faith Religious Education in the 1970s," *History of Education: Journal of the History of Education Society* 41 (3): 381–404.

Shewell Cooper, I. (1940), "What Our Pupils Think," *Religion in Education* 7 (1): 44.

Tatlow, T. (1940), The Results of an Enquiry on Evacuation," *Religion in Education* 7 (3): 140.

The Times, Religion and National Life, February 17, 1940.

Yeaxlee, B. (1941), "Once that Call Is Sounded," *Religion in Education* 8 (1): 2.

27

"A new sense of God": British Quakers, Citizenship and the Adolescent Girl

Siân Roberts

Siân Roberts is a postdoctoral research fellow at the University of Worcester, and an Honorary Fellow in the School of Education at University of Birmingham, UK. Her research encompasses women's history, and the history of childhood and youth. In this chapter, she examines the history of Camp Fire Girls organization, founded in the USA in 1910 by a network of progressive reformers, educators, and youth workers. She looks at how the movement was brought to England by Quaker women from Birmingham between 1912 and 1914 as part of a broader culture of participation by Quakers in idealistic and utopian non-militaristic youth movements in the early twentieth century.

Introduction

And so, with the scents of the pine trees and the burning fire, with the shadowy forms of our friends about us and the fitful gleam of the fire upon their faces, there sank into each soul a new sense of God, a new love of beauty, a new joy in possibilities of service.

This highly evocative description appeared in *The Sunday School Chronicle and Christian Outlook* on October 27, 1921.[1] It was one of a series of articles hailing the importance of youth work in Sunday schools for developing the moral and spiritual welfare of the young, and the benefits of a relatively new organization, The Camp Fire

Girls, for young women in particular. As an extract it captures some of the key features of the organization's appeal—its use of ceremony and ritual, its focus on fellowship and friendship, and its emphasis on a practical Christianity rooted in ideals of citizenship and service for others in the interwar period.

The Camp Fire arrived in Britain some two years after its initial establishment in the USA in 1910 by a network of progressive reformers, educators, and youth workers. It promoted a model of citizenship for girls based on discourses of domesticity and maternalism supplemented by outdoor camping activities and civic engagement in the wider community. By the 1920s, it had become the most popular organization for girls in the USA and had expanded internationally to nearly thirty countries (Buckler et al. 1961; Helgren, 2010). Although precisely when and where the first British Camp Fire was founded is unclear, the organization's magazine the *Camp Fire Journal* of November 1934 allocated a pivotal role to Bournville, the garden village suburb established by the Cadbury family to house workers in their chocolate factory, declaring that "it was largely from Bournville that the news was spread abroad."[2] The founding narrative was rehearsed in this particular issue to mark the retirement of the British Camp Fire Girls' first president, and the woman credited with the establishment of the organization in the UK, Margaret A. Backhouse or "Meluit" to give her ceremonial Camp Fire name. It was, the *Journal* insisted, due to her "inspiration and enthusiasm and to her guidance that the Camp Fire became a British institution," going on to recount the adventurous story of Meluit's discovery of the Camp Fire in 1912 during a train journey across Canada. Before we turn to this story and a closer look at the Camp Fire Girls, however, we need to divert briefly to explore Margaret's connection to Bournville and its Sunday school, a connection which is inextricably bound up with the establishment of the British Camp Fire Girls.

A model Sunday school

Born in Darlington to a wealthy and well-known Quaker family, Margaret was by her own account "a very bad" Sunday school teacher when she met the charismatic Canadian Sunday school reformer George Hamilton Archibald.[3] Archibald had arrived in England in 1902 and rapidly made an impression on religious educators of various denominations through his writings and public lecture tours for the Sunday School Union. In 1905, he accepted a challenge from the Quaker businessman George Cadbury to take on the leadership of the Sunday school at Bournville as a way of proving the efficacy of his child-centered reform agenda. Archibald stayed in the Backhouse family home during one of his frequent lecture tours, this one probably taking place in early 1907. Margaret recalled being "thrilled" by his lectures and by the end of his stay had promised to be one of the inaugural students at his new training college for Sunday school teachers at Westhill, established in 1907 by Birmingham Quakers as a vehicle to disseminate Archibald's theories and methods. Bournville Sunday school became a "model" demonstration school for Westhill led by Archibald's

FIGURE 27.1 *Margaret Backhouse (left) in her ceremonial dress,* British Camp Fire Girls, *January 1926, Friends' Library, Temp MSS 370 © Religious Society of Friends (Quakers) in Britain.*

daughter and teaching colleague Ethel Archibald. Although the Archibalds were not Quakers at this time and both Westhill and Bournville Sunday school were officially non-denominational, both institutions were Quaker led (with the Sunday school coming under the direct supervision of Bournville Quaker Meeting) and the Archibalds moved in Quaker circles. Ethel later married the missionary Andrew Johnston in 1922 and the couple spent time at the Quaker Mission in Pemba, East Africa, where Ethel ran a school before returning to her lecturing post at Westhill. She and her parents were formally accepted as members of the Society of Friends in 1926.[4] Following two terms at Westhill in 1907–1908, Margaret returned to Darlington to put her training into practice but was a regular visitor to Westhill and in close contact with Ethel with whom she had become friends. In 1915, Margaret formally returned to Westhill as a member of staff and to Bournville Sunday school as a teacher and member of the management committee.[5]

In April 1912, Archibald accepted an invitation to undertake a six-month lecture tour of Australia, New Zealand, and Canada to disseminate the Westhill model of Sunday schooling. In addition to his wife Clara, he was accompanied by Ethel and Margaret who gave practical demonstrations of method following his lectures. On the return journey across Canada, Margaret and Ethel read an article in *The Ladies Home Journal* on a new youth organization the Camp Fire Girls, a moment captured in later autobiographical accounts by both women. In her account, Margaret described the attraction of the movement, suggesting that its appeal lay in its originality and distinctiveness from existing provision, and in a particularly gendered model:

> When we were crossing Canada, Ethel and I had read of a rapidly spreading movement in USA for out of school activity for girls called Camp Fire Girls. The scheme seemed to us much better worked out than Girl Guides—which at that time was a copy of Boy Scouts. We organised two groups of Camp Fire Girls in Bournville and as our students saw our work, the movement spread and in the course of years I became the recognised leader in England.[6]

Ethel later recalled that they realized immediately that the Camp Fire movement "would be ideal for Bournville girls" (Johnston 1945: 134). But why? What was it about the organization that so captivated the imagination of two teachers in a Quaker Sunday school?

A significant element of the Westhill-Bournville model was the extension of formal Sunday focused schooling into informal religious and moral education delivered through weekday evening youth groups, and the College minutes in the early period illustrate Archibald's preoccupation with establishing a suitable organization for the boys of the Sunday school and a related programme of training in youth leadership at Westhill. "Boy psychology" figured largely both in his published writings and on the Westhill curriculum, and by 1913, a group of "Peace Scouts" had been formed in the Sunday school, which differed from Baden-Powell's Boy Scouts in a typically Quaker rejection of military characteristics. It is no surprise therefore that Ethel and Margaret had been looking out for a comparable organization for girls and the Sunday school records note that by early 1914 two Camp Fires, Kienach and St. Bride, were in existence for teenage girls.[7] A group of "Bluebirds" targeted at younger girls under 12 was also formed (Bailey 2002: 210).

Practical Christianity and citizenship

The overall aim according to the Sunday school's annual report was character formation, and to "help the young people to fill spare moments with useful pursuits and service for others."[8] How this aim was achieved is illustrated by the citizenship activities of the Bournville Camp Fires as described in the Sunday school's records. During 1915, for example, they undertook collections and made clothing for Belgian refugees and war victims in France, they attended talks from a local nurse on aspects of health, they gathered blackberries and made jelly which they sold in aid of local causes, they collected money for African and Indian missions, they played hockey and went on camping trips, and they presented public entertainments in aid of good causes. On the 14th April, for example, thirty-two members gave an entertainment for the benefit of Dorothy Wheelwright, a patient at the local orthopedic hospital, during which the girls presented six tableaux representing the rules of the Camp Fire—seek beauty, give service, pursue knowledge, be trustworthy, hold on to health, glorify work, and be happy. Developing this tradition of service for others was seen as a fundamental part of instilling the spiritual ethos of the Sunday school; as the annual report presented to Bournville Meeting in 1916 maintained:

> The guardians of the two camps are feeling that great strength for this work comes from the binding together of the girls through the common spiritual aims of the Sunday School.[9]

The emphasis on cultivating character occupied a central role in pedagogy in this period, particularly for boys, and was an aim that Bournville Sunday school held in common with other youth organizations and schools (Roberts 2004; Olsen 2015). Service-based leisure activities rooted in a Christian ethos had become a fundamental part of the "club" work developed by settlements and other providers of informal education, with the multiple aims of contributing to the common well-being, equipping members to participate in a democratic society and cultivating religious sensibility and spirituality (Snape 2015).

The Camp Fire extended this citizenship mission to adolescent girls. Its aim was to demonstrate to its members that "they as girls can take their share of the responsibilities of citizenship" (Camp Fire Girls 1933: 9). Its slogan was "Give Service," which members fulfilled through the study of seven "crafts"—Home Craft, Health Craft, Camp Craft, Hand Craft, Nature Lore, Business, and Citizenship. Each "Camp Fire" included 10–12 girls and was led by a "Guardian," usually an adult or older girl. Their watchword was "Wo-he-lo," a combination of the first two letters of the words work, health, and love. Each group chose a name which expressed its ideals or a "distinguishing historical interest," and each girl chose her own symbolic name and designed her own symbol, both of which were to express "the essence of her ideal" (Camp Fire Girls 1933: 113–4). Although the ordinary uniform comprised of a tussore-colored middy jumper accompanied by a dark brown blazer, skirt, tie, and hat, on ceremonial occasions a special costume based on Native American dress was worn and each girl made her own. Like other utopian youth organizations in the period, Camp Fire's symbolic identity, group rituals, ceremonial dress, and reward system were all based upon a perceived concept of Native American culture and we will return to the significance of symbolism for the organization shortly.

There was a strong emphasis on "the natural pursuits of girls" and on rewarding everyday domestic tasks, handcrafts, child care, and service to others. Rewards were allocated along a complex system of "honours" involving awards of "native" beads, and girls could progress through four "ranks"—"runner," "wood gatherer," "fire maker," and the fourth and highest rank of "torch-bearer." Activities glorified ideals of female domesticity, the family, and the "natural" aptitudes of woman prevalent in the period particularly home making and child care, and the organization repeatedly cast its girls as mothers and wives of the future. As the "modern girl" had less time to "cultivate the art of home making" than her predecessors, a new approach was necessary, one that rewarded "tasks often thought of as drudgery," and infused day-to-day activities with adventure, romance, and colorful ritual. In common with many other women's and girls' organizations of the period, Camp Fire preached a discourse of citizenship where women were equal, but different. As the organization's handbook explained although:

> The girl must take an equal share with the boy [...] her fundamental nature together with the training of the past ages point to the fact that the share must be different from that of her brother. Each must give the best so that the combine is unique and fuller than the contribution offered by either party [...] Nevertheless, there remains the racial urge towards marriage and home-making; the desire to create, and to create beauty; the attraction of little children, and sympathy for the infirm and ailing. (Camp Fire Girls 1933: 11)

Tasks which were rewarded included, for example, making bread, planning a vegetarian menu for a week, keeping a thrift chart, saving money, and undertaking voluntary work in a playground, settlement or Sunday school (Camp Fire Girls 1933: 113–4). Given this stress on motherhood, it is ironic that Margaret herself never married but spent most of her life with another Westhill student and Quaker, and from 1921, national secretary of the British Camp Fire Girls, Norah Ackerley, with whom she shared a home from 1934 until Norah's death in 1974.

Great emphasis was placed on camping, outdoor activities, and nature study, all of which were linked to physical and emotional health, or what David Pomfret has described as the "discourse of nature as educator and regenerator" prevalent in the period (Pomfret 2001: 411). However, for Margaret and Ethel, who had trained at the Froebel Institute, nature was also a means of encountering the divine, a significant element in Froebelian ideas and approaches (Thomson, 117). This was clearly articulated in their book *Nature Talks*, first published by the Pilgrim Press in 1914 and written by

Ethel with illustrations by Margaret. In the foreword Ethel drew on Ruskin to explain that it was "intended for the Primary Department leaders in our Sunday Schools who have found the great book of Nature to be for them a word of God, and who believe that the children under their care can be given, through this wonder-book, 'certain sacred truths which by no other means can be conveyed'" (Johnston [1914] 1926).

Margaret and Ethel's adoption of the Camp Fire Girls' ideals of character building and service, nature and healthy outdoor living, combined with the romance of "primitive" cultures and ritualized ceremony reflects a wider culture of enthusiastic participation by Quakers in idealistic and utopian youth movements in the early twentieth century. Mark Freeman has argued that Friends felt they could make a distinctive contribution to youth work by stressing social service, character building, and spiritual well-being together with a non-military or pacifist focus (Freeman 2010). The Camp Fire belongs in a similar tradition as the Order of Woodcraft Chivalry, for example, established in 1916 by two Quakers influenced by the ideas of American Ernest Thompson Seton which used similar Native American ritual in its camps (Wilkinson 1969; Freeman 2010).

In November 1926, the Quaker periodical *The Wayfarer* included an article by Margaret in which she articulated the appeal of the "practical citizenship of Camp Fire" for a Quaker audience. The Camp Fire taught responsibility and was financially self-supporting providing an opportunity to "learn the value of money and economy." The lack of military insignia and drill was emphasized, replaced by democracy as a means of developing leadership skills through the girls' participation in decision making. Competition was not encouraged, rather collaboration and teamwork was fostered through organized expeditions and games, and the sharing of home responsibilities around the camp fire. Camp Fire honors were awarded for things that were "worth doing and so give dignity to the little things." All of this contributed to providing a foundation for a girl's future life as a wife and mother, and an educated responsible citizen who could play her part in the civic and religious life of her local community in a post-suffrage society. Margaret wrote that "Right living is the result of the formation of right habits" which were "essential to the smooth running of community life" (Backhouse 1926). Similarly a Camp Fire attached to a Friends Hall in London in 1935 stated that its aim was "to give the girl a good time, and while so doing, to help her to realise that woman has a distinctive part to play in the world, and to help her to develop her personality that she may make the best possible contribution to the life of the home, the nation and the world" (Rooff 1935: 13–14).

The "Problem" of the adolescent

Like other Froebelian and progressive educators in the period, Margaret had a profound interest in the ideas and discourses of the emerging social sciences, and in particular the "new psychology" of the early twentieth century (Thomson 2006). Ideas about adolescence as a specific developmental phase distinct from childhood which brought particular problems and needs had been in circulation since the late nineteenth century, and had proliferated anew following the publication of G. Stanley Hall's study of adolescence in 1904 (Dyhouse 1981: 115–17; Hendrick 1990: 3–10). Margaret and her male colleagues at Westhill were preoccupied with the insights that this new knowledge brought to bear on religious education and how it might inform the development of Sunday schools and the spiritual welfare of young people. Her search for a suitable youth organization and her utilization of the Camp Fire Girls is a manifestation of that aim.

In March 1925, Margaret was elected as the first woman president of the Birmingham Sunday School Union. In her presidential address delivered to an audience of 400 Sunday school workers in Birmingham, she pleaded with Sunday schools to respond to contemporary concerns:

"The young people of today are every bit as good, and have as much goodness in them as the young people of our day," said Miss Backhouse in her presidential address. "Have faith in them. Give them plenty of responsibility, plenty of work to do, and let them do it by their own methods."[10]

Her speech marked the launch of her special presidential campaign for the coming year—"Our Work for the Adolescent."

A conference in December 1925 held at Westhill and attended by teachers from 54 Sunday schools was reported in some detail in the local press. In her opening address, Margaret argued that "the problem of the adolescent was so vital that the Church had to face it." In the same way that Sunday schools had recognized the particular needs of very young children, so they had to grapple with the equally specialized needs of the adolescent, needs that had a psychological basis but were exacerbated by the demands of a modern, industrialized society. The reporter paraphrased her arguments about the responsibility of Sunday schools toward young people, and the opportunity that adolescence presented for the movement:

Adolescence was also a time of chopping and changing; there was an unfinished sense of religion and right living [...] one of the big aims of Sunday school workers should be to help adolescents face life as it is, and to keep a hold of them until they had a right attitude towards life. If they wanted to help adolescents they should supply them with work. It was the work of the Sunday school to give the adolescent something to do, so that he could put into practice the truths of the Christian life [...] It was useless to judge adolescents by thinking of how they felt at the same period, because circumstances had so changed that the conditions were not similar, and they had to face the world as it now is. Boys and girls were better educated to-day than they were years ago, and did not live the same kind of lives. They read the newspapers and knew far more about the world. In days that were gone young people went out as apprentices or into small businesses, but now they went into great factories or big concerns where parental and maternal guidance was lacking.

It was for the Sunday Schools to rouse Birmingham to the tremendous task that awaited it respecting the adolescent population.[11]

Youth groups such as the Camp Fire Girls provided a means for Sunday schools to fulfill this mission. Camp Fire provided a means of harnessing the "social impulses" and idealism of adolescence, and translated it into a practical living religion under the wise guidance of a "guardian" who would be both friend and adviser (Backhouse 1926).

In the same vein, the 1933 British Camp Fire Girls handbook, produced during her period as president, goes into some detail on the psychological needs of the adolescent girl. The Camp Fire was a means of developing a girl's self-knowledge and confidence through the exercise of her "controlled imagination." Every person, it argued, was "endeavouring to find some means of self-expression," without it people become "pent-up, nervy and unstable." Camp Fire provided an opportunity for girls to find this means of expression through physical activity, handcraft, song and other "normal" girl pursuits. However, the handbook contended, something deeper was required for those the parts of a personality that were "most deeply rooted" and therefore difficult to express. The answer was symbolism which, it argued, had been in use "since time began" to express "ideals and religion." It fulfilled the adolescent girl's "extreme craving for beauty," and through beauty and pageantry the girls would "find fellowship and religion through symbolic form." The overall symbolic emblem was fire which represented both the home and the family which gathered around it. Traditionally in the "care of the woman," fire also "stood for power and progress" together with "protection and communication." Equally significant was fire's religious associations; for the Camp Fire it "symbolised the mysterious, and tongues of flame stood for the Spirit of God." The Guardian tended not only the physical fire of the camp but also the inner psychological and spiritual fire of her girls (Camp Fire Girls 1933: 9, 12, 113, 117–18). Partaking in Camp Fire ceremonies on a Sunday would help to "focus the girls' religious life and strengthen the link between the activities of the Camp Fire and the church" and suggestions for hymns and Bible readings were provided to supplement the readings of Camp Fire "desires" (Camp Fire Girls 1933: 189–90). These "desires" also had a religious tone, in particular that of the Fire Maker and Margaret closed her *Wayfarer* article by quoting its last lines: "The core of the movement is expressed in the Fire Maker's Desire, 'I will tend … the fire that is called the love of man for man, the love of man for God.'" (Backhouse 1926).

It was this model of citizenship and service with a Christian ethos that appealed to Quakers and to other religious denominations. Another article in *The Wayfarer* a few years later reiterated the appeal: "It adds colour and healthy romance to club work. Through it school mistresses have grown to know the girls better, and it makes an excellent week night activity for Sunday Schools because it helps to translate ideals into practical living" (Harris 1932).

Although the initial Bournville Camp Fires were closely associated to Quaker initiatives, the organization obviously appealed to other non-conformist denominations

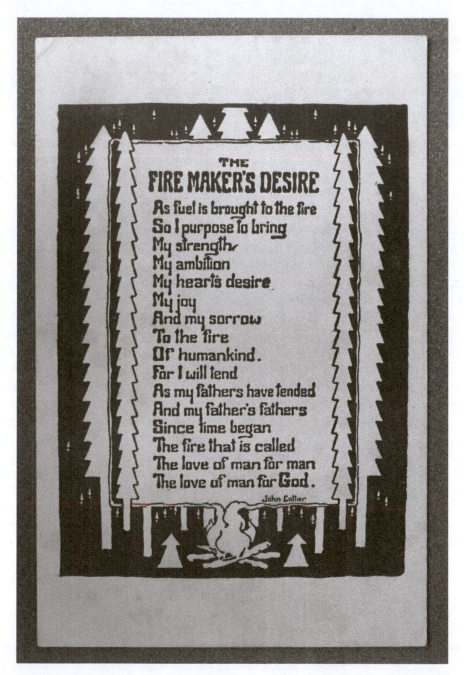

FIGURE 27.2 *Postcard of The Fire Maker's Desire, Friends' Library, Temp MSS 370 ©
Reserved, from the collections of Religious Society of Friends (Quakers) in Britain.*

"I greet you". (The Hand-sign of the fire).

FIGURE 27.3 *"I greet you" from The Record Book of the Lehiro-Tanda Camp Fire, 1923– 1946, Friends' Library, Temp MSS 370 © Religious Society of Friends (Quakers) in Britain.*

as well. Indeed, a survey of girls organizations in England and Wales published in 1935 found that most Camp Fires were attached to churches (Rooff 1935: 13). The Friends Library holds the records of Nellie Jackson, or "Mora-itai," Margaret's successor as President from 1934, which illustrates all aspects of Camp Fire life for groups associated to Congregational churches in the Lewisham area.[12] Camp Fire was promoted at Westhill's annual Easter School of Method at Swanwick, and through the pages of *The Sunday School Chronicle*. In 1917, an article described a display by the South Shields Camp Fire complete with ceremonial dress, ceremonial candles, and Morris dancing.[13] Similarly an article on the 1919 Swanwick School demonstrated how symbolism was used to convey the ideals of the movement in a portrait of a "semi-ceremonial assembly" held by Ethel and one of the Bournville groups:

> The girls were considering how they could make the influence of their "fire" brighten the lives of others. They spoke of their own homes first, then of neighbours, then of some Serbian children, and after that of a large family of Belgian refugees who had just gone back to their own country, and the girls decided not to break the bond which had held them together during the dreadful war years. Miss Archibald, who, by the way, made an excellent "Guardian" of the Camp Fire, told her girls how the Camp Fires of America had supported war orphans.[14]

Another author concluded that through such ceremonies and activities, the Camp Fire was "bound to make God and Religion more real to the girls" as well as draw in those who were outside the church.[15]

Conclusion

By 1935, when Margaret resigned as Chief Guardian, national membership of the Camp Fire Girls was approximately 2,500 girls organized in 157 Gamp Fires and 44 junior Bluebird groups (Rooff 1935: 13–14). It never therefore presented a serious challenge to the other better established girls' organizations such as the Girl Guides or the Girls' Friendly Societies. Despite this, the involvement of Quakers at Bournville Sunday school and Westhill with the Camp Fire Girls represents an interesting attempt to re-energize Sunday school activities for young people in the light of contemporary discourses on informal learning for citizenship. By harnessing the new social science of psychology, they hoped to make an intervention in the religious education of adolescent girls and thereby equip a generation for young women to take an active, if highly gendered, role in the spiritual life of their local churches and communities.

Notes

1   *The Sunday School Chronicle and Christian Outlook*, October 27, 1921: 656, Cadbury Research Library (CRL), NCEC D73.

2   *Camp Fire Journal*, November 1934: 62, Friends Library (FL), London, Temp MSS 370.

3   Autobiographical account, Margaret Backhouse Papers, FL, Temp MSS 10868.

4   Minutes Warwickshire North Monthly Meeting, Central England Quakers' Archives, Birmingham Archives & Collections (BA&C), SF/2/1/1/1/1/31, December 14, 1926.

5   Minutes Bournville Meeting, BA&C, SF/3/3/1/1, November 1915. For more on Margaret's life as an educationist and humanitarian activist see Roberts (2013).

6   Margaret Backhouse Papers, FL, Temp MSS 10868.

7   Minutes Bournville Meeting, BA&C, SF/3/3/1/1, November 1913 and November 1914.

8   Minutes Bournville Meeting, BA&C, SF/3/3/1/1, February 1914.

9   Minutes Bournville Meeting, BA&C, SF/3/3/1/1, November 1916.

10   Records of Birmingham Sunday School Union, CRL, LCEC 13, pp. 243–4.

11   *Birmingham Post*, December 13, 1925, BA&C "Churches" newscuttings: 91.

12   Papers of Nellie Jackson, FL, Temp MSS 370.

13   *The Sunday School Chronicle and Christian Outlook*, June 7, 1917, CRL, NCEC D69.

14   *The Sunday School Chronicle and Christian Outlook*, May 1, 1919, CRL, NCEC D71.

15   *The Sunday School Chronicle and Christian Outlook*, October 27, 1921, CRL, NCEC D73.

References

Backhouse, Margaret A. (1926), "British Camp Fire Girls," *The Wayfarer: A Record of Quaker Life and Work*' 5 (11): 181–182.

Bailey, Adrian R. (2002), *Constructing a Model Community: Institutions, Paternalism and Social Identities in Bournville, 1879–1939*. PhD thesis, University of Birmingham.

Buckler, Helen, Fiedler, Mary F., and Allen, Martha F. (1961), *Wo-He-Lo: The Story of the Camp Fire Girls, 1910–1960*, New York: Holt, Rinehart and Winston.

Camp Fire Girls (1933), *British Camp Fire Girls*, London: Camp Fire Girls.

Camp Fire Girls (November 1934), *Camp Fire Journal*.

Dyhouse, Carol (1981), *Girls Growing Up in Late Victorian and Edwardian England*, London: Routledge & Keegan Paul.

Freeman, Mark (2010), "Muscular Quakerism? The Society of Friends and Youth Organisations in Britain, c. 1900–1950," *English Historical Review* 125 (514): 642–669.

Harris, May (1932), "The British Camp Fire Girls," *The Wayfarer: A Record of Quaker Life and Work* 11 (8): 144–145.

Helgren, Jennifer (2010), "'Homemaker' Can Include the 'world': Female Citizenship and Internationalism in The Postwar Camp Fire Girls," in Helgren, Jennifer and Vasconcellos, Colleen A. (eds), *Girlhood: A Global History*, 304–322, New Brunswick: Rutgers University Press.

Hendrick, Harry (1990), *Images of Youth: Age, Class and the Male Youth Problem, 1880–1920*, Oxford: Clarendon Press.

Johnston, Ethel Archibald (1914; 1926), *Nature Talks*, 2nd edition, illustrated by Margaret A. Backhouse, London: Pilgrim Press.

Johnston, Ethel Archibald (1945), *George Hamilton Archibald: Crusader for Youth*, Wallington: The Religious Education Press Ltd.

Olsen, Stephanie (2015), *Juvenile Nation: Youth, Emotions and the Making of the Modern British Citizen, 1880–1914*, London: Bloomsbury.

Pomfret, David (2001), "The City of Evil and the Great Outdoors: The Modern Health Movement and the Urban Young, 1918–40," *Urban History* 28 (3): 405–427.

Roberts, Nathan (2004), "Character in the Mind: Citizenship, Education and Psychology in Britain, 1880–1914," *History of Education* 33 (2): 177–197.

Roberts, Siân (2013), "Backhouse, Margaret Ann (1887–1977)," *Oxford Dictionary of National Biography*, Oxford: Oxford University Press. Available online: http://www.oxforddnb.com/view/article/103381 (accessed August 16, 2016).

Rooff, Madeline (1935), *Youth and Leisure: A Survey of Girls' Organisations in England and Wales*, Edinburgh: National Council of Girls' Clubs.

Snape, Robert (2015), "Voluntary Action and Leisure: An Historical Perspective 1830–1939," *Voluntary Sector Review* 6 (1): 153–171.

Thomson, Mathew (2006), *Psychological Subjects: Identity, Culture, and Health in Twentieth-Century Britain*, Oxford: Oxford University Press.

Wilkinson, Paul (1969), "English Youth Movements, 1908–30," *Journal of Contemporary History* 4 (2): 3–23.

28

"When we get out of here ..." Children, Faith-Based Schools, and the Society That Warrants Their Attention

Sally Anderson

*S*ally Anderson is an associate professor in the Department of Education at Aarhus University, and the author of Civil Sociality: Children, Sport, and Cultural Policy in Denmark (Information Age Publishing, 2008). In this chapter, she considers ongoing debates about faith-based schooling in Europe, and how these relate to the Danish context. Drawing on fieldwork with a Jewish private school in Denmark, Anderson engages here with how such schools act as "incubators" that allow children to develop a religious stance and a like-minded circle of friends before engaging in the generalized peer sociability of "out there in society." The chapter opens up understanding of spatial discourses and practices of "school" and "society" and addresses how sociability among religious peers is expressed as being "in here" as opposed to "out there" among others.

Pedagogical questions of childrearing and childhood education and the role of religion in this are deeply political, as many chapters in this volume illustrate. Extensive debates among Enlightenment philosophers of the role of religion in moral and intellectual inculcation, of how best to both cultivate the "true nature" of the child and meet the needs of states for educated, moral, and loyal citizens was, and still is, at the heart of these debates. Over the last centuries, European states have forged diverse responses to the question of how to organize that troublesome trinity of children, religion, and school. While Spain and Malta have drawn the Catholic Church into public schooling, France has enforced a strict division between the church and state education. While the Netherlands fashioned a pillarized system of Catholic, Protestant, and secular schools, Scandinavian countries initially gave Evangelical Lutheranism sole sway over public schools, although the church's influence is now greatly reduced (Smyth et al. 2013)

The free school in Denmark

In Denmark, the right of parents (*forældreretten*) to choose how to educate their child is old, established at the same as universal public schooling. In 1814, two royal orders proclaimed public schooling for all children, specifically for (*almue*—peasant) children living in rural village and towns, whose parents could not afford "house teachers."[1] Although these orders obliged parents to educate their children, they did not oblige parents to send their children to school. This principle of *skolefrihed*—or freedom of schooling—allowed for the continuation of elite education in private schools and homes, but also opened the door for less well-to-do parents to establish free-schools, *free* as in free of state meddling, not free of charge.

The nineteenth-century Danish free school movement was inspired by the teachings of a Danish priest, N.F.S. Grundtvig (1783–1872), and developed by an "awakened" teacher, Christen Kold (1816–1870), in the 1850s—in the midst of a Christian revival. This grassroots movement championed the common man's right to establish local religious and educational communities in opposition to centralized state control of church and school. Proponents staunchly maintained the principle that parents are both capable of deciding what is best for their children and have the right to educate their children as they see fit.

The first free school, set up by Christian Kold in 1851, was, thus, the child of revivalist lay-assemblies (*gudelige forsamlinger*), which, interestingly, were one of the earliest expressions of *civil society* in Denmark. Comprised of rural villagers and townspeople, lay assemblies were highly critical of the state–church's understanding of Christianity, and of its pedagogy, requiring rote learning of Luther's little catechism in order to graduate. Inspired by Grundtvig's critique of rote learning as "dead book knowledge," Kold taught through storytelling, a practice he claimed spoke naturally to the fantasies and, thus, to the hearts and spirits of children, creating cheerful rather than fearful learners. Kold aimed to instill in children a "living belief" and awaken their desire for an active life, for the good of society, Denmark and the Danish people. Because of his aim to awaken the "spirit of the Danish people," the Danish historian Ove Korsgaard argues that Kold's grassroots "free schools" were the first nationalistic educational institution in Denmark (2002, retrieved 16-10-07 http://www.kristeligt-dagblad.dk/artikel/192181).

Several years after Denmark became a constitutional monarchy (1849), the government passed a Free School Law (1855), reinforcing the right of all parents to educate their children privately. The state relinquished its right to specify teacher qualifications and require specific teaching methods, as long as free schools taught the same subjects, and produced educational results comparable to public schools. Later laws (1899, 1946) again endorsed state subsidies to all free private schools.

I have dwelt on this bit of Danish history because it highlights issues important for understanding present controversies over free schooling. First, it stresses (*forældreretten*) the legal right of parents to choose how to educate their children (*skolefrihed*). Second, it reveals the central role that religious education played in parents' desire to claim these rights. Third, it highlights the role "lay-religious assemblies" and "free schooling" played in institutionalizing civil association among the rural population. Through participation in "godly assemblies," country men and women gained valuable experience in voluntary and cooperative association: organizing themselves, calling meetings, establishing meeting etiquette, acquainting themselves with political issues, speaking out and arguing for a cause. They also gained experience in associating freely across social divides of gender, age, and occupation.

Today, the Danish constitution (*Grundloven* 1953) guarantees parents' rights to establish schools, and school laws provide the framework for a wide variety of state-free private schools. Although often grounded in opposition to specific pedagogical, social, or corporeal demands of "the common school" (*folkeskolen*) (Nissen 1973; de Coninck Smith 2000), free schools receive subsidies of up to 73 percent of what public schools receive. Groups of parents with small means can, thus, start schools premised on their own educational preferences. The government, in turn, oversees these schools to ensure educational quality and, at present, loyal orientation toward Danish society (Rudolf 2003).

Whereas the original free schools were based on religious and pedagogical freedom for the rural classes, free schools established in the twentieth century more often grew out of alternative pedagogical, political, or philosophical movements in urban areas. Schools started by religious[2] and ethnic minorities[3] are some of the oldest and most recent additions to the free school arena. Whereas well-established Jewish, Catholic, French, and German schools no longer arouse much debate, more recent Muslim, Arab, and Christian schools have attracted much public attention.

Controversies regarding religion in school

European countries have legitimized the teaching of religion in public schools variously as national cultural heritage, moral and spiritual anchoring, and objective knowledge of religions as human social phenomena. Teaching religion in a school—whether public or private—is however a careful balancing act, not least because families, even when of similar religious observance, have different practices and opinions about the content and intensity of religious teaching. Moreover, critics are quick to complain that animating an omnipotent God may deter children from developing critical "minds of their own" and thus undermine the proper fashioning of autonomous individuals. The risk of being called out for indoctrination is also present as many assume that modern schools should be committed to critical thinking and to emancipating young minds from "the darkness of received opinions," including those of their parents (Glenn 2003: 62).

Controversies over children, religion, and school (both public and private) are commonly driven by conflicts over parental versus state rights to decide the formal education and moral upbringing of children. Modern nation-states, albeit to different degrees, "share" children with parents across public and private spheres of care and inculcation. In Denmark, this sharing is extensive, as children from ages one to sixteen make their daily rounds between public and publicly funded private schools, after school clubs, day-care institutions, and home. The question of which—the state, professional educators or parents—has the authority to determine what is best for a child is under constant negotiation. Yet ultimately parents must "give the gift of the child," and hand over their children to society as citizens (Fortes 1984: 118; Carsten 1991: 435).

Controversies regarding religion, school, and children are also driven by disparate understandings of what is and should be *common* to *all* children—and through this *common* to society at large (Glenn 1988). As ideas of public schooling developed in Europe in the nineteenth century, one aim was to replace religious particularism, and local norms and loyalties with an emerging national identity and culture (Glenn 2003: 62). Glenn suggests that the powerful myth of the common school is not altogether benign, as it shores up a deeply held view that enlightenment and the inculcation of national life and character is the exclusive province of public schools. It also shores up the view that religious schooling per definition generates discord, disharmony, and strife among a people (2003: 62). Today there is widespread concern that faith-based schools disparage democratic values, promote gender inequality, and teach in ways not always conducive to turning out free, democratic citizens. Critics maintain that sectarian schools, established by religious minorities in the name of educational freedom and minority rights, in fact promote segregation and inequality, and thus challenge the state's obligation to ensure social integration and children's rights to an equal education. By allowing children to live "totally parallel lives" (Curtis 2004), private faith-based schools are damaging to local and national cohesion (James 2002; Rudolf 2003). Arguing that fanaticism can reside on both sides of the secular–sectarian divide, Glenn asserts the fundamental right of parents to choose the education and schooling that will shape their children's understanding of the world, particularly when state educational systems grow "unresponsive to what parents want for their children" (Glenn 2003).

Whose company is "good" company?

At the heart of the concern that faith-based schooling leads to social segregation and education inequality, and thus threatens national cohesion, is the age-old question of whose company children should keep, a question of import to parents and states, to schools and to children themselves. For children, it raises questions of which classmates to sit beside, look up to, rival or befriend, ignore or invite home. For parents, it is a matter of placing one's child among classmates of fairly similar background upbringing, manners, attitudes, and interests with regard for the child's social and intellectual life. For schools, it is a matter of forging a coherent and cooperative student body across classes and age-grades. For states, it is a matter of forging an integrated and cohesive society by encouraging and facilitating *generalized* or *cosmopolitan sociability* across social, economic, political, and religious differences (Birenbaum-Carmeli 1999; Glick Schiller et al. 2012).

In Denmark, this includes attempts to hinder the establishment of endosocial enclaves of so-called "parallel society" by encouraging parents to send their children to public *folkeskoler,* schools for *all* children, and not just for *particular* children. Many politicians and educators are critical of faith-based private schools, seeing them as small, and comparatively homogenous, endosocial enclaves of like-minded families and children. When parents choose small, private faith-based schools for their children's education, this choice does tend to narrow the range of "other" children encountered in school. Public schools are considered more heterogeneous social arenas than faith-based schools, which generally provide a more homogenous range of classmates and potential friends. Thus, organizing schools around a particular religion greatly affects the "company" children keep both at school and at home.

School, society, and the world

In Alan Peshkin's thoughtful ethnography (1986) of a private fundamentalist school in Illinois, the school community takes particular stock of two opposing worlds, a heavenly world of God and a worldly world full of Satan's temptations. Students are encouraged to act in ways that ensure their deliverance from Satan's clutches and smooth transition to their ultimate place in God's world.

In Denmark, schools in general, including faith-based schools, are differently worlded. People often speak as if formal school education takes place "in here," in a place less real that the "*real* world out there," often evoked as "society." Upon leaving "here," children enter "the real world out there in society." What goes on in formal educational settings is imaged as a kind of *practicum* that readies one for a more real world in society at large, the world that *really* counts. The religious overtones of this worlding are clear.

In a sense, faith-based schools are doubly hit by these spatial and temporal metaphors, in that the *real world* being invoked is beyond both school and religion. Moreover, the religious minorities who run faith-based schools are thought to reside on the "margins" of society, from where they must work to assert their compliance with national education policies and their affiliation and loyalty to mainstream society. Common spatial metaphors that place both schools and minorities beyond, or at best on the outskirts of, society conjure up a rather amusing image of religious minority schools teetering on society's edge, while cosmically attempting to balance their relation to past, present, and future godly and real worlds, as well as national societies. The political and relational realities of this metaphorical positioning are of course not such a laughing matter.

In Denmark, and most likely in other modern nation-states, society is imagined in Durkheimian fashion as a set of parts integrated into an organic, and preferably harmonious whole. The imagined societal whole is ideally maintained through a robust civil society premised on generalized sociability among all kinds of people from all walks of life. Family and individual concerns with personal relationships and sociabilities are thus never entirely private, but of deep concern to states responsible for the social cohesion of society at large (Anderson 2015). Controversies over faith-based schooling in Denmark are thus less about parent versus state rights, public funding, or religious indoctrination and more about whose society children attending these schools eventually will keep. The concern here is that private faith-based schools and the religious communities that sponsor them will decouple children from dominant national society, detach them from mainstream values and loyalties, promote identification with insular global religious communities, and fail to properly inculcate the desire and capacity to take on "part" in "Danish society."

Refuge, incubator, and *osteklokke*[4]

This chapter draws on fieldwork carried out in a small Jewish private school established in 1805. Founded by The Jewish Community of Denmark for the purpose of educating poor Jewish children, the school today incorporates both "secular" and "religious" Jews. It is affiliated with the Free School Association and governed by the Danish Free School and Private School Law. Run by a small Jewish community with approximately 2400 members, few newcomers and convertees, the school's role in promoting the well-being, identification and affiliation of upcoming generations is of great import to the community's ongoing existence. Teachers at the Jewish school often joked that the school's early mission to integrate children of Jewish immigrants into Danish society had been so successful that the school now had to reintegrate the children of assimilated Jews into Jewish society.

Teachers could also be heard depreciatingly describing the school as "Lilliputian" and "village-like" shot through with kin ties, petty gossip, and conflicts among the different fractions. More positive accounts portrayed the school as an *incubator*, or a sheltering *refuge*, where everyone knew everyone else, and children felt at home. Teachers argued that the sheltered environment allowed children to "take stock of their own origins and foundations, as human beings and as Jews." Developing a mind of one's own here involved developing a personal standpoint as a Jew, because, as the headmaster put it: "when they get out of here, they risk meeting all those who are not fond of Jews." Both teachers and students saw the school as a place where being Jewish was physically and existentially safe and normal, a place where children could both be themselves and be different as Jews, without constantly having to defend their heritage and identity, explain their values and actions, and not least the actions and stances of Israeli governments. As one teacher explained to me:

> These kids are Jews. They'll need to be able to hold their own out in society. It's not become any easier to be a Jew in Denmark, and they'll run into discussions out in society. They need to know a lot about themselves, and to have the courage to join in the debate.

The Jewish school thus provided a sheltered social space that could withstand an increasingly inhospitable political environment, produce a desire to contribute to the maintenance and safety of the community, and the courage to voice one's own mind in the inevitable conflicts (and very real dangers[5]) to come "out in society."

Thus while this particular faith-based school, insular in the sense that it is surrounded by a chained fence and watched over by armed guards, focuses on imparting knowledge of Judaism, religious practice, and diasporic history as well as teaching normal school subjects, its mission is also to instill self-knowledge, *civil courage*, and a proclivity for engaged participation in Jewish, Danish, and global society.

School leaders, well aware that the school provided a sheltering enclave "in here, among Jews," worried that it could feel claustrophobic, like being under a cheese bell. The school was open only to children of Jewish descent whose parents were members of the organized community. The ethno-religious segregation resulting from this was generally viewed as beneficial to children who soon enough would have to deal with their minority status, their controversial Jewish heritage and identity "out there" in wider society. From the school's point of view, this arrangement was not about thwarting societal cohesion through segregation or indoctrination, but about providing refuge and incubation for children belonging to a small and vulnerable religious minority.

Children's views of "in here" and "out there"

During conversations and interviews with pupils, I asked for their views on the school. One young boy told that he was very happy to be here, because here he did not feel like he had to keep his "secret"—that he was Jewish. Others who had also previously attended other schools, spoke of the wonderful feeling of not sticking out, of feeling normal among people who understood what Shabbat, kosher food and the celebrations of Rosh Hashanah or Yom Kippur entailed. Here were classmates who also played on Jewish football teams, traveled to Nordic Jewish football weekends, celebrated *bar and bat mitzvahs,* who also had grandparents or great grandparents in Theresienstadt or Sweden during the war, and now had family in Israel and spread out over the world. Here children felt they shared religious and cultural knowledge, a common history, holidays, minority status, and a sense of vulnerability.

Some of the eighth-grade students did express that after almost nine years, the small school had begun to feel extremely claustrophobic. Some could not wait to escape, and spoke excitedly about "getting out of here," as they were looking forward to going to other schools where they would be with "all kinds of people." A first-grade boy characterized public school as "those kinds of school where all children go." Picking up on the gist of my questions about whose company she kept, a fourth-grade girl assured me that she often went "out among Danes." The children's expressions illustrate a clear sense that only enclosed social spaces could be full of Jews, because social space "out there" in Danish society was full of Danes and all kinds of people.

As noted, older students looked forward to "getting out," but they also spoke of carefully choosing which secondary schools to attend. They were trying to avoid schools with many Muslims, and schools where teachers were known to have "negative attitudes towards Jews." Several boys had personal experience of verbal and minor physical abuse on buses and in the streets, and admitted that they did not feel quite safe wearing kippahs in public or football jerseys sporting the Star of David when playing league games in particular parts of town.

Learning to be "in here" among Jews

Although states and educators are interested in children learning the ins and outs of convivial, generalized sociability, "out among all," children are arguably also learning important lessons about being Jews together "in here." The following story of an unhappy girl, told by her class teacher, reveals what may be learned about peer sociability, about oneself, about religious difference, and how to deal with this. The story begins:

> I had a girl in my class, who, all the way through, had tremendous existential problems with her religion. We have a rule here at school that everyone must be able to eat any sweets distributed in class, but sometimes things go pretty quickly, and kids hand out candy that's not kosher. This girl refused the candy herself, because she knew she shouldn't eat it, but there she stood with tears running down her cheeks, crying: "How come they can eat it? Why can't I have any?" I went in and talked with her about how religion was a choice and that her parents had made a choice on her behalf, and that later on, she would be able to choose for herself. I could see how this problem affected her, how it existed in her over the years—and how she later was able to use it. Because she gained a strong sense of herself and what it was like to be an outsider—right in here, in this little group. And she learned something about social acceptance and non-acceptance from others. Because the others had

a very different lives. On Saturday mornings, when the other girls went into town, to the walking street to shop, she couldn't go with them. Nor would she, because she was marked by her parents' religion and accepted it. She wouldn't dream of breaking the rules, but she did complain loudly and she did cry. It was very rough on her—being a religious child.

This story is about a girl who had to learn to stand alone with her difference, even in the safety of a school, where all were Jewish, but not all were orthodox, and thus religious to the same degree.

The following story is about the upsetting experience of being forced to withdraw from a national science competition, when just on the verge of winning.

When I first met the fourth grade, they were practicing a play. They'd been working hard on this play for several weeks—taking time out from many classes to get it right. They were trying to win first prize—a class trip to Waterland—by participating in the Science Theater Festival at the Museum of Science. To win, they had to stage a play called "Salmonella attacking" about Bacto and Lacta, two feuding families, whose children Otto and Bibbi fall in love and wish to marry against their families' wishes. The class did such a professional job on the play that they made it to the finals, with a good shot at first place. But because finals were held on Saturday afternoon during Shabbat, two orthodox families refused to allow their children to participate. Needless to say, this caused much furor among the children, their parents, the school board, the rabbi and The Jewish Community. In the end, the rabbi announced that the 4th graders would have to withdraw. To make amends, the Jewish Community would give them a trip to Waterland.

When I later asked the children how they felt about having to withdraw from the finals in this way, most admitted to being very upset, but they also spoke of not blaming their classmates whose parents stopped the show by refusing to let their children do the play on a Saturday. A girl from a religious family, whose parents had refused to let her participate, told the following:

In the beginning I felt pretty badly because in a way I felt it was my fault, because I am not allowed to ride in a car and such. Brad goes to the synagogue a lot, too. A lot go there on the holidays but we go almost every Saturday and my Dad said I wasn't allowed to participate, so I was very upset and felt the whole thing was my fault. Brad's Mom told my Mom that some of the girls had told him it was our fault that the class couldn't go and I felt really bad. But the next day, quite a few said they couldn't either, so I felt better. They said that if the whole class couldn't go, then they were not allowed to go either.

Her friend added: "We all emailed each other and there were some who said: Can't we do it without them? And there were others who said: 'No, we're on their side. We won't do it when there are some who can't.' And then it became agreed that none of us would." *This attitude was confirmed by other children. While interviewing two boys, one pointed out:* "I understood the reason why some couldn't, and I think it would have been unfair if we did it without them". *The other agreed:* "I think the decision was fair enough for the others because even if you have only one line, if that person can't come, then we shouldn't do the play. We shouldn't keep the other kids out, just because we can do it." *Then both boys grinned:* "Besides we got at trip to Waterland anyway—without having to win the contest!"

This story points up strong school-class solidarity, not found in the other story—as well as an acceptance of a fair solution to this religious drama *within* the school. Taken together the stories show how through experiences of exclusion—one's own, and that of others—this faith-based school provides first-hand knowledge of problematic religious differences and possible ways of tackling these. The stories illustrate that while providing Jewish children with a refuge, the school also exposes them to very real dilemmas of religious difference, and forces them to reflect on and to come to terms with these.

Conclusion

Exploring the troublesome trinity of children, religion and school raise important questions about how both school and religion complicate children's lives. It also raises questions of how children, who belong to particular parents and who must be treated universally and equitably in public contexts of education and care, pose problems of how to forge childhood commonality and equality in private as well as public school communities.

Answers to the very real problem of whose company should children keep before entering society for real, of which peers and forms of peer sociation are good for children, religious communities and civil societies, do not point in one direction, as proponents of the open sociation of public schooling would have it. Indeed there appears to be something about the ideal of open sociation, all with all, that can make religious minority children, those with different lifestyles, clothing and "secrets" feel uncomfortable. Given the extensive freedom of religion in Denmark, one may wonder why public schools are not more adept at extending the "gift of communality" (Hage 2002) to those children whose daily lives are religiously oriented.

The role religion plays in this conundrum is tricky. Given the example of the Jewish school, religion here seems to be less about fashioning true believers through orthodox indoctrination, and more about forging personal and collective stances, that allow children to survive both school politics and the geopolitics of religiously inflected conflict. How should children be taught to "'make room for everybody" when "everybody" does not make room for them? How should children understand the admonishing maxim: "We all have to be able to be here," when they are excluded from downtown shopping sprees dues to religious observance (Anderson 2003, 2008). Do such experiences, in themselves, easily come by in both public and private schools, ready children any *less* for "taking part in" society? Conversely, what "part" of society must a citizen ultimately take part in? In querying whose society children should keep while preparing for society, it is important to note that children are born into worlds *not* of their own making, worlds full of contested national ideology, complicated spatial cosmology, compelling mainstream moralities and geopolitical realities that all warrant their attention. Whether children pay closer attention to these in small faith-based schools than in larger mainstream public schools is an open question. But as we have seen, faith-based school cannot cordon off "the real world." Children attending such schools may still find themselves—like the Jewish students who took part in their classmate's bat mitzvah on the night of the second fatal "Copenhagen shooting"—in the eye of the storm in a world where to be openly religious makes one socially and physically vulnerable.

Notes

1 The establishment of universal schooling was a consequence of many factors: Enlightenment thinking, the abolition of adscription and subsequent emergence of a free peasantry, and political awareness of the need to transform peasant children into enlightened and economically useful citizens.

2 Jews, Catholics, Muslims, Scientologists and Pentecostals

3 German, Moroccan, Somali, Pakistani, Turkish, French.

4 This term, meaning cheese bell or cheese dome, connotes a protective environment hermetically sealed off from its surroundings.

5 This refers to the cold-blooded shooting on February 15, 2015 of a Jewish civilian, a volunteer guarding the main gate of the synagogue during the Bat Mitzvah party of a young Jewish girl.

References

Anderson, S. (2003), "Bodying Forth a Room for Everybody: Inclusive Recreational Badminton in Copenhagen," in N. Dyck and E. Archetti (eds), *Sport, Dance and Embodied Identities*, 23–53, Oxford: Berg.

Anderson, S. (2008), *Civil Sociality: Children, Sport and Cultural Policy in Denmark*, Charlotte, NC: Information Age Publishing.

Anderson, S. (2015), "Sociability: The Art of Form," in V. Amit (ed.), *Thinking Through Sociality: An Anthropological Interrogation of Key Concepts*, 97–127, New York and Oxford: Berghahn.

Birenbaum-Carmeli, D. (1999), "'Love Thy Neighbour': Sociability and Instrumentality among Israeli Neighbors," *Human Organization* 58 (1): 82–93.

Carsten, J. (1991), "Children in Between: Fostering and the Process of Kinship on Pulau Langkawi, Malaysia," *MAN* 26 (3): 425–444.

Curtis, P. (2004), "Teachers Lack Faith in Muslim Schools," *The Guardian Review*, June 9, 2004, EducationGuardian.co.uk © Guardian Newspapers Limited 2004.

De Coninck Smith, N. (2000), *For barnets skyld—byen, skolen og barndommen 1880–1914*, Copenhagen: Gyldendal.

Fortes, M. (1984), "Age, Generation, and Social Structure," in D.I. Kertzer and J. Keith (eds), *Age and Anthropological Theory*, 99–122, Ithaca, NY: Cornell University Press.

Glenn, C.L. (1988), *The Myth of the Common School*, Amherst MA: University of Massachusetts Press.

Glenn, C.L. (2003), "Fanatical Secularism," *Education Next: A Journal of Opinion and Research* 1: 60–65.

Glick-Schiller, N., Darieva, T., and Gruner-Domic, S. (2012), "Defining Cosmopolitan Sociability in a Transnational Age. An Introduction," in T. Darieva, N. Glick-Schiller, and S. Gruner-Domic (eds), *Cosmopolitan Sociability: Locating Transnational Religious and Diasporic Networks*, 1–20, London: Routledge.

Hage, G. (2002), "The Differential Intensities of Social Reality: Migration, Participation and Guilt," in G. Hage (ed.), *Arab Australians Today: Citizenship and Belonging*, 192–205, Melbourne: Melbourne University Press.

Nissen, G. (1973), *Bønder, skole og demokrati. En undersøgelse i fire provstier af forholdet mellem den offentlige skole og befolkningen på landet i tiden ca. 1880–1910*. Copenhagen: Institut for Dansk Skolehistorie.

Peshkin, A. (1986), *God's Choice. The Total World of a Fundamentalist Christian School*, Chicago: Chicago University Press.

Rudolf, T.S. (2003), *En analyse af de offentlige danske debatter om tørklæder og friskoler*, Copenhagen: Institute of Political Science, University of Copenhagen.

Smyth, E., Lyons, M. and Darmody, M. (2013), *Religious Education in a Multicultural Europe: Children, Parents, Schools*, London: Palgrave Macmillan.

PART FOUR

Media and the Materialities of Childhood Religion

Introduction

In their introduction to the *Materialities of Schooling: Design, Technology, Objects, Routines*, Martin Lawn and Ian Grosvenor make the point that there is often a false dichotomy made between objects and people and between imagination and action in historical studies of schooling. In reality, they argue, objects and how they are used, technologies and routines of actions, the materiality of settings, together constitute the learning and life contexts of children (Lawn and Grosvenor 2005). This is no less true of the relationship between the materialities and media around children which invoke for them the religious as an aspect of life. Media and forms of materiality are part and parcel of the religious lifeworlds of children, even in religious traditions which might see themselves as eschewing the material dimension of life, for instance certain puritan forms of Christianity. Just as the act of looking itself contributes to religious formation, according to David Morgan (1998), from the chapters below it is clear that other actions—such as of play, reading, story-telling, listening, and singing—may similarly socialize children into religious ideas, language and forms of practice. Objects that make up the world around children—the toys, books, radio, and other electrical and digital devices, indeed classrooms themselves—may be designed or appropriated by adults to invoke the religious for children. As Robert Orsi (2005) has observed, the religious is constituted for children in their use of, and their relationship with, the material culture and the sacred it is made to represent to them. Moreover, it is in the intersubjectivity of adults with children and the material—or children alone in interaction with a medium or material object—that the religious may be invoked. Religion is always and inherently a relational phenomenon.

The chapters below explore the ways in which the media and material realities of childhood are so implicated in constituting the religious for children. The extract from one of John G. Williams broadcasts at the BBC provides an early example of the ways in which modern media were used to inform adults and children about religion. In this instance it is a didactic piece about the kind of relationship adults/parents and children have in relation to religion. It invokes responsibility on the adult's part to be an example to the child, and construes the child as one who can spot disingenuity in adults a good distance away. A sort of cautionary tale to adults on how not to religiously educate, it assumes the relationship between the domestic and the formally religious to be in harmony in children's religious socialization.

This construction of the relationship between adults and children illustrates what John Gillis writes of here as the idealization of family life from the nineteenth century onwards. In a context of rising doubt in some societies, the family became "proof of the existence of the divine"; children came to be seen as "priceless possessions"; and motherhood and fatherhood took on distinctive characteristics in relation of child-rearing and spiritual guidance. Family life became the locus of the sacred.

Four chapters in this section, by Henry Jenkins, Pat Pinsent, Jodi Eichler-Levine, and Naomi Wood, examine the ways in which children's literature are implicated in mediating particular values to children. The extract from Jenkins' examines the case of Dr. Seuss, showing how the concerns of children's authors, and of the wider social setting in which such texts are written, may be conveyed by the stories written for children's consumption. This is not to argue that children's stories are simple devices to communicate directly with children, reading as a process is much more complicated than that. Children's fictional literature is not a manual of morals. Rather stories often hide coded messages of the kinds of ideas and values authors wish to convey, as in the case of Dr. Seuss, a radical utopian vision of society. Pinsent's chapter traces the development of children's literature from the overt form of moral and religious guide from the seventeenth century onwards, to the nineteenth-century heyday of the genre, through to the ways in which religion is dealt with as a subject for children through to the present. Eichler-Levine's chapter opens up the question of the monstrous in Jewish children's literature through a close reading of books by Eric Kimmel and David Wisniewski, revealing how reading American Jewish children's literature with an eye for darkness shows the ways in which anxieties over past persecutions and trauma and future uncertainties become "projected onto the imagined bodies of children and the spaces they inhabit." Naomi Wood's focus is upon two children's authors in particular C.S. Lewis and George MacDonald. These two highly popular authors conveyed ideas of the religious through fantasy stories. Their work reveals that ideas and ideals can be conveyed through story almost invisibly, through metaphor and allusion. This intrudes so little it is almost impalpable.

A chapter by Stephen Parker explores the history of the BBC's provision of radio worship for children in schools. In particular, he examines a conscious change of discourse on the part of broadcasters to a new hymnody for children at a time of apparent de-Christianization of British society. The extent to which such radio provision of collective worship truly impacts upon children, and how they respond to it is explored in the chapter by Rachael Shillitoe.

Laura Arnold Leibman's chapter points out that religious games and toys are nothing new, and that games in general communicate both competitive and collaborative values. Focusing upon a Jewish community in particular, she examines two toys (building blocks and toy figures similar to their secular alternatives) designed in a collaboration with manufacturers in order to convey "messianic" non-competitive values to children, "reworking American popular culture" to fit the particular Haredi, ultra-Orthodox Jewish worldview.

A further chapter by Parker argues that study of materiality of classrooms historically and in the contemporary gives us access to the everyday religious education occurring there. He makes the point that religious education is much more than the knowledge defined by curricula, it is the whole of spatial, material, visual, and auditory culture of the classroom too.

References

Lawn, M. and Grosvenor, I. (eds) (2005), *Materialities of Schooling: Design, Technology, Objects, Routines*, Cambridge: Symposium.

Morgan, D. (1998), *Visual Piety: A History and Theory of Popular Religious Images*, Berkeley: University of California Press.

Orsi, Robert A. (2005), *Between Heaven and Earth: The Religious Worlds People Make and the Scholars Who Study Them*, Princeton: Princeton University Press.

29

Training Children in Religion

John G. Williams (1957)

*J*ohn G. Williams was an Anglican cleric, broadcaster, and religious educator particularly active between the 1940s and 1960s. He pioneered religious broadcasting for children at the BBC, as well as someone who contributed to ideas about how to lead worship in schools when Collective Worship became compulsory in Britain in the post-Second World War period. In this extract from his book Worship and the Modern Child, *Williams addresses the issue of religious education in the domestic context.*

A small boy of nine was polishing his boots in the scullery after breakfast one Sunday morning, getting ready to go off to church. His father, settling back comfortably in his armchair by the kitchen fire and opening his Sunday newspaper, called out: 'Look sharp there, Tom, or you're going to be late for church', and the boy, with a boot in one hand and the blacking-brush in the other said: 'Dad, when shall I be old enough not to have to go to church any more – like you?'

That kind of situation is repeated in thousands of homes every Sunday. What reply can the father make, in all honesty, to the child's question? There are only two possible answers. One is: 'You stick to the Church, my boy. It's the right thing. I ought to be going myself, but I'm just a slacker – so don't take any notice of what *I* do.' The other is: 'Well, frankly, Tom, I think religion is all right for youngsters like you – I had my share of it when I was your age – but when you get as old and wise as I am… well, you can drop it.' But the important thing to notice is that, whatever the father *says*, it is what he *does* that is going to carry the real weight. The boy is bound to argue, quite naturally, 'If my father doesn't think much of all these things the vicar is always talking about, then I suppose there can't be much in them …'

This takes us immediately to the heart of all problems connected with the explicit training of children in religion. It is not going to be just a simple question of giving them religious *instruction* – Bible stories, prayers, ethical teaching, and so on (though of course it will involve that incidentally). During those early formative years from infancy to the age of ten or so, the really vital thing is going to be, not what they learn about religion objectively, but what they come to *feel* about it from their contacts with older people. It is going to be the general impression, pleasant or unpleasant, real or bogus, that will determine whether, in later years, the child will find God or will throw overboard (perhaps scornfully) everything he imagines religion to be; and the general impression he gets of it will be derived almost entirely from the religious atmosphere of his home, positive or negative. If religion means little or nothing to you, then, however much good sense you may talk, the chances are hundreds to one that your child will be infected by your unspoken attitude....

How does this work in practice? Let us look at it from the earliest beginnings. We cannot be certain how soon a child begins to receive impressions. It may be quite soon after he is conceived and certainly some time before he is born. He may be profoundly affected by his mother's state of mind during the period of gestation; so his religious training may well begin as early as that, in the very atmosphere of prayer and dedication with which his mother then surrounds him. Let the child be (so to speak) steeped in an atmosphere of prayer and healthy thinking from the moment of his conception. You may in fact surround him with prayer before he is even conceived and is still only a hope. Prayer is not closely tied to the time-scheme! The mother's thoughts and aspirations will have a quite immeasurable effect on the whole psychic development of the unborn child....

As soon as the child is born his religious education begins in real earnest. At this stage it is impossible to differentiate between religious and any other kind of education – it is *all* religious. The child's first and most formative experience is his relationship with his mother. From this relationship he derives the complex of impressions which will later become his attitude and response to the world at large – and to God. That is an added reason why Mother is such a very important person. To a tiny baby his mother *is* God. She is the source and ground of his existence. She is Providence, supplying all his physical wants and giving him the security, comfort and encouragement he needs. His whole existence and welfare depend entirely upon her. She is his whole Universe. What mother is and does are giving the child, all unconsciously, his first glimpse of what God is like; those early impressions are terrifyingly powerful and deep-seated and may in fact be indelible. The more we understand about juvenile delinquency, for example, the more we see it as a form of 'rejection' which derives in most instances from an unstable and insecure home background, and chiefly from an unhappy relationship with the mother. It is, in a sense, the total rejection of the universe at large, and therefore of God. This underlines most powerfully the point I am making here. The Mother and Child relationship is a profoundly sacred one for more than merely sentimental or emotional reasons. It mediates God to the child.

This is the first step in religious training … our whole relationship must be imbued with gentleness and firmness combined, for firmness is a part of true love, though it need never be ungentle. Above all, let the whole relationship be, as far as possible, completely balanced … whatever discipline we need to exert should always be evident to the child as part of our love for him – not something that temporarily suspends our love. It is a terrible thing to say to a young child, 'If you do that, Mummy won't love you any more'; still more damaging to say, 'If you do that, *God* won't love you anymore.' Remind yourself constantly, 'I am all the time introducing this child to God.' It is a chastening thought.

30

A World of Their Own Making

John R. Gillis (1996)

*J*ohn Gillis's A World of Their Own Making *explores how contemporary ideas of 'family values' and the idealization of the home are recent phenomena, drawing attention to how 'The Family' becomes mythologized and idealized through particular historical practices. In this extract, Gillis describes the material practices that sustained the sanctification of family life, with children becoming increasingly central, from family portraits to the keeping of family photograph albums.*

Middle-class Victorians turned the family into an object of worshipful contemplation. As a result of the crisis of faith that had caused so many to have serious doubts about the existence of God and his transcendent order, the family became proof of the existence of the divine. In what would have appeared to earlier generations as a pagan if not papist inversion of the divine order, Victorians on both sides of the Atlantic began to worship through their families. Family life became a kind of sacrament for those, like Charles Kingsley, who declared that 'fully to understand the meaning of "Father in Heaven" we must be fathers ourselves; to know how Christ loved the Church, we must have wives to love, and love them'. Fatherhood was thus sanctified, but the image of motherhood was even more exalted, for to men like Kingsley women were 'most divine because they are most human'. Henceforth, they would be assigned a role in the family analogous to the role of the clergy in the church – becoming its guide and most perfect incarnation.

The archetypes had been brought down to earth, but in turning away from the cosmos and the community for families to live by, the Victorians had taken on the cultural project of creating and sustaining their own symbolic universe. Their imagined families could no longer be taken for granted but needed constant attention. This fundamental transformation opened up vast new possibilities for individuals to construct identities, marriages, and family worlds to their own specifications, but it also placed huge burdens on marriage and family to produce those models of behaviour – the saintly mother, the good family man, the perfect child – that had previously been found only in a divine original or communal exemplar, never in the family itself.

Cut off from the old cosmic and communal archetypes by the combined forces of secularism and individualism, the Victorian middle classes would turn those they lived with into their significant others, attributing to them qualities that previously had been associated with divine or communal archetypes. What religious and communal rituals, images, and symbols had previously provided, these household gods and goddesses would now be responsible for. To the challenge of sustaining the material basis of family life was now added the awesome task of providing for its spiritual requirements. A revolution in family life occurred; in a few short decades during the second half of the nineteenth century, the household ceased to be like any other place and became an enchanted world populated by mythic figures ... .

Previously unadorned domestic space had become representational. Mirrors invited reflection; portraits and photographs guaranteed the presence of family even in its absence. More and more of what people came to think of as family life was not so much the lives that family members actually lived but the representations of that life they produced for one another. Alain Corbin has noted that, in the nineteenth century, 'visual contact became more important than physical contact'. In a shift that presaged in some ways the 'virtual reality' being talked about today, the simulacra of family became the measure of family. The copy took on a reality that had previously belonged to the thing itself.

The image of family, which had been blurred and indistinguishable from the larger collectives of friends and neighbours, now took on a new sharpness. Family had put itself on display. Mothers and children, rarely the focus of family portraits in earlier periods, were henceforth the icons of family life, present on all its important occasions and in all its representations. Previously valued for their labour and earning capacity, children took on symbolic value to the point that by the end of the nineteenth century they were seen as priceless possessions whose loss could never be compensated for. While children had always played a minor role in religious and communal rituals, they were now central to all those occasions on which the family represented itself to itself. Christian baptism, previously a communal event, became home-centred for the first time. And not accidentally, the Jewish rite of circumcision, the *bris*, was shifted from the synagogue to the house in the same period. Children's birthdays, of no significance previously, became a centrepiece of the family calendar, and by 1900 Christian confirmation and the Jewish bar mitzvah were such major family occasions that religious authorities began to worry that they were losing their religious meaning.

By the twentieth century, middle-class families could no longer imagine themselves without children. Offspring were kept at home longer, and even when they left, they remained a powerful symbolic presence. Their pictures were kept in family albums, and their toys and school things carefully stored away in attics and basements, Children were never allowed to leave the mental worlds that families now inhabited.

Even their rooms were kept as they were, an object of nostalgia for young adults, but equally important insurance against the loss of parental identity for those whose time of parenting was over. By the twentieth century, a couple without children no longer qualified as a family. It even became common to say of those whose children had grown up that their family had left them.

Motherhood assumed a similar iconic function. In Victorian images of the good family life, mothers occupied an increasingly central position, displacing the father figure to a very large extent. By the end of the century, men were more likely to be behind the family camera than in front of it. They became the missing presence, literally and figuratively, in a family world that was increasingly organised around the symbolic interaction between women and children.

As mothers became the central symbols of generational continuity, the image of the grandmother underwent a remarkable transformation. In previous centuries, grandparents had rarely appeared in the family imaginary, and when they did, it was usually the male ancestor who figured most prominently. Grandmothers had once been viewed as meddling, even threatening figures, but now they were seen in a much more favourable light. By the end of the nineteenth century, the older woman had lost her image as a wilful, sexual being and become the epitome of a loving presence. The grandfather image also softened to the point that, despite continued high mortality, which often prevented grandparents from playing much of a role in their grandchildren's lives, the symbolic importance of elders was enormously enhanced, even as the generations grew further apart in every other respect.

With the rise of these new icons, the patriarchal figure was largely displaced. Just as the nation-state was now represented by the female form, the house was more likely to be identified with the wife than the husband. Yet men were keener than ever to see themselves as part of the family circle, even though much more of their lives was now spent outside the home. 'The child and its mother are no longer relegated to the woman's apartments as in the past', noted a French observer. 'The child is shown while still an infant. Parents proudly present the child's nurse. It's as if they were on stage, making a great show of their production. In short, a man is father today as he would have been a citizen a little less than a century ago – with a great deal of show.' The fact that fathers were more of an absence than a presence in the everyday life of the household only made the display of fatherhood that much more urgent. As with everything else connected with family life, the representation of fatherhood became as important, if not more so, than fathering itself.

Families not only saw but spoke of themselves in an entirely new manner. By the mid-nineteenth century, the definition of the word *family* distinguished it from *household* or any other residential unit. The idiom of parenthood and siblingship was reserved to flesh and blood alone, and children ceased to address their parents as 'Sir' and 'Madame'; the terms they had once used in speaking to all adults now seemed inappropriate for those special persons they were calling 'Daddy' and 'Mommy' for the first time. Such terms of endearment, together with the pet names Victorians became so fond of using, swathed each family with a language of its own making, as transparent to them as it was opaque to those who spoke another family tongue. Language defined the boundaries of particular families just as it defined the borders of nations. Caught up in their own rhetorics, in the stories they told themselves and nobody else, imagined families took on a life no less real than the imagined communities that had come to underlie the national consciousness.

Names too were endowed with a magic they had not had previously. In the eighteenth century, naming had ordinarily not taken place until there was assurance that the newborn would survive, and the names given were symbolic of ties other than those of family. Catholics chose from a limited stock of saints' names, while Protestants preferred names that were emblematic of virtue – Patience, Preserved, Chastity – rather than family connections. Frequently, the same name was used more than once, transferred from a dead to a living sibling. But from the mid-nineteenth century onward, names took on unprecedented significance, and the christening ceremony, previously a relatively minor part of Christian baptism, became its most meaningful moment, an important family occasion, a rite of passage not into an extended spiritual community but into the family world itself. Thus, a rite that once symbolised the inadequacy of the flesh and blood became one of its principal celebrations.

Only the nobility had been able to lay sure claim to a family name in earlier centuries. As late as the eighteenth century, the connection between the individuals and surnames was tenuous, even for males. Names were more likely to be attached to land than to family, one of the reasons it was customary in some places for the man to take the surname of his bride when marrying into a landed family. Many men would never have this good fortune, and many among the poor were called solely by their first name or nickname for their entire lives. However, by the end of the nineteenth century, the possession of a surname divided people by gender rather than by class. It would be some time before women would gain (or regain) the right to retain their own name in marriage, but already the family name was the first thing a child learned, the first sign of its intelligence, and its initiation into the mysteries of its own special family world.

Names became the family's symbolic link with its past and the promise of its future. They were carefully recorded in family Bibles and entered into the family trees that in the Victorian era became a sure sign of membership in the middle class. While the aristocracy had always invested itself in its pedigrees, the middle-class passion for genealogy was entirely new. In the second half of the century, dozens of genealogical societies were founded on both sides of the Atlantic. What had been considered a vanity and an affectation earlier became an indispensable emblem of connection for family members who found themselves increasingly isolated from one another. A mass search for roots would not occur until a century later, but already American's obsessive quest for ancestry had reached the point where Mark Twain could satirise it in *Huckleberry Finn* by having 'the rightful duke of Bridgwater' and the 'pore disappeared Dauphin, Looey the Seventeenth', join Huck and Jim on the raft.

What earlier generations had kept alive in 'loving hearts' and 'edifying conversations' now found concrete expression in myriad household objects and in the house itself. There was a long tradition of aristocratic attachment to particular houses, but the middle class had never before felt the need to represent itself through its dwellings. Now they too found comfort in bricks and mortar. The house became a status symbol and, more important, a memory palace, the repository of all that united families mentally even when they were physically apart.

Furniture, silver, and other household objects that had been assigned only economic significance earlier were magically transformed into priceless possessions. Known in prior centuries as 'lucks' by the aristocracy, who had jealously guarded them as legal proof of their rights of inheritance, heirlooms entered into middle-class life only in the middle of the nineteenth century. By the nineteenth century, even though they had lost their legal standing, household objects handed down over the generations had increased immensely in their symbolic capacity to link past and present. By the 1880s antiques had become 'narcissistic equivalents of self' for the upper middle classes, and even quite ordinary objects came to carry great symbolic weight as the passion to collect and preserve spread rapidly during the next few decades. And when the genuine article did not exist, it could always be invented. In Marcel Pagnol's story *My Father's Glory*, an old rifle bought in a second-hand shop becomes for the boy his grandfather's gun, creating a bond across generations that no longer had much contact with one another.

Objects served as mnemonic devices capable of recalling family even in its absence. By the end of the century, animals were serving a similar purpose. They had become the 'sovereign masters of domestic space', symbolising those qualities that families often found wanting in themselves. Dogs had become man's best friend, and cats were idealised for their supposedly familial qualities. The middle classes were the first to thoroughly domesticate their pets, to transform them into the equivalents of human significant others. The image of loyal Fido refusing to leave his master's grave could be found in parlours and bedrooms on both sides of the Atlantic. Families mourned their pets as they mourned their own relations, consoled by the thought that the family dog or cat would be waiting for them in heaven. By the 1870s there were pet cemeteries in France and elsewhere, constituting yet another family plot where the symbols of family remained forever safe in stone even if family itself seemed perpetually endangered....

The middle classes developed family life to the level of an art, but an art that was heavily dependent on a gendered division of labour: men were the producers, and women were the directors of the family drama. In earlier centuries, it was he head of the household who served as master of ceremonies, but men now readily ceded that role to their wives.

Women's work, previously inseparable from that of men, was given new names – 'housework' and 'homemaking'– and a new meaning. No longer associated with toil, it came to be seen as 'an emanation of Woman's nature', something that women should find revitalising. Among the better off, the real toil of housework was being assumed by domestic servants, but where the woman of the house did most of the domestic tasks, convention demanded that she represent it as a labour of love. To the beneficiaries of female domestic labour, ironed shirts and elaborate dinners appeared as if by magic. 'Like a mechanic at the opera, she controls everything that happens, yet no one sees her do it', was the way one contemporary characterised it....

By then an increasing amount of women's work was devoted to the creation of the rituals, myths, an images on which the newly enchanted world of family had come to depend. Women were the ones who facilitated the symbolic communication among family members. They were the ones who told the family stories, remembered the birthdays and anniversaries of distant relatives, organised family holidays, and were most involved in mourning and commemoration. Women became the keepers of the family' schedule and its calendar. While men's diaries constituted a record of their own personal accomplishments, women's diaries, devoted to family events, constituted a running chronicle of marriage, births, and deaths. As such, women's diaries, like women's letters, were not protected by the same rights of privacy as a man's. They were assumed to be open to the inspection of a father or husband, who considered it to be as much his as hers.

In the eighteenth century, family correspondence had been the husband's responsibility, and personal messages shared the page with news and business matters. By the mid-nineteenth century, the family letter had come into its own and fell increasingly within the feminine domain. It was then that family letters took on the novel symbolic dimension they have retained ever since, less valued 'for what they said as [for] the regularity of their exchange'. The ritual of writing became far more significant than what was written. The quality of the paper, the care of composition, all contributed to the symbolic weight of the family letter. Meant to be kept and reread, it constituted a presence in the absence of a lover or family member. Over the course of the Victorian era, family correspondence became both more frequent and more formal. Facilitated by the newly created national and international postal systems, the family letter facilitated the kind of intimacy at a distance that since then has become so characteristic of modern family life that we are scarcely aware of how its forms have changed over time.

The first holiday and greeting cards that circulated among kin were handmade. By the end of the century, however, bought cards accounted for an increasingly greater share of family correspondence as people took advantage of this relatively cheap form of symbolic interaction to extend their family worlds still further. In the early twentieth century, telephonic technology added still more possibilities for symbolic communication. The ritual of calling replace to some extent the exchange of cards and letters. The desire for tangible signs of connection persisted, however, and conversation, by itself, never regained the place it had once had in the life of families.

Cards and letters found their way into the albums that were the conversation pieces of every Victorian parlour. Babies' locks, dried flowers from wedding bouquets, the souvenirs of family vacations – all became sacred objects, relics too precious to part with. When photography became more accessible after the 1850s, family pictures took on a similar magical power, capable of bringing the past into the present, Family photos were then, as now, less a statement of what the family actually was than what it imagined itself to be. They assured the Victorians, as they continue to assure us, of family solidarity and endurance.

31

"No matter how small": The Democratic Imagination of Dr. Seuss

Henry Jenkins (2002)

Henry Jenkins is a scholar of media and children's culture. In 1998, he edited The Children's Culture Reader, *which explored children's popular culture, child-rearing, and other areas in which adults attempted to influence children's lives. In this excerpt, Jenkins argues that intermingled with the nonsense rhyming words and the captivating pictures, Dr. Seuss's work had a strong political and social agenda, for Seuss understood that children's books not only serve to inculcate values into their young audience, but also work to reshape their adult readers.*

When Horton the elephant in Dr Seuss's *Horton Hears a Who* (1954), listens to the 'very faint yelp' of a microscopic civilization living on a dust speck and tries to rally his neighbours to protect the endangered Who village, he gets caught between two different democratic communities. On the one hand, there is the conformist world of his own friends and neighbours, 'the Wickersham Brothers and dozens/Of Wickersham Uncles and Wickersham Cousins/And Wickersham In-laws', who use chains and cages to crush individualistic tendencies: 'For almost two days you've run wild and insisted/On chatting with persons who've never existed./Such carryings-on in our peaceable jungle!/We've had quite enough of your bellowing bungle!'. On the other hand, there is the civic-minded community of Whoville, 'a town that is friendly and clean'. Faced by a crisis that threatens their survival, the Whos rally together to ensure that their voices are heard: 'This is your town's darkest hour!/The time for all Whos who have blood that is red/To come to the aid of their country!'

Horton's situation encapsulates the dilemmas that many liberals faced in postwar America – torn between the conflicting values of community and individualism, frightened by mob rule and, yet, dedicated to democracy. *Horton* expresses a nostalgia for the Whoville-like America of the war years, when political differences were forgotten in the name of a common cause and fear over the rigid Wickersham-like conformity of the 1950s ....

Seuss's outrage over the community's pillorying of the non-conformist Horton (a liberal out of sync with his community) contrasts sharply with his disgusted response to Jo-Jo the 'very small, *very* small shirker' (who places personal interests ahead of the larger cause). The heroic Horton challenges his community to show greater concern for the weak and powerless. The contemptible Jo-Jo endangers his community by withholding his small voice from their noise-making efforts. Only when Jo-Jo contributes his voice 'the Smallest of All', do the Wickershams and the other animals hear the Whos and commit themselves to their preservation. *Horton* is not only a plea for the rights of the 'small', but also an acknowledgment that even the 'small' have an obligation to contribute to the general welfare. Yet, what the story never really addresses – beyond a commonsensical assurance that we all know the right answers – is who gets to define what constitutes the general welfare, the right-thinking Horton or the fascistic Wickershams. Here, as so often in his stories, Seuss trusts the child to find his or her way to what is 'fair' and 'just'....

Permissive writers looked with horror at the way that adult problems – the Depression, the Second World War – had introduced desperation and brutality into the lives of America's children; they looked upon the children who would be born into the postwar world as holding a fresh chance for social transformation. Born free of prejudice, repression, and authoritarianism, one writer argued, the 'Baby Boom' child 'comes into the world with a clean slate, needing only to guided aright to grow into an adult with the highest ideals to which man has attained'. Childhood was imagined as a utopian space through which America might reinvent itself.

Children's fiction, in this context, became a vehicle for teaching both children and adults this new mode of democratic thinking. As child-rearing expert Mauree Applegate explained: 'If the democratic process is to improve or even continue, the skills of living together must be taught children with their pablum'.

As McCarthyism foreclosed the prospect of meaningful political change within the public sphere, many leftists turned towards the family as a site where the culture could be shifted from below. In doing so, they retained the 'Popular Front' habit of framing their social critiques in the language of 'democracy' and 'Americanism', terms we find it difficult today to disentangle from the nationalistic rhetoric of the cold war. A close reading of these books, however, reveals that their core impulses are progressive (struggling to transform and 'democratize' American society) rather than conservative (preserving American institutions from outside challenge).

Dr. Seuss was, in many ways, the poet laureate of this 'permissive' culture, with many parents clutching a copy of Dr. Spock in one hand and Dr. Seuss in the other. Seuss wrote five of the ten best-selling children's books of this century. By 1954, when he wrote *Horton*, Seuss was already gaining national recognition as a distinctive voice in children's literature. However, he had spent most of his professional life writing for adults, translating what he had learned from an apprenticeship cartooning for popular humor magazines into the tools for persuasion – first, working in advertising, then, doing editorial cartoons for the Popular Front newspaper PM, and finally, scripting propaganda and training films for Frank Capra's Signal Corps unit. The postwar period saw a gradual narrowing of his attention toward children's writing…a transition which parallels the emergence of this postwar discourse of 'democratic' parenting….

Renewed interest in the project of 'radical democracy' forces us to think about how an empowered citizenship might be fostered on the most local levels – not only by changing politics within our communities or our work places, but also by rethinking the politics of the family…There is much about permissiveness we might well want to reject. Feminist critics note that permissive approaches often disempowered women even as they sought to empower children, that permissiveness was linked to the domestic containment of women and that writers like Spock helped to 'naturalise' dominant conceptions of gender roles and normative sexual identities. Permissiveness often mystified the power relations between children and adults, making authority seem to disappear when its mechanisms had only been masked. Permissiveness placed impossible expectations on parents, which are still being felt was we confront an economic reality that makes postwar models impossible to maintain. Permissiveness romanticizes the child as a Rousseauian ideal. No, permissiveness won't do at all!

Yet, there is something else we can learn from permissiveness writers like Dr. Spock and Dr. Seuss – the process of rethinking the family, of re-imaging the power relations within the home, and of seeing childhood as vitally linked to the political transformation of American culture. The utopian futures envisioned by permissiveness writers were never fully achieved. Social institutions and attitudes proved too deep-rooted to be transformed by simply changing the ways parents raised their young…however, rediscovering the democratic imagination of Dr. Seuss should remind us that 'fairy tales' can become powerful tools for political transformation.

32

"Making disciples of the young": Children's Literature and Religion

Pat Pinsent

Pat Pinsent, Senior Research Fellow at the University of Roehampton, UK, has published widely on themes related to religion and children's literature. In this chapter she outlines how the development of English language children's literature has been inextricably intertwined with the desire of many writers to influence young readers towards the kind of beliefs and behavior appropriate to their variety of Christianity.

Introduction

The desire to teach children the elements of their religion was until the twentieth century one of the most important factors behind the production, sale and distribution of children's books in English. Much of the material intended for young readers was either directly religious in origin, or took the form of stories calculated to motivate them towards behavior regarded as appropriate to young Christians. From the earliest books in English until the end of Victoria's reign, the majority of British writers envisaging a child audience were themselves Christian, and generally regarded "indoctrination" as part of their vocation. This was nothing new; Seth Lerer observes that "Medieval children learned to read and write from alphabets and prayer books, psalters and primers... [they] would find their ABCs imbued with Christian teaching from the start" (Lerer 2008: 61). As a greater range of writing for young people emerged, the emphasis remained the same, though the situation was rendered more complex by the religious controversies of the ensuing centuries.

While the twentieth century witnessed a significant decrease in children's literature with an overtly religious agenda, the didactic impulse still remained common, even in works by writers who would have disavowed it. Today the same impulse is often also exhibited in non-Christian and indeed anti-religious literature; these frequently advocate qualities which in the past would have been regarded as consequent upon religious belief, such as valuing all human beings and accepting those who differ from us in race, class, gender or belief. There is also an increasing focus in children's literature on what might be termed the spiritual value of respect for the environment.

The beginnings of children's literature

While some earlier material addressed to children exists, the production of both prose and poetry for young readers or subsequently adopted by them becomes more evident in the seventeenth century. Notorious among the prose writings is James Janeway's *A token for children: being an exact account of the conversion, holy and exemplary lives, and joyful deaths of several young children* (1672): its title accurately describes its subject matter. As Mary V Jackson points out, the popularity of Janeway's book can partially be accounted for by the recent great plague and Fire of London, together with widespread infant death; Janeway nevertheless faced criticism because some of his biographies "were partial or complete fictions and therefore were unreliable and dangerous" (Jackson 1989: 13, 25). Suspicion of fiction did not however prevent Puritans from accepting John Bunyan's *Pilgrim's Progress* (1678), while not specifically addressed to the young it contains many elements attractive to them, notably Christian's fight with Apollyon. Margaret Spufford (1997: 58) suggests that Bunyan's writing for children may well have been among the earliest deliberately to attempt to substitute wholesome texts for the "fanciful histories" which he and others had delighted in before their conversions. This children's classic speedily became one of the few non-biblical books that could be read on Sundays.

Bunyan's collection of poetry, *A Book for Boys and Girls or Country Rhimes for Children* (1686), later known as *Divine Emblems*, was not the first verse work addressed to children. It was preceded by versifications of parts of the bible, such as *Little Timothy His Lesson* (1611) by Edmund Graile, a physician who (rightly) disclaims any poetic skill. Bunyan's short reflections on child friendly subjects such as "Upon the Boy and his Paper of Plumbs [sic]", "Upon the Boy on his Hobby-horse" and "Upon the whipping of a Top" would however have provided more entertainment than Graile, the moral admonitions being easy to ignore. The popularity of Bunyan's poetry, which is to be found not only in this frequently reprinted collection but also in *Pilgrim's Progress*, may well have encouraged Isaac Watts to produce *Divine Songs for Children* (1715); many of his edifying verses remained sufficiently well known to be parodied one hundred and fifty years later in Lewis Carroll's *Alice*. Among them are "'T is the voice of the sluggard" and "How doth the little busy bee"; Alice transmogrified these characters respectively into the Lobster and the Crocodile. Perhaps Watts' greatest posthumous achievement was inspiring William Blake's use of hymn-like meters for his ostensibly simple *Songs of Innocence* (1789). Whether or not Blake's frequently analysed lyrics are to be regarded as part of the corpus of religious verse for children depends on how narrowly the terms "religion" or indeed "children's poetry" are defined: Humphrey Carpenter and Mari Prichard comment: "Blake ... departed utterly from the moralistic conventions of almost all 18th-century versifiers for children" (1984: 66).

The eighteenth century witnessed a considerable increase in the publication of stories written specifically for young readers. Many of these, inevitably in a period dominated by the conviction that children should be brought up to be God-fearing, include a significant element of religious and moral teaching. Thomas Day's influential *Sandford and Merton* (1783–1789) consists of edifying stories told to the two boy protagonists by a local clergyman. More explicit Christian teaching is provided by two energetic women campaigners, Sarah Trimmer and Hannah More. Both were devout members of the Church of England and active in the Sunday School movement. Trimmer wanted to preserve children from the dubious morality of fairytales, which she saw as fostering undesirable emotions like jealousy and vanity. Instead she offered them *The History of the Robins* (1786), a fable which preaches good behavior as well as kindness to animals. She also published a *Journal* to make mothers familiar with edifying reading for their children. More's influence is best displayed in her series of pamphlets, the Cheap Repository Tracts, intended to replace chapbooks which she regarded as depicting morally dubious values liable to corrupt the young. Her initiative indirectly led to the formation of the more evangelically inclined Religious Tract Society which throughout the nineteenth century was a major source of inexpensive reading material for children.[1]

The heyday of religious writing for children

The nineteenth century is marked by a proliferation of religious children's literature not to be seen before or since.[2] The most prolific children's writer of the first half of the nineteenth century, Mary Martha Sherwood, held Evangelical convictions: behind nearly all her writing lies her belief that all those who had not acknowledged that they were miserable sinners and accepted the redemption offered by Christ, would perish in hellfire, however young they might be. She spent several years as an army wife in India, where *Little Henry and His Bearer* (1814) is set. It is marked by the piety of the title character, who, before his early death, succeeds in converting his servant, Boosy. Also apparent is Sherwood's horror not only at the religious practices of Hinduism and Islam, but also at the absence among their devotees of British standards of hygiene.[3] She does however seem to have been fascinated by the exotic environment with its diverse trees, a feeling she "baptises" by imagining how idyllic it would be if only it was filled with knowledge about the Lord.

Sherwood's sensitivity to natural settings is also evident in the stories in her best-known work, *The History of the Fairchild Family* (1818), children's editions of which continued to appear well into the twentieth century. In "Story on the Sixth Commandment", the devoutly Christian father takes his squabbling children to a place in the forest where they may learn that arguments like the one they have just been having could result in fratricide. She builds up a sinister atmosphere; as they walk through the wood they see a desolate ruined house next to which stands "a gibbet, on which the body of a man [who had killed his brother] hung in chains: It had not yet fallen to pieces, although it had hung there some years" (Sherwood 1818: 57–8). It is likely that many children enjoyed her stories for elements of pleasing horror like this but skipped the long prayers and hymns which conclude each chapter.

The quantity of fiction written for children increased considerably during Victoria's reign. While the explicitly religious elements remain, there is a gradual appreciation that entertainment.is also necessary. Caroline Sinclair's *Holiday House* (1839) presents child protagonists whose naughty behavior does not result in awful warnings about eternal hellfire. In Sinclair's "The terrible fire," Harry, who mischievously but almost inadvertently burns down the nursery, is punished by having to sleep in the ruined room, covered by burnt blankets; his fate however is milder than that of Sherwood's similarly guilty Augusta Noble, who dies in the fire she has caused and is, in the judgment of the adults who speak about her fate, undoubtedly consigned to the flames of hell for her disobedience. Nevertheless Sinclair rounds off her book with a stereotypical climax when Harry's brother Frank edifies his less than perfect siblings by his pious death.

Directly religiously motivated fictional works continued to appear throughout the century. The mid-century writings of A.L.O.E. (A Lady of England: Charlotte Tucker) followed in the Evangelical footsteps of Sherwood. By contrast, Charlotte Yonge, a High Church devotee, was as committed to religious literature for children as were A.L.O.E. and Sherwood. Yonge's *The Daisy Chain* (1856), serialized in *The Monthly Packet,* the magazine she founded in 1851 and edited for forty-two years, is about a family of eleven children; like Yonge herself, they have strong connections with the local parish church.

Yonge's work influenced the development of the family saga genre which soon became popular. Among the best known examples are Louisa Alcott's *Little Women* (1868) and Susan Coolidge's *What Katy Did* (1872). Both novels include explicitly religious and moral elements, and both engendered series about the same characters. Mrs March encourages her children to model themselves on the pattern of Christian behavior portrayed in Bunyan's *Pilgrim's Progress,* while Coolidge's disabled Cousin Helen gives Katy a lesson about enduring her suffering after she falls from a swing: "The Teacher is always at hand … If things puzzle us, there He is close by … don't be afraid to ask Him for help if the lesson gets too hard." Katy then has a dream-like vision reinforcing Helen's admonition (Chapter 9).

Later readers have often felt uneasy about these explicit messages, which reveal that popular children's writers of the period ensured that their stories contained religious teaching. Most of the family fiction of the ensuing period before World War One is however much less dominated by the desire to influence readers towards Christian practice. Significantly its most notable exponents, Edith Nesbit and Frances Hodgson Burnett, were rather less orthodox in their own practices and beliefs.[4]

While most of the fiction so far mentioned is set within families, some later Evangelical writers of children's stories, perhaps influenced by fiction for adults by Dickens and Gaskell, present young readers with a broader social perspective. The best known of the sixty or so stories by Hesba Stretton (Sarah Smith) are *Jessica's First Prayer* (1867) and *Little Meg's Children* (1868), both set among the London poor. The protagonist of the earlier of these, the daughter of a drunken actress, transcends her background: her innocence contrasts with the worldliness of the caretaker and congregation of a fashionable chapel, and even makes the minister aware of his own shortcomings. An innocent child is also an agent of conversion in *Little Meg,* which additionally warns about the dangers of drink.[5]

A number of Victorian women also produced hymns and religious poetry for the young. Probably the best known of the hymn writers is Cecil Frances Alexander, whose carol "Once in royal David's city" is still inextricably associated with Christmas, while Christina Rossetti's "In the bleak midwinter" is nearly as well-known. Rossetti's strong religious convictions are indirectly reflected in the morality which is the basis of both her fantasy narrative poem, *Goblin Market* (1862) and the short and simple verses collected in *Sing-Song* (1872).[6] The didacticism of her poetry is less explicit than in that of many other writers, which helps to account for her enduring popularity.

All the nineteenth-century literature discussed above was written by women, with an appeal largely to girls. This "feminization" is often seen as applying to children's writing as a whole, not only to that which conveys a religious message. Children's poetry and prose of this period probably exhibit a greater degree of gender dichotomy than that written either before or since. Edifying fiction was also however produced for boys, though its religious messages tend to be set into either adventure or boarding school narratives. Back in the eighteenth century, Daniel Defoe's *Robinson Crusoe* (1719), another work adopted as part of the children's canon because of the current absence of a literature of their own, includes some very pious admonitions. Crusoe penitently recalls his failure on arrival at the island to be sufficiently grateful to God for his deliverance, a deficiency he speedily remedies by reading a bible fortuitously saved from shipwreck. On the advent of Man Friday, Crusoe wastes little time before starting to teach the "savage" about the necessity of a divine redeemer, with the result that Friday wants to go off and instruct his own people.

Even more explicitly religious is Johann Wyss's *Swiss Family Robinson* (1819), one of the few translated texts (other than the fairytales) to make an impact on young British readers. Wyss, himself an army chaplain, makes his central character, the father of the family, a pastor, and loses no opportunity to incorporate moral and religious teaching. This model inspired Frederick Marryat, of whose *Masterman Ready* (1841–1842) Carpenter observes, "Mr Seagrave, like his counterpart in *The Swiss Family Robinson*, is attentive to the demands of religion, and Ready himself is prone to moments of sermonizing" (1984: 344). This trait is perhaps less immediately obvious in one of the most influential "robinsonades," R.M.Ballantyne's *The Coral Island* (1858), which nevertheless includes numerous references to the Bible. Near the end of the book the savages who are threatening our heroes with a violent death are suddenly converted to Christianity. The boys are told by one of the "natives": "The Lord has unloosed the bands of the captive and set the prisoners free. A Missionary has been sent to us, and Tararo [the chief] has embraced the Christian religion! The people are even now burning their Gods of wood" (1858: chapter 34). Overt piety is less evident in most of the later adventure fiction, such as R.L.Stevenson's *Treasure Island* (1881/3), G.A.Henty's tales of empire, and the stories of Rudyard Kipling.

Another opportunity for authors to disseminate the Christian message to male readers was provided by the increasing popularity of boys' boarding school stories. The most famous of these, Thomas Hughes's *Tom Brown's Schooldays* (1857), though not the first such chronicle was probably the most influential.[7] It was speedily succeeded by F.W.Farrar's *Eric or Little by Little* (1858). As indicated by Robert Fitzgerald, the purpose of both these books was to preach to boys (2000: 2). Hughes emphasizes the value of personal prayer and proper preparation for confirmation, while Farrar's eponymous hero is only redeemed from his drunken and debauched behavior by his pious death. Talbot Baines Reed's *The Fifth Form at St Dominic's* (1887), originally serialized in the evangelical *Boys' Own Paper* (1881–1882), also emphasizes the importance of retaining integrity in the face of wrongful accusation.

The greatest amount of nineteenth-century realist children's literature was inspired by Christian didacticism. Adventure and school stories (for girls as well as for boys), together with family sagas and novels seeking to ameliorate poor social conditions, were all dominated by moral and religious values. The situation with fantasy, in the wake of the translations of the fairytales of the Grimms and Hans Andersen, as well as (the Reverend) Charles Kingsley's *The Water Babies* (1863), is more complex.[8] *Alice in Wonderland* (1865) transfers the severe moralising to various anthropomorphic animals, showing how Lewis Carroll could satirize didactic moral fiction and verse in the confidence that his readers would be familiar with this material. George MacDonald's contributions to the genre are discussed elsewhere in the present volume.[9]

The religious writing of Roman Catholic writers for children is less familiar. Greater freedom after the Emancipation Act of 1829 and the increasing numbers of Catholics, both converts and the laboring Irish poor, led to realization about the importance of providing suitable religious reading for children. In emulation of the Religious Tract Society (RTS) with its largely Evangelical output directed to young readers, the Catholic Truth Society (CTS), founded in 1884, produced a good many pamphlets for the young. While many of these were lives of the saints, others consisted of fictional stories with edifying messages. Often written by aristocratic women, these pamphlets, together with longer works from other publishers, are sometimes obviously addressed to the lower classes, perhaps reflecting the fear that poor Catholics might well succumb to the temptations resulting from living in a Protestant country, thus losing their faith. The Catholic journal, *The Tablet,* describes an anonymous tract, *Bessy: Or the*

Fatal Consequences of Telling Lies as "a very good tale to put in the hands of young servants."[10]

The need to produce reading matter for boys was not forgotten by the Catholic community. Monsignor Robert Hugh Benson, the convert son of an Archbishop of Canterbury,[11] wrote a number of books to inspire the young; the best known, *Come Rack, Come Rope* (1906), features the heroic deeds of the Catholic martyrs of the reign of Elizabeth. Also notable on the educational scene was the literary involvement of members of religious orders, notably the Jesuits, who had been guided by pedagogical motives since their foundation. A school story by R.H.Garrold S.J., *A Fourth Form Boy: A Day School Story* (1910) is clearly an attempt to translate the qualities that characterize the nineteenth-century boarding school fiction of Hughes, Farrar and Read into a twentieth-century Catholic setting, based on Garrold's own teaching experience in Liverpool.

Children's literature after the First World War

The decline in realist children's fiction with an explicitly religious message accelerated throughout the twentieth century, at least as far as mainline Anglicanism was concerned. Whereas most of the earlier fiction seems to have had as its aim the reader's adherence to Christian doctrine and behavior, there is an increasing tendency for later children's fiction, if it mentions religion at all, to adopt what could be described as a more sociological approach, taking church as part of the background of the characters; in the latter part of the century, this portrayal is sometimes negative. Religious practice does not feature significantly in the school, adventure, or domestic stories of the popular authors of the inter-war period or immediately after the Second World War (Blyton, Brazil, Buckridge, Ransome, Streatfeild etc.), any more than in the work of the major writers of the ensuing "second golden age" of children's literature (Boston, Garner, Pearce, Sutcliff et al.).[12]

Two Catholic school-story writers, Elinor Brent-Dyer and Antonia Forest, are however exceptions to this marginalization of religion: Brent-Dyer's "Chalet School" series reveals her desire to normalize the Catholic devotions sometimes mentioned, while Forest provides both her characters and her readers with information not only about Catholic recusancy but also (to the surprise of some characters) the fact that Jesus and his companions in the Christian Gospels were all Jewish. Many of the relatively few Catholic children's writers of the latter part of the century are by now unfamiliar.[13] Robert Cormier however is well known for his focus on a Catholic boys' day school in *The Chocolate War* (1975); his treatment of moral and religious issues has often evoked ambivalent responses from readers.[14]

Didactic Protestant children's fiction of this period is often Evangelical in authorship, as with Patricia St John, whose work spans a long period, including *Treasures of the Snow* (1950) and *Friska My Friend* (1985). The explicit message of the latter, which uses the story of the rescue of a dog by a young boy, Colin, as a means of instructing readers about the theology of redemption, is very different from mainstream children's literature of the period. A quite different, and oppositional, angle on religion is taken by the more distinguished Robert Swindells, who in *Unbeliever* (1995) and *Abomination* (1998) presents some horrific warnings about the danger of religious sects.

It is arguable that some of the most interesting twentieth-century treatments of religious and spiritual themes have been in the area of fantasy. While the outstanding instances of these are of course C.S.Lewis's "Narnia" books (discussed elsewhere in the current volume), the religious element in the work of Lewis's friend and Oxford confrère, J.R.R. Tolkien, is sometimes overlooked. Tolkien's Catholic beliefs can be detected in all his fiction, notably in the way in which the virtuous life as epitomized in good hobbits such as Bilbo, Frodo and Samwise reflects the ideals of Cardinal Newman, the founder of the Birmingham Oratory, to which Tolkien's guardian, Father Francis Xavier Morton, belonged.[15]

In rather different ways, religion is relevant to the fantasy novels of both the best-selling late twentieth-century children's writers, J.K.Rowling and Philip Pullman. Both have come under fire from right wing religious groups, largely in the United States—Rowling for the magic, witches and wizards in her Harry Potter novels, Pullman for the hostility towards established religion in his "Dark Materials" trilogy. This is most virulent against the Roman Catholic church, satirized in Lyra's world where the Magisterium keeps a tight hold on people's beliefs and practices. Pullman's opposition to Lewis's "Narnia" books, on the grounds that they are life-denying, is notorious. It has been argued however that the underlying message of the work of both authors is by no means as obviously anti-religious as their opponents would claim: Rowling's novels uphold traditional moral values, while aspects of what might be described as Pullman's "anti-theology" are not inconsistent with the ideas of some radical Christian theologians.[16] Within the borderland between fantasy and realism, the novels of David Almond frequently evince the effect of his Catholic upbringing, both in transmuted autobiographical material and in the engagement with "spiritual" issues, though never from an orthodox religious standpoint. For a number of writers, fantasy seems to provide a means for exploring the nature of the universe in a way less easily open to realist writers.

Joan Lingard's "Kevin and Sadie" series

It has been suggested above that most of realist novels from the 1950s onwards, other than those written from a specific denominational commitment, tend to depict church membership as a social phenomenon rather than advocating specific beliefs or behavior. Many of the authors concerned seem to take a broad view of religio-spiritual elements, and to encourage their readers towards the creation of a peaceful and tolerant world. The five "Belfast" novels by Scottish writer Joan Lingard fit this pattern, focusing on the relationship between two young people from Northern Ireland during the 1970s, a period dominated by "The Troubles." Neither Catholic nor Protestant factions appear superior; rather, as suggested by Darja Mazi-Leskovar, Lingard puts forward for emulation 'how Sadie and Kevin manage to outgrow the bias-based way of viewing the world and turn into admirable adults "able to show they can live together in peace and harmony (*A Proper Place*.p.31)"' (2004: 306).

In the first book of the series, *The Twelfth Day of July* (1970), the tribal aspect dominates religion: the emphasis is less on belief or churchgoing than on the signifiers of difference between the communities in the lead-up to the July marching season. The slogans painted on walls, "GOD BLESS THE POPE" versus "NO POPE HERE" (1985: 47), epitomize the two communities. Against this background, Sadie, from a Protestant Unionist family strongly supportive of the partisan marches, and Kevin, from a Catholic Republican background opposed to them, begin a friendship that three years later, in *Across the Barricades* (1972), develops into love. Their mixed fortunes once they have left Northern Ireland, married and started a family, are the subject of *Into Exile* (1973), *A Proper Place* (1975), and *Hostages to Fortune* (1976).

Church professionals receive relatively little attention in the series; their conciliatory though ineffectual attitude is epitomized by a Protestant minister, the Reverend Gracey, who describes the presence of two Catholic boys in the Protestant streets as "nice…most encouraging" without inquiring as to their original intention in being there (1985: 61). While the marching, the bunting and the wall slogans mark the Protestant community, readers are also made more aware of the visible manifestations of Catholic devotion. On visiting Kevin's parents' house, Sadie notices, with a mixture of "distaste" and "thrill," the "Popish images": "the Sacred Heart picture above the fire and the Lourdes statue in the window" (1985: 49–50). As indicated by J. Demos in a different context, the Protestant emphasis on the "absolute sovereignty of God" means that many of the outward trappings of religion are not available to them, so that such Catholic "accoutrements" are inevitably likely to be much more apparent.[17] It is therefore easier for the novelist to use objects to signify the Catholic ethos visually.[18]

In the final book of the sequence, *Hostages to Fortune* (1976), set in Wales and Cheshire, the issue of whether Kevin should go to Midnight Mass when Sadie, now his wife, is heavily pregnant with their second child, is central to the future of their relationship. Almost perversely, in her resentment at his attendance at the Catholic church, she climbs a ladder to straighten a Christmas tree ornament, and falls, thus losing the baby. Shortly afterwards, Kevin visits his family in Ireland and brings back a crucifix left to him by his dead father. To Sadie it is an emblem of all she hates in Catholicism, so that it externalizes the barrier between them: "Whenever she came into the room now it was the first thing she saw. It drew her eyes like a magnet. It seemed to grow bigger as she looked, to leer at her. It was only six inches high, four across, with a tiny replica of Christ crucified attached to it; yet it dominated the room" (1995: 165–6).

Readers have already encountered the hostility of Sadie's mother to Catholicism (1995: 141) so it is easy to understand how deep-seated is Sadie's prejudice. Although she rationalizes that the cross cannot hurt her, she is relieved when Kevin takes it down from the bedroom wall; this very removal of an important symbol suggests that despite difficulties, their relationship will survive.

Lingard originally intended to write a final volume to the series, re-establishing the couple in Northern Ireland, but felt unable to do so because the political situation there has itself not been sufficiently resolved in the last forty years.[19] Despite not offering closure, *Hostages to Fortune* does present several positive elements. The final scene shows the protagonists undertaking the restoration of a ruined cottage, symbolically signifying their own constructive approach as well as providing an ecological note. Sadie reads their son "a bedtime story about a cottage in a field full of snowdrops" (1995: 174). Even more significantly, they are visited by Kevin's uncle Albert who, despite having lost his legs in the pub bombing that killed Kevin's father, seeks reconciliation by visiting this mixed religion family. Without any sentimentality, Lingard in this series presents the hope that religion need not be a barrier between people.

Conclusion

The focus in this brief survey has inevitably been on Christianity. The only other religion to figure significantly in English fiction, for both adults and children, was, until recently, Judaism. The situation of Jewish children's fiction is made more complex as a result of the historical fact of anti-semitism, culminating in the Holocaust, though as Madelyn Travis (2013) reveals, there exists in English literature a much older tradition of portraying Jewish characters.[20] In today's multicultural society children's books increasingly portray other ethnic and religious minority groups, and the interaction of Islam in particular with established religion and culture has been given attention by a number of children's writers. Muslim author and critic, Rukhsana Khan, has provided both a useful list of children's novels and her own critique.[21]

Children's authors today have a very different perspective from their predecessors of two hundred years ago; unless a book, whether with a religious focus or not, has believable characters and a gripping plot, it will succumb to the competition currently provided by so many other media outlets. While blatantly didactic texts like those of Sherwood would be unlikely to attract readers, it is arguable nevertheless that most writers of serious children's fiction have an agenda. Today that is unlikely to be that of forming believing Christians; rather, many of them seek to convey a message of acceptance and understanding of those from different religious traditions. Beyond this is an increasing tendency for fiction to present the ideals of peace and the future of the planet, aims which also appeal to the large sector of readers who lack any religious affiliation. In this context, children's literature concerned with spirituality, if not explicitly with religion, is probably more important today than ever before.

Notes

1   This later developed into the Lutterworth Press, still extant today.
2   For more information on this flourishing, see Pinsent in (eds) De Maeyer et al. (2005: 125–144).

3   For further information about *Little Henry*, see Pinsent in (ed.) Pinsent (2005: 36–53).

4   Nesbit was involved domestically in a "menage á trois" and Burnett was a Christian Scientist.

5   A further instance of the same genre is *Froggy's Little Brother* (1875) by "Brenda" (Mrs G Castle Smith).

6   As a devout Anglican, she rejected a suitor on religious grounds because he was a Roman Catholic. Nevertheless, the latent sexuality underlying the temptation to eat the fruit in *Goblin Market* means that this poem has not always been regarded as suitable for children.

7   Robert Kirkpatrick (2000: 1) points out that it had had at least sixty predecessors.

8   This is not to imply that fantasy is without a spiritual and sometimes an explicitly religious element—see Pinsent in (eds) Gavin and Routledge (2001: 14–31).

9   Reference to chapter on fantasy/MacDonald etc.

10   See Pinsent in (eds) De Maeyer et al. (2005: 145–164), for further information.

11   His brothers A.C.Benson, who wrote the words of "Land of Hope and Glory," and E.F.Benson, whose work includes the "Mapp and Lucia" series, wrote prolifically for adults.

12   A writer who does not sideline his characters' religious background however is William Mayne, whose four choir school novels recall his own experience as a boy-chorister at Canterbury Cathedral, but to describe these as religious fiction would seem to be stretching the term.

13   See note 11 and Pinsent in (ed.) Pinsent (2006: 185–202).

14   See Pinsent in (ed.) Gavin (2012: 48–63).

15   See Pinsent in (ed.) Lee (2014: 446–460).

16   As indicated in "New Casebook" series volumes, edited respectively by C.J. Hallett & P.J. Huey (2012), and C. Butler & T. Hallsdorf (2014) plus (eds.) Lenz with Scott (2005).

17   J.Demos, quoted by Em McAvan in (ed.) *J.K. Rowling 'Harry Potter'*, Palgrave Macmillan New Casebook, 2012: 105.

18   The nineteenth-century Anglo-Catholic revival of devotional pictures and practices is no part of the Protestant setting in Northern Ireland of the 1970s.

19   See www.heraldscotland.com/the-story-continues-for-joan-lingard-s-star-cross-d-lovers-1.10408327 (accessed March 17, 2015).

20   See also Pinsent in (ed.) S Porter (2000: 311–328).

21   Available online: http://www.rukhsanakhan.com/muslimbooklist/Muslimbooklist.pdf (accessed 20 August 2016).

References

Ballantyne, R.M., (n.d., first published 1858), *The Coral Island*, London: Blackie.

Butler, C. and Halsdorf, T. (eds) (2014), *Philip Pullman: His Dark Materials*, Basingstoke: Palgrave Macmillan.

Carpenter, H. and Prichard, M. (1984), *The Oxford Companion to Children's Literature*, Oxford: University Press.

Coolidge, S. (1985; first published 1872), *What Katy Did*, Harmondsworth: Penguin.

De Maeyer, J., Ewers, H.H., Ghesquiere, R., Manson, M., Pinsent, P., and Quaghebeur, P. (2005), *Religion, Children's Literature and Modernity in Western Europe 1750–2000*, Leuven: University Press.

Gavin, A. (ed.) (2012), *Robert Cormier*, Basingstoke: Palgrave Macmillan.

Gavin, A. and Routledge, C. (2001), *Mystery in Children's Literature: From the Rational to the Supernatural*, Basingstoke: Palgrave Macmillan.

Hallett, C. and Huey, P. (eds), (2012), *J.K.Rowling: Harry Potter*, Basingstoke: Palgrave Macmillan.

Jackson, M. (1989), *Engines of Instructionm, Mischief and Magic*, Lincoln: University of Nebraska

Kirkpatrick, R. (2000), *The Encyclopedia of Boys' School Stories*, Aldershot: Ashgate.

Lee, S. (ed.) (2014), *A Companion to J.R.R.Tolkien*, Chichester: WileyBlackwell.

Lenz, M. with Scott, C. (2005), *His Dark Materials Illuminated: Critical Essays on Philip Pullman*, Detroit: Wayne State University.

Lerer, S. (2008), *Children's Literature: A Reader's History from Aesop to Harry Potter*, Chicago & London: University of Chicago Press.

Lingard, J. (1985; first published 1970), *The Twelfth Day of July*, Harmondsworth: Puffin.

Lingard, J. (1995; first published 1976), *Hostages to Fortune*, Harmondsworth: Puffin.

Mazi-Leskovar, D. (2004), "Children's Literature and Human Rights," *Vestnik Letnik* 38 (1–2): 303–307.

Pinsent, P. (2005), *East meets West in Children's Literature*, Lichfield: Pied Piper.

Pinsent, P. (2006), *Out of the Attic: Some Neglected Children's Authors of the Twentieth Century*, Lichfield: Pied Piper.

Porter, S. (ed.) (2000), *Christian-Jewish Relations through the Centuries*, Sheffield: Sheffield Academic Press.

Sherwood, M. (n.d., first published 1818), *The History of the Fairchild Family*, London: Ward Lock.

Spufford, M. (1997), "Women Teaching Reading to Poor Children," in Hilton et al. (eds), *Opening the Nursery Door*, 47–62, London: Routledge.

Travis, M. (2013), *Jews and Jewishness in British Children's Literature*, New York: Routledge.

33

Golems and Goblins: The Monstrous in Jewish Children's Literature

Jodi Eichler-Levine

Jodi Eichler-Levine is an associate professor of Religion Studies and serves as the Berman Professor of Jewish Civilization at Lehigh University. She is the author of Suffer the Little Children: Uses of the Past in Jewish and African American Children's Literature (NYU Press, 2013). In this chapter, she offers close readings of Jewish children's books by Eric Kimmel and David Wisniewski, exploring forms of fantastic monstrosity in these texts and how they relate to anxiety over past traumas and future uncertainties.

On the cover of David Wisniewkski's award-winning picture book *Golem*, readers face a dramatic image. A white-haired, be-robed rabbi clutching a Torah scroll is dwarfed by the shadow of a massive monster: the golem, or animated clay man, who looms up over two thirds of the illustration. In the background, the medieval cityscape of Prague appears, both candy-coated and sinister, with pale blues, oranges and browns outlined against a pitch-black sky. Throughout this text, the unformed mud of the golem "child" mirrors the notion of human children as amorphous clay that must be shaped and molded by adult hands. Like other monsters, the golem reveals "the otherness within" ourselves. As Timothy Beal writes, "The voice of the monster is the audacious voice of theodicy" (Beal 2001: 3). This darkness haunts both Jewish history and children's literature. As childlike monsters, both golems and goblins stand in for the uncontrollable nature of children and the continuity fears that surround their place in Jewish life.

This chapter engages in close readings of Jewish children's books in order to work through fantastic monstrosity as it bursts forth in literature geared towards young people. Because of *Ashkenazi* (Eastern European) Jews' history of persecution, their stories for children heighten the already fraught stakes of inculcating religio-ethnic identity and grappling with both internal and external stereotypes. The monstrous in Jewish children's literature refracts central tensions in childhood studies and religion: the play between "innocence and experience"; the stakes of religious and ethnic diversity in picture books; and the longstanding study of the fearsome, *awe*-ful-ness in both dark children's tales and religious narratives, accompanied by grown-up debates over the appropriateness of such content (Blake 1901; Bettelheim 1977; Zelizer 1985). If, as Jeffrey Cohen argues, "monsters are our children," then the Jewish monsters we create for and out of children are one facet of American Jewish identity (Cohen 1996). Reading American Jewish children's literature with an eye for darkness shows us how anxiety over past traumas and future uncertainties is projected onto the imagined bodies of children and the spaces they inhabit.

Jewish children's literature: A very short introduction

I define the category of "Jewish children's literature," capaciously, including work both about or written by Jews, directed at young people ages 0–16, and encompassing numerous genres, including picture books, schoolbooks, nineteenth-century "catechisms," poetry, biblical adaptations, young adult novels, and more. The category emerges in the nineteenth century, coinciding with two Christian influences: namely, the developing Sunday School movement and the growth of children's literature as a distinct category. Both of these come to fruition in the twentieth century, and the children's book industry grows dramatically from the mid-twentieth century to the present as the notion of youth itself becomes more distinctly understood and even subdivided. Jewish children's literature is also deeply influenced by medieval and modern Jewish folklore, as well as biblical tropes (Boylan 1990; Bottigheimer 1996; Gold 2004).

What makes Jewish children's literature "Jewish" is an open question. Jewish authorship and/or Jewish themes are the most likely candidates. In the case of the golems and goblins discussed below, some books explicitly discuss a Jewish legend using Jewish history, symbols, or holidays (Cummins and Toder 2000, 2003; Kimmel 2003; Gross 2014). Today, the Jewish children's book market comprises hundreds of titles, official recognition of outstanding authors through awards programs, and a host of other trappings. Jewish juvenile literature has moved beyond the Hebrew school or synagogue Judaica shop and into the mainstream market place, assisted, in part, by online retailers, and growing (if limited) interest in multicultural literature. The field of Jewish children's literature remains entangled with concerns over Jewish continuity. Through books and programs like the PJ Library, which I discuss further below, Jewish parents and communal leaders hope to inculcate a sense of Jewish religio-ethnic identity "l'dor v'dor," or "from generation to generation."

Golems: Jewish difference, Jewish power

Ironically, the golem—an early modern, Old World monster—is used to welcome twenty-first century American Jewish children into the fold. Legends about the golem, a clay man created and animated by Rabbi Judah Lowe of Prague, have been part of Jewish folklore for centuries, but their popularity increased markedly over the last two hundred years. Today, the golem is "one of the most broadly recognized signifiers of modern Jewish popular culture ... the construct of the golem as an authentic signifier of Jewish culture, arising from popular traditions among the Jewish people, inadvertently betrays the brittleness of ethnicized constructs of culture" (Gelbin 2011: 13).

The details of the tale vary, but the golem is always made of clay, river mud, or earth, echoing early meanings of the Hebrew root to mean "unformed." It is sometimes envisioned as a protector of the Jews, particularly in the context of blood libels; at other points it is created as a helper or servant. In one way or another, the golem's power becomes uncontrollable. This sometimes leads to its destruction or deactivation.

Both David Wisniewski and Eric Kimmel have reinvigorated the presence of the *golem* in the picture book world.[1] Wisniewski's *Golem*, which was awarded the Caldecott medal in 1997, retells the myth in vivid paper cut illustrations. Here, the golem provides a cautionary tale on the limits of power and creation, demonstrating how that power can go awry once it is uncaged. Although the golem is created to protect the Jewish community from anti-Jewish violence and blood libels, when he encounters vigilante anti-Jewish mobs, he quickly becomes a destructive force, smashing huge structures throughout Prague. Quite intentionally and painfully, Wisniewski's golem is also figured as a child. He refers to Rabbi Loew as "Father" and has a juvenile curiosity about the world (Wisniewski 1996).

This book is a dark one, with vivid fires, angry mobs, and haunting cityscapes. Near the climax of the text, as the Golem confronts a vicious crowd, his gigantic, enraged face and hands evoke a comic book character—a Hulked-out Incredible Hulk. The rabbi is overwhelmed by "too much destruction" and death. The next morning, he vows to destroy the golem, who heartbreakingly asks: "Father, will I remember this?" "No, you will be clay," Rabbi Loew replies. Then, he unmakes his "child" with magical wordplay: he erases the letter *aleph* from the word *emet* (truth) that graces the golem's forehead, turning the word to *met*, or death. As the golem dies, he cries out for his father, an early modern Isaac whose sacrifice is carried through.[2]

In contrast with Wisniewski's tragic tale, Kimmel's *The Golem's Latkes* is a humorous tale with a friendly, if still uncontrollable, golem (Kimmel 2011). In interviews, Kimmel has stated that his text was influenced by *The Sorcerer's Apprentice* and *Frankenstein* (Reading Today 2012). Here, the rabbi creates a mildly androgynous, quietly obedient Golem. The only problem is that this golem continues any household task *ad infinitum* until told to stop with the phrase, "Golem-ENOUGH!". The rabbi's housekeeper, Basha, tells the Golem to make the Hanukkah *latkes* (fried potato pancakes)—but then goes off to gossip with a friend. Like Mickey Mouse's brooms or the Energizer bunny, the golem keeps going … and going … and going, for so long that, "Latkes began piling up in the streets of Prague. They topped the city walls. People began fleeing from the mountain of latkes that grew higher and higher." Ultimately, rather than a tale of destruction and tragedy, we witness a story of table fellowship and celebration: all the people of Prague, including Emperor Rudolf (!), share in the latkes. Fried delicacies trump anti-Judaism, and we can all go home happy.

As a pseudo-child, the golem embodies the idea that "monsters are our children" (Cohen 1996). He carries tremendous symbolic weight. On the one hand, in various early modern and romantic European notions, the monster—including the golem—was seen as abnormal and potentially an abomination, just as the Jewish body itself was suspect (Gelbin 2011). Simultaneously, however, some scholars of children's literature argue that there is:

> a subtle reason for our use of fear to control children; that is, because we fear children ourselves. We fear them because they appear to be fundamentally different from us. We don't always understand them, we cannot always control them, and they sometimes do the very things that we want to do, but cannot or will not do, such as act upon antisocial impulses or act out angry or hate-filled fantasies. (Stallcup 2002, 130)

In other words, as Jackie Stallcup and numerous others argue, the child represents the monster within: that which we cannot control. Wisniewski's golem oversteps his boundaries: he takes his protection of the Jews too far, leading to violence and fire. Kimmel's golem repeats the steps of latke making—"Peel! Chop! Mix! Fry!"- mimicking a child's uncontrollable appetite and, in turn, our fears of our own unmitigated desires for consumption. The golem also fulfills many children's desire for darkness, or "a predilection for what we now characterize as the Gothic" (Jackson et al. 2007: 2).

Hershel and the Hanukkah Goblins: Humor and Horror

Though his golem tale is a light one, Eric Kimmel has also brought much darker aspects of Jewish folklore and history into his picture books. In his *Hershel and the Hanukkah Goblins,* the title character uses his wits to exorcise goblins from a town where they had curtailed all Hanukkah celebrations (Kimmel 1989). Like many Jewish folk tales, *Hershel* features the notion that brainy cleverness, rather than muscular brawn, saves the day. The goblins of the title mix the grotesque with the humorous. Paralleling Maurice Sendak's goblins, they resemble Christian medieval and early modern paintings and etchings of various regions of hell or of sneaky spirits entering innocent spaces, particularly homes (Sendak 1981). Thus, Jewish pictures books are also inhabited by Christian beasts, whether threatening or comic, medieval or modern.

Indeed, the premise of *Hershel* brings to mind the central tension of the popular Dr. Seuss tome *The Grinch Who Stole Christmas*: a happy winter holiday celebration is foiled by external forces.

At the same time, *Hershel* uses both Jewish humor and classic tropes of the underdog winning against the odds. These goblins are play-acting: they perform fierceness but are easily defeated by a trickster figure. The tale, originally published over two decades ago, remains popular; it is now part of the PJ Library series, which distributes free books to Jewish children around the country.[3]

To defeat the goblins who prevent the villagers from celebrating Hanukkah, Hershel must manage to light the menorah in the old synagogue on each night of the festival, without being stopped by them. Every evening after sunset, he stops the greedy ghouls with ever more ridiculous feats: one goblin gets his hands stuck in a pickle jar; another falls into (and loses) a game of *dreidel*, evoking cinematic chess games with the Grim Reaper.

On the final night of the holiday, Hershel sees "a monstrous shape in the doorway, a figure too horrible to describe." In this climactic episode, Hershel appeals to standard formulas of Jewish prayer: "Master of the world....Thou who created the heavens and the earth and the spirits of the air, stand by me now." But he defeats the goblin by playing upon the dark thing's pride. He declares that he cannot *tell* that he has met the King of the Goblins because the room is too dark...and then he tricks the goblin into lighting the menorah, so that Hershel can see that it is truly him. Once the candles are lit, the goblin declares:

NOW, HERSHEL, DO YOU KNOW WHO I AM?
I know you're not Queen Esther.
VERY FUNNY! ENJOY THE JOKE! IT WILL BE YOUR LAST!

But, of course, it is not. Jewish humor wins the day, the goblin turns into a whirlwind, and Hershel walks back down to the village, where every window now glows with Hanukkah lights. Goblins are tricksters, representing fears and what lurks in the darkest corners. Are goblins Jewish? Not uniquely, no. They are, however, reflections of Jewish immersion in Western gothic and horror cultures.

Jewish monsters: The consumption of difference and the imperatives of heritage

The resurgence of interest in golems and goblins parallels the explosive growth of children's literature (as a whole) over the last two centuries. Kimmel and other authors of his generation have rapidly moved Jewish children's literature from a primarily didactic genre to highly creative one.

This is not to say that acculturation anxieties are absent from today's Jewish book world. Far from it. Though Kimmel revels in the creative advances of the field, the advent and tremendous popularity of the PJ Library demonstrates how major donors and community institutions are eager to inculcate Jewish identity through picture books (Kimmel 2003). Framed as a "A Gift for Jewish Children and Their Families," this program, which began in 2006, sends age-appropriate free children's books and CDs to any Jewish child whose parents sign them up; the group's website provides sample activities and lesson plans; it also advertises the fact that over five million books have been mailed to date. Numerous Eric Kimmel works, including both *The Golem's Latkes* and *Hershel and the Hanukkah Goblins*, are featured in the series. The book's guide includes questions such as "Does the golem in this story seem funny or comforting or scary?" and "Would you like to have a golem? If you had a golem, what would you have it do to help people?" In other words, the golem explicitly becomes a site of imagined power for children, with an emphasis on help, not harm, but an acknowledgment that fear might accompany the text. The suggestion of making latkes is also, of course, present; interestingly, children and parents are encouraged to "Give them a Cajun or Asian flair." Golems might signify Jewish difference, but latkes become a site to consume *other* people's difference (PJ Library 2015).

Jewish children's literature is also not just for Jews. Non-Jews read this book too. In this way, the monstrous—specifically the *Ashkenazi* ghetto monstrous—continues to signify Jewish difference—but also universal appeal. One Amazon.com reviewer states that, "Children of any faith will enjoy this lovely story." Another adds that "I read it to a group of young children (none of whom are Jewish), and they loved the story." One writes that the book is "Highly recommended—and not only throughout the Jewish population. This Catholic Christian enjoyed it thoroughly (as did the entire family!)" (Amazon 2015). Jewish children's books have truly arrived. The winter holidays are no longer just a time when Jews emulate Christmas traditions or experience "tree envy"; they are also a moment when Christians and other non-Jews partake in Jewish folklore and gastronomic delights.

Studying children and religion requires us to cast a broad net, one that encompasses the myriad representations surrounding both Jewish and non-Jewish children and the adults around them. The ascendence of golems and goblins in such books also coincides with the popularity of monster culture, from *Twilight* to *Monsters, Inc.*, in American youth culture more generally. Perhaps this is a particularly Jewish American way in to this phenomenon. Jews, who for so long were figured as monstrous in the Euro-American imagination (a stereotype that still lingers globally), now get to present their own monsters as a site of not just fear, but also humor and seduction. The golem and fantasies of Jewish power have been harnessed, even domesticated … at least between the covers of children's books.

Notes

1   There are previous picture books about the golem, dating back to the 1970s, and we must not ignore the fact that children were undoubtably some of the recipients of older, non-illustration folktales and oral traditions (Sonheim 2003). However, the Wisniewski and Kimmel volumes have garnered awards and enjoy very wide popularity.

2 In Genesis 22, the Hebrew Bible contains a famous story in which Abraham is told to take his son Isaac and bind him upon an altar, then sacrifice him to God. At the last moment, an angel stays Abraham's hand. This episode is central in Jewish tradition, where it is referred to as the *akedah,* or "binding" of Isaac; in Christian tradition, where it is most commonly called the "sacrifice" and seen as a prefiguration of God's willingness to sacrifice his son Jesus; and in Islam, where Ishmael is the intended sacrifice.

3 This is a grand irony, since Kimmel has discussed how difficult it was to get the book published–it was, like Sendak's work, considered too dark and nontraditional (Kimmel 2003).

References

Amazon.com (2015), "The Golem's Latkes Reader Reviews." Available online: http://www.amazon.com/The-Golems-Latkes-Eric-Kimmel/product reviews/0761459049/ref=cm_cr_pr_btm_link_1?ie=UTF8&showViewpoints=1&sortBy=byRankDescending&reviewerType=all_reviews&formatType=all_formats&pageNumber=1 (accessed October 30, 2015).

Beal, T. (2001), *Religion and Its Monsters*, New York: Routledge.

Bettelheim, B. (1977), *The Uses of Enchantment: The Meaning and Importance of Fairy Tales*, New York: Vintage.

Blake, W. (1901), *Songs of Innocence and Songs of Experience*, London: R. Brimley Johnson.

Bottigheimer, R. (1996), *The Bible for Children: From the Age of Gutenberg to the Present*, New Haven: Yale University Press.

Boylan, A. (1990), *Sunday School: The Formation of an American Institution, 1790–1880*, New Haven: Yale University Press.

Cohen, J. (1996), "Monster Culture: Seven Theses," in Jeffrey Jerome, Cohen (ed.), *Monster Theory: Reading Culture*, Minneapolis: University of Minnesota Press.

Cummins, J. (2003), "Becoming An All-of-a-Kind American: Sydney Taylor and Strategies of Assimilation," *The Lion and the Unicorn* 27 (3): 324–343.

Cummins, J. and Toder, N. (2000), "The Jewish Child in Pictures Books?" *The Five Owls* November–December, 15 (2): 38–40.

Gelbin, C. (2011), *The Golem Returns: From German Romantic Literature to Global Jewish Culture, 1808–2008*, Ann Arbor: The University of Michigan Press.

Gold, P.S. (2004), *Making the Bible Modern: Children's Bibles and Jewish Education in Twentieth-Century America*, Ithaca: Cornell University Press.

Gross, R. (2014), "Objects of Affection: The Material Culture of American Jewish Nostalgia," PhD dissertation, Princeton University New Jersey.

Jackson, A., Coats, K., and McGillis, R. (2007), *The Gothic in Children's Literature: Haunting the Borders*, New York: Routledge.

Kimmel, E. (2003), "Joy on Beale St.," *The Lion and the Unicorn* 27 (3): 410–415.

Kimmel, E. (2011), *The Golem's Latkes*, Aaron Jasinksi: Two Lions.

Kimmel, E. (1989), *Hershel and the Hanukkah Goblins*, Ill. Trina Schart Hyman, New York: Holiday House.

PJ Library (2015), "*Reader's Guide, The Golem's Latkes.*" Available online: https://pjlibrary.org/assets/2/books/readingguides/11bd0a27-3d8e-412e-9728-066fcace10b9.pdf (accessed November 10, 2015).

"Reading Today: Interview with Eric Kimmel," (2012), Available online: http://www.reading. org/reading-today/classroom/post/engage/2012/12/07/5-questions-with-eric-a-kimmel- hershel-and-the-hanukkah-goblins (accessed November 14, 2014).

Sendak, M. (1981), *Outside Over There*, New York: HarperCollins.

Sonheim, A. (2003), "Picture Books About the Golem: Acts of Creation Without and Within," *The Lion and the Unicorn* 27 (3): 377–393.

Stallcup, J. (2002), "Power, Fear, and Children's Picture Books," *Children's Literature* 30: 125–158.

Wisniewski, D. (1996), *Golem*, New York: Clarion Books.

Zelizer, V. (1985), *Pricing the Priceless Child: The Changing Social Value of Children*, Princeton, NJ: Princeton University Press.

34

Childhood, Imagination, Consecration: Romantic Christianity in C.S. Lewis and George MacDonald

Naomi Wood

Naomi Wood is Associate Professor of English at Kansas State University. She specializes in literature for and about children, with a particular interest in Victorian literature and culture. This chapter explores the relationship of C.S. Lewis and George MacDonald's theories of childhood to the Romantics who influenced them, such as Wordsworth, Coleridge, and Novalis. This literature presents the message that only by recovering the eyes and the spirit of childhood can an adult enter the kingdom of heaven. Their success in persuading readers of the peculiar closeness of children with divine wonder through the imagination offers death as culmination rather than maturity, is a thesis many twentieth- and twenty-first-century readers find troubling.

In the fantasy worlds of C.S. Lewis (1898–1963) and George MacDonald (1824–1905), children enjoy intimate relationships with the divine. While adults are restricted to the mundane, children soar over stormy seas with a personified north wind, ride God in the form of a magnificent lion, and witness the origins and deaths of worlds. These relationships cannot endure the passage of time, however, and both writers depict a necessary withdrawal from divine intimacy during adolescence and adulthood, unless the child is "taken" beyond life, never to return.

As "people of the book," Protestant Christians have long emphasized childhood literacy to lead children to faith (Pinsent 2005). Whether their stories emphasize realistic settings or imaginary ones, they stress belief in the Christian God and reliance on the Bible for guidance. This text-centered orientation often assumes a single authority (the Bible) and a single truth (Christianity). Yet in the Christian metaphysical fantasies of C.S. Lewis and George MacDonald, religious significance emerges from play with what Lewis called "supposals," thought experiments that reframe, retell, and make more imaginatively powerful Christian tenets dulled, perhaps, by habit and custom.[1] In the work of both writers, the personal belief characteristic of Protestant Christianity is strongly associated with childhood and not easily attained by adults. Moreover, characters' spiritual development between child- and adulthood is disjointed, as childlike faith seems inappropriate for adulthood and yet is strongly preferable in intensity and conviction. Their religious fantasies defy conventional expectations and values about growth, change, and development and test the boundaries of consensus reality. Lewis, following MacDonald, crafts a Romantic Christianity that rebels against two kinds of literalism: fundamentalism on the one hand and positivism on the other.

This chapter examines Lewis and MacDonald's depictions of childhood and religious maturation in children's fantasies. Both writers began with strong affinities for Romanticism, particularly its use of folklore, fairy tales, and other romance forms. Associated with past times and the peasantry, fairy tales were thought to express primal human identities, simultaneously individual childhood and the "childhood of the race," ontogeny recapitulating phylogeny (Boas 1966: 64–5; Andrews 1994: 9–26). Some English Romantics saw children as naturally gifted possessors of a free imagination permitting untrammeled connection with the eternal (Plotz 2001: 4–5). MacDonald continued this strand of Romanticism by affirming children's imaginative power in his works for children and implying that adults' relationship to faith is compromised and flat. Only by recovering the eyes and the spirit of childhood can an adult enter the kingdom of heaven. Lewis did not participate in this Romantic cult of childhood, though he granted the strong association of children with fairy tales. Both insisted that chronological age is beside the point: what matters is the capacity of fantasy to infuse the mundane with spiritual significance. Yet, in their works for children, certain children develop special apprehension of the divine: Lewis's Lucy Pevensie and MacDonald's Diamond are clear models. Both reject worldly concerns for divine bliss, and death is life's culmination rather than adulthood, a thesis many twentieth and twenty-first century readers find troubling. The more well-known Lewis has been particularly criticized for this narrative choice; however, his acknowledged "guide" was MacDonald, who "baptise[d]" his Romanticism with "a certain quality of Death, *good* Death" (Lewis 1947: 21).

Religious educators have not always endorsed the expression of Christianity in fantasy. Though John Bunyan's *Pilgrim's Progress* (1678) was enthusiastically read by child and adult alike, many educators and parents agreed that religious tenets were more reliably conveyed through realistic stories (Pinsent 2005: 127). But Lewis recalled his Sunday school as actively "harmful": it "paralysed much of my own religion in childhood" (1966: 37). Because of Sunday-school insistence upon reverence and "obligation[s] to feel," Lewis as a child associated religion with "something medical" rather than with awe or joy (1966: 37). Offering relief from off-putting piety, George MacDonald's *Phantastes* (1858), which Lewis purchased when he was eighteen, arrested him with what he came to call "Holiness," a "bright shadow coming out of the book into the real world and resting there, transforming all common things and yet itself unchanged" (Lewis 1955: 179). Neither completely allegorical nor completely realistic, literary fantasy allowed Christian writers to "steal past [the] watchful dragons," as Lewis termed them, of conventional piety (Lewis 1966: 37).

Lewis and MacDonald's rebellion against a disenchanted world has roots in both German and English Romanticisms (Gray 2009). In the early nineteenth century, British readers eagerly read the fantasies emerging from Germany. Both Samuel Taylor Coleridge (1772–1834) and Thomas Carlyle (1795–1881) discovered in German Romantic philosophy and literature an alternative to dry Enlightenment rationalism, and translated German Romantic works into English (Prickett 2005; Gray 2009). Like others of his generation, George MacDonald was entranced by the fantasies of Novalis (Friedrich von Hardenberg 1772–1801), Friedrich Schiller (1759–1805), and Friedrich de la Motte Fouqué (1777–1843). Of Fouqué's most famous story, *Undine* (1811), MacDonald wrote, "Were I asked, what is a fairytale? I should reply, *Read Undine: that is a fairytale*" (1893: 313). According to MacDonald's biographer William Raeper, "Novalis's mysticism and piety, expressed in disturbing and beautiful symbols, … appealed strongly to MacDonald" (Raeper 1987: 107), and he took as a frequent motto Novalis' "Our life is no dream, but it ought to become one and perhaps will" (1858: 182). MacDonald appreciated the German Romantics' fascination with the realm of the spirit and their expressions of *poetisch*—Schiller's word for art-fantasies' "theoretical, abstract, and spiritualized flavor" (Prickett 2005: 188)—in both poetry and prose. Prickett convincingly argues that even Goethe's seminal Bildungsroman *Wilhelm Meister's Apprenticeship* (1795–1796) provided a key model for MacDonald's understanding of childhood development and maturation, in that it articulated the problem of conventional maturity as a goal and gestured toward a spiritual resolution.

Among the most potent symbols in the English Romantic repertoire was the child, which represented prelapsarian freshness, originality, and imaginative receptivity (Abrams 1971: 380). William Wordsworth (1770–1850) and Coleridge articulated for English readers the link between the imagination and childhood as both natural and desirable, separate from the taint of original sin. Coleridge asserted that folk tales and romance encourage children's awareness of the transcendent. They nurture the imagination to rise above the limits of the senses and the fragmenting effect of isolated facts to comprehend "the Great" and "the Whole":

> Should children be permitted to read Romances, & Relations of Giants & Magicians, & Genii?—I know all that has been said against it; but I have formed my faith in the affirmative.—I know no other way of giving the mind a love of "the Great," & "the Whole."—Those who have been led to the same truths step by step thro" the constant testimony of their senses, seem to me to want a sense which I possess— They contemplate nothing but *parts*—and all *parts* are necessarily little—and the

Universe to them is but a mass of *little things*. ("To Thomas Poole," October 16, 1797, Coleridge 1956: 354)

Critiquing rational education as offering a fragmented and partial version of reality, Coleridge here advocates for fantasy as offering coherence, and, along with coherence, a species of religious awe. Coleridge's apprehension of "the Great" and "the Whole" is strongly associated with childhood reading, and seems inaccessible to adults, except, perhaps, to poets. Wordsworth's "Intimations Ode" offers the most explicit statement of childhood's special relationship to the divine:

> Our birth is but a sleep and a forgetting:
> The Soul that rises with us, our life's Star,
> Hath had elsewhere its setting,
> And cometh from afar:
> Not in entire forgetfulness,
> And not in utter nakedness,
> But trailing clouds of glory do we come
> From God, who is our home:
> Heaven lies about us in our infancy!
> Shades of the prison-house begin to close
> Upon the growing Boy,
> [...]
> At length the Man perceives it die away,
> And fade into the light of common day.
>
> (ll. 58–68;75–6)

In the Intimations Ode, children experience Heaven as a matter of course, as a "home"; but growth and enculturation inevitably draw a shade between them and the light of eternity. This loss of "glory" and the construal of adulthood as an inevitable "fading" into the "light of common day" encapsulate the narrative trajectory of the classic Bildungsroman, the movement from innocent faith in the promises of Romance to disillusionment and acceptance of experience's forced acceptance of Reality's limits (Buckley 1974).

Lewis and MacDonald learned from the Romantics to see the fairy tale not only as an expression of childlike imagination, but also as an epistemological tool. MacDonald, who studied chemistry and natural philosophy at university (Raeper 1987: 43), contested the dismissal of fantastic and imaginative writing as childish and of children as of no account, arguing, like Coleridge, that imaginative literature and language were a legitimate form of knowing. Indeed, he proposes that language structures knowledge, and that childlike "humility" is essential to scientific discovery: "the poetic relations themselves ... may suggest to the imagination the law that rules its scientific life. Yea, more than this: we dare to claim for the true, childlike, humble imagination, such an inward oneness with the laws of the universe that it possesses in itself an insight into the very nature of things" ("Imagination," 12–13). Against the double pressure of empiricist skepticism on the one hand and rigid religious literalism on the other, MacDonald and Lewis offer escape—escape from the prison-house of diminished possibilities, diminished joy. In this, they challenge children's literature's default "moral": that returning "home" is always the best resolution. The best "happy ending" was not one in which chastened children learn submission and look forward to a life just like their parents'. Instead, their Christian Romanticism extends the possibility that the greatest joy is not to return to consensus reality, but to go beyond it.[2] For these late Christian Romantics, the "eucatastrophe,"[3] the happiest turn, is the "good death" that allows return to Wordsworth's "clouds of glory."

Nonetheless, the convention of disillusionment—or, at least, of return to reality—even drives most fantasy narratives, especially portal fantasies that feature children from "our" world traveling to marvelous lands elsewhere. As compensatory fantasies that allow children to act out their psychological issues before returning, subdued, to the world of social reality, most portal fantasies offer only temporary escape. Max, in *Where the Wild Things Are* (1964), learns that he really wants to be "where someone loves him best of all" instead of being King of all the Wild Things; *The Wizard of Oz*'s (1901) Dorothy rejects the pleasures and adventures of Oz because "there's no place like home." E. Nesbit's children in the *Psammead* trilogy (1902–1906) initially enjoy but are more frequently perplexed by their magical adventures, and breathe collective sighs of relief when the magic comes to an end. As U.C. Knoepflmacher points out, children's fantasy operates "from the vantage point of experience, an adult imagination re-creates an earlier childhood self in order to steer it towards the reality principle" (Knoepflmacher 1983: 497). In Sarah Gilead's account of the return convention, such fantasies offer Bildung—social and personal development—in exchange for submission to the status quo (1991: 285).

Lewis's Narnia books initially conform to this convention. The four Pevensie children, even after having grown up as Kings and Queens in Narnia, return to the Professor's house during the war a moment after they had left. Nothing has changed, not even their clothing, as Pauline Baynes' illustration makes clear (The only evidence of Narnia on this side of the wardrobe is the missing fur coats that the children abandon there near the beginning of their adventure [*Lion*, 187]). The narrator promises more adventures in Narnia; however, the Pevensie children and their successors not only are forced to return to their home world, but also told there is an age limit. Peter and Susan learn, at the end of *Prince Caspian* (1951), that they are "getting too old" to return to Narnia, and Edmund and Lucy likewise at the conclusion to *The Voyage of the Dawn Treader* (1952). It appears that "shades of the prison house" must impinge even on the fortunate Pevensies. Aslan offers as consolation: "there [in England] I have another name. This was the very reason why you were brought to Narnia, that by knowing me here for a little, you may know me better there" (*Voyage*, 247). How losing Aslan, his physical presence as a lion, his beauty, strength, softness, and aw(e)fulness; and Narnia, with its magic, its divine trees and speaking animals, its adventures and pageantry, is to be compensated for in this world is left unstated. And though various critics have attempted to unify the developmental tasks set in each volume of the Chronicles (Ward 2008 10–11), none has provided a definitive interpretation. Still, the omission of goals such as marriage, procreation, householding, and vocation is noteworthy. By the *Last Battle* (1956), it is evident that those favored enough to have a connection to Narnia continue talking about it, thinking about it, and feeling an investment in its welfare. Ironically, Susan's exclusion from the final scenes is a result not of her apostasy to Christianity, but to Narnia. She "is no longer a friend of Narnia" because she ceased to "come and talk about Narnia or do anything about Narnia" (*Last*, 154), following Aslan's lead about age-limits by concluding that the whole experience was merely childish "funny games" (*Last*, 154).

Reversing the convention that fantasy's secondary world is expendable and dependent upon the primary world, *The Last Battle* moves to what Stephen Prickett calls the Todsroman, "death-romance," a genre that posits development beyond earthly, material life (Prickett 2005: 188–92). The Todsroman, according to Prickett, solves the Bildungsroman's problem that "the very process of self-formation and the gaining of worldly wisdom, essential as it is to growth and maturity, is actually toward a goal that is fundamentally less interesting and less morally worthy than the raw immature idealism that preceded it!" (2005, 189). According to Prickett, George MacDonald learned from Goethe's *Wilhelm Meister* to remove self-development from a temporal, mundane context and into the context of eternity. Rather than submitting to necessity and relinquishing the ideal, MacDonald's romances strategically *un*fit protagonists for life in consensus reality: his denouements pose radical questions not only about moral value but also about epistemology, exhibiting a profound skepticism about objective reality. Thus, the death-romance moves the sphere of action from daily life to spiritual pilgrimage, offering an alternative to the mundane world so inadequate to human desire. Lewis's widely condemned decision in *The Last Battle* (1956) to kill and then move his characters to "the Real Narnia" solves the theological problem of the "contradiction between moral idealism and worldly accommodation" endemic to the Bildungsroman (Prickett 2005: 192) while "stealing past the watchful dragons" of conventional piety.

George MacDonald's classic *At the Back of the North Wind* (1871), his only portal fantasy, goes even further than Lewis's *Last Battle* in offering the romance of death as the best finale to a story of spiritual self-development through fantasy.[4] The protagonist is a young son of a coachman named Diamond, who becomes friends with the North Wind, personified as a beautiful woman with long streaming hair. She takes him on adventures and, at his request, to the country "at the back of the North Wind," where time ceases and "nothing [goes] wrong" (*Back* 122–23), a vision of heavenly bliss connected to Dante's *Paradiso* and James Hogg's "Kilmeny." On his return, Diamond learns he has nearly died from a fever. From this point forward, though Diamond's family struggles to survive in a Dickensian urban setting peopled by drunken coachmen and destitute street-sweepers and the occasional benevolent sponsor, Diamond never ceases to radiate goodness and joy garnered from his recollection of the back of the North Wind.

Diamond's maturation has little to do with growing up to be a householder and everything to do with advancing beyond the "prison-house" shadows of mortality. When Diamond first encounters North Wind, he objects to being cold and is frightened when she suddenly leaves him alone in the dark in the garden. Despite this inauspicious beginning, Diamond learns to love North Wind for her beauty, her power, and her mystery and to have complete faith in her care for him, no matter what appearances may suggest. Under North Wind's guidance, Diamond witnesses individual hardship and mass disaster, which enlarges his sympathies and gives him a supernatural view of the mortal world. He makes friends with a street-sweeper Nanny, whose caregiver old Sal forces her to sleep on the streets and uses her wages to buy spirits, and he learns of North Wind's mandate to sink a ship with all passengers aboard. North Wind teaches Diamond to make no distinctions of scale between the blowing open of a flower and the sinking of a ship. North Wind explains her hope that eventually things will come out right, and her trust that worldly appearances are only apparent, not final.

After Diamond's return from the back of the North Wind, the narrator emphasizes Diamond's noticeable difference from other children, from his family. Diamond's otherworldly serenity earns him epithets variously loving or scornful: a drunken coachman calls him "God's baby," while his friend Nanny calls him "silly." When Diamond's mother worries about tomorrow's food, Diamond reminds her that they have food enough for today, and when Diamond's father objects to a gentleman's "hard bargain" with him, Diamond expresses his faith that there is "some good reason" for it (*Back*, 262). Diamond's spirit soars over and triumphs against the material world's anxiety, rage, and despair. Though Nanny is only a month older than he, she is far advanced in disillusionment: she has no faith in Diamond's marvels and has succumbed to conventional cynicism and realism, seeing dreams as mere illusion and metaphysics as nonsense. In her words: "she wasn't such a flat as to believe all that bosh" (*Back*, 78). Against Nanny's disillusioned development, *At the Back of the North Wind* calls conventional maturation into question by undermining its assumptions about reality. North Wind's other name is "death" as she strongly suggests, but in this death-romance Diamond's experiences, far from ending his story, extend both his spirit and his influence far beyond the realistic parameters of an unemployed coachman's son. Worldly class distinctions are merely another appearance that conceals moral status: "all emperors are not gentlemen, and all cooks are not ladies—nor all queens and princesses for that matter, either" (*Back*, 56).[5] Real gentility emerges from the interior, which in its turn relies on a sanctifying imagination. Like the protagonist of MacDonald's *Lilith* (1895), Diamond's "task is not to inhabit one world or the other, but rather constantly to straddle the two and to insist (despite appearances) on their ultimate congruity" (Prickett 2005: 202).

If the goal of development is to fit seamlessly into pre-existing social structures and to fulfill conventional expectations, the fairy tales of both MacDonald and Lewis obviously miss the mark. But if a goal of development might be to imagine new pleasures and new ways of connecting to the seen and unseen worlds, they succeed marvelously. Though his focus was frequently on spiritual matters, Lewis also argued that imagining other worlds could allow new appreciation of this one: the fairy tale "stirs and troubles [a child] (to his life-long enrichment) with the dim sense of something beyond his reach and, far from dulling or emptying the actual world, gives it a new dimension of depth … the reading makes all real woods a little enchanted" ("Three Ways," 29–30). For Lewis, the fairy tale thus becomes "an *askesis*, a spiritual exercise" ("Three Ways," 30). And this enchantment of "real" things is part of the point: it offers a sort of seasoning—his alimentary image is of otherwise tasteless meat that becomes "more savoury for having been dipped in a story" ("Tolkien's," 525). Dipped in story, reality is rejuvenated. "If you are tired of the real landscape," he writes, "look at it in a mirror" ("Tolkien's," 525). Whether mirror or salt, stories add rather than subtract. More than this, for Lewis, they gesture to infinity. When, in *The Last Battle*, Jewel the Unicorn urges the characters to go "further up and further in," the possibilities for story extend beyond the parameters of the text, as the conclusion underscores:

> All their life in this world and all their adventures in Narnia had only been the cover and the title page: now at last they were beginning Chapter One of the Great Story which no one on earth has read: which goes on forever: in which every chapter is better than the one before. (*Last* 210–11)

The characters never arrive—the goal is always beyond. But rather than being a source of anxiety, this deferral allows greater pleasure, greater opportunities. There is no need for an end to childhood, an end to play. Even death does not conclude self-development.

Not all critics of children's literature endorse the notion that the religious imagination can or should override concerns about this world and material life. David Rudd contends that in breaching the "fourth wall" between our world and his fictions, Lewis reveals more about Narnia's "ideological roots in a rather curmudgeonly old don" (Rudd 36) than transcendent reality. Lewis himself at times fell prey to literalism of a kind, closing off alternate readings with orthodox ones. In 1955, C.S. Lewis assured the mother of nine-year-old Laurence Krieg that he needn't worry that Narnia was more appealing than the Gospels:

> Laurence can't *really* love Aslan more than Jesus, even if he feels that's what he is doing. For the things he loves Aslan for doing or saying are simply the things Jesus really did and said. So that when Laurence thinks he is loving Aslan, he is really loving Jesus: and perhaps loving Him more than he ever did before. (May 6, 1955, *Collected Letters*, Vol 3.)

Yet this consolatory restriction on meaning belies the experience of many other readers who feel betrayed by the assertion that Aslan is "really" Jesus (Rudd 2002; Spufford 2002; Miller 2008). If the imaginative story is merely sugar coating for some otherwise unpalatable religious pill, all claims for its psychological or spiritual truth might well be suspect.

In the "watchful dragons" metaphor for religious and hermeneutic control, Lewis contrasts "harm" done by extorted "reverence" with the "real potency" that emerges if gospel is retold as fairy tale. For Lewis, romance could realize—in the sense of converting something imagined into reality—the feelings that historical or doctrinal orthodoxy failed to achieve. More subversive and certainly less orthodox, George MacDonald imagines a boy achieving heavenly bliss not through a saving relationship with Christ or observance of sacraments and ritual, but through a relationship with a nature spirit. "What does it mean?" the fundamentalist might ask alongside the positivist. And to both MacDonald would reply, that if the reader is "true," "he will imagine true things; what matter whether I meant them or not?" ("Fantastic," 320). The fairy tale's reliance on image provides more imaginative flexibility and opportunities for a freer range of emotional response. The success of MacDonald's and Lewis's mythopoeic approach to children's literature lies in this Romantic latitude, this willingness to allow fantasy not to "teach" but to "waken" the reader's imagination. Their thought experiments demand attention not only to the "little things" of everyday life but also the "Vast" and the "Great," the idea of connection beyond species and order, beyond the limits of space and time. Nurturing reverence and wonder in this version of Romantic Christianity makes available the possibility of ecstasy even for the "post-secular" child—or adult—willing to play along.[6]

Notes

1 For his more literal-minded readers, often but not exclusively children, Lewis distinguished between allegory and "supposal," which he explained as a thought experiment wherein he places the story of incarnation and redemption in another world. To a class of fifth-graders in Maryland, he wrote

> You are mistaken when you think that everything in the book "represents" something in this world. Things do that in The Pilgrim's Progress but I'm not writing in that way....I said "Let us suppose that there were a land like Narnia and that the Son of God, as He became a Man in our world, became a Lion there, and then imagine what would happen." (May 25, 1954, CSL Collected Letters Vol III, 479–80)

2 An extended discussion of Lewis' "romantic religion" and his inspiration in Coleridge can be found in Reilly (1971).

3 The term "eucatastrophe" was coined by Tolkien in "On Fairy Stories" to describe the happy "turn" for the better fairy tales take when all seems lost (1983, 153).

4 MacDonald's other fantasies are secondary-world fairy tales that do not feature traffic between the worlds (*The Princess and the Goblin, The Princess and Curdie,* "Day Boy and Night Girl, The Light Princess," etc.)

5 Admittedly, MacDonald collapsing the moral and class valences of "lady" and "gentleman" does not go far enough to undercut class hierarchies, yet he regularly diminishes upper-class pretensions to superiority as he does in this quotation, while acknowledging the difficulty of being both poor and virtuous in a middle-class sense.

His realistic depiction of the effects of Nanny's hard life on her character is convincing by realist tenets.

6 For "post-secular" children and religion, see Davis (2014).

References

Abrams, M.H. (1971), *Natural Supernaturalism: Tradition and Revolution in Romantic Literature*, New York: W.W. Norton.

Andrews, Malcolm (1994), *Dickens and the Grown-up Child*, Iowa City: University of Iowa Press.

Boas, George (1966), *The Cult of Childhood*, London: The Warburg Institute.

Buckley, Jerome (1974), *Season of Youth: The Bildungsroman from Dickens to Golding*, Cambridge, MA: Harvard University Press.

Coleridge, Samuel Taylor (1956), "To Thomas Poole," in Earl Leslie Griggs (ed.), *Collected Letters of Samuel Taylor Coleridge, Vol. 1, 1785–1800*, Oxford: Clarendon Press.

Davis, Robert A. (2014), "Religion, Education and the Post-secular Child," *Critical Studies in Education* 55 (1): 18–31.

Gilead, Sarah (1991), "Magic Abjured: Closure in Children's Fantasy Fiction," *PMLA* 106 (2): 277–293.

Gray, William (2009), *Fantasy, Myth and the Measure of Truth: Tales of Pullman, Lewis, Tolkien, MacDonald and Hoffmann*, Houndmills, Hampshire: Palgrave Macmillan.

Knoepflmacher, U.C. (1983), "The Balancing of Child and Adult: An Approach to Victorian Fantasies for Children," *Nineteenth-Century Fiction* 37: 497–530.

Lewis, C.S. (1947), *George MacDonald: An Anthology*, New York: Macmillan.

Lewis, C.S. ([1950] 2000), *The Lion, the Witch and the Wardrobe 1950*, New York: HarperCollins Publishers.

Lewis, C.S. ([1951] 2000), *Prince Caspian*, New York: HarperCollins Publishers.

Lewis, C.S. ([1952] 1966), "On Three Ways of Writing for Children," in Walter Hooper (ed.), *Of Other Worlds: Essays and Stories*, 22–34, London: Geoffrey Bles.

Lewis, C.S. ([1952] 2000), *The Voyage of the Dawn Treader*, New York: HarperCollins Publishers.

Lewis, C.S. ([1954] 2000), "Tolkien's *Lord of the Rings*," in Lesley Walmsley (ed.), *C.S. Lewis: Essay Collection and Other Short Pieces*, 519–525, London: HarperCollins Publishers.

Lewis, C.S. (1955), *Surprised by Joy*, San Diego: Harcourt Brace.

Lewis, C.S. ([1956] 2000), *The Last Battle*, New York: HarperCollins Publishers.

Lewis, C.S. ([1956] 1966), "Sometimes Fairy Stories May Say Best What's to Be Said," in Walter Hooper (ed.), *Of Other Worlds: Essays and Stories*, 35–38, London: Geoffrey Bles.

Lewis, C.S. (1966), "On Juvenile Tastes," in Walter Hooper (ed.), *Of Other Worlds: Essays and Stories*, 39–41, London: Geoffrey Bles.

Lewis, C.S. (2007), *The Collected Letters of C.S. Lewis. Vol. 3 (1950–1963)*. Ed. Walter Hooper, San Francisco: HarperSanFrancisco.

MacDonald, George ([1858] 1999), *Phantastes*, Grand Rapids, MI: Wm. B. Eerdmans.

MacDonald, George ([1871] 2011), *At the Back of the North Wind*, Peterborough, ON: Broadview Press.

MacDonald, George (1893), "Fantastic Imagination," in *A Dish of Orts: Chiefly Papers on the Imagination and on Shakspere*, 313–322, London: Sampson Low Marston & Company.

MacDonald, George (1893), "The Imagination: Its Functions and Its Culture," in *A Dish of Orts: Chiefly Papers on the Imagination and on Shakspere*, 1–42, London: Sampson Low Marston & Company.

Miller, Laura (2008), *The Magician's Book: A Skeptic's Guide to Narnia*, New York: Little, Brown and Co.

Pinsent, Pat (2005), "The Varieties of British Protestant Children's Fiction: Severe Moralising versus Flights of Fancy," in Jan De Maeyer, Hans-Heino Ewers, Rita Ghesquière, Michel Manson, Pat Pinsent, and Patricia Quaghebeur (eds), *Religion, Children's Literature and Modernity in Western Europe 1750–2000*, 125–144, Leuven: Leuven University Press.

Plotz, Judith (2001), *Romanticism and the Vocation of Childhood*, New York: Palgrave Macmillan.

Prickett, Stephen (2005), *Victorian Fantasy*, second edition, Waco, TX: Baylor University Press.

Raeper, William (1987), *George MacDonald*, Tring, Herts: Lion Publishing.

Reilly, R.J. (1971), *Romantic Religion: A Study of Barfield, Lewis, Williams, and Tolkien*. Athens, GA: University of Georgia Press.

Rudd, David (2002), "Myth-Making—Or Just Taking the Myth? The Dangers of Myth Becoming Fact in Lewis's Narnia Series," *Papers* 12 (1): 30–39.

Spufford, Francis (2002), *The Child That Books Built*, London: Faber & Faber.

Tolkien, J.R.R. ([1947]1983), "On Fairy-Stories," in Christopher Tolkien (eds), *The Monsters and the Critics and Other Essays*, 109–161, London: George Allan and Unwin.

Ward, Michael (2008), *Planet Narnia: The Seven Heavens in the Imagination of C.S. Lewis*, New York: Oxford University Press.

Wordsworth, William ([1807] 1947), "Ode: Intimations of Immortality from Recollections of Early Childhood," in E. de Selincourt and Helen Darbishire (eds), *The Poetical Works of William Wordsworth*, vol. 4, 279–285, Oxford: Clarendon Press.

35

The BBC's *Religious Service for Schools*, "Come and Praise", and the Musical Aesthetic and Religious Discourse Around the Child

Stephen G. Parker

*S*tephen Parker has published on other aspects the history of worship for children at the BBC (Parker 2010; Parker 2015). In this chapter he shows how, from its beginnings, broadcast worship for schools was avowedly Christian, supplying children with a language and experience akin to that of adult religious broadcasting, and the worship of the mainstream Christian churches. However, by the late 1970s this approach seemed no longer tenable, leading to the development of a new hymn book for schools to resource the changing need. 'Come and Praise', first published in 1978, proved enormously popular, allowing the continued circulation of traditional orthodoxies whilst offering a new, open language, which affirmed certain moral commitments aside from the religious. That it also successfully elided the distinctions between the religions cemented its success beyond the scope of the radio service itself.

Introduction: The historical and legal situation

Prayer and worship in schools (religious observances as they were sometimes called) have been customary practice since the beginnings of state-funded education in England in 1870. Even so, they were made a statutory requirement by the 1944

Education Act, in the context of the provision of wider compulsory religious education (including Religious Instruction). Although this legal requirement has been much debated in the intervening decades, most vigorously in the 1960s and 1970s (Parker 2015), the 1988 Education Act prescribed that this legal requirement be a continuous expectation upon schools in England and Wales, and that collective worship be of a 'Christian character'. This minor liberalization of the law (the use of the terminology of a 'Christian character' does not necessarily mean Christian *per se*) the legal mandate for collective worship remains. The emphasis upon the 'Christian character' of that worship, in the rhetoric of those who instituted it, reflects the historic national religious situation, a strong linkage between Christianity and British identity, and that England has an established church (Copley 2008).

Despite arguments against statutory worship in schools, based upon philosophical, ethical and practical objections, its usefulness as an 'assembly' of the school to celebrate communal life and affirm particular values is widely understood (see for instance Hull 1975; Cheetham 2004). Moreover, in practise schools negotiate the mandated religious requirement, taking into account local needs and the consciences of all those involved. Although numerous schools fail to meet the legal requirement, many schools continue to see collective worship as providing space for students' personal and moral reflection and growth (Smith and Smith 2013). Even so, pressure is currently mounting to remove the statutory requirement for worship, replacing it instead with an assembly for 'reflection' aimed at the development of the spiritual, moral and cultural development of pupils (Clarke and Woodhead 2015).

This chapter traces the history of the British Broadcasting Corporation's (BBC) involvement in providing broadcast collective worship programmes for schools from the 1940s onward. It describes how these were avowedly Christian in content, ritual shape, discourse, hymnody and musical aesthetic, this remaining the case for some decades. In particular, the chapter focuses upon a time, in the late 1970s, when, driven by debates going on about place of worship in schools, the need to provide a service of relevance to the schools, and the changing social and religious circumstances, the BBC commissioned a new song book and music around which a revised form of worship could be constructed. The origins, development, implications and lasting impact of the resultant book 'Come and Praise' will be discussed in some detail.

The BBC and its *Religious Service for Schools*

Under the its founding Director General, John Reith's, guiding influence, the BBC saw itself as engaged in promulgating the Christian message to a Christian people utilising the new technology of radio (Bailey 2007; Wolfe 1984). The public service broadcaster's cultural mission included the Christianizing of children as well as adults, and was a resilient feature of its stated purpose in religious broadcasting until at least the 1950s (Parker 2015). In many respects this support for the mainstream denominational Christianity has continued, albeit in an adapted form, right up to the present day (Noonan 2013). The aims and development of religious broadcasting to children, particularly in schools, latterly took a different trajectory, as will be detailed below.

Broadcast worship for children began with a regular radio Sunday children's service in September 1926 – deliberately scheduled later on Sunday afternoon to avoid a clash with the timing of Sunday Schools. A broadcast radio service for schools began much later, in September 1940, at the height of the blitz, when it seemed most appropriate that all – including children – should be galvanized to some kind of spiritual endeavour, and it also led to the establishing of a prayer time for children as an epilogue to the BBC's flagship children's broadcast *Children's Hour* (Parker 2010; Parker 2012). The Anglican clergyman, John G. Williams, who led both programmes, did so for the decade following, having an influence on the tenor of the familial and school broadcasts, but also in shaping practice in collective worship in schools generally (see the section of his book Worship and the Modern Child elsewhere in this volume) (Parker 2015).

The initial BBC *Religious Service for Schools* was aimed at a broad audience 8–12 year olds. In 1961 a further programme was added to the schedule for older children (12–16 year olds), the *Act of Worship*. The normal order of service for these 'live' broadcasts were music, a hymn, a dramatic 'interlude', reflections led by the presenter followed by a prayer, a further hymn, and a closing prayer – with a blessing – given by a clerical broadcaster. The thematic programme of the broadcasts generally followed the Christian calendar. The hymnody was chosen by broadcasters (in the schools and religions departments of the BBC) in conjunction with teachers in schools, the respected listening audience to which the BBC always paid attention (Bailey 1957). Eventually, a hymn booklet was produced by the BBC for use in school, its 'Hymns and Prayers'. This slight pamphlet, of just 28 of the most popular hymns of the period, such as: 'At the name of Jesus, every knee should bow'; 'Lord of all hopefulness, Lord of all joy'; and 'When a knight won his spurs in the stories of old', were deemed appropriate for children to sing.

'Come and Praise': The creation and preservation of a 'community of the air'

The Christian character of broadcast worship was continuous across this period. As late as 1977 stated BBC policy was that its *Religious Service for Schools* should 'affirm the continuing reality of Christian truths,'[1] and schedules remained thematically structured around the Christian year. In 1975, however, consideration began to be given to a new hymn book to align with the 'changing texture of the programmes'.[2] At this stage it was decided to adopt a 'quiet gradualism'[3] in commissioning and introducing new songs, to allow children to learn brand new material, and because producing an entirely new hymnbook would be expensive for the BBC and schools. Indeed, broadcasters planned the introduction of new material so carefully they were concerned to monitor the regularity with which songs were sung (traditional and new) and the style of new songs (folk and traditional), seeking to achieve a balance.[4] A piece of listening research carried out by the BBC in June 1976 found that all schools supported the use of folk-modern songs, such as 'He's got the whole world in his hands', or songs with a 'lively modern tune', which contributed to the 'corporate feeling of the morning service'[5]. Broadcasters found that the pattern and style of the weekly programmes was akin to how schools worshipped during the rest of the week, suggesting an influence on the wider worship practice that school programming was having.

In 1978 the BBC returned to the question of publishing a new hymn book. The cost to schools of purchasing a large number of hymnbooks was resolved by regarding this as a 'special' purchase outside normal costs, the BBC were able go ahead with commissioning almost a million-copy initial print run of the volume, which it anticipated would resource the religious broadcast to schools for the following ten years.[6] This initial print-run was regarded as a conservative estimate of demand by producers, given sales of existing hymn booklets, and the listening audience of nine thousand schools, some nine-hundred and twenty-thousand school pupils[7], nearly half of the schools across the nation. It was decided by producers, however, that the descriptor 'hymn book' should not be used of the new volume, instead referring to it as an "song book", which was thought preferable because the book 'may well live through a period when the audience shifts from "a service" to an "assembly" preference'.[8] The rejection of the word 'hymn' reflected a wider debate going on at the time about the continuing justification for compulsory school worship, assembly being a less religiously laden term (Hull 1975). The BBC commissioned an artist to produce a cover for the new hymn, and it was agreed that the new book should have sixty to seventy hymns (50 new ones, around 20 traditional), be reviewed after three or four years when schools had had time to assimilate its use.[9] It was decided to call the new assembly song book, 'Come and Praise'.

The new song book proved immediately popular with schools and children, indeed churches and cathedrals began to use it.[10] Even so, despite the evidently huge popularity of the new book and some of the largest audiences on radio at the time, the BBC began an investigation into the appropriateness of the provision in an increasingly multi-faith society, and where children and teachers listening to broadcasts had little background knowledge of Christianity.[11] However, the idea of a multi-faith (or single-faith) worship service was rejected as impractical and unacceptable, though 'tales from other religions' could be used without disrupting the worship element. It was concluded by broadcasters that 'any changes at all would be hurtful to a good number of people. Not to make changes would be regarded as failing to face to facts of life by many others'.[12] In the end, the use of differing kinds of story and the songbook 'Come and Praise' seems to have represented an ideal compromise, which acknowledged the changing times but still preserved a sense of the 'community of the air' which the Religious Service for Schools stood for in the minds of broadcasters.[13]

What was the nature of the compromise, and what were the children being asked to sing? Two examples of the most popular songs in the 'Come and Praise' repertoire were 'Autumn days when the grass is jewelled' by a former nun turned religious education teacher, the other 'One more step along the world I go' by the famous hymn writer Sydney Carter.

Autumn days when the grass is jewelled
And the silk inside a chestnut shell.
Jetplanes meeting in the air to be refuelled.
All these thing I love so well

So I mustn't forget
No, I mustn't forget.
To say a great big
Thank You
I mustn't forget

Clouds that look like familiar face
And the winters moon with frosted rings.
Smell of bacon as I fasten up my laces
And the song the milkman sings

So I mustn't forget
No, I mustn't forget.
To say a great big
Thank You
I mustn't forget

Whipped-up spray that is rainbow-scattered
And a swallow curving in the sky
Shoes so comfy though they're worn out and they're battered
And the taste of apple pie.

So I mustn't forget
No, I mustn't forget
To say a great big thank you
I mustn't forget.

Scent of gardens when the rain's been falling
And a minnow darting down a stream
Picked-up engine that's been stuttering and stalling
And a win for my home team.

So I mustn't forget
No, I mustn't forget
To say a great big thank you
I mustn't forget.

ESTELLE WHITE

One more step along the world I go,
one more step along the world I go;
from the old things to the new
keep me travelling along with you:
[Refrain:]
And it's from the old I travel to the new.
keep me travelling along with you.

Round the corners of the world I turn,
more and more about the world I learn;
all the new things that I see
you'll be looking at along with me. [Refrain]

As I travel through the bad and good
keep me travelling the way I should;
where I see no way to go
you'll be telling me the way, I know: [Refrain]

Give me courage when the world is rough,
keep me loving though the world is tough;
leap and sing in all I do,
keep me travelling along with you: [Refrain]

You are older than the world can be,
you are younger than the life in me.
ever old and ever new,
keep me travelling along with you: [Refrain]

SYDNEY CARTER

Both songs appeal to nature without reference to a deity (or a specifically Christian deity at least). Certainly 'songs were designed to be inclusive', and it is the noticeable slippage between the traditional Christian language and the non-specific language of these songs – and those drawn from the folk groups like 'The Spinners' – which appears to have popularized the song book to such a degree that within five years it had sold 3 million copies[14] and had become the main hymnbook in many schools for the whole of the school week. According to the Producer responsible for the *Religious Service for Schools* at the time, Geoff Marshall-Taylor, before 'Come and Praise' children sat passively listening to 'churchy' hymns; with its advent they became joyful participants. 'Come and Praise' and the changes to the Religious Service for Schools invited children 'to respond on different levels', to 'reflect', to 'pray *if you wish*' (emphasis added).[15]

The producer, Geoff Marshall-Taylor, hoped to create a 'community of the air', and he stated, for instance, that he took heart that children of different religious backgrounds, Roman Catholic and Protestant, were singing the same religious songs at the same time during the 'troubles' in Northern Ireland.[16] Additionally, another song 'Spirit of Peace, come to our waiting world' was said to be of reassurance to children of parents fighting in the South Atlantic during the Falklands War.[17]

A second volume of songs was commissioned by the BBC in 1988, and the song book remains a mainstay of religious music and discourse in schools (and churches) across the United Kingdom, songs popularized by it appearing in other hymnbooks also.

In 1996 a survey carried out on 520 schools found that nine of the ten favourite songs of children were from 'Come and Praise'. The author of three of these, Sydney Carter, said he thought that their popularity was owed to them being 'not so doctrinal' as other hymns.[18] As a measure of its influence upon generations of children Geoff Marshall-Taylor recounted a not untypical story of a telephone call he had received in the recent past from someone planning a wedding with a couple. The couple, who had no other contact with the church, wanted to sing a song from a 'blue hymn book they remembered from school', which was 'Come and Praise'.[19]

Conclusion: Styling children's spirituality by radio at the end of the twentieth century

The 'Come and Praise' song book has entered the folklore of broadcasting, and was clearly a hugely successful initiative.[20] Along with the radio programme which it grew out of, it had mass appeal within schools because it appeared to meet the need to sing songs which were both enjoyable and meaningful to a broad and diverse audience. The meaning derived from the songs appeared to be the openness of their language, which in schools populated by children of many religions and none was deemed more appropriate than a diet of Christian hymnody. By providing a combination of both songs of this ilk and traditional Christian hymns in the same song book, broadcasters could claim to be meeting the legal and cultural requirements in which they were working, whilst also preserving the sense of a 'community of the air' they sought to serve. Moreover the slippage between 'Christian' and 'open' and 'reflective' made possible by the 'Come and Praise' phenomenon has arguably shaped the spirituality of generations of children in the UK in the latter part of the twentieth century, providing young people with a distinctive and memorable religious language and musical aesthetic.

Notes

1   BBC Written Archive Centre (WAC) R165/64/1 The School Broadcasting Council for the United Kingdom Programme Committee II, 7 November 1977.

2   BBC WAC R165/64/1 Memo J.P. Reid Assistant Head of Schools Broadcasting Radio to Head of Schools Broadcasting Radio, 18 November 1975.

3   BBC WAC R165/64/1 Memo J.P. Reid to Head of Schools Broadcasting – Religious Service for School – the hymns, 18 February 1976.

4   BBC WAC R165/64/1 Uses of Hymns/Songs in a Service for Schools, undated.

5   BBC WAC R165/64/1 The School Broadcasting Council for the United Kingdom, Programme Committee I & II, June 1976, A Service for Schools, information paper based upon fieldwork carried out by SBC officers in 1975/76.

6   BBC WAC R165/64/1 Suggested print order for sales to schools for new edition of pupils' hymn booklet for a Service for Schools for 10 years from 1978–79, May 1977.

7   BBC WAC R165/64/1 Senior Assistant Education Broadcasting to Geoff Marshall-Taylor, Statistics for audience for a Service to Schools, 16 May 1977.

8   BBC WAC R165/64/1 J.P. Reid to Geoff Marshall-Taylor, New Hymnbook for a Service for Schools, 1 June 1977.

9   Ibid

10 BBC WAC R165/64/1 J.P. Reid to Head of School Broadcasting, Come and Praise Church Edition, 8 February 1979.

11 BBC WAC R165/64/1 Senior Education Officer (Schools) to All Education Officers, Fieldwork Enquiry, Acts of Worship in the Primary School, 28 February 1981.

12 BBC WAC R165/64/1 Multi-faith Material and a 'Service for Schools', undated paper c.1980.

13 The phrase 'community of the air' comes from Geoff Marshall-Taylor, producer of the Religious Service to Schools, with the author on 31 March 2014.

14 Interview with Geoff Marshall-Taylor, 31 March 2014.

15 Ibid.

16 Ibid.

17 See the televised celebration of Come and Praise here: http://www.bbc.co.uk/programmes/p00h2fb2 (accessed 15 October 2015).

18 John O'Leary Education Editor. "Folk singer strikes chord with young worshippers." Times [London, England] 29 Aug. 1996: 6. The Times Digital Archive. Web. 15 Oct. 2015.

19 Interview wtih Geoff Marshall-Taylor, 31 March 2014.

20 http://www.bbc.co.uk/programmes/p00h2fb2 (accessed 15 October 2015).

References

Bailey, K.V. (1957), *The Listening Schools: Educational Broadcasting by Sound and Television*, (London: British Broadcasting Corporation).

Bailey, M. (2007), '"He Who Has Ears to Hear, Let Him Hear": Christian Pedagogy and Religious Broadcasting During the Inter-War Period', *Westminster Papers in Communication and Culture*, 4(1): 4–25.

Cheetham, R. (2004), *Collective Worship: issues and opportunities*, London: SPCK.

Clarke, C. and Woodhead, L. (2015), *A new settlement: religion and beliefs in schools*, London: Westminster Faith Debates.

Copley, T. (2008), *Teaching Religion: sixty years on*, Exeter: Exeter University Press.

Hull, J. (1975), *School Worship: an obituary*, London: SCM Press.

Noonan, C. (2013), 'Piety and Professionalism: the BBC's Changing Religious Mission', *Media History*, 19 (2): 196–212.

Parker, S.G. (2010), '"Teach them to pray Auntie': Children's Hour Prayers at the BBC, 1940–1961"', *History of Education: journal of the History of Education Society*, 39(5): 659–676.

Parker, S.G. (2012), 'Reinvigorating Christian Britain: the spiritual opportunities of the war, national identity, and the hope of Religious Education', in Parker, S.G. and Lawson, T. (eds), *God and War: the Church of England and Armed Conflict in the Twentieth-century*, (Aldershot: Ashgate).

Parker, S.G. (2015), 'Mediatizing childhood religion: the BBC, John G. Williams, and collective worship for schools in England, c.1940–1975', *Paedagogica Historica: international journal of the history of education*, 51(5): 614–630.

Smith, G. and Smith, S. (2013), 'From values to virtues: an investigation into the ethical content of English primary school assemblies', *British Journal of Religious Education*, 35(1): 5–19.

Wolfe, K. (1984), *The Churches and the British Broadcasting Corporation, 1922–1956*, London: SCM Press.

36

The Construction of Religion and Childhood in Broadcast Worship

Rachael Shillitoe

Rachael Shillitoe is a doctoral student at the University of Worcester, UK, where she is completing an ethnographic study on children's perspectives on Collective Worship in school. Here she uses the BBC's current radio provision for Collective Worship for schools ("Something to Think About" and "Together") as the basis for her analysis. She critically examines the meaning of childhood and religion as depicted in such shows.

Introduction

It has been well argued that media and popular culture takes an increasingly influential role in society and has become intertwined with other institutions and spheres of public life (Couldry 2003; Hjarvard 2008, 2013). One such field is religion, and as Lynch et al. (2012) observe, it is increasingly difficult to think of religion without considering how it is constructed and portrayed in media forms. The practice of everyday religious life, knowledge about religion and the nature and authority of religious institutions, are increasingly becoming reliant on media logics. When considering this relationship a number of core issues emerge, including how religion is constructed and conceptualized in such spaces. However, such debates rarely consider media as created for children and instead rely on products intended for an adult audience. Ridgely (2011, 2012), La Fontaine and Rydstrøm (1998) and Bunge (2006) note that research on religion is predominantly adult-centric, relying on adult-generated analytical categories to understand phenomenon and experiences found within the lives of adults. In considering these two areas of emerging interest, I will examine how both notions of childhood and religion are constructed in media outputs.

This chapter will specifically investigate how religion and childhood are understood and constructed within a small sample of recent broadcast collective worship programmes for children at the BBC. It will examine how religion is approached within such outputs, while considering how producers conceptualize the imagined child audience intended for this programme. By exploring broadcast collective worship through a media lens, which also attends to both the sociologies of religion and childhood, this chapter will highlight the need to pay greater attention to the adult-generated constructions of *religion for children*, arguing that much can be learnt about both religion and childhood in this context.

Collective worship and broadcast worship at the BBC

Collective worship has been a compulsory feature of maintained schools in England and Wales at least since the 1944 Education Act. The legal requirement stipulated by this Act has caused decades of confusion and controversy, with many questioning its educational suitability and relevance in an increasingly plural and diverse society (Cheetham 2000). Despite a multitude of reports, commentaries, and papers on the subject, many teachers have historically found great difficulty in meeting the legal requirement, with reports and studies revealing considerable noncompliance when it comes to collective worship (Durham Report 1970; Hull 1975, 1984, 1989; Swann Report 1985; OFSTED 1994).

As there is no curriculum which stipulates how collective worship should be approached and delivered, a multitude of resources and materials have been created for schools in order to meet this demand. The BBC has broadcast a regular schools service since the early 1940s and, as shown by Stephen Parker (2010, 2015), the BBC has historically, been a key provider of religious broadcasting for schools as part of this service. This provision should be viewed within the greater context of the BBC's overall outputs and its close relationship with the church. Kenneth Wolfe (1984), by his historical research on broadcasting and the church, demonstrates the intertwined relationship between these two institutions and how they in turn shaped and affected each other's development. Noonan (2013) has since shown how this relationship changed between 1960–1979, as the broadcasting institution and those who worked there increased their professional standing as broadcasters and how ultimately, the church's authority gave way to that of media logics.

The BBC currently provides collective worship for children aged 6–11, through their *Schools Radio* department. Within this provision, the BBC offer two sets of podcasts, one for children aged 6–7 called *Something to Think About* and one for children aged 7–11 called *Together*. In addition to this the BBC provide songs for collective worship and audio visual resources which are organized thematically into "Festivals," "Special

Days" and "SEAL Themes" (Social and Emotional Aspects of Learning). For the purposes of this chapter, I will be focusing on the podcasts produced by the BBC with specific reference to *Together*. The BBC states the podcast series can be used to fulfill the legal requirement regarding collective worship, while drawing upon a wide range of resources from various cultural and faith groups. According to the guidance notes for teachers, which accompany each series, the aim of the podcasts is to "provide assemblies which relate to children's own experiences and concerns while exploring a wide range of moral, spiritual and religious issues celebrating the different social, cultural and religious backgrounds of the audience" (Hill 2014).

The *Together* series covers various themes from coding and computing, to healthy living and caring for the environment. These themes are carefully chosen and relate to the children's everyday lives while responding to news and events in the wider world. They are not random or abstract but are designed to be relevant and meaningful to the child listener. Such themes are then packaged and presented through a podcast which is usually made up of a song, voxpops, a story or drama, moment of reflection and occasionally a prayer. Every week the child, if a regular listener, would grow accustomed to the programme's structure and style. Each programme is organized thematically and usually grouped with one or two other programmes connected to this theme. The types of stories, dramas and songs used will draw upon a wide range of religious and non-religious sources. To investigate this in more depth, we will now take a look at some of the key features of the podcasts and consider how religion and childhood are constructed in such spaces.

Construction(s) of religion in broadcast collective worship

This section considers the various ways in which religion and childhood are constructed within broadcast collective worship. It will examine both religious and non-religious resources, the spiritual and reflective dimensions of the programmes and the adult-centered motivations behind the production process.

Throughout the course of an academic year, the BBC's collective worship outputs cover a wide range of themes, drawing upon a diverse assortment of religious and non-religious sources. The BBC claim this resource can be used to help fulfill the legal requirement of collective worship, stating that the "material" is of a "broadly Christian character," reflecting the "broad traditions of Christian belief" (Hill 2014: 1).

The 1988 Education Reform Act requires all schools to provide for a daily act of collective worship which is "wholly or mainly of a broadly Christian character" (section 7). However, as Graham argues, "such a provision is less about the observance of Christian heritage and more about negotiating the pluralism of religious beliefs and practices in a multi-cultural society" (2012: 229). This negotiation is one that will also face the producers of broadcast collective worship. Broadcasters are tasked with creating a resource that is suitable for a diverse audience while meeting the legal requirement of collective worship which privileges Christianity over any other faith or non-faith.

To meet this requirement, many of the religious sources contained within these outputs are predominately drawn from the Christian tradition. This may be in relation to the stories and dramas featured, the songs used, the opportunities for prayer or by the overall liturgical structure of the programme. However, the programme makers still need to produce a programme that is accessible and relevant to a diverse audience made up of all faiths and none. As such, the programme makers produce their outputs in such a way that does not require previous knowledge of, or affiliation with, any particular faith tradition. For example, in a programme focused on self-belief, the story of Moses and the burning bush is used (BBC 2015a). The children are provided with enough detail to understand the context and characters of the story before being entertained with a drama centered on overcoming challenges and believing in yourself. As a result, any awareness of the Christian tradition or biblical understanding is not necessary. The story is used as a vehicle to address the theme of self-belief rather than in any confessional sense.

In another episode about personal development and growth, the podcast is made up of a variety of religious and non-religious material (BBC 2014). The podcast begins with voxpops of children describing what they are proud of, and what makes them unique, before being introduced to the programme's story. The presenter informs the children that today's story is from the bible and is about a man called Zacchaeus. The story is told in the form of a modern day news report, featuring interviews with "witnesses at the scene" and live reporting of events as they unfold. The programme does not provide specific information as to the exact reference of the story nor a theological interpretation of the text. The story is used as a way to demonstrate to the children the importance of changing for the better and how we are all capable of this. In this context, the religious is used in a variety of ways; for entertainment, storytelling and importantly, self-development.

When understanding how religion is constructed and framed within such media, Stig Hjarvard's (2008, 2013) work on the mediatization of religion can prove useful. According to Hjarvard (2013), as religious authority declines, the media takes an increasingly influential role in terms of defining and constructing religion. This process is known as mediatization and in his typology Hjarvard (2013) outlines three forms of mediatized religion. Firstly there is religious media; this would usually be controlled by religious institutions and often for the purpose of providing religious services for a religious audience. A second form of mediatized religion is journalism on religion. In this instance the institution in control is journalism and the purpose of such media is to provide news, debate and current affairs concerning religion. Finally, Hjarvard (2013) observes that the mediatization of religion can take one other form, banal religion. As opposed to using this term in the pejorative sense, Hjarvard (2013) appropriates the term in much the same way as Billig (1995) originally did with banal nationalism. It is in this final form of mediatized religion that we can think of the BBC's construction and representation of religion in broadcast collective worship. The use of religious stories for narrative fiction and entertainment, the focus on self-development and the "bricolage of religious representations" which provides a framework for the cultural knowledge about religion, all provides for a banal mediatization of religion (Hjarvard 2013: 84). The BBC constructs an idea of religion through a series of representations which have little or no connection with formal institutionalized religion. Constructing religion in this way can have its strengths. Through harnessing religion to meet the needs of the narrative fiction, the programme makers are both able to produce a show that is accessible and relevant while also meeting the legal requirement of collective worship. If the religious elements of the programmes were constructed so that they were to fall into the other two categories of mediatized religion, there is a risk that the podcast series would become far less entertaining and accessible for children.

However, such stories and dramas are not the only ways in which religion features in these programmes. Towards the end of the podcast, children will be asked to contemplate the theme of the show. Set to calming or new age instrumental music, the presenter, speaking in a soft tone with a slow pace, asks the children questions; encourages them to consider the issues explored in the show, and how these may apply this to their everyday lives. Occasionally, the BBC will also provide for a short prayer in addition to this moment of reflection which will either be read by the presenter or by children. If a prayer is read, the presenter would not assume that the children listening would be familiar with this or wish to take part. As such, before the prayer is read, the presenter informs the children of what is about to happen and, if they would like to, how they can participate in this: "I'm going to say a short prayer now. You can make it your own by joining in with Amen at the end or you can just listen to the words" (BBC 2015b).

The prayer would be short, address God, usually be one of thanks and always end in amen. For example, in an episode on growing your own food, the presenter reads the following prayer: "*Dear God, Thank-you for the seasons of the year. All the fruits and vegetables that grow through the spring and ripen in summer. Help us enjoy food that is good for us, to keep us healthy and strong. Amen*" (BBC 2015c). The inclusion of prayer in these podcasts blurs the edges between Hjarvard's (2013) cluster of communicative practices. Earlier in the programme, we can see a more banal mediatization of religion; however, these prayers do not fit so easily within this category due to serving a more explicit religious purpose. It would also not demonstrate religious media, as the primary institution in charge is still that of the BBC, and not a religious organization. As a result of the constraints imposed by the law surrounding collective worship and the need for the podcasts to be suitable for a diverse audience, the programme makers are then left with continually constructing and reconstructing religion in order to meet these different requirements. What these podcasts demonstrate is that within one single fifteen minute show, we can have multiple constructions or mediatizations of religion.

However, as mentioned earlier, it is not only religious stories and sources that are used in these programmes, a wide range of non-religious resources are also employed.

As argued by Lee, it is vital that we consider such non-religious content in order to help "round out our understanding of 'religion' in society, which is necessarily exclusive or incomplete if the secular is neglected" (2015: 3). Within this context, to neglect such themes would overlook a large section of the BBC's provision for collective worship. Some episodes focus on computing and technology, while others may reflect on family and friends. Such themes may not utilize stories drawn from religious traditions; instead they explore the theme through a fictional drama. As the BBC cannot make any assumptions on the part of its listeners in terms of their religious or non-religious commitments, the programme makers need to produce a programme that speaks to all children and as such, will also need to include non-religious content in addition to a diverse representation of various religious traditions. This diversification can also be found within the BBC's wider outputs as Noonan demonstrates with the "changing religious mission" of the BBC and how religion, especially Christianity, has lost the monopoly it once had (2013: 207).

However, as opposed to simply reducing the religious content of the programme altogether, the programme makers have drawn upon a bricolage of religious and non-religious sources in order to appeal to the audience they imagine are listening. Knott and Mitchell note that "representations of religion in the media have diversified rather than disappeared and that the BBC still plays a major role" (2012: 243). The inclusion of non-religious sources does not disrupt or jar with the wider provision of collective worship at the BBC due to the banal quality of the religious material. It allows the BBC to therefore meet both the legal requirement of collective worship, while also attending to the perceived diversity of its listening audience. It is this diversity and banality which allows the podcast series to be accessible for all children, irrespective of their religious or non-religious beliefs.

Adult-centered motivations

When examining how religion is framed and approached in such media, it is vital we consider how, in turn, the intended audience is constructed and perceived. As has been pointed out by Jenkins (1998), the concept of childhood is culturally and historically contingent. Ariès (1962) shows how the notion of childhood has changed over the centuries, demonstrating how prior to the middle ages the concept of childhood did not exist. Various scholars (James et al. 1988; James and Prout 2015) have traced the development of childhood and shown how certain taken for granted notions of what it means to be a child are laden with adult assumptions and perceptions which do not give rise to the everyday realities of childhood. Writers such as Walkerdine (1998) and Rose (1998) have demonstrated how popular culture and children's literature promote certain definitions of childhood. Jenkins (1998), through attending to the material worlds that children live in, demonstrates the need to investigate such materials created for and used by children, as these in themselves are imbued with various ideas of what it means to be a child. As Kline (1998) observes, children's culture is always inflected with the needs and wants of a given society at a given time. Culture is a means by which societies can maintain and uphold certain positions and children's culture is therefore intrinsically linked to the desires adults have for children as well as their beliefs and practices (Kline 1998).

In her work on religious toys and childhood, Sachs-Norris (2011) argues that we need to cast a critical gaze over the products and materials created for children and question the motives and agendas behind the resources that are developed. Toys, media and other materials created for children are not themselves reflective of what it means to be child nor does it reveal an accurate picture of the worlds that children inhabit; such products are the result of adult's motivations for children (Bado-Fralick and Sachs Norris 2010, Sachs Norris 2011). They are adult-generated constructions created for children. Far from politically neutral, such materials will carry various meanings of not only childhood, but also race, gender, class and religion.

Throughout the podcast series, each programme provides opportunities for reflection and contemplation. The BBC explicitly states that their programmes are intended to support children's spiritual development as well as contributing towards other areas of the curriculum (Hill 2014). Such moments of contemplation are perhaps more revealing of the "motivational complexity" of the outputs, demonstrating that the programme makers are equally aware that their programmes need to appeal to adults as well as children (Sachs Norris 2011: 191). Children will only be able to access this resource once it has been accepted and authorized by the adult gatekeeper, the teacher. The programme makers can therefore sell their product through the branding of spirituality, which as Carrette and King (2005) demonstrate, can result in many benefits. Noonan notes that producers are aware of the increasing "appetite for the spiritual" amongst the viewing audience (2011: 731). But the question remains, whose appetite are we feeding? The subjective turn featured in the *Together* podcasts not only responds to the changes within wider programming and therefore media logics, it also speaks to pedagogical ones too (Heelas et al. 2004). In recent years, there have been both therapeutic and contemplative turns within education and it can be argued that the moments of reflection in the podcasts are motivated by such pedagogical imperatives (Ecclestone and Hayes 2008; Todd and Ergas 2015).

The resources produced for this part of the school day, by the BBC and beyond, are infused with certain messages and ideas of what adults want for children. The themes of the programmes are intended to reflect the children's everyday lives and concerns. However, such concerns are more revealing of the concerns adults have for children then perhaps concerns that children have themselves. This is not to say that such products are unethical or that the children themselves lack the agency to reconstruct and negotiate the messages presented to them. Rather, it is to highlight that the materials and media created for children do not themselves represent childhood. They represent how adults perceive childhood and in this particular case, how adults perceive of *religion for children*.

Conclusion

This chapter has briefly explored broadcast collective worship for children as produced by the BBC. By integrating insights from the sociology of religion, sociology of childhood, and media studies, we have been able to see how various factors influence the production and construction of religion for children. Rather than simply viewing such media as neutral outputs created for children, this chapter has demonstrated how different forms of religion emerge in such contexts and what such constructions reveal about notions of childhood amongst the adults involved in producing broadcasts. It also considers the various logics which govern such materials and the multifaceted nature of such media. Ultimately, this chapter calls for more attention to be paid to religion and childhood, while also taking account of the adult-generated constructions which inhabit children's worlds. In addition to this, we need to think critically about who the intended audience for such media outputs are and what this reveals about the construction of religion contained in such media.

References

Ariès, P. (1962), *Centuries of Childhood*, London: Pimlico Press.

Bado-Fralick, N. and Sachs Norris, R. (2010), *Toying with God: The World of Religious Games and Dolls*, Texas: Baylor University Press.

Billig, M. (1995), *Banal Nationalism*, London: Sage.

Bunge, M. (2006), "The Child, Religion, and the Academy: Developing Robust Theological and Religious Understandings of Children and Childhood," *Journal of Religion* 86 (4): 549–579.

Carrette, J. and King, R. (2005), *Selling Spirituality: The Silent Takeover of Religion*, Abingdon: Routledge.

Cheetham, R. (2000), *Collective Worship: Issues and Opportunities*, London: SPCK.

Couldry, N. (2003), *Media Rituals: A Critical Approach*, London: Routledge.

Durham Report (1970), *The Fourth R: The Report of the Commission on Religious Education in Schools*, London: National Society and SPCK.

Ecclestone, K. and Hayes, D. (2008), *The Dangerous Rise of Therapeutic Education*, Oxon: Routledge.

Graham, E. (2012), "Religious Literacy and Public Service Broadcasting: Introducing a Research Agenda," in G. Lynch, J. Mitchell, and A. Strhan (eds), *Religion, Media and Culture: A Reader*, 228–235, Oxon: Routledge.

Heelas, P., Woodhead, L., Seel, B., Szerszynski, B., and Tusting, K. (2004), *The Spiritual Revolution: Why Religion Is Giving Way to Spirituality*, Oxford: Blackwell Publishing.

Hjarvard, S. (2008), "The Mediatisation of Religion: A Theory of the Media as Agents of Religious Change," *Northern Lights* 6: 9–26.

Hjarvard, S. (2013), *The Mediatization of Culture and Society*, Oxon: Routledge.

Hull, J. (1975), *School Worship: An Obituary*, London: SMC Press.

Hull, J. (1984), *Studies in Religion and Education*, Sussex: The Falmer Press.

Hull, J. (1989), *The Act Unpacked: Meaning of the 1988 Education Reform Act for Religious Education*, Birmingham: University of Birmingham and Christian Education Movement.

James, A. and Prout, A. (2015), *Constructing and Reconstructing Childhood: Contemporary Issues in the Sociological Study of Childhood*, third edition, London: Falmer Press.

James, A., Jenks, C., and Prout, A. (1988), *Theorising Childhood*, Cambridge: Polity Press.

Jenkins, H. (1998), *The Children's Culture Reader*, London: New York University Press.

Kline, S. (1998), "The Making of Children's Culture," in H. Jenkins, *The Children's Culture Reader*, London: New York University Press.

Knott, K. and Mitchell, J. (2012), "The Changing Faces of Media and Religion," in L. Woodhead and R. Catto (eds), *Religion and Change in Modern Britain*, London: Routledge.

La Fontaine, J. and Rydstrøm, H. (1998), *The Invisibility of Children: Papers Presented at an International Conference on Anthropology and Children*, Sweden: Linköpings Universitet.

Lee, L. (2015), *Recognizing the Non-Religious: Reimaging the Secular*, Oxford: Oxford University Press.

Lynch, G., Mitchell, J. and Strhan, A. (2012), *Religion, Media and Culture: A Reader*, Oxon: Routledge.

Noonan, C. (2011), "Big Stuff in a Beautiful Way with Interesting People: The Spiritual Turn in UK Religious Broadcasting," *European Journal of Cultural Studies* 14 (6): 727–746.

Noonan, C. (2013), "Piety and Professionalism: The BBC's Changing Religious Mission (1960–1979)," *Media History* 19 (2): 196–212.

OFSTED (1994), *Religious Education and Collective Worship, 1992/1993*, London: OFSTED.

Parker, S.G. (2010), "'Teach them to pray Auntie': Children's Hour Prayers at the BBC, 1940–1961," *History of Education: Journal of the History of Education Society* 39 (5): 659–676.

Parker, S.G. (2015), "Mediatising Childhood Religion: The BBC, John G. Williams and Collective Worship for Schools in England, 1940–1975," *Paedagogica Historica: International Journal of the History of Education* 51 (5): 614–630.

Ridgely, S. (2011), *A Methods Handbook: The Study of Children in Religions*, London: New York University Press.

Ridgely, S. (2012), "Children and Religion," *Religion Compass* 6 (4): 236–248.

Rose, J. (1998), "The Case of Peter Pan: The Impossibility of Children's Fiction," in H. Jenkins (ed.), *The Children's Culture Reader*, London: New York University Press.

Sachs-Norris, R. (2011), "The Battle for the Toy Box: Marketing and Play in the Development of Children's Religious Identities," in S. Ridgley (ed.), *A Methods Handbook: The Study of Children in Religions*, 189–201, London: New York University Press.

Swann Report (1985), *Education for All*, London: HMSO.

Todd, S. and Ergas, O. (2015), "Introduction," *Journal of Philosophy of Education* 49 (2): 163–169.

Walkerdine, V. (1998), "Popular Culture and the Eroticization of Little Girls," in H. Jenkins (ed.), *The Children's Culture Reader*, 254–264, London: New York University Press.

Wolfe, K. (1984), *The Churches and the British Broadcasting Corporation 1922–1956. The Politics of Broadcast Religion*, Norwich: SCM Press.

Legislation

Education Act 1944, section 25.

Education Reform Act 1988, section 7.

Online Sources

Hill, D. (2014), "BBC School Radio Teacher's Notes: Together" Autumn 2014. Available online: http://downloads.bbc.co.uk/schoolradio/pdfs/together_autumn_2014.pdf (accessed: October 26, 2014).

Podcasts

BBC (2014), "Together: Proud to Be Me: Old Me, New Me." Available online: http://www.bbc.co.uk/programmes/p025lr8q (accessed: November 22, 2014).
BBC (2015a), "Together: Moses" (podcast). Available online: http://www.bbc.co.uk/programmes/p02mpjvp (accessed: June 21, 2015).
BBC (2015b), "Together: Growing with Granddad, Part 1." Available online: http://www.bbc.co.uk/programmes/p02mpjk8 (accessed: April 8, 2015).
BBC (2015c), "Together: Growing with Granddad, Part 2." Available online: http://www.bbc.co.uk/programmes/p02mpjmw (accessed: April 16, 2015).

37

Children, Toys, and Judaism

Laura Arnold Leibman

Laura Arnold Leibman is a Professor of English and Humanities at Reed College in Portland, Oregon (USA). Her fields of interest are Jewish American studies and religion and American culture prior to the American Civil War. Her publications include Messianism, Secrecy and Mysticism: A New Interpretation of Early American Jewish Life (Vallentine Mitchell 2012). Her current research uses material culture to explore the topic of Jews and race during the emancipation debates that swept the Americas in the 1790s–1830s. In this chapter, she explores the tools scholars have used for analyzing toys, and recent ultra-Orthodox Jewish engagements with the toy industry.

Introduction

His small, round face has all the innocence of a Renaissance putti: red lips in a tight bow, a faint blush on his cheeks, pug nose, upward-turned blue eyes, and a slight smile even an archaic Greek statue would envy. Yet rather than sprouting wings or wearing a modestly poised loin cloth, this little darling is "all dressed up for Shabbos" and wears an argyle vest, long pants, white shirt, *kippah* (skull cap), *tzitzit* (ritual fringes), and glossy black shoes. His hand holds no bow and arrow, but rather a green book of *Zemirot Shabbat*—Jewish hymns to be sung around the Sabbath table. His name is Yossi, and he is a *Mitzvah Kinder*, a toy designed and marketed by ultra-Orthodox Jews for their children. Like his twin Yanky (dressed the same but with a pink book), Yossi's purpose is religious. As his packaging explains, you can "Teach your child the importance of Shabbos Kodesh [the holy Sabbath], and even a few zemiros [songs], with these adorable figurines." While Christians in America have used toys for centuries to promote religious values, Yossi and Yanky are part of the relatively new—but flourishing—world of ultra-Orthodox Jewish toys.

Toys help us assess how religion is taught to children. Toys provide a hands-on way for young practitioners of religion to learn their religion's values. In this chapter, I overview the tools scholars have used for analyzing toys, and then look at recent ultra-Orthodox ("Haredi") Jewish engagements with the toy industry. Haredi affiliations with the toy industry might at first glance seem anachronistic, for while Orthodox Judaism is not intrinsically opposed to toys, ultra-Orthodox Jews tend to see religion and secular culture as incompatible. Orthodox Jews in general believe both the written and oral Torahs were revealed at Mount Sinai. Thus Orthodox Jews consider Jewish law binding. Consequently Orthodox practice is characterized by refraining from the thirty-nine categories of activity prohibited on the Sabbath, keeping kosher, and a variety of other Torah-based commandments. Ultra-Orthodox Judaism is an offshoot of Orthodoxy that created protective circles ("fences") around Jewish practice in response to the Enlightenment and Jewish emancipation. Thus Haredi Jews not only adhere to Jewish law, but also see modern secular life as a threat to Orthodox practice. Hence they tend to separate themselves from modern society. Ultra-Orthodox Judaism is composed of a diverse range of groups, including various Hasidic sects, Litvak (Lithuanian) Jews, and certain Sephardic Jews (Jews of Iberian origin). While not all ultra-Orthodox sects are fervently messianic, they all adhere to the medieval Jewish philosopher Maimonides' Thirteen Principles of Faith, which include a belief in God's providence, and the arrival of the Messiah in the messianic age. Consequently Haredi Jews believe following of *mitzvoth* (Jewish commandments) will hasten the Messiah's arrival. In keeping with their desire to build a fence around the Torah, ultra-Orthodox Jews are also united by an emphasis on modest dress, head and hair coverings, family values, gender separation, cohesive neighborhoods, and a distrust of secular media.

In the past, Haredi communities have also often rejected certain modern toys because of the secular values the toys convey (Slifkin 2006: 36). Recently, however, Haredi Jews have changed their tactics and started creating toys that reinforce rather than undermine their religious traditions and values. Importantly these toys provide an alternative to the typical understanding of American Judaism in American mass culture. Haredi toys envision American Judaism as revolving around adherence to Jewish law in the home and synagogue, and by reading sacred books and helping people. That is, the toys promote religious, rather than cultural, Judaism. Toys represent one example of American fundamentalists' ability to adapt modern forms even as they adhere to a traditional way of life.

As early as the nineteenth century, American religious communities have used toys to maintain identities. Playthings, as Cross points out, introduce "the young to the tools, experiences, and even emotional lives of their parents" (1997: 14), including their religious lives. In an odd way, toys are extremely dependent upon adult desires. Although toys are designed to appeal to children, adults typically purchase toys. Hence appealing to parents' "hopes and fears" has become a multi-million dollar industry (Norris 2011: 190). Norris reminds us that the "idea that children *need* to have the correct toys in order to develop properly is now well developed in American and

British cultures" (2011: 192). When looking at the intersection of religion toys, two different levels of analysis are important: (1) the gaming strategies taught by toys, and (2) the theological narratives toys impart. In the following sections, I use these two levels to analyze several two recent popular Haredi toys: *Binyan Blocks* and *Mitzvah Kinder*. I conclude by thinking about how toys structure plausibility alignment between generations.

Gaming strategies and *Binyan Blocks*

Religious toys, like other games, present a microcosm of how people understand the structural order and regulation of the universe. As literary critic Gregory Jackson remarks about the 1875 *Pilgrim's Progress Board Game*, children's games simplify and "crudely schematize" the rules through which life is understood (2013: 453). In this sense, toys implicitly value specific game theories. Most broadly understood, "game theory" refers to the science of understanding how humans, or animals, or computers make logical decisions. Board games such as *Life* or *Monopoly*, for example, present the adult world as a "zero-sum game," in which players battle for limited resources. If one participant is to win, all others must lose. In contrast, certain newer games, such as the *Lord of the Rings Board Game*, require collaborative work to win. Like many role-playing games, the *Lord of the Rings Board Game* teaches children that succeeding in life and defeating evil requires cooperative strategies. While Bado and Norris found that many Christian games were modeled on secular zero-sum race games (2015: 262), the ultra-Orthodox toys I discuss in this article encourage children to envision life as a non-zero-sum game. Yet, unlike the *Lord of the Rings Board Game* and non-zero-sum secular role-playing games that transport children into an alternate, imagined, and ultimately unreal realm, ultra-Orthodox toys insist upon the importance of playing the game of life in a world resembling our own. Moreover, unlike secular games, the play embedded in ultra-Orthodox toys is presented as radically transformative. In this section, I use the toy *Binyan Blocks* to show the non-zero-sum principle in action, with an eye towards the toy's messianic subtext.

Binyan Blocks encourage collaborative, coordinated acts as winning strategies that can better the world. Like their secular kin *LEGOS*, *Binyan* or "building" blocks are a plastic construction toy consisting of colorful, interlocking bricks and miniature figurines (Indeed *Binyan Blocks* can interlock with *LEGOS*). As the education branch of *LEGO* explains, *LEGOS* encourage "creative development through collaboration," as well as "problem solving, decision making, and remembering" (Whole-child development 2015). Indeed, the ShareCollab foundation in Columbia has used a "*LEGO*® SERIOUS PLAY®" methodology" not only to "enhance innovation and business performance," but also to "facilitate the creation of a community that thinks and acts for collaborative Economy" (Palacios, 2015). Similarly *LEGO* therapy has been used to improve collaborative behaviors in children on the autism spectrum (Huskens et al. 2015).

Binyan Blocks' collaborative message is serious play. As Hasidic theologian Crispe (2010) explains, in ultra-Orthodox Judaism, humanity's goal is *not* to live life as a zero-sum-game. Although a materialistic, primitive, "hunter-gatherer principle" may encourage people to see resources as finite, a higher, spiritually-based vision of the world reveals that only when we coordinate and collaborate that we can grow spiritually. Indeed, in this spiritual vision of the universe, the pool of resources *increases* any time humans engage in positive collaboration. Thus in order for the higher levels of an individual's soul to develop, collaboration is necessary. Equally significant, while the unredeemed world is characterized by zero-sum game activities, we need to use non-zero-sum strategies to bring about the messianic age (Crispe 2010). The redemptive power of the non-zero-sum game underscores the play's power: mundane acts such as playing with toys allow children to do world-altering labor.

The collaborative projects fostered by *Binyan Blocks* reinforce the potentially transformative significance of building together. Like *LEGOS*, *Binyan Blocks* are themed. *LEGOS* have combined collaborative building with role playing, by marketing themed sets such as space, castles, robots, pirates, trains, dinosaurs, as well as storylines tied to popular children's books and media. Like secular role-playing games more generally, LEGO themes generally take children out of this world, and into a fantastical, fictional settings inhabited by non-human or "super human" beings. In contrast, the *Binyan Blocks* themes are set in the everyday world: a *shul* (synagogue), school bus, *sukkah* (temporary hut built for use during the week-long Jewish festival of Succot), "Shabbos Table," or Israeli rescue vehicles. Importantly these scenes all require collaboration once built: a synagogue requires a *minyan*–that is, a quorum of ten adult men–for prayer, and hence includes "10 *Heimishe* [friendly] people." Likewise the Sabbath dinner table and *sukkah* all are explicitly designed to be places families and friends can congregate. The *shomrim, chaverim*, and *hatzolah* rescue-working volunteers are all engaged in protecting and aiding communities. All of these collaborative activities center around completing *mitzvoth*, that is doing acts that will help redeem and perfect the world. *Binyan Blocks* teach children that to win the game of life, one must collaborate and help others. When we collaborate, we all win, and we bring about the age of the messiah.

The theological narratives of *Mitzvah Kinder*

In addition to teaching children the rules governing life and the universe, religious toys teach children important theological narratives. Through play, children perform these narratives, and thereby practice life stories. Games often teach children religious narratives through a board game structure. The first American board game *The Mansion to Happiness* (1843), for example, led children through a story of life in which "players hop along the spiral board, moving forward toward the mansion of happiness if they land on temperance or generosity, backward to the pillory if they land on idleness or immodesty" (Early Board Game 2010). Likewise games such as the *Pilgrim's Progress*

Board Game (1875) "emphasize the incremental nature of the Christian journey by highlighting a spatiotemporal landscape that mapped the space between the material life and spiritual consequences" (Jackson 2013: 461). Yet games do not need to have a board in order to convey theological narratives. In this section I look at the toy sets to which Yossi and his *Mitzvah Kinder* companions belong. *Mitzvah Kinder*, I argue, contain important theological narratives about gender and diversity within the Haredi world.

Mitzvah Kinder encourage children to perform ultra-Orthodox religious narratives that contrast with the narratives embedded in secular toys. The name "*Mitzvah Kinder*" combines the Hebrew *mitzvah,* meaning a divine commandment or "good deed," with the Yiddish word for children, *kinder*. If *Binyan Blocks* rethink *LEGOS* to fit within a Haredi worldview, *Mitzvah Kinder's* closest secular cousins are the Fisher Price *Little People*. Like *Little People*, *Mitzvah Kinder* are small plastic figurines aimed at toddlers. Also like *Little People*, *Mitzvah Kinder* come in sets or "themes," many of which have embedded narratives. *Little People* themes include, farm, city and town, zoo, Disney Princess, Disney Movie Classics, and Holidays sets. While in the past Fisher Price has reached out to Jews by creating Jewish holiday sets, in 2015 all of the Holiday sets were either explicitly Christian (Nativity, Christmas Tree, Easter), or secular American (Halloween, Thanksgiving, St. Patrick's Day, Fourth of July). Although none of the *Little People* themed sets are narrative neutral, the Disney Princess sets most explicitly teach secular stories about gender. As Karen Wohlwend explains, "During play with Disney Princess toys, children reenact film scripts and expectations for each princess character, quoting memorized dialogue or singing songs from the films as they talk in-character" (2009: 57–58). Disney Princess play sets teach children gendered stories. Although children are always free to improvise with given narratives and revise expectations for "character actions," in general the dolls, "index identity texts from damsel-in-distress fairy tales with princess victims and princely rescuers, a classic trope in children's literature and play that "prepare[s] the ground for the insertion of the little girl into romantic heterosexuality'." (Wohlwend 2009: 59). In addition, the princess narrative emphasizes "gendered talk" that includes "*wearing femininity, body movements* [e.g. twirling (hair or skirt), curtseying], *make-up, beauty,* and *fashion talk*" (Wohlwend 2009: 60; emphasis in the original).

While *Mitzvah Kinder* themed sets also often contain narratives, their narratives are explicitly religious. *Mitzvah Kinder's* holiday themes, for example, are Jewish: for example, Purim, Chanukah, and Shabbat. Other themes include families, a *Seforim* [religious book] Room, *Shul* [synagogue], *Chasuna* [Engagement], Mommy Mentchees, Totty [Father] Mentchees, *Chosson/Kallah* [Groom/Bride], and a mixed gender group of "Mitzvah Mentchen." These names suggest roles for children to enact. *Mentch* (pl. *menches or menchen*), for example, is Yiddish for "human being," but is used colloquially for a good person, or a person who is good to other people. Thus, the Mommy and Totty Mentchees sets suggest that being a Haredi mother or father is connected to performing good deeds.

Like the Disney Princess *Little People* sets, many of the *Mitzvah Kinder* sets are embedded with gender narratives. However rather than encouraging children to perform a "princess narrative," these sets encourage young girls to enact the narrative of the *Eshes Chayil* (Woman of Valor) from Proverbs 31, a parable familiar to all Haredi children from the Friday night song sung at the beginning of the Sabbath meal. As Rebbetzin Tziporah Heller notes, the "*Eshes Chayil* is the ideal woman" (1993: 67). She is "a woman whose spirituality is totally reflected in her deeds, and this is part and parcel of her being" (1993: 67). Such a woman is strong, not weak, and has an "equal right to influence others," albeit in ways that are deemed appropriately feminine (Aiken 1992: 29). While much has been made about the restrictive nature of ultra-Orthodox gender roles, ironically *Mitzvah Kinder* provide more active–and positive–gender roles than secular Disney Princess sets. In contrast to *Little People*, for example, older women are explicitly honored as "Mentchees" who fulfill important social roles, pray, and do *mitzvoth*. Moreover, *Mitzvah Kinder* reveal less of a youth-centric vision of female beauty. Although all adult *Mitzvah Kinder* women cover their hair, some do so with attractive gray wigs. Adult women are depicted as pleasantly plump *and* happy. This contrasts sharply with the Disney Princess storyline in which "Older women are either backgrounded as loving (preferably deceased) mothers...[or] vilified as evil femme fatales or ugly hags" (Wohlwend 2009: 59). Moreover, the *Eshes Chayil* actions are cosmically important, since she makes a "fundamental contribution that brings the Messiah" every time she performs acts of loving kindness, whether giving charity, being a good host, visiting the sick, encouraging learning, and raising Jewish children (Aiken 1992: 62). The "gendered talk" of *Mitzvah Kinder* does not involve make-up, beauty, fashion, or being rescued by men; rather, women are envisioned as partners in reforming the world.

In addition to encouraging women to see their actions as important, the sets reinforce theological narratives about diversity. While *Little People* tend to promote racial diversity, *Mitzvah Kinder* promote the religious diversity found in the Haredi world, and encourage a non-competitive, collaborative model of Haredi observance. For example, certain collections, such as *Totty Menchees Go To Shul* display a wide range of male headgear from *streimels* to *kolpiks* to *spodiks* to fedoras to homburgs and suggest such diversity might be found within a single Haredi congregation. This diversity is more than a marketing ploy, but rather reflects both a respect for different customs within Orthodoxy and an increasing religious sense of the bonds connecting ultra-Orthodox Jews together politically and socially. *Mitzvah Kinder* women, for example, accurately display the diversity of opinions within Haredi communities about how laws regarding the covering of hair can be kept, whether women use a *sheitl* (wig), *tichel* (head scarf), *snood* (thick hair net), or *sheitl* topped with the type of small cap. While the nuances of the clothing codes distinguishing various subsets of Haredi families available in the figurines should be fairly obvious to insiders, *Mitzvah Kinder* also usefully identifies what type of Haredi family presented in each set, for example Litvish, Hasidic, Yeshivishe, and Lubavitch. This attention to the diversity among Haredi Jews reflects the upswing of pan-Haredi political, cultural, and religious organizations in the twentieth and twenty-first centuries. In Israel, for example, Haredi Jews have bonded together politically in the *Agudat Israel* and *Degel HaTorah* parties in order to have more sway in the Knesset. Likewise the pan-Haredi organization *Agudath Israel*, established in 1912, helps connect Haredi Jews in the United States. *Agudath Israel* not only serves as a political lobby, but also oversees synagogues, camps, and many educational institutions. Pan-Haredi magazines such as *Mishpacha* (Family) help reinforce a sense of a collective mission in changing the world, while simultaneously respecting and embracing the diversity of the Haredi experience as modeled in *Mitzvah Kinder*. Just as non-zero-sum games encourage collaboration, so too toys like *Mitzvah Kinder* allow children to begin the work of Haredi community-building at an early age.

Conclusion

Although many Haredi communities in Europe were destroyed during the Holocaust, remnants of these communities fled to the United States and Israel, and following the war they began the important work of rebuilding what was lost. By creating toys that embody religious values and narratives, Haredi Jews maintain a vision of the world that they brought with them to these new locations. Toys are a crucial example of "plausibility alignment": they are a way Haredi Jews can maintain a correspondence between their own worldviews and "information impinging on the group from the social context in which it resides" (Piff and Warburg 2005: 86). By reworking American popular culture to meet Haredi worldviews, ultra-Orthodox Jews pass along to their children the important role Haredim play in the post-Holocaust world. Through toys, children learn that even their most mundane acts can change the world for the better and hasten redemption.

References

Aiken, L. (1992), *To Be a Jewish Woman*, Northvale, NJ: Jason Aronson.

Bado, N. and Norris, R.S. (2015), "Games and Dolls," in J. Lyden and E. Mazur (eds), *The Routledge Companion to Religion and Popular Culture*, 261–280, New York: Routledge.

Crispe, A. (2010, December), *From Zero to Non-Zero Sum Games—Globalization & the End of Work. Lesson 2 -Globalization & the End of Work* [Video File]. Available online: http://www.chabad.org/multimedia/media_cdo/aid/912270/jewish/From-Zero-to-Non-Zero-Sum-Games.htm (accessed 8 August 2016).

Cross, G. (1997), *Kids' Stuff: Toys and the Changing World of American Childhood*, Cambridge, MA: Harvard University Press.

Early board game (reason): American treasures of the Library of Congress (2010). Available online: http://www.loc.gov/exhibits/treasures/trr171.html

Heller, T. (1993), *More Precious than Pearls: Selected Insights into the Qualities of the Ideal Woman*, Jerusalem: Feldheim.

Huskens, B., Palmen, A., Van de Werff, M., Lourens, T., and Barakova, E. (2015), "Improving Collaborative Play Between Children with Autism Spectrum Disorders and their Siblings: The Effectiveness of a Robot-mediated Intervention Based on LEGO(®) Therapy," *Journal of Autism and Developmental Disorders* 45 (11): 3746–3755. Available online: doi: 10.1007/s10803-014-2326-0.

Jackson, G.S. (2013), "A Game Theory of Evangelical Fiction," *Critical Inquiry* 39 (3): 451–485. Available online: doi:10.1086/670041.

Norris, R.S. (2011), "The Battle for the Toy Box: Marketing and Play in the Development of Children's Religious Identities," in S.B. Ridgely (ed.), *The Study of Children in Religions: A Methods Handbook*, 189–201, New York: New York University Press.

Palacios, G. (June 22, 2015), "Lego Serious Play & Collaborative Economy—Collaborative Consumption," Available online: http://www.collaborativeconsumption.com/2015/06/22/lego-serious-play-collaborative-economy/

Piff, D. and Warburg, M. (2005), "Seeking for Truth: Plausibility Alignment on a Baha'i Email List," in M. Hojsgaard and M. Warburg (eds), *Religion and Cyberspace*, 86–101, London: Routledge.

Slifkin, N. (2006), *Man and Beast: Our Relationships with Animals in Jewish Law and Thought*, Bet Shemesh, Israel: Zoo Torah.

"Whole-child development: creative development through collaboration" (2015), Available online: https://education.lego.com/en/lesi/preschool/getting-started/whole-child-development

Wohlwend, K.E. (2009), "Damsels in Discourse: Girls Consuming and Producing Identity Texts Through Disney Princess Play," *Reading Research Quarterly* 44 (1): 57–83.

38

Classrooms as Spaces of Everyday Religious and Moral Education and Socialization

Stephen G. Parker

Stephen Parker began to explore the implications of the spatial dynamics of schools in values formation in an article entitled "Theorizing sacred space in educational contexts: a case study of three English Midlands Sixth Form Colleges" (Parker 2009). In this chapter, he focuses upon classrooms as sites of learning about religion, providing some examples of historic and present-day examples religious education classrooms from the English context. He concentrates particularly upon the spatial and material culture and aesthetics of classrooms, and argues that religious education classrooms offer indications of the "everyday" of religious education and pedagogy, which need to be taken into account in any reconstruction of the actualities of the subject.

Introduction

I still recall many of the details of the most striking of religious education (RE) classrooms of the comprehensive secondary school I attended in late 1970s Birmingham.[1] Despite the shifts in emphasis in the RE curriculum occurring at the time, from one dubbed as confessional to another denoted a world religions approach (Parker and Freathy 2011,2012), Christianity remained the major focus in my experience as a pupil. My classroom walls were quite literally plastered with posters—sourced, I would think, from the local Christian bookshop—along with a few pieces of children's writing and art. One poster I vividly remember was of a famous footballer surrounded by adoring fans, which rhetorically questioned, "so you think you don't worship?"; another of a cute animal reassured everyone present of God's love. The former resonated with a phenomenological approach to RE, the latter made an appeal to any latent Christianity.

For every lesson, the teacher, who was particularly skilled at drawing, had pre-prepared chalk-drawn characters from the Bible story to be studied that day onto a sliding blackboard, which enabled him to hide or reveal the next stage of the lesson. On another occasion tables were neatly laid out—as if for an exhibit in a shop or museum—with books and objects relating to a particular religion for students to discover and handle. Further, making use of a red telephone and a reel-to-reel tape recorder—which he then left on display as a reminder—the teacher enacted a "phone conversation to God." A slide projector was sometimes used to show us images of the "Holy Land," and other places of religious association that came up during lessons.

Although we did not sing in every RE period (we had just one hour's religious education per week), the guitar was always close to hand. The popular Christian choruses "Give me Oil in My Lamp" or "Lord of the Dance" were amongst the favorites. The Bible was always on the teacher's desk, and sets of Bibles were shelved and available for all to consult. In many respects the classroom enacted the RE on offer, as well as the values of the teacher who taught it. The teacher was earnest in his presentation of religion as something to be seriously engaged with; thoughtfully, and in a spirit of respect, whatever one in the end concluded. Although we generally sat in rows (the teacher wanted our gaze and concentration to be upon him and what he had to say), his interactions were individual and caring, all communicated by the warm and interactive classroom environment he had created. On reflection, it mattered to me that what I experienced in my lessons did not jar too much with the religious education I had received at church. Christianity was the curricular norm in the discourse, and in the visual, material and even aural culture of the classroom, and this offered some reassurance to my young self.

I mention these recollections to underline the principal argument of this chapter, that the RE I received was more than my few brief lessons (which I recall very little of). Rather the RE I experienced in that classroom was one which impacted upon and was imbibed by all of my senses. This was enacted within the spatial, material and aesthetic culture of the particular classroom, the environment and technologies of which were orchestrated by the teacher. Moreover, the everyday religious education performed there was complex, multi-faceted and multi-layered: knowledge about religion was mediated in multiple ways using the technologies of the time (by chalk-board, slides and tape recorder, for instance), but at the same time reflected elements of the discourse going on beyond the classroom, both in terms of the study of religion, and debates going on within religious education (Parker and Freathy 2012).

This chapter addresses the everyday religious education potentially discernible from such memories, and other more tangible sources of RE classrooms in photographs and film. Such evidence of the everyday details of RE classrooms, I argue here, has the potential to lay bare the hidden agenda behind such contemporary notions of the religious education classroom as "sacred space" or "safe space."

The classroom as a technology and window onto pedagogy

It is now widely acknowledged, drawing upon Foucault and also Actor-Network-Theory, that the architecture and layout of schools and classrooms is powerful in shaping the work of teachers, as well the learning and social experiences of students (Grosvenor et al.1999; Lawn and Grosvenor 2005; Simons and Masschelein 2008; Parker 2009; Masschelein and Simons 2013). When viewed as part of the "social technology" of schooling, that is as "an actor in a network of which it is part" (Lawn 1999: 78), including teachers, rules, artifacts, displays, computers, and so on, classrooms can be seen to provide rich insights for understanding the character of education in particular times and places. Of course, this observation is no less true of religious education classrooms, both historically and in the contemporary. My remembered classroom is a case in point. From the emphases underlined by the content of the visual culture (for instance, posters and blackboard art), the aural culture (for instance, Christian choruses sung), and the material culture (for instance, the use of new technologies to reinforce the possibility of a "conversation with God"), much can be discerned about the nature of religious education I as a pupil was invited to participate in and engage with. This recollected experience, for instance, belies the arguments going on outside classrooms of the period around the place of world religions in the religious education curriculum. Nor was the problematic of teacher commitment and bias in teaching the subject, much in the wider discourses of religious education (see for example, Hulme 1979), an apparently troublesome feature of classroom life at the time. Was this due to sluggishness in the appropriation of curriculum reform, or does it indicate a resistance on the part of the school/department/teacher to these agenda?

Everyday religious education is not simply what teachers do (their teaching methods), or what they teach (the curriculum), it is what actually happens within the classroom, the artifacts teachers deploy, and the physical, material and aesthetics of the environment they create (or which are created for them) that make up their pedagogy: it is these, together with the responses of students, which constitute everyday religious education. With a focus upon what happens between the teacher and the child, and the emphases in religious education upon the nature and character of the curriculum, the wider dynamics are often forgotten by educationalists.[2] Such spaces can, however, be "read" and investigated. They reveal the sometimes unarticulated values and principles operating around the religious education teacher, as well as those actioned by them.

From the Edwardian Sunday School to the contemporary classroom

The Sunday-School reformers of the early twentieth century, George Hamilton Archibald, and his daughter Ethel Archibald, understood and stressed the importance of the physical environment to the religious and moral education reforms they sought. "It is harder for a child to be naughty in a clean, bright, attractive place" wrote Ethel Archibald in her book of 1912, "where the child feels that all around him is beautiful and at peace, he is far less likely to be peevish or perverse" (Archibald 1912: 34–5). Writing in considerable detail to describe the classroom space which needed to be created for religious education, she penned:

> at least 35 feet square. All rooms should have high ceilings, and be bright and well-ventilated. The walls should be decorated in such a way that the pictures which the children love may show up to the best advantage. Noiseless block floors are preferable to any others, but where these cannot be had the floor should be carpeted or covered with matting or linoleum. For seating there should be a hundred small chairs of at least three heights. The feet of each child should rest upon the floor, while he sits well back in the chair. The teachers' chairs should be of the same height as those of the children in their classes....There should be no platform of any sort in any of the rooms....The rooms in which the children meet for their service should be beautiful and comfortable. The colour-scheme of a room is a most important consideration. Pictures should be there, pictures of nature's beauties, pictures of heroes, pictures which the children can appreciate and which silently retell stories of noble deeds and tender emotions. It is well to have at least some of these in colour; bright things appeal strongly to the children; but the colouring must be good, for it is possible to kill all sense of colour harmony in the children by allowing them to gaze upon crude and harsh colour combinations...the chairs must be the right size, so that the little ones will not be wearied and driven to ill-temper by awkward or cramped position. It is most desirable that both children and teachers should remove cloaks and hats before the school session. In this way much physical inconvenience and one great cause of fussing and restlessness are done away with. It is exceedingly difficult to get an atmosphere of reverence and devotion in a room where children are allowed to talk and play before the beginning of the session. Such a room cannot be turned instantly into a place of worship...our rooms must be orderly. Everything should be ready beforehand (Archibald 1912: 20–1; 35–6).

Prioritising children and their religious education in Sunday Schools for the Archibalds meant investing in purpose-built spaces and the latest resources, which at least half the Sunday Schools of the period managed to achieve (Cliff 1986: 221). For the Archibalds the classroom surroundings helped to shape children's moral and religious sensibilities. In this they also paid attention to children's physical bodies and to the feelings invoked by being in the classroom space. The images below of the model Edwardian Sunday

School the Archibalds established at Bournville in Birmingham in the early 1900s indicate this. The photographs create the impression of a pristine environment with which the Archibalds' model pedagogy was being trialled. Figure 38.1 shows it to be a well-lit space: light having many connotations, including being associated with enlightenment and the natural world, in opposition to industrialization since Rousseau (Burke 2005: 130). Its flexible arrangement shows it can be set up when necessary to have the children sitting around an only slightly raised teacher's dais. These stand-alone desks on some occasions fix the children's gaze on the teacher, and on what the teacher wishes the children to attend to, which the teacher can display in chalk-on-board. Unlike the fixed, stiff rows of desks one might typically see in iconic photographs of the period, the Archibalds' classroom is intimate, individual, and has a degree of informality. The classroom is marked by spaciousness, high ceilings, and the potential freedom to move around. The French doors enable the classroom to be opened to the world beyond it. In George Archibald's understanding of religious education (as can be seen from Chapter 13) play and access to the natural environment were essential. Nature here is brought into the classroom by way of flowers and plants. The classroom is equipped with a piano and regular singing was a regular feature of any Sunday School, and a fundamental part of everyday religious life of the period.

FIGURE 38.1 *Image of the model Sunday School classroom at Westhill, Birmingham supplied courtesy of the Cadbury Research Library, University of Birmingham, UK, reference: WC Box 217.*

George Hamilton Archibald's focus upon the child (influenced by Friedrich Froebel), is strongly conveyed by Figure 38.2, which depicts interaction between teachers and children, as well as group and individual activities. Differentiation of activity, dependent upon the age and interest of the child, were part of the graded approach the Archibalds promoted. In this context the ideal was that the teacher worked with different, small, groups of children. Ethel Archibald suggested a high staff ratio to children to enable this, one adult for every two children (Archibald 1912: 19). The focus in these "graded" (differentiated) lessons was upon nature study and Bible stories, discussion, imaginative play, and creative responses. Ethel Archibald provided a detailed list of the "requisite paraphernalia" for the classroom, basic by today's standards but clearly a significant investment of resource, each item functioning within the pedagogy being proposed. They were a piano, a table for the secretary and superintendent, a cupboard to hold materials for teaching and those produced by the children, a blackboard, white and coloured chalk, dusters, white paper for drawing, pencils and crayons, "mill-boards" for drawing (one for each child), a large sand-tray and 48 individual trays, sand, small blocks for the sand-trays, plasticine, cradle-roll materials, pictures for wall decoration, cards and books for recording attendance, vases for flowers and nature specimens, small tables for the kindergarteners.

Here the classroom walls have children's art clearly on display, mounted on paper to professionalize its impression. Other pictures adorn the walls, noticeably at child's eye-level. Though the content of these is hard to make out, undoubtedly, from Ethel

FIGURE 38.2 *Image of the model Sunday School classroom at Westhill, Birmingham supplied courtesy of the Cadbury Research Library, University of Birmingham, UK, reference: WC Box 217.*

Archibald's comments above, these would relate to reinforcing the subject-matter children had been discussing with their teachers. These sepia images belie an intention to create a visually appealing environment, perhaps one which brought colour into the lives of children.

The contemporary RE classroom

The furnishings and space as depicted by image three, of a contemporary English Secondary school (age 11–18) RE classroom, provide a contrasting impression of everyday religious education. Children in this space are meant to be seated at grouped desks, and it is this furniture which takes up the majority of the available area of the room. School desks have their own design history, reflecting changing pedagogical imperatives (Martinez 2005). The standard design here, of a flat shared desk, is commonplace in contemporary classrooms. Grouping children in RE classrooms reflects discussion as a key practice in the subject. Indeed, one of the reasons for the subject's popularity amongst students is the opportunities it presents for discussion and debate (Conroy et al. 2013: 96). Noticeably, the children's gaze is set towards one another, not the teacher or the electronic whiteboard, even the blackboard here having lost its original use. This physical setting implies that knowledge about religion and morality is formed in the discourse between children. Much of this reflects how the RE teacher is currently constructed as a professional, someone who promotes reasonable debate, respect for others, and a non-judgmental attitude.[3]

The wall displays in the classroom, on understandings of community, branches of philosophy, and "challenge wall" activities to rehearse knowledge towards the completion of an exam in the subject, function to stimulate thinking and reinforce learning (see Figure 38.3). Again these codify the subject as open and exploratory,

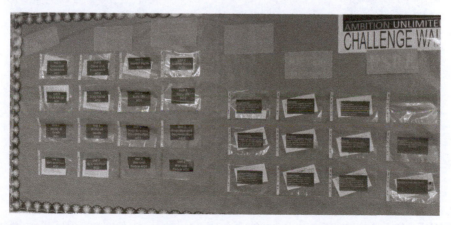

FIGURE 38.3 *Wall display in a contemporary RE classroom. With thanks to Danielle Evans for this image from her RE classroom.*

one which places the initiative in learning upon the child as an individual in pursuit of investigative questions. The teacher's role and function in a very similar discursive-oriented classroom space is aptly depicted in the recruitment video for RE teachers to be found here: https://www.youtube.com/watch?v=SzvZTFmp6qc&sns=em (accessed October 2015).

In the corner of the classroom (Figure 38.4) are a range of artifacts from differing religions presented together where children may study and handle them. The use of religious artifacts as a vehicle for religious education has been a recommended practice for some time (Gateshill and Thompson 1992). Though not without critique for its tendency to abstract sometimes venerated objects from the religious context which makes them meaningful (Homan 2000), the practice is now widespread as a way of bringing the ostensibly religious into the classroom. The classroom thereby becomes a site in which the phenomenon of religion, and the multiple religious and moral questions around it, can be explored, investigated and debated "safely." Indeed, the notion of the religious education classroom as a "safe space" is one used to describe the political and pedagogical position of religious education classrooms across Europe at a time when religion is perceived to be problematic (Miller 2013; Jackson 2014). Even so, it is far from certain whether students find their classrooms to be safe spaces, or indeed that the everyday religious education enacted in the classroom coheres with that experienced beyond the school (Moulin 2015).

FIGURE 38.4 *A contemporary Religious Education classroom, England 2015. With thanks to Danielle Evans for this image from her RE classroom.*

Religious education classrooms as "sacred space"

Where religious education classrooms are extensions of a religious community (Sunday Schools or madrasa, for example) they might legitimately be described as "sacred spaces," it is clearly more problematic to extend such a definition of them to religious education classrooms in state-funded non-religious schools. However, as Lily Kong has posited of museums, perhaps religious education classrooms may be regarded as "unofficial sacred spaces," particularly in the sense that they are "implicated in 'story-telling' about religions and religious groups, and are sometimes the site of display of religious art and artefacts" (Kong 2005: 496). That religious education classrooms be regarded as "safe spaces" lends support to their unofficial sacredness, imputing them with a quasi-confession like ethic of secrecy. This blurring of the distinction between the sacred and the secular is even more acute in English schooling because of the persistent legal requirement to provide a daily act of collective worship in all maintained schools.

Conclusion

Everyday religious education can be read and known by adopting a critical gaze upon extant photographic and filmic examples of them. In this context, much can be learned about the dynamics of the religious education on offer in such spaces, and by extension the genealogy of influences which the social technology of the classroom serves to enact in the dynamic of teacher and pupils.

Notes

1 The term "religious education classroom" is here understood to mean those sites dedicated to religiously education (whether permanent or temporary) in a context for formal learning (a school, Sunday school or madrasa, for instance), whilst understanding that there are espoused differences between such sites.

2 Perhaps this is also bound up with the Protestant history of the construction of religion, which focuses on "belief" at the expense bodies/practice/objects, so that RE has tended to focus on beliefs, and therefore so has research on RE.

3 See for instance how the Practice Code for Teachers of RE constructs the professional role of teachers: http://religiouseducationcouncil.org.uk/media/file/Practice_Code_for_Teachers_of_RE.pdf (accessed October 2015).

References

Archibald, Ethel J. (1912), *The Decentralised Sunday School Primary Department*, London: Pilgrim Press.

Burke, C. (2005), "Light: Metaphor and Materiality in the History of Schooling," in M. Lawn and I. Grosvenor (eds), *Materialities of Schooling: Design, Technology, Objects, Routines*, Cambridge: Symposium.

Cliff, P. (1986), *The Rise and Development of the Sunday School Movement in England, 1780–1980*, Surrey: National Christian Education Council.

Conroy, J. et al. (2013), *Does Religious Education Work? A Multidimensional Investigation*, London: Bloomsbury.

Gateshill, P. and Thompson, J. (1992), *Religious Artefacts in the Classroom*, London: Hodder and Stoughton.

Grosvenor, I., Lawn, M., and Rousmaniere, K. (eds) (1999), *Silences and Images: The Social History of the Classroom*, New York: Peter Lang.

Homan, R. (2000), "Don't Let the Murti Get Dirty: The Uses and Abuses of Religious 'artefacts'," *British Journal of Religious Education* 23 (1): 27–37.

Hulme, E. (1979), *Commitment and Neutrality in Religious Education*, London: Geoffrey Chapman.

Jackson, R. (2014), *Signposts: Policy and Practise for Teaching About Religions and Non-religious Worldviews in Intercultural Education*, Oslo: Council of Europe.

Kong, L. (2005) "Re-presenting the Religious: Nation, Community and Identity in Museums," *Social & Cultural Geography*, 6 (4): 495–513.

Lawn, M. and Grosvenor, I. (eds) (2005), *Materialities of Schooling: Design, Technology, Objects, Routines*, Cambridge: Symposium.

Martinez, P.L.M. (2005), "History of School Desk Development in Terms of Hygiene and Pedagogy in Spain (1838–1936)," in M. Lawn and I. Grosvenor (eds), *Materialities of Schooling: Design, Technology, Objects, Routines*, Cambridge: Symposium.

Masschelein, J. and Simons, M. (2013), *In Defence of the School: A Public Issue*, Leuven: Education, Culture and Society Publishers.

Miller, J. (2013), "Religious Extremism, Religious Education and the Interpretive Approach," in J. Miller, U. McKenna, and K. O'Grady (eds), *Religion in Education: Innovations in International Research*, London: Routledge.

Moulin, D. (2015), "Reported Schooling Experiences of Adolescent Jews Attending Non-Jewish Secondary Schools in England," *Race Ethnicity and Education* 19 (4): 683–705, published online.

Parker, S.G. (2009), "Theorizing Sacred Space in Educational Contexts: A Case Study of Three English Midlands Sixth Form Colleges," *Journal of Beliefs and Values: Studies in Religion and Education* 30 (1): 29–39.

Parker and Freathy (2011), "Context, Complexity and Contestation: Birmingham's Agreed Syllabuses Since the 1960s," *Journal of Beliefs and Values: Studies in Religion and Education* 32 (2): 247–263.

Parker and Freathy (2012), "Ethnic Diversity, Christian Hegemony and the Emergence of Multi-faith Religious Education in the 1970s,'" *History of Education: Journal of the History of Education Society* 41 (3): 381–404.

Simons, M. and Masschelein, J. (2008), "From Schools to Learning Environments: The Dark Side of Being Exceptional," *Journal of Philosophy of Education* 42 (3–4): 687–704.

PART FIVE

Religious Discipline and the Agency and Domination of Childhood

Introduction

We learned in 1978 in Jonestown, Guyana, and again on September 11th in Manhattan's financial district that "religion is not nice; it has been responsible for more death and suffering than any other human activity" to quote Religious Theorist Jonathan Z. Smith, writing in response to the mass suicide/murder in Jonestown (1982: 110). Of course, some people knew this simple fact already in large and small ways, but for many others it took large-scale events to start to decouple morality and religion. By the turn of the Millennium, the sex abuse scandal in the Catholic Church also began to get widespread coverage, first in Ireland, then the US and elsewhere. Evidence seemed to be mounting that religious people did not posses exclusive access to morality; in fact adherence to a particular dogma might just as easily be leading them away from righteousness and towards it.

At the same time that institutional religions seemed to be losing some of their appeal, America and much of the secular West seemed fascinated by conservative, traditional, and group-oriented religious communities. For instance, in 2008, the cable television station TLC switched to a reality format that would soon bring its viewing audience a glimpse at the lives of children in non-liberal religious groups including the Amish, the conservative Christian Duggar family, the Fundamentalist Mormons, and the Gypsies seven nights a week. Each of these shows existed because of outsider interest in these traditions, yet the shows normalized their characters by largely ignoring their religious beliefs.

The desire to hear stories of religious lives without the theology, while we waded through tale after tale of the wrongdoings of priests (and Cardinals as they attempt to make the original criminal action disappear) seems a strange juxtaposition. Yet there were similarities: the stories of abuse tended to focus on the needs of the perpetrators more than the children who suffered the abuse; the stories of religious conservatives tended to emphasize authority and conformity within the family over strife and individual desires. As these stories were told day after day on television and in print, the lines between religion, discipline, submission, and domination seemed to blur.

What were we looking for in each television episode and newspaper headline? James Kincaid's *Erotic Innocence* (1998), excerpted in section one, argues, "Our storytelling has become so formulaic and so 'natural' that it channels far too much of our concern into self-gratification....Through the stories of what monsters are doing to our children, we find ourselves forced (permitted) to speak of just what it is they are doing....We denounce it loudly but never have done with it" (1998: 7). Nearly twenty years on, it seems, little changed. TLC was still telling the same story every half hour and religious communities were still struggling to find ways to ensure that their children were safe. The struggle came perhaps, from the media's choice to begin with the same old formula in an effort to try to find a new outcome. Kincaid argues, for instance, that we need different stories, different formulas, if we are to reach new conclusions.

The selections in this section are a first step to creating those new stories, stories that center children, their rights, and their desires. Three essays in this section deal specifically with issues of abuse. Gordon Lynch address the broad issues of abuse and neglect as a subject for inquiry in religious studies, particularly in how religious organizations are implicated in the abuse of children, how power dynamics within religious practices can lead to childhood trauma, and how religion or religious frameworks might be used in the expression of childhood trauma. While Lynch centers abuse generally, Zayn Kassam offers a specific examination of how Islam might be used to end the practice of recruiting child-soldiers and abusing girls and woman in the Sudan and elsewhere.

While the previous two essays offered a broad foundation to discuss abuse, the next two pieces focus specifically on the sex abuse crisis in the Roman Catholic Church. Susie Donnelly examines on how the changing definitions of childhood within the Catholic Church contributed to the abuse of young Catholics in Ireland. Similarly, Robert Orsi's piece explores American Catholic Culture from the 1950s through the 1980s and how it might have contributed to the sex abuse scandal that was made public in the 2000s. Further he offers insights into how a greater acknowledgement of children as Catholics in their own right might protect future generations of young practitioners.

Protecting and advocating for and with children is the theme of the three other essays in this section. In Rachel Taylor's piece, she examines the inherent tensions in the UNCRC between the rights of parents to rear their children according to their tradition and the child's right to religious freedom. Further, she queries whether this adult-authored document can adequately address the changing needs and alternate perspectives of children. Maya Mayblin continues that theme exploring children's perspectives in her study of child labour in Brazil. She examines the symbolic dimensions surrounding children's engagement in productive endeavours pushing for children's cultural contributions to be recognized by researchers as much as their economic contributions are currently. The excerpt from Ayala Fader's *Mitzvah Girls: Bringing Up the Next Generation of Hasidic Girls in Brooklyn* shifts the perspective of the previous essays from that of adult researchers advocating for children to how a young girls growing up in a strict, communal setting advocate for themselves through play, proper questioning, and other subtle, if effective, means.

References

Kincaid, James (1998), *Erotic Innocence: The Culture of Child Molesting*, Durham, NC: Duke University Press.

Smith, Jonathan Z. (1982), *Imagining Religion from Babylon to Jonestown*, Chicago: University of Chicago Press.

39

Historical Abuse, Trauma, and Public Acts of Moral Repair

Gordon Lynch

*G*ordon Lynch is Michael Ramsey Professor of Modern Theology at the University of Kent. He has written widely on moral meanings in modern societies, including The Sacred in the Modern World: A Cultural Sociological Approach *(Oxford University Press, 2012). His most recent book is* Remembering Child Migration: Faith, Nation-Building and the Wounds of Charity *(Bloomsbury Academic, 2015). In this chapter, he considers how we might conceive of public responses to historic child abuse drawing on concepts from the study of religion.*

Since the mid 1980s, the abuse of children in religious contexts has received increasing public attention. Much of this has focused on cases relating to the sexual abuse of children by individuals or groups working within religious organizations (see, e.g., Keenan 2012). But alongside this a growing number of inquiries and truth commissions have addressed wider forms of historic institutional abuse in which religious organizations operated in forms of child-care intervention with other State and voluntary agencies that have since been recognized as having caused significant and unjustifiable trauma (see, e.g., Daly 2014; Sköld and Swain 2015). Notable cases of these are native assimilationist policies in Canada and Australia (see Royal Commission on Aboriginal Peoples 1996; Human Rights and Equal Opportunity Commission 1997), including the role of native residential schools run by churches and religious orders (Truth and Reconciliation Commission of Canada 2015), child migration schemes (Parliamentary Health Select Committee 1998; Senate Community Affairs Committee 2001) and systems of residential child-care such as the industrial and reformatory school system in Ireland (Ryan Commission 2009). The public significance of these developments should not be under-estimated. Whilst the numbers of individual criminal convictions for historic child abuse in religious contexts has not been high, other forms of censure for religious organizations has had significant implications. In some cases, compensation packages have been offered to former victims of abuse amounting to substantial financial liabilities for churches and religious orders. The moral authority of religious organizations has also been challenged not only as cases of abuse have come to light, but greater scrutiny has been paid to the ways in which some organizations have sought to manage cases of abuse covertly to preserve their institutional reputation. The figure of the paedophile priest has come to symbolize the loss of moral standing for religious organizations in the context of a wider cultural turn away from deference to traditional institutional forms of authority. Alongside this, the institutional autonomy of religious organizations has been placed within clear limits of wider standards of child-care and protection to be implemented by the State. As the "Murphy Report" into clerical sexual abuse in the Archdiocese of Dublin concluded:

> The Commission has no doubt that clerical child sexual abuse was covered up by the Archdiocese of Dublin and other Church authorities over much of the period covered by the Commission's remit.... The State authorities facilitated the cover up by not fulfilling their responsibilities to ensure that the law was applied equally to all and allowing the Church institutions to be beyond the reach of the normal law enforcement processes.... It is the responsibility of the State to ensure that no similar institutional immunity is ever allowed to occur again. This can be ensured only if all institutions are open to scrutiny and not accorded an exempted status by any organs of the State. (Commission of Investigation into Catholic Archdiocese of Dublin 2009: 28)

Given the profound social, political, economic and cultural implications of these public responses to child abuse in religious contexts, it is remarkable that this has received relatively little attention amongst scholars of religion during this period. Whilst pastoral, practical and feminist theologians have written on this subject, there has been far less work done within the discipline of religious studies about how child abuse might be understood in relation to the contemporary and historical religious contexts in which it has taken place.

The aim of this chapter is not to engage in that particular task, which is addressed by other chapters in this Reader. Instead, it offers an alternative way in which we might conceive of public responses to historic child abuse drawing on concepts from the study of religion, in particular neo-Durkheimian approaches to the study of the sacred (see Alexander 2003; Lynch 2012a). The sacred, in this theoretical perspective, is understood in terms of symbols, practices and social interactions structured around deeply-charged moral meanings that can evoke shared moral emotions, generate compelling claims over individual and collective action and shape collective identities. These processes take place not simply in relation to assumed moral realities that are regarded as sacred, but in relation to forms of the evil-profane that threaten to pollute or destroy these sacred forms. Working within this approach, this chapter will introduce the argument that inquiries, truth commissions, apologies and redress schemes for historic child abuse operate not simply as legal or policy processes, but as symbolic interventions in public memory which seek to offer forms of moral repair against the profanation of child abuse. Understanding them in this way makes it possible to situate them in the broader context of projects of moral and civil repair that attempt to "fix the past," as well as to reflect on the implications of these normative intentions for their methods and outcomes. In doing so, it becomes possible to broaden the religious study of public responses to historic child abuse beyond those cases in which children experienced abuse in religious contexts (although these remain an important focus of study), to consider how public responses to child abuse more generally have become an important site for the performance of sacralized moral meanings.

This approach can be situated within a much wider scholarly interest in what Jeffrey Olick (2007) refers to as "social acts of remembering," public practices through which representations of the past are constructed and circulate. Within this wider interest in the study of public memory, the role of such social acts of remembering for achieving ameliorative political and social goals has become of particular interest in work on transitional justice. A central concern of the study of transitional justice is how institutionalized historic injustice may most appropriately be addressed. Whilst commonly discussed in the context of societies that have moved from authoritarian to democratic governments, in which earlier governance was characterized by systematic abuses of human rights, the notion of transitional justice is now also being applied to discussions of contemporary responses to historic injustices in established democracies (Winter 2014). Alongside discussion of the most appropriate legal responses to such historic injustices (Teitel 2000), there has also been interest in social practices of remembering, exemplified by the South African Truth and Reconciliation Commission, which provide public narrations of past trauma in order to effect therapeutic, symbolic or moral resolution in the present (Neumann and Thompson 2015). Inquiries, apologies, redress schemes and memorials are thus understood, in this context, in terms of a "politics of memory" in which social actors seek to shape public memory of historic trauma and injustice for normative ends (Barahona de Brita et al. 2001; Buckley-Zistel and Schafer 2014). Torpey (2006) has argued that these reparative acts constitute a relatively new expression of progressive politics, in which projects of social justice are focused on material compensation and symbolic recognition through the idiom of the past rather than the present or future. Alongside a growing number of individual case studies of these processes, efforts have also begun to be made critically to analyse wider issues and patterns across them, for example in relation to the forms and politics of public apologies for historic trauma (Celermajer 2009; Nobles 2008).

Inquiries, apologies and redress schemes relating to the historic abuse of children in out-of-home care have become an increasingly prevalent example of such reparative projects of public memory (see, e.g., Daly 2014; Sköld and Swain 2015). Although some of the earliest examples occurred in Australia and Canada, the majority have since been undertaken in Europe, which has now become a major hub of such work. Whilst usually performed within a clear legal framework, they do not usually lead directly to criminal prosecution and, in many cases, intentionally anonymize identities of individuals accused of perpetrating abuse. Instead, their aim is typically to provide a context in which victims of historic abuse are able to narrate their experiences in the hope that this will be both personally therapeutic and socially useful in developing public understanding of children's suffering. They are intended to function as morally reparative acts of public memory by identifying the broad class of social actors, structures and policies culpable for this suffering, offering statements of regret and recommending actions considered necessary for restitution of past wrong and prevention of future harm. Such inquiries into the abuse of children in out-of-home care have often, but not always, led to formal apologies by governments, churches, charities and other care providers, and, even less consistently, to systems of financial redress. Redress has varied from substantial financial settlements managed by quasi-legal reviews of individual cases to smaller and more purely symbolic financial gestures of restitution. These interventions function in a wider context of acts of public memory in relation to historic child abuse including news stories, documentaries, fictional films, plays, novels, autobiographies and memoirs which, in a number of cases, have created the social and political conditions in which inquiries, apologies and redress schemes have come to be seen as appropriate reparative acts.

As normative interventions into public memories of historic child abuse, intended to provide moral reparation for victims, these processes can be understood as performances of sacralized, humanitarian moral emotions. Humanitarian piety, directed towards the relief of human suffering, has become an increasingly influential form of moral emotion in the contemporary world, structuring social practices and identities, framing the construction of news media narratives and legitimising (or de-legitimising) public actions (Fassin 2011; Lynch 2012b). In this context, public recognition of specific instances of trauma for innocent victims has become an important means through which the moral emotions of humanitarian concern find expression (Fassin and Rechtman 2009). In the case of inquiries and truth commissions into historic child abuse, a central concern has been to create processes in which former victims feel able to come forward and narrate their own experiences of personal trauma, either through public hearings recorded for public dissemination or private, confidential hearings of which transcripts are not disseminated but more general findings are allowed to inform final conclusions. It is precisely this process of recognition that constitutes the moral reparation that inquiries, truth commissions, apologies and redress schemes claim to offer.

Recognition can, as Axel Honneth (1995) has argued, be seen as a central social and psychological basis for human well-being. Abuse in childhood constitutes a powerful failure of recognition because of the ways in which the child's experience is radically subsumed to adults' indifference, needs, desires or moral claims. Instances of childhood trauma involving separation from parents, siblings or friends (for example, through child migration schemes, native assimilationist programmes or other forms of incarceration in institutional care) constitute another significant rupture in which many children were displaced from relationships in which they experienced recognition to new relationships in which they did not. Recognition of individuals' historic suffering thus becomes the moral transaction at the heart of these interventions into public memory, a transaction infused with humanitarian intent. As Ronald Niezen (2013) has observed, in the context of the Truth and Reconciliation Commission of Canada's investigation of Indian Residential Schools, an explicit aim of its work was to deepen public understanding of former residents' suffering in these schools. The inability of the Commission to instigate criminal investigations of individual cases of abuse meant that its role, instead, become one of psychological and social recognition to those who had experienced trauma, humiliation and shame through this system of child-care. Inquiries and truth commissions are thus established as mechanisms through which recognition can take place, with apologies and redress schemes (in which financial compensation functions as much as a symbolic as material form of reparation) established as further remedial acts.

If a central aim of this moral transaction is to give recognition to victims, an inevitable accompaniment is to pass the moral censure implied in their humiliation and shame on to those held culpable for their abuse. Although not always the case, these processes typically seek to attribute blame less to individuals than to organizational actors (whether State, religious or other voluntary agencies) who are held responsible for operating systems in which children experienced trauma or for failing to respond appropriately to evidence of their abuse and neglect. As Bernhard Giesen (2004) has argued, the ability to absorb such moral censure and to recognize complicity in trauma is socially and psychologically challenging and is easier for subsequent generations who were not directly involved in the censured acts. The difficulty of this task is illustrated in the ways in which institutions respond to such moral censure. Whilst some offer complete apologies or damning indictments of their past practices, others provide apologies that are framed in general terms (whilst refuting most individual allegations of abuse) or situate the trauma in the memories of victims ("we are sorry if this is how you experienced it") rather than in their harmful actions or policies. Alternatively the trauma of accepting culpability for past abuse is institutionally managed by arguing that such abuse and neglect took place in a morally-distant past which, whilst abhorrent to our standards today, reflected how children were often treated "back then." Such attempts to contain past trauma in a morally-distant past typically neglect evidence that those child-care practices or systems were criticized at the time or that alternative approaches to child-care were possible (see, e.g., Lynch 2015).

It can be argued, then, that inquiries, truth commissions, apologies and redress schemes relating to historic child abuse are not simply acts of material compensation or historical record. They are also symbolic acts, moral rituals in which sacralized humanitarian intent underpins normative interventions in public memory to provide recognition to victims and censure to perpetrators. They merit further study amongst researchers working in religion and childhood because, as such, they represent key sites in which sacralized moral meanings shape the ways in which the experience of childhood is publicly represented. The ways in which religious organizations address the challenges of moral censure for their culpability in historic abuse also deserves more scholarly attention that it has so far received. But in addition to this, it is also important to reflect on whether these sacralized acts of moral repair for historic abuse necessarily achieve the positive normative outcomes to which they aspire. In cases, where inquiries and redress schemes are established on the basis of anonymising individuals alleged to have committed acts of abuse or institutional immunity from further legal action, does this unhelpfully foreclose the possibility of further criminal investigations or victims' ability to pursue legal redress? When inquiries access archival information from organizations under investigation, but rely on organizational summaries of that material or fail to make archival material available to public scrutiny (for example through placing it in closed repositories), does this hinder, rather than help, open processes of public reflection about these histories? If these acts of public memory are premised on moral transactions of recognition and censure, can this encourage public representations of historic child-care practices which emphasize traumatic experiences and occlude more positive ones, or which focus on childhood trauma more than on resilience? Can the intention to provide recognition of individual trauma run against the development of nuanced historical understanding? Do redress schemes necessarily achieve their reparative intent if they expose applicants to the further traumatising effects of adversarial questioning about their past experiences from review panels or legal representatives of accused organizations? What are the implications of highly public attempts to offer reparation for historic child abuse for those whose contexts or forms of childhood abuse and neglect are excluded from the terms of reference of inquiries, apologies or redress schemes?

To ask these questions is not to suggest that inquiries, truth commissions, apologies and redress schemes for historic child abuse have no value. Their underpinning moral impulse to provide reparation to people who have experienced profound humiliation, shame and misrecognition through childhood abuse and neglect is important, and many former victims of abuse have spoken about the positive role that such public acts of recognition have played in their lives. But when these interventions function as moral rituals there is also a risk that they become self-evident goods, acquiring an almost sacramental quality in determining public memories of historic child-care practices or creating an impression of moral resolution and closure for past trauma that may not accord with former victims' actual experience. In cases where this happens, scholars of religion have an important role to play in reflecting on how sacralized moral meanings shape these interventions into public memory and give moral authority to processes that at times may not fulfill their reparative intent or provide the best historical knowledge of children's past lives.

References

Alexander, J.C. (2003), *The Meanings of Social Life: A Cultural Sociological Approach*, New York: Oxford University Press.

Barahona de Brita, A., Gonzalez-Enriquez, C. and Aguilar, P. (eds) (2001), *The Politics of Memory: Transitional Justice in Democratizing Societies*, Oxford: Oxford University Press.

Buckley-Zistel, S. and Schafer, S. (eds) (2014), *Memorials in Times of Transition*, Cambridge: Intersentia.

Celermajer, D. (2009), *The Sins of the Nation and the Ritual of Apologies*, Cambridge: Cambridge University Press.

Commission of Investigation into Catholic Archdiocese of Dublin (2009), *Report into the Catholic Archdiocese of Dublin*, Dublin: Department of Justice and Equality.

Daly, K. (2014), *Redressing Institutional Abuse of Children*, Basingstoke: Palgrave MacMillan.

Fassin, D. (2011), *Humanitarian Reason: A Moral History of the Present Times*, Berkeley: University of California Press.

Fassin, D. and Rechtman, R. (2009), *The Empire of Trauma: An Inquiry into the Condition of Victimhood*, Princeton, NJ: Princeton University Press.

Giesen, B. (2004), *Triumph and Trauma*, Boulder, CO: Paradigm Publishers.

Honneth, A. (1995), *The Struggle for Recognition: The Moral Grammar of Social Conflicts*, Cambridge: Polity.

Human Rights and Equal Opportunity Commission (1997), *Bringing Them Home: National Inquiry into the Separation of Aboriginal and Torres Strait Islander Children from Their Families*, Sydney: Human Rights and Equal Opportunity Commission.

Keenan, M. (2012), *Child Sexual Abuse and the Catholic Church: Gender, Power and Organizational Culture*, New York: Oxford University Press.

Lynch, G. (2012a), *The Sacred in the Modern World: A Cultural Sociological Approach*, Oxford: Oxford University Press.

Lynch, G. (2012b), *On the Sacred*, London: Acumen.

Lynch, G. (2015), *Remembering Child Migration: Faith, Nation-Building and the Wounds of Charity*, London: Bloomsbury.

Neumann, K. and Thompson, J. (eds) (2015), *Historical Justice and Memory*, Madison: University of Wisconsin Press.

Niezen, R. (2013), *Truth and Indignation: Canada's Truth and Reconciliation Commission on Indian Residential Schools*, Toronto: University of Toronto Press.

Nobles, M. (2008), *The Politics of Official Apologies*, Cambridge: Cambridge University Press.

Olick, J. (2007), *The Politics of Regret: On Collective Memory and Historical Responsibility*, New York: Routledge.

Parliamentary Health Select Committee (1998), *The Welfare of Former British Child Migrants*, London: House of Commons.

Royal Commission on Aboriginal Peoples (1996), *Report of the Royal Commission on Aboriginal Peoples*, Ottawa: Canada Communication Group.

Ryan Commission (2009), *Final Report of the Commission to Inquire into Child Abuse*, Dublin: Commission to Inquire into Child Abuse.

Senate Community Affairs Committee (2001), *Lost Innocents: Righting the Record (Report on Child Migration)*, Canberra: Senate Community Affairs References Secretariat.

Sköld, J. and Swain, S. (2015), *Apologies and the Legacy of Abuse of Children in "Care,"* Basingstoke: Palgrave MacMillan.

Teitel, R. (2000), *Transitional Justice*, Oxford: Oxford University Press.
Torpey, J. (2006), *Making Whole What Has Been Smashed: On Reparation Politics*, Cambridge, MA: Harvard University Press.
Truth and Reconciliation Commission of Canada (2015), *Honouring the Truth, Reconciling for the Future*, electronic report available online: http://www.trc.ca/websites/ trcinstitution/File/2015/Honouring_the_Truth_Reconciling_for_the_Future_July_23_2015. pdf.
Winter, S. (2014), *Transitional Justice in Established Democracies: A Political Theory*, Basingstoke: Palgrave MacMillan.

40

Child Soldiers and the Militarization of Children: A Muslim Ethical Response to the Situation in the Sudan

Zayn Kassam

Zayn Kassam is the John Knox McLean Professor of Religious Studies at Pomona College, California. Her research is in Islamic Studies, particularly the study of women and Islam, and on religion and migration. In this chapter, she discusses the extent and nature of child militarization in Sudan, and presents an ethical response to this issue, grounded in Muslim beliefs.

The problem of child soldiers is not restricted to any one continent, country, ethnicity, or faith tradition. Reports vary as to the number of countries recruiting and/or utilizing child soldiers, but estimates range from twenty-six[1] to thirty-six countries[2] across the world. For instance, UNICEF reports that the number of children who are members of illegal armed groups in Columbia, South America could be as high as 14,000. In Nepal, there were as many as 7,000 children abducted by Maoists for indoctrination and service to Maoist cadres. The Sudan, Sierra Leone and Uganda are identified in several different reports as guilty of child abduction and forced conscription. However, legal recruitment of children aged 16 and 17 into the armed forces also occurs in countries such as Australia, Austria, Germany, the Netherlands, the United Kingdom, and the United States of America,[3] with the USA deploying seventeen-year-old soldiers in military operations in the Gulf, Bosnia, Somalia, and Kosovo.[4]

Although the problem of child soldiers is widespread and clearly knows no religious or ethnic boundaries, it is a serious problem within Muslim communities that are engaged in conflict. Works such as those of Ishmael Beah's *A Long Way Gone: Memoirs of a Boy Soldier* point to the extent of the use of child soldiers in the conflict in Sierra Leone in the 1990s. Some Muslims acknowledge the problem and are attentive to it; others do not. Many people, both Muslim and non-Muslim, believe that in some Muslim countries child soldiers are recruited for armed conflict in an attempt to Islamize the children within a larger context of Islamist revivalism, or they are indoctrinated into a particular understanding of *jihad* and their role in it. Yet, in Beah's account of the conflict in Muslim contexts such as Sierra Leone, Islamic education appears to play no role at all in recruiting child soldiers there, and even in the Sudan, many other factors in addition to religion appear to feed the recruitment of child soldiers.

The aim of this chapter is to outline some of the primary sources of the problem by focusing on the example of child soldiers in the pre-2005 Sudan, and to offer an ethical response to the issue of child militarization in the Sudan and other countries that is grounded within core Muslim beliefs. The chapter is divided into two parts. Part one focuses on root causes of the problem in the Sudan, showing that although Islamic education does play a role in the recruitment of child soldiers, it is a corollary, and not the primary source, of the problem there. Part two then attempts to answer the question posed by the intersection of violence and children's lives, particularly in the Sudan: in what ways might Islam guide a response to the situation of children in the Sudan, both male and female?

The Sudan: A case study

By turning now to the particular case of child soldiers in the Sudan pre-2005, this section of the chapter helps underscore the seriousness and complexity of the problem; its multiple causes; its impact on both boys and girls; and the possible role of religion in the militarization of children. Practices in the Sudan utilizing children for purposes of supporting conflict, whether through conscription or household or sexual slavery, violate both the United Nations Convention on the Rights of the Child (UNCRC) as well as foundational Islamic precepts.

Pre-2005, Sudan's government was a military regime brought to power by the National Islamic Front (NIF), at war with the Sudan People's Liberation Army (SPLA) whose rebel platform consisted of seeking a united secular Sudan and autonomy for the southern third of the country and the Nuba mountains. The NIF considered the war against rebel forces a *jihad* or holy war for Islam, and its soldiers as holy warriors.

Procuring child soldiers and sex slaves

The capture of children in the Sudan from that time falls into three categories: (1) street children, mostly southerners and Nuba children, who were rounded up by the government and sent to camps at which they were given new Arab names and subjected to forced conversion; (2) Dinka and Nuba children, captured in raids on their villages and taken into household slavery; and (3) children forcibly recruited into the army or government-sponsored militias.

The so-called street children of the first group were a mixture of homeless children and children with families. Those with families were captured while simply out on the street, often running errands for their families. These children were rounded up and taken to closed camps that did not admit visitors, including parents looking for their lost children.

In the case of children in the second category, southern and Nuba children were captured during raids on their villages by Arab militias and soldiers, and suffered one of two fates: either they were retained as unpaid household servants, and often beaten or sexually abused; or, if they were not retained, they were sold into slavery to other households. If not pressed into household service, captured children could end up drafted as soldiers in the army, thus directly contravening Sudanese law, which sets the age of conscription at 18. Other children were drafted into the government-sponsored militias. Such children were forcibly Islamized and trained by military trainers to become "holy warriors," by characterizing the conflict as a *jihad* against the south. Such a characterization of the conflict is highly problematic as it pulls religion into playing a role in justifying the unethical treatment of children, and of legitimating the conflict, which, as will be explored below, has been brought about through a complex of factors that far outweigh religious considerations.

Armed militias in the so-called Christian south were found equally to be culpable in their recruitment of children, which relates to children falling under the third category. The SPLA, the key armed militia and resistance group in the south, had long had the practice of recruiting children from Ethiopian refugee camps on the promise of providing education to them, only to substitute education with military training. Another militia, the Southern Sudan Independence Army (SSIA), recruited children from the Upper Nile, again promising education, but instead sending them to military camps for weapons training. No mention of religious indoctrination is found in the Human Rights Watch or other reports in the forced militarization of children in Southern Sudan.

All of these children were unwittingly rendered vulnerable to being made unwilling accessories to the civil wars in the Sudan. Their presence was, and in conflicts around the world deploying children as soldiers, continued to be facilitated by the ready availability of small arms, manufactured in the United States, Italy, and the former USSR. In the Sudan, their inclusion in military training and duties was further facilitated by longstanding social conventions by which raids for replenishing military groups were common and children were socialized into a military profession through placement in a military camp.

The conflict in the Sudan was less a religious war than it was a series of civil wars fought for control over resources, land, and oil, in which the parties to the conflict exploited ethnic and religious divisions. A program of vast dislocation, brutality, and murder was carried out by the ostensibly extra-governmental but in fact government-trained and sponsored militia known as the Janjaweed, in order to quell the aspirations of the southern Sudanese to exercise control over their resources, on the one hand, or in the case of Nubians and Darfurians, to drive them out of areas that are being drilled for oil. The violence against women and female children whether in the form of murder, rape, and household or military slavery is endemic to the conflict situation and not the explicit result of intended Islamization of southern Sudanese or Nubians and Darfurians, although the latter was often cited as justification for these barbaric acts.

The displacement caused by the need to clear land for oil drilling, as well as the conflicts over political power-sharing and control of natural resources creates refugee populations that are vulnerable to the raiding of children and their subsequent mobilization as child soldiers.

Islamization is simply the most readily available ideological tool for depriving these children of their natal identity, creating a religious and with it a cultural distance between the children and the familial and communal populations they will be asked to fight, and an ideology to be marshaled in justification of the dislocation of peoples whose control over their resources is being stolen from under them.

Women, girls, and war

The gender components of the conflict cannot be overlooked; while male children are conscripted, older female children and women are raped and taken to military camps to service the soldiers and the commanders. In this respect such inexcusable behavior is seen to have been no different from any other conflict in which women are raped both to satisfy male soldiers and as a form of psychological warfare intended to humiliate the enemy, despite the fact that international UN sanctions exist against the use of rape as a weapon in war.[5] Indeed, one report dated October 2004 states that "Contemporary armed conflicts in Africa, Eastern Europe, Asia and Latin America have seen systematic sexual violence rise to an unprecedented level."[6] In a 2005 report released by Médecins San Frontiers (Doctors Without Borders), which has been active in West, North, and South Darfur since December 2003, over 700 rape victims had been treated, a figure that does not accurately reflect the magnanimity of the actual number of women and girls raped, ranging in age from 12 to 45 years old,[7] while another report places the women subjected to such violence as being aged anywhere from under 10 years old to over 70.[8]

Oftentimes the women or girls were taken to military compounds and kept there for several days while they were gang raped. Villagers or family members who attempted to stop the raping were beaten, themselves raped, or subjected to brutal physical violence. In some instances, Janjaweed military forces either attacked women and girls as they left their villages in search of firewood or water; entered the villages and raped women and girls from house to house, killing the men; or rounded up the villagers and separated the men and boys from the women and girls, killing the former and raping the latter. In addition, ethnic superiority is often reported as being deployed in the taunts made by Janjaweed rapists—that an impregnated woman will be "freed" through her Arab-blood-bearing child, suggesting that all non-Arab Muslims (by which they mean the people of Darfur) are "slaves" to "Arab" Muslims.[9] The depiction of the Sudanese civil war as a war perpetrated by Arabs on Africans has been shown to be a gross misunderstanding of the situation on the ground. In its report released on February 25, 2005, the UN Commission on Darfur countered the Arab/African dichotomization by noting that "many Arabs in Darfur are opposed to the Janjaweed, and some Arabs are fighting with the rebels" while simultaneously, "many non-Arabs are supporting the government and serving in its army." Further, tribes such as the Fur, Massalit, and Zeghawa that are the targets of assault are attacked by those who speak the same language (Arabic), are also Muslim, and whose ethnicity cannot be differentiated from that of their victims. The commission also noted that political events are now causing new nomenclatures to emerge: tribes that support the government are being called Arab even though they are African, such as the Gimmer, while those that support the rebels are being called African, whether they are nomads or Arabs from the Misseriya and Rizeigat tribes.[10]

The consequences for the women and children that have been raped are often severe, including being ostracized from their community, jailed for having an illegal child, and being infected with HIV. A further concern is whether the children born as a result of rape will be nurtured by their mothers or abandoned to their fates.

Boy soldiers

With respect to male children, an investigation of the connection between Islam and child militarization shows that Islam was invoked by the northern armed forces, whether governmental or not, to socialize children rounded up in street raids or in raids into southern Sudanese territories, by giving them new, Islamic names, requiring their participation in Islamic ritual observances, with some scant evidence that the new Muslim identity was expected to justify to children why they should fight against their families and former communities. Other tactics utilized were to separate children from their families, such that no visitations were allowed to families seeking their lost children, or children were forced to commit killings to alienate them from their southern village communities. Reunification programs by international agencies have met with some success, but pastoral and retraining and employment programs that would support the return of former child soldiers to civilian life are sorely lacking. Religion is mentioned in one of the Human Rights Watch reports of the raids conducted in the south, facilitated by government-sponsored programs of ethnic division, especially among the Nuer tribes and other government-sponsored militias such as the agrarian Baggara peoples who are identified as Arab but utilized by the government to dislocate the Dinka and Nuer peoples sitting atop the oilfields. Here, girls and boys taken into household slavery were taught Islam but not in as stringent a manner as they were in the camps in the north.[11]

An Islamic ethical response

Religions can be utilized both to initiate and perpetuate violence against children, and Islam was certainly being mobilized in that manner in the training of captured children in the Sudan. Further, Muslim discourses and identity were mobilized in order to pit as well as to represent the conflict in the Sudan as either a religious war (northern Muslims against the Christian and animist south) or as an ethnic conflict (Arab Muslim against African Muslim in Darfur).[12] As we have seen, representing the conflicts in the Sudan in such a manner masks the power struggles over resources that fueled the conflict, while key parties involved in the conflict simultaneously deployed religious and ethnic formulations to lend justification to their violent practices. Thus, it is essential to examine what Islam could contribute as an ethical response.

The Sudan

The outright contravention of the UNCRC in the Sudan[13] is in several instances also contrary to Qur'ānic principles of freedom of religion, injunctions against aggression and killing, and the ethnic and religious pluralism that is acknowledged in a positive manner by the Qur'an. With respect to the Sudanese case, the imposition of an Islamic identity on non-Muslim, most likely Christian and children belonging to indigenous traditions (since many of the Dinka and Nuer follow Christianity along with tribal Nuer and Dinka religions), is completely unnecessary, according to Q. 2:62, "Those who believe, and those who follow the Jewish scriptures, and the Christians, and the Sabians, any who believe in God and the Last Day, and work righteousness, shall have their reward with the Lord; on them shall be no fear, nor shall they grieve." Further, Q. 2:256 expressly declares "Let there be no compulsion in religion." Inviting people to consider Islam as their faith of choice through peaceful education is an altogether different activity from imposing Islamic names, rituals, and ideologies through coercive means, or on children of different religious faiths who have no means to resist such measures.

Freeing slaves is explicitly viewed in the Qur'ān as an opportunity to exercise righteousness; Q. 2:177 states: "But it is righteousness…to spend of your substance…for the ransom of slaves…." Thus, the incorporation of children as unpaid soldiers in military groups, whether governmental or not, or as unpaid household labor or sexual slaves whether for the military or the household, is in principle and in practice unacceptable to the Qur'ān. Q. 2:244, "Fight in the way of Allah," is a verse that is misused by those who utilize it to motivate the killing of hapless folk as a religious mask for economic gain, as is well illustrated by the Sudanese example. Had there been a real need to convert southern Sudanese to Islam, then this could have been carried out through peaceful *da'wah* (exhortation and missionary activity) rather than through the military options of death, seizure, and rape, actions whose intent is to terrorize a population as it is driven off its lands and separated from its flocks and pastures.

A Qur'ānic verse (2:233) that is explicitly about a mother's responsibility to suckle her child for a full two years, and a father's responsibility to feed and clothe nursing mothers in a seemly manner goes on to state: "A mother should not be made to suffer because of her child, nor should he to whom the child is born (be made to suffer) because of his child." While this verse refers specifically to the issue of maternal and paternal duties, it also lays the charge of social responsibility on the community, to ensure that no mother or father [the verse does not limit the charge to Muslim mothers or fathers, so it could be read as applicable to any mother, Muslim or not, and any father, Muslim or not] suffers from their inability to nurse or provide for the nursing mother. Simultaneously, as a wider application, the verse suggests that no mother or father should be subject to preventable suffering on account of their child. The forcible capture of children by armed groups, and their subsequent militarization, slavery, or sexual abuse, cannot but inflict untold suffering on their parents.

With respect to the gendered aspects of the conflict in the Sudan, nowhere in the Qur'ān or in Islamic teaching is the Arab race rendered superior to any other human race or ethnicity. For rape to be used as weapon of ethnic purification or assertion of ethnic superiority is an outright disregard of the Qur'ānic injunction that all humans are equal before God and can only be distinguished from one another on account of their righteousness (*taqwa*) (Q. 49:13). A Qur'ānic verse addressed to the children of Adam relates that God has forbidden indecencies, whether manifest or hidden, and sin and oppression. Rape, whether utilized as a weapon of war or not, contravenes the words of the Qur'ān, as does the broader oppression of civilians in Darfur by government and government-supported militias. Further, all the injunctions against adultery in the Qur'ān assume consent from both partners; the conflation of rape with adultery, and the viewing of pregnancy resulting from rape as proof of adultery are gross forms of patriarchal injustice that victimize and stigmatize the female for acts of male violence, whether carried out during a time of war or not.

Applying lessons about the Sudan to other contexts and countries

Some lessons that can be drawn from the Sudanese case in consideration of the use of child soldiers in other global, including Muslim majority contexts. The UNCRC provides an international direction of state responsibilities toward children. However, religious and secular humanist ideologies and practices must support it to ensure the well-being of children throughout the world. The Sudanese case teaches us to look beyond the popular depiction of any conflict that has been labeled an ethnic or religious war to an examination of the deeper causes and material supports fueling the conflict. One must identify the specific causes of the conflict in order to examine whether any use of religious rhetoric to commit acts of violence or coercion against children, or using children to commit acts of violence toward others can, in fact, be justified on religious grounds. For instance, was the use of children as minesweeps during the 8-year Iran–Iraq war justified through the argument that such children would be martyrs for the faith if killed? Or is such rhetoric created to use faith itself as a resource or weapon to support the war at a time of labor shortage? Similarly, can the use of Christianity in mobilizing children to serve in the Lord's Army in Uganda be justified in suggesting that this is the role Christ would have wanted for His children? As conflicts occur within and/or involving people belonging to one faith or another, a religious ethic of war, whether developed through interfaith consultations and conversations, or whether developed specific to a particular religious tradition, that takes into consideration all aspects of how children are recruited, mobilized, and affected by war is a critical discourse that must engaged.

As the case in the Sudan suggests, the gendered aspects of war in how they affect children are also an important facet that need to be addressed. In countries where Islamic law prevails, the distinction between rape and adultery must be made very clear in order to stop the further victimization, social and legal, of girl children, and women who have been raped, or male children and men who have been sodomized. Ostracizing raped females and abandoning children of rape run counter to righteousness as defined in the Qur'ān, 2:177:

> it is righteousness ... to spend of your substance out of love for [God], for your kin, for orphans, for the needy, for the wayfarer, for those who ask, and for the ransom of slaves; to be steadfast in prayer, and practice regular charity; to fulfill the contracts you have made; and to be firm and patient, in pain (or suffering) and adversity, and throughout all periods of panic. Such are the people of truth, the God-fearing.

Similarly, ethical religious responses from other faiths must be developed in order to help survivors of sexual crimes committed during times of war.

Finally, religious traditions need to work with each other in order to address the use of religion as a cover for wars that are fought over resources. Once again, the case of the Sudan shows that religious identities are often the visible markers of groups at opposite ends of the conflict, and that religious rhetoric is often utilized in order to incite people to fight for the cause. Such identities and rhetoric then serve in misnaming or masking the real reasons for the conflict by casting it solely or primarily as a *religious* conflict rather than a conflict over political control, or land, or other resource, which is aided and abetted by religious identities and rhetoric. Examples of such misnamings in the more recent past include the conflicts in Ireland, Bosnia, Israel, and more recently, in Nigeria, among others. Members of religious traditions need to stop allowing the vilification of members of other faiths for such purposes, through a clear examination of the causes and factors fuelling the conflict. Such vilifications, as we have seen with horrendous effect in the last century with respect to the Holocaust visited on Jews,

Gypsies and others, do very little to attend to the real causes of conflict, and thus imperil the many children whose lives are adversely affected by war, whether they are militarized or not.

Notes

1   For the State Department's 2004 Human Rights report.

2   For the Human Rights Watch report.

3   Amnesty International Press Release dated November 17, 2004.

4   Center for Defense Information (2001).

5   Rape of civilians during a time of conflict has been entered as a crime against humanity and as a war crime in the Rome Statute of the International Criminal Court, which entered into force July 1, 2002, U.N. Document A/CONF.183.9 (1998).

6   Physicians for Human Rights.

7   http://www.doctorswithoutborders.org/publications/reports/2005/sudan03.pdf Physicians for Human Rights has cited figures as high as 9,300, or double that figure as of October 2004. While it is difficult to verify any of these figures, there is no doubt that rape is being deployed as a significant weapon in the conflict, as reported by UN Secretary-General Kofi Annan: "In Darfur, we see whole populations displaced, and their homes destroyed, while rape is used as a deliberate strategy." United Nations, "Secretary-General's Address to the General Assembly," September 21, 2004,http://www.un.org/apps/sg/sgstats.asp?nid=1088. See also https://s3.amazonaws.com/PHR_Reports/nowhere-to-turn.pdf

8   Physicians for Human Rights (15).

9   Physicians for Human Rights (18).

10 See Mamdani (2007).

11 Human Rights Watch report (1995).

12 Such a claim is once again graphically portrayed in the documentary titled, *The Devil Came on Horseback*, in which the former US Marine Captain Brian Steidle chronicles his observations of the atrocities taking place in the Sudan. http://www.thedevilcameonhorseback.com/

13 Article 16 of the UNCRC states: "No child shall be subjected to arbitrary or unlawful interference with his or her privacy, family, home or correspondence, not to unlawful attacks on his or her honour and reputation." Article 19 further charges the State "to protect the child from all forms of physical or mental violence, injury or abuse, neglect or negligent treatment, maltreatment or exploitation, including sexual abuse, while in the care of parent(s), legal guardian(s) or any other person who has the care of the child." When a child is temporarily or permanently deprived of his or her family environment, as in times of conflict, Article 20 of the UNCRC calls upon the State to provide "special protection and assistance" to the child.

Article 29 provides for respect of ethnic differences within nations by calling for education to be directed toward the "preparation of the child for responsible life in a free society, in the spirit of understanding, peace, tolerance, equality of the sexes, and friendship among all peoples, ethnic, national and religious groups and persons of indigenous origin." Article 30 is explicit in stating that people of different ethnicities must be allowed to exercise the full dignity of co-existence and equality with other groups:

> In those States in which ethnic, religious, or linguistic minorities or persons of indigenous origins exist, a child belonging to such a minority or who is indigenous shall not be denied the right, in community with other members of his or her group, to enjoy his or her own culture, to profess and practise his or her own religion, or to use his or her own language.

Thus, to use rape as a weapon of ethnic cleansing, or to suggest that a member of an ethnic group is lower in stature to a member of another ethnic group, clearly contravenes both the spirit and the letter of the UNCRC.

The use of female children as laborers in military camps contravenes Article 32 that states it is the right of the child "to be protected from economic exploitation and from performing any work that is likely to be hazardous or to interfere with the child's education, or to be harmful to the child's health or physical, mental, spiritual, moral or social development." The strongest protection for children in matters of their sexuality comes in Article 34:

> State Parties undertake to protect the child from all forms of sexual exploitation and sexual abuse. For these purposes, State Parties shall in particular take all appropriate national, bilateral and multilateral measures to prevent: (a) The inducement or coercion of a child to engage in any unlawful sexual activity; (b) The exploitative use of children in prostitution or other unlawful sexual practices.

Article 36 further states: "State Parties shall protect the child against all other forms of exploitation prejudicial to any aspects of the child's welfare."

References

Center for Defense Information (October 15, 2001), "Children and Armed Conflict."

For the Human Rights Watch report. Available online: http://www.humanrightswatch.org/campaigns/crp/where.htm: http://www.pogoarchives.org/straus/cdi_archive/2004-state-hrr-child-soldiers.pdf.

For the State Department's 2004 Human Rights report. Available online: http://www.state.gov/g/drl/rls/hrrpt/2004/.

Human Rights Watch report (September 1995), *Children in Sudan: Slaves, Street Children and Child Soldiers*. Available online: http://hrw.org/doc/?t=children_pub&document_limit=300,20 HRW Index No.: 1-56432-157-6.

Mamdani, Mahmood, (March 8, 2007), "The Politics of Naming: Genocide, Civil War, Insurgency," *London Review of Books*, 29 (5): 5–8.

Physicians for Human Rights. http://physiciansforhumanrights.org/library/documents/reports/the-use-of-rape-as-a-weapon.pdf (accessed May 16, 2016).

41

The Learning Curve of Clerical Child Sex Abuse: Lessons from Ireland

Susie Donnelly

Susie Donnelly received her PhD from University College Dublin. She has worked in the media industry as a researcher and journalist, and taught sociology at the University of Edinburgh. Her research explores institutional power and social change by examining the cultural conditions under which clerical scandals emerged in contemporary Irish society. In this chapter, she traces policy and attitudes around the reporting of child sex abuse cases in Ireland, and the role of the media in reporting it.

The way we think about child abuse has greatly evolved throughout the twentieth century. Public consciousness of the issue and understanding of its effects has developed gradually since the 1960s. In recent years, as religious and residential child care institutions have been subject to child abuse scandals, it has been increasingly pertinent for sociologists to understand the social climate in which institutional child abuse has taken place historically and the context in which it eventually emerged. This chapter takes the opportunity to look at the emergence of child abuse through a contemporary lens. It considers the extent to which, at times, the media have filled the gap in knowledge around the issue; shaping and informing public understanding.

Child abuse is a modern concept and one which has developed as our understanding of child welfare has evolved. Throughout the early to mid-twentieth century, various forms of child abuse were normalized in homes, schools, and by judiciary. Corporal punishment was considered a necessary tool for raising a healthy and happy child. Instead child abuse was generally associated with neglect and poverty. In his analysis of the discovery of child abuse, Pfohl suggests that while there were a number of important movements such as the society for the Prevention of Cruelty to Children and the rise of juvenile courts in the twentieth century, "… prior to the 1960's sociolegal reactions were sporadic" (1977: 311). As legislation around civil rights developed in the latter half of the twentieth century in the West, so too did legislation of the rights of children. The UN Convention on the Rights of the Child was introduced as a binding agreement in 1989 and corporal punishment was widely outlawed. Advancements in behavioral sciences began to provide a greater understanding of the long lasting consequences of traumatic and abusive experiences in childhood.

However, levels of awareness and levels of understanding have not always developed in tandem. In the case of child sex abuse by clergy, Keenan asserts that while bishops were on a "steep learning curve" in relation to child sex abuse, so too were medical, social work, and criminal justice professionals (2012: 207). Responses from social, political, and religious institutions have been slow to keep up with the rate and scale of media exposés. Indeed Goddard and Saunders suggest that at times the media have led the way and appeared "to have [had] more influence on child protection policy and practice than professionals working in the field" (2001: 1). The emergence of child sex abuse scandals in the Irish Catholic Church is a clear example of this. This chapter considers how the media have often played a vital role in raising public awareness.

Uncovering child abuse

With the benefit of hindsight, we know that the sexual abuse of children by clergy was taking place within Irish communities for many decades. However the discovery of the systematic abuse of children only emerged in the mid-1990s. So why then? For much of the twentieth century journalists and editors were cautious of coming into conflict with the Church. In 1994 the scandal surrounding a sexual offender Fr Brendan Smyth, opened the floodgates of clerical abuse in Ireland and began the "drip-by-drip never ending revelation about child sexual abuse and the disastrous way it was handled" (Archbishop Diarmuid Martin quoted in Cooney 2012). The Smyth case was initially a scandal involving the unpopular appointment of the Attorney General who failed to deal with an extradition order for Smyth to face charges of the indecent assault of children in Northern Ireland. The coalition government collapsed as a result of the scandal and Smyth eventually faced seventy-four charges in the Republic. As journalists began to investigate and survivors increasingly came forward, it appeared that the silence around child abuse had been broken.

In response, the Church established an advisory committee in 1994 whose remit included publishing guidelines for procedures to be followed when responding to complaints. In 1996, "Child Sexual Abuse: Framework for a Church Response" recommended that allegations of clerical child sex abuse should be reported to civil authorities. Three years later the Department of Health and Children produced statutory guidelines for notifying the police and social services of allegations of clerical sexual abuse and assisting people in identifying and reporting child abuse (Department of Health and Children 1999). These documents laid the foundation for developing clearer policy in relation to third party child sex abuse in Ireland. While the Church was integral to the advancement of policy, a study commissioned by the Bishop's Committee on Child Protection found "little public awareness of actions the Church has taken in recent years to address the issue of child sex abuse by clergy" with only 10 percent of respondents in their survey reporting to have heard of "The Framework Document" (Goode et al. 2003: xxviii).

Child abuse inquiries

When journalists in Ireland began to investigate allegations of clerical abuse from the mid-1990s, stories of heinous acts of abuse appeared with great intensity. It started with reports of individual abusers but as the accountability of the Catholic hierarchy was questioned, it became clear that systematic abuse had been taking place (Donnelly and Inglis 2010). Public inquiries were established to investigate the extent of child abuse in dioceses throughout Ireland. One of the earliest was set up in 2001 following the suicide of Fr Seán Fortune, a prolific child abuser in the South West of the country. The publication of The Ferns Report in 2005 was a critical moment in capturing the understanding of child sex abuse in the Catholic Church. It identified over 100 allegations of abuse involving twenty-one priests dating back to 1962. The report examined how the Church as well as the Health Board and An Garda Síochána (police) responded to complaints. A number of recommendations were made, such as Garda vetting and increased regulations around reporting abuse.

"The Ferns Report" recognizes that prior to the Smyth case, awareness of child sex abuse in Ireland was confined to families, particularly in light of a number of high-profile incest cases in the early 1990s. While these cases raised awareness of child sex abuse as a crime "perpetrated by apparently upright and decent members of the community," it was not until the publicity around the Smyth case that "Irish society was fully exposed to the phenomenon of the systematic abuse of children by third parties who were in a position of trust and authority over those children" (Murphy et al. 2005: 12). The report asserts that while third-party abuse may only represent a small proportion of abuse "it is a major problem for any organisation entrusted with the care of children in which it becomes manifest" (Murphy et al. 2005: 12).

The Commission to Inquire into Child Abuse was established in 1999 following the government's apology to victims. This Commission had a much broader remit to inquiry into the causes, nature and extent of physical and sexual abuse in Irish institutions from 1936 onwards. It heard from 1500 witnesses and provided victims with an opportunity to recount the abuse they had suffered and to claim for compensation. In 2009, it reported on sixty Reformatory and Industrial Schools operated by the Church, and funded and supervised by the Department of Education. More than

90 percent of witnesses reported being physically abused and approximately half reported sexual abuse as well as frequent instances of neglect and emotional abuse. Known as "The Ryan Report", it concluded that sexual abuse was endemic in boys' institutions in particular. In terms of disclosing abuse, witnesses reported "a culture of secrecy and isolation and the fear of physical punishment [which] inhibited them in disclosing abuse" (Ryan 2009: 14). Although protective action was taken at times, in other instances complaints were "ignored, witnesses were punished, or pressure was brought to bear on the child and family to deny the complaint and/or to remain silent" (Ryan 2009: 14). The report concludes that complaints were managed by the Church in order to minimize the risk of public disclosure and that this policy resulted in the protection of perpetrators.

The detailed testimony contained in the five volumes of "The Ryan Report" were debated and discussed in the Irish media. A few months later, the findings of another report into child abuse were published. Following publicity surrounding an investigative documentary *Cardinal Secrets* in 2002, an inquiry was set up to examine how Church and State authorities handled clerical child sex abuse in the Dublin archdiocese between 1975 to 2004. Unlike "The Ryan Report", "The Murphy Report" was confined to sexual abuse and had no specific remit to make recommendations. The report strongly rejects the Church's claim to have been on "a learning curve" in relation to child sex abuse prior to the late 1990s. Its investigation found that complaints were internally managed within the Archdiocese from the 1950s. Indeed it reveals that in 1987 insurance was purchased to cover potential compensation claims. "The Murphy Report" found evidence to suggest that sexual abuse was a kind of hornet's nest— there was suspicion of sexual abuse but it was rarely acted upon, stating "Some priest witnesses admitted to the Commission that they had heard various reports 'on the grapevine'" (Murphy et al. 2009: 7).

The problem of child sex abuse

At a human level, it is unfathomable that abuse was identified but ignored. As far back as the 1970s, an expert group established by the Department of Health unanimously agreed that there was "a significant problem" of child abuse in Ireland and that "coordinated efforts should be made to remedy the situation" (Murphy et al. 2005: 11). Consequently, in 1977 they issued a "Memorandum on Non-Accidental Injury to Children" (Department of Health 1977). Yet crucially this report did not mention the *sexual* abuse of children. Further guidelines were produced in 1983 but again sexual abuse was not addressed. It was not until 1987 that the Department of Health produced "Guidelines on Procedures for the Identification, Investigation and Management of Child Abuse". However these guidelines did not consider sexual abuse carried out by a third party (i.e., a member of the clergy). They also failed to address how complaints made by victims in later life should be handled (i.e., those abused as children but lodging a complaint as an adult). Despite indications from the 1970s that child abuse was a significant problem in religious organizations, guidelines for responding to complaints were only developed in the late 1990s under the scrutiny of the media's gaze and substantial public and political pressure.

In terms of accountability for the cover-up of clerical child sex abuse, the Church is an obvious place to start. But this does not give us a full picture of the many actors involved. "The Ferns Report" reminds us that it is not one single institution that can be held to account, stating "With the benefit of hindsight it is possible to see that the Church authorities, the medical profession and society generally failed to appreciate the horrendous damage which the sexual abuse of children can and does cause" (Murphy et al. 2005) Similarly, "The Ryan Report" concludes that there were failings at many levels of Irish society from government inspectors, medical practitioners, teachers to local people and members of the public, asserting that "Awareness of the abuse of children in schools and institutions was believed to exist within society at both official and unofficial levels" (Ryan 2009, Vol. III §19.3: 394). The task falls to social scientists to unpack the social context under which child abuse is ignored. In the case of Ireland, this requires examining the extent to which other actors struggled to challenge the authority of the Catholic hierarchy. In this respect, the media is a useful site of analysis as it has played an integral role in making child abuse visible.

Undue deference

Until the 1990s, there existed a degree of deference toward the religious organizations that ran child welfare institutions. Cultural sociologists, such as Lynch (2012) and Inglis (1998), have recognized the sacred position traditionally held by the Church and a pervasive moral authority which shaped social institutions in Ireland, from education to criminal justice and social welfare. Deference to the Church and clergy is key to understanding how institutional child abuse did not emerge until the 1990s. Traditionally the Church played a primary role in providing child welfare in Ireland. By the middle of the nineteenth century the only public provision for children was in the workhouse. It was proposed that industrial schools, which had been successfully established in Scotland, should be introduced in Ireland. However Local Authorities were unwilling to contribute and instead religious organizations took on the role of providing care for juvenile offenders in the form of the reformatory school system. In 1970, "The Kennedy Report" on reformatory and industrial schools found this system of care to be "completely inadequate" and recommended that it be abolished (Kennedy 1970: 6). While the Department of Education held responsibility for children in these schools, "The Ryan Report" later commented that the Department "was woefully lacking in ideas about policy" (Ryan 2009, Vol. IV §1.231: 43). At a public hearing the Department's Secretary General remarked that the Department had shown a "very significant deference" toward the religious Congregations which according to the Commission, impeded change (Ryan 2009).

The role of the police has also been considered. "The Murphy Report" (2009) points to failings on the part of An Garda Síochána, including undue deference to the Catholic Church. It states:

A number of very senior members of the Gardaí, including the Commissioner in 1960, clearly regarded priests as being outside their remit. There are some examples of Gardaí actually reporting complaints to the [Dublin] Archdiocese instead of investigating them. (Murphy et al. 2009: 24)

The inquiry found until 1995, the Church did not routinely report complaints to the Gardaí.

While the role of the media is not extensively explored in these reports, it is part of the story. Prior to the 1970s, the limited coverage of clerical abuse reflects a lack of public consciousness around the issue, as well as journalistic practice at that time which, when it came to matters involving the Church, often lacked critical analysis. Indeed, it was common to reproduce papal encyclicals, letters, and communications from clergy in full without editing. Arguably, Irish journalism has at times shown undue deference toward the Church in relation to stories with the potential for scandal. According to Patsy McGarry, religious affairs correspondent with *The Irish Times*, "The relationship between the media and the establishment was far too close here in Ireland ... and that applied to the Church as well. And forgive me for saying it, it applied to some of my predecessors ... in that they were too enamoured by their contact with senior clergy in particular" (Donnelly 2012: 111). Scholars have noted that, with some exceptions, the limited coverage of the [Reformatory] Schools in the Irish media was treated "either with nostalgic gloss ... or as simple reportage devoid of analysis" (Keating 2002: 275). In "The Ryan Report" it is remarked that "Even if a skeleton made its way out of its cupboard, the newspapers could be persuaded to turn their back" (Ryan 2009, Vol. IV §3.99: 231). A former reporter and editor of the *Evening Herald*, Brian Quinn, recalled an incident in the 1950s whereby a Christian Brother pulled an article which mentioned a court case involving an Industrial School. Quinn reflected that, "Those requests should have alerted journalists to start inquiries into what was happening ... . That we did not is a heavy burden" (Ryan 2009, Vol. IV §3.99: 230). There are similar accounts of direct censorship imposed upon journalists by members of the clergy in the 1950s and 1960s (see Donnelly 2012). But as Conor Brady, former editor of *The Irish Times* concludes "... the real story is not that it happened but that [journalists] never wrote about it" (Donnelly 2012: 70).

Public watchdog

There is no doubt that the media have played an important role in exposing clerical child sex abuse. Irish clergy and Church personnel have commented that "If it hadn't been for good journalists, a lot of this [clerical child abuse] would not have come out"

(Goode et al. 2003: 183). Clergy and Church personnel have described the avoidance of scandal as a feature of how complaints were managed. While the media can be accused of moral panic with regard to the "pedophile priest" (Ferguson 1995; Breen 2004), scholars have recognized the important role the media has played in child protection. Goddard and Saunders have argued that "media coverage is vital if public concern for children is to remain on the political agenda, and if child protection services are to remain accountable" (2001: 1). In this sense, the media fulfill their role as a public watchdog and a key cornerstone within a democratic society (Curran 1991; Meyer 2006).

In an issue such as institutional child abuse where understanding and acceptance is slow to develop, the media play an equally vital role in informing the public. Goode, McGee et al.'s study published in 2003 following a sustained period of abuse scandals, found that almost all (95 percent) of those surveyed reported "the media as their main source of knowledge about child sexual abuse in general" and in terms of knowledge regarding sex abuse perpetrated by clergy, "almost all (94 percent) cited non-religious sources, mainly television, and print media, with 5 percent obtaining knowledge from both religious and non-religious sources" (2003: 65). The clergy themselves were also informed and educated about child abuse through the media. The authors concluded that "Most clergy interviewed for this study reported only recent awareness of the problem of child sexual abuse and this was based on media reports" (Goode et al. 2003: 59). Media coverage has also helped to inform policymakers. A spokesman for the Department of Education recounted how they generally became aware of child abuse as a public issue following the broadcast of investigative documentaries such as *Dear Daughter* and *States of Fear*, which captured the experiences of abuse survivors (Ryan 2009).

Conclusions

Analysing the awareness and understanding of clerical child abuse in the latter half of the twentieth century reveals a society which at many levels struggled to assert itself, particularly in terms of shedding a tradition of deference toward the Church. The reports produced by various child abuse inquires have provided an important historical record of the scale of abuse in Irish communities. Journalists have played a vital role in raising public awareness and educating the public, policymakers, and clergy on the issue. The Ryan Report states that "Civil society has a responsibility to ensure the safety of children" (Ryan 2009, Vol. III §19.8: 396). It is clear that advancements have indeed been made in the development of procedures for reporting and responding to clerical abuse, particularly since the 1990s. Yet there are concerns over the extent to which procedures are adhered to; as recently as 2009, it was found that guidelines in the Cloyne Diocese "were not fully or consistently implemented" (Murphy et al. 2010: 5). Moreover, there have been few criminal convictions as a result of public inquiries, the names of offender are often redacted from reports and there is still no specific offence in law in relation to child abuse.

While public inquiries provide a degree of justice for survivors, it is likely that the impact of clerical child abuse on wider society will take time to be fully appreciated, particularly in the context of a predominantly Catholic society such as Ireland. Confronting the many layers of accountability is an unpalatable task but a most important one. As "The Ryan Report" states, "Many people, including extended family members, neighbours, staff in schools, hospitals and other health services, had some awareness of the abuse of children in schools and institutions in the past and failed to act to protect them" (Ryan 2009, Vol. III §19.8: 396). Historians and sociologists have a responsibility to illustrate and explain the lack of intervention by various actors within society.

References

Breen, M.J. (2004), "Depraved Paedos and Other Beasts: The Media Portrayal of Child Sexual Abusers in Ireland and the UK," in P. Yoder and P.M. Kreuter (eds), *Monsters and the Monstrous: Myths and Metaphors of Enduring Evil*, 285–291, Oxford: Inter-Disciplinary Press.

Cooney, J. (2012), "Dark Forces Hiding Truth over Abuse, Says Martin," *The Irish Independent*, May 11, 2010.

Curran, J. (1991), "Mass Media and Democracy: A Reappraisal," in J. Curran and M. Gurevitch (eds), *Mass Media and Society*, 82–117, London: Edward Arnold.

Department of Health (1977), *Memorandum on Non-Accidental Injury to Children*, Dublin: Department of Health.

Department of Health and Children (1999), *Children First: National Guidelines for the Protection and Welfare of Children*, Dublin: The Stationery Office.

Donnelly, S. (2012), 'The Media and the Catholic Church in Ireland: Clerical Sex Scandals and Shifts in the Balance of Power,' PhD thesis, University College Dublin, Dublin.

Donnelly, S. and Inglis, T. (2010), "The Media and the Catholic Church in Ireland: Reporting Clerical Child Sex Abuse," *Journal of Contemporary Religion* 25 (1): 1–19.

Ferguson, H. (1995), "Paedophile Priest: A Deconstruction," *Studies: An Irish Quarterly Review* 84 (335): 247–256.

Goddard, C. and Saunders, B.J. (2001), *Child Abuse and the Media 14*, Melbourne.

Goode, H., Mc Gee, H., and O' Boyle, C. (2003), *Time to Listen: Confronting Child Sexual Abuse by Catholic Clergy in Ireland*, Dublin: Liffey Press.

Inglis, T. (1998), *Moral Monopoly: The Rise and Fall of the Catholic Church in Modern Ireland*, second edition, Dublin: University College Dublin Press.

Keating, A. (2002), "Secrets and Lies: An Exploration of the Role of Identity, Culture and Communication in the Policy Process Relating to the Provision of Protection and Care for Vulnerable Children in the Irish Free State and Republic, 1923–1974," Phd thesis, Dublin City University, Dublin.

Keenan, M. (2012), *Child Sexual Abuse and the Catholic Church*, New York: Oxford University Press.

Kennedy, E.D.J. (1970), *Reformatory and Industrial Schools System Report 1970 Chaired by District Justice Eileen Kennedy*.

Lynch, G. (2012), *The Sacred in the Modern World*, Oxford: Oxford University Press.

Meyer, B. (2006), *Religion, Media, and the Public Sphere*, Bloomington: Indiana University Press.

Murphy, F.D., Buckley, H., and Joyce, L. (2005), *The Ferns Report*, presented by the Ferns Inquiry to the Minister for Health and Children, Dublin: Stationery Office.

Murphy, Y., Mangan, I. and O'Neill, H. (2009), *Commission of Investigation—Report into the Catholic Archdiocese of Dublin*. Dublin: Stationery Office..

Murphy, Y., Mangan, I., and O'Neill, H. (2010), *Commission of Investigation—Report into the Catholic Diocese of Cloyne*. Dublin: Stationery Office..

Pfohl, S.J. (1977), "The 'Discovery' of Child Abuse," *Social Problems* 24 (3): 310–323.

Ryan, S. (2009), *The Report of the Commission to Inquire into Child Abuse*. Dublin, The Stationery Office.

42

A Crisis About the Theology of Children

Robert A. Orsi (2002)

*R*obert Orsi is the Grace Craddock Nagle Chair in Catholic Studies at Northwestern University and has written widely on children in relation to American Catholicism. In this chapter, Orsi reflects on the place of children in the Catholic sex abuse crisis, arguing that the debate on the crisis on this has yet to consider the real, flesh and blood children who suffered at the hands of these priests. This seeming oversight, he argues, get to the heart of the problem: although present in congregations, children are largely absent as real beings with knowledge, hopes, and experience. In what ways then, Orsi asks, do Catholic and other theologies contribute to the erasure of children?

Whatever else the dreadful crisis still unfolding in the American Catholic Church is about – and the news media, the courts, the Church hierarchy in Rome and in the United States, and an increasingly infuriated laity have offered different interpretations – it is fundamentally about children. It is about children's vulnerability to adult power and to adult fantasy in religious contexts and it is about the absence of real children in these settings – real children as opposed to 'children' as the projections of adult needs and desires or 'children' as extensions of adult religious interiority. The necessary response to the crisis must be about children, too.

The most common interpretations of clerical pedophilia have been biological. The issue is celibacy – if priests were allowed to marry and have families none of this would have happened.... Such bio-political interpretations effectively accomplish several things. They make this a completely Catholic problem, first of all, because only Catholic clergy are celibate, which means, in turn, that there is nothing to learn from this crisis about children's risk and fate in other Christian contexts. They also naturalize the problem: pedophilia is about sexual urges. This implies either that nothing can be done about it (because who can stem the forces of nature?) or else that the only way of dealing with the crisis is representation. Naturalization also takes the crisis out of culture, making it a matter of bodies and not of history or theology. Most important, bio-political interpretations completely deflect attention away from children and from the nature of children's lives in the church....

This interplay of children's absence and presence also characterizes the Vatican's response to the crisis. Roman officials say clerical pedophilia is an American problem; as a Cardinal spokesman slyly pointed out at a Vatican press conference, questions about child abuse are invariably addressed in English. Then, shamefully – is there any end to the shame of all of this? – Rome asserted that this distinctly American crisis was about gay priests. Taken together what these statements mean is that in Rome's understanding the rape of children is the product of liberal democracy, certainly of movements for gay rights, but more generally of a rights-based and democratically open political culture. Then Vatican officials called for a purge of gay priests. So the violated bodies of children are to be mobilized for the reactionary ends of the curia and for the demonizing of liberalism. Children are present in these imaginations only long enough so that the pain in their bodies can be appropriated for Rom's political ends, a variant of the logic of torture, and then they disappear....

What accounts for the strange doubleness of children in Catholic culture, for their simultaneous presence and absence?

There has always been a deep ambivalence in Christianity about the spiritual and moral status of children. St. Augustine thought that children were naturally depraved; other theologians suggested that children were good only because they lacked capacity and opportunity for sin; others found children angelic and innocent. Christian conceptions of children throughout the Middle Ages 'oscillate between extremes,' writes church historian Janet L. Nelson, 'because children's behavior was taken to indicate good or bad supernatural power: on the one hand, lack of control suggested diabolical influence, on the other, weakness and unprotectedness suggested access to the divine.' Nelson concludes that the child was a protean figure to be 'exploited in legal or political as well as moralizing contexts.' In the Christian imagination, the child-as-holy-innocent and the child-as-demonic-other have spun around each other in an unsteady dance.

It was the child-as-holy-innocent, however, that came to dominate European and American Christian under-standing in the modern era. Children were brutalized in industrial workplaces; in European colonies they suffered the same fates as their parents (modern times have not been kind to children). And in these same years, the European and American middle classes elaborated an extensive fantasy of childhood innocence in the idioms of romanticism, religion, and consumerism.

Among Catholics, the nineteenth and twentieth centuries were the age of the child. Catholics thrilled to the sight of children in ecstatic communication with the Virgin and to the sound of their voices speaking her messages of consolation and warning.

That Mary chose to reveal herself to children at Lourdes and Fatima and elsewhere was taken by the Church as proof of the validity of the events – because how could innocent children deceive anyone – and by critics as proof of the Church's intolerable and decadent corruption of the minds and hearts of simple people. The age of the child had its pope, Giuseppe Sarto, Pius X, who was determined to bring children into full participation in the life of the Church. Pius radically lowered the age at which children might make their first communion (in a widely reported story, the pope himself gave the host to a 4-year-old boy), encouraged youngsters to receive often, and promoted the cult of the baby Jesus (to whom the Pope was devoted).

Catholics prided themselves on offering their children direct access to the sacred, not what they imagined as the scaled-down, make-believe, Sunday-school version of Christianity given Protestant children. Childhood became the model of adult faith in the age of children. In an allocution in 1929 on St. Theresa of the Little Flower, whose autobiography was a major inspiration for the age of the child, Pope Benedict XV summed up the ethos of the period: 'In spiritual childhood is the secret of sanctity for all the faithful of the Catholic world'. This was how the challenges of modernity would be met, by the politics of innocence.

Pope Pius told an audience of French children in April 1912 that their guardian angels every day beheld the face of God 'in the souls of these little ones where God is reflected as in the mirror of their innocence, their splendor, their purity.' The comment reveals the dilemma of real children in the age of the child: Innocence is a mirror – but there is nothing in a mirror other than what is reflected in it. Innocence is empty. 'Childhood can be made a wonderfully hollow category', literary historian James Kincaid writes of Victorian fantasies of the innocent child, 'able to be filled with anyone's overflowing emotions, not least overflowing passion'.

Kincaid refers to the discourse of innocence as the 'hollowing out of children'. What is hollowed out? The child hollowed out by adult religious fantasies is denied agency and will. The discourse of innocence precludes children having their own wants, needs, and desire, and their own understandings of things different from what adults propose for them. Innocence ironically functions more effectively as discipline than religious tropes of childhood depravity because while the latter acknowledge (even if only hyperbolically) the existence of childhood needs and behaviors that enrage or frighten adults, the discourse of innocence simply and authoritatively denies children any existence at all. The emptiness of innocence deprives children of the authority and integrity of their own experience ('tell the child to forget about it'). Ironically, the discourse of innocence puts children at the greatest risk because the emptiness of innocence creates a space into which adult desire can be projected. The innocent child is bound to adult desire; he or she does not exist apart from this.

This is not to say that there were not countervailing modern accounts of the child in Catholic and Protestant cultures. When Christians aligned with progressive political initiatives in defense of young people's rights, for example, they developed richer accounts of children's real lives that challenged normative religious views. Nor am I saying that the hollowing out of the child in modern Christian culture is the only source of children's distress and oppression. Many of the children abused by the priests assigned them by Boston's bishops were poor and dark-skinned; in these cases, race and class deepened children's invisibility. The demon child endured into modernity, moreover, the necessary shadow of the holy innocent. The innocent child is uncanny, and adults are made anxious by the emptiness they themselves have imposed on children. When this happens, innocence is transposed into evil. But the major trope of the modern Christian conception of the child is innocence, with all that this brings with it.

Let me give an example of children as the objects of adult desire in modern Catholic culture. The 1884 decision of the Third Plenary Council of Baltimore virtually to mandate that American parents send their children to parochial schools under penalty of sin ensured that Catholic youngsters and the adult religious assigned the task of forming them in the faith spent a great deal of time together, much more so than religious figures and children in any other American religious culture. Children and adults watched one another very closely in this world, the inevitable result of their daily proximity, and one of the things that adults searched children for were signs of religious vocation. (Children looked back too, but this is another matter.) It was common before the Second Vatican Council for youngsters to enter religious life at a very early age, directly out of elementary school; these special children – 'priests-in-the-making', in a popular phrase for altar boys, or little nuns – were identified as such by adult religious, sometimes taking hold of children's own religious fervor, sometimes imposing their vision on children.

The children singled out for this special kind of religious attention were marked off from the rest of their peers and usually found themselves relentlessly pursued, the objects of a long and complex seduction process that involved special privileges in school, little gifts of religious objects, special field trips, and the delight of adult attention. Some children found this intense religious scrutiny flattering, but many others were terrified by it. Little priests and nuns in the making experienced the attention as a constraint on their behavior – they could no longer be themselves among their peers. It was very hard to dissuade the adults involved, moreover, to convince them they were mistaken about a child's destiny. The boundary between these specially designated children and the adult religious around them had been dissolved by adult fantasy and projection.

None of this is distinctive to Catholicism, however. The hollowing dynamics of innocence and the absent/present 'child' generated by them are evident across American Christianity. There are two dominant discourses about children among contemporary American Christians and post-Christian practitioners (in New Age and Pagan groups, for instance). The view that children are innately spiritual, which develops out of the nineteenth-century discourse of the holy innocent, holds liberal imaginations; the view of children as weak and in need of adult religious authority and protection holds conservative imaginations. In popular understanding and practice there is considerable fluidity between the two (apparently dissimilar) accounts of childhood because they are shadows of each other, the holy child and the demon child chasing each other across the American Christian landscape.

It is a widely held assumption among Christian educators and writers on children's religion today that children are naturally religious, as Protestant and Catholic educators insisted to me again and again at a conference recently. Children are endowed with an innate spirituality that is more authentic, more open and more gracious than adult religiosity. There is a real gnosticism of childhood in the contemporary United States. Prominent religious theorists claim that children have greater spiritual insight than adults and that children speak with prophetic voices. In such fantasies of childhood spirituality, maturation can only be seen as a fall from grace; holy children cannot really grow up. Adult fantasies of innately holy children deny youngsters the full range of human experience and emotion. The fantasy is predicated on children not having normal lives (normal lives are the privilege and prerogative of the adults who nostalgically situate children in a pre-social space of holiness). The fear that children may indeed have more complicated lives, emotions, experiences than is allowed them by fantasies of their natural holiness- that in fact they might be just like adults in this regard – produces the damned children that populate the American gothic as well as the moral hysteria that periodically grips American Christians, liberal and conservative. The discourse of the holy child generates as its necessary counterpart the fantasy of the dark teenager that so haunts contemporary imaginations; the dark teen is the holy child come to adolescence. (Sometimes, as in the Christian retelling of Columbine, sacred children and damned teenagers are arrayed against each other in cosmic combat.) The trope of innocence, the hollowing out of children's own interiorities, desires, and autonomy, the blurring of boundaries between adult religious fantasies and the lives of children – this is children's fate in Christian modernity. Children may have been safer in premodern Christian contexts where they were not burdened by adult fantasies of their sacredness or by the peculiar attentions that follow the imposition of holiness.

Adults tell themselves (with great urgency and often enough fearfully) that they must pass on their religious beliefs and values to their children; to this end, they organize catechism classes, Sunday school programs, after-school religious instruction, special children's rituals, and so on. The fear is that without such instruction children will be bereft and alienated on the deepest levels. But this is disingenuous. Children represent the vulnerability and contingency of a particular religious world and of religion itself; in exchanges between adults and children about sacred matters, the religious world is in play. On no other occasion except perhaps in times of physical pain is the fictive quality of religion – the fact that religious meanings are made and sustained by humans – so intimately and unavoidably apprehended as when adults attempt to realize the meaningfulness of their religious worlds in their children. This is why discussions of what children lack religiously – and most often children's religious development is framed precisely as a narrative of lack – are fraught with such fear, sometimes sorrow, and sometimes ferocity, among adults, especially in times of social dislocation. Fear *for* children is invariably accompanied by fear *of* children. The apparently commonsensical and straightforward nature of the enterprise of religious training – we want to pass our religious beliefs onto our children – naturalizes a far more complex relationship. Children's bodies, rationalities, imaginations, and desires, rendered accessible to adult imposition by the fantasy of innocence, have all been privileged media for giving substance to religious meaning, for making the sacred present not only *for* children but *through* them too for the adults in relation to them.

The problem, then, is not celibacy, homosexuality, or liberalism but the unstable presence/absence of children in a religious and political culture that denies then the full complexity of their experience and renders them porous to adult need and desire. The necessary response to the crisis in the church is to find ways of making children more authentically and autonomously present in contemporary Christian contexts and of genuinely protecting them. Genuine protection here means protecting their autonomy rather than putting in place safeguards that only serve to locate children ever more completely under adult authority and protection. The issue at stake, in other words, is children's rights in religious environments. (I have not read a single commentator on the Catholic crisis say that what is needed are mechanisms for giving children greater voice in the Church.) Making children truly present means recognizing first of all their separateness from adults (at the same time honoring the bonds of love, responsibility, and dependence that form between the generations). Clearly defined boundaries between children and adults are essential *especially* in religious contexts where not only the boundaries tend to be weak but also the absence of such boundaries between generations is often seen as morally and spiritually good. Children are not extensions of their parents' religious worlds. Churches might begin a season of reflection on their own theological traditions and moral practices (the resources for this are becoming available in the emerging study of children's religious history) to examine how theology and denominational practices deny children's lives and experience and what they have affirmed of children's lives. Christians might also reflect on the relationship between their theological and ecclesiastical traditions, on the one hand, and discourses and practices relating to children in the culture around them, on the other.

It may be possible to stop the endlessly spinning modern Christian dialectic of children's absence/presence by opening a space in Christian contexts for real children with lives not constrained by adult fantasies (of children's innate spirituality and holiness), grief (for a lost golden age of innocence), fear (of children), or desire (for children). This calls for a new season of honoring children in their fullness and complexity of their real lives in the circumstances of the present and in their autonomy.

43

The Child's Right to Religion in International Law

Rachel Taylor

Rachel Taylor is a Tutor and Fellow in Law at Exeter College, Oxford and an Associate Professor in Law at Oxford University. Her interests lie in child law, family law, public law and human rights. She has written widely on children's rights and rights within the family, with a particular emphasis on religion. In this chapter she discusses tensions surrounding children's rights to religion in international law.

Introduction

The question of whether children have a right to religious freedom and, if so, what this might mean is one of the most contentious for children's rights law. The issue brings together inherent uncertainties both in what it means for a child to have a right and in what it means for a child to have a religious identity. There remains significant theoretical disagreement as to whether children are capable of possessing rights that equate to those of adults. In particular there remains deep conceptual debate on the extent to which any such rights are dependent on the autonomous role of the child rights-holder or are merely means of protecting that child's interests as defined by others, most notably the child's parents.[1] These uncertainties are echoed in the field of children's religious rights by the debate as to how children experience religious identity, belief, and belonging. As demonstrated by the contributions to this volume, there remain significant differences as to emphasis that diverse writers, nations, cultures, and faith traditions place on the relative importance to the child's religious identity of individual belief, religious instruction, participation, identity, and socialization within the family and wider religious community. These uncertainties are also dynamic in that what it means for a child to possess a right and to possess religious identity and understanding will vary both between children and for the individual child as she matures. For these reasons, while the right of the child to freedom of religion is clearly stated within the texts of international and regional human rights treaties, the extent and meaning of that right is not yet clearly defined.

This chapter will start by identifying children's right to religion within the text of the most significant human rights treaties, most importantly the United Nations Convention on the Rights of the Child (UNCRC). It will then proceed to analyse the meaning of that right both within the text itself and in its subsequent interpretation. This analysis demonstrates that the drafting of the text represents an uneasy tension between a vision of the child as possessing an independent right to determine her own faith and an understanding that the child's right is primarily a right to be brought up in the faith of her parents without state interference. Given the constraints of space this analysis will focus primarily on the relationship between the rights of parents and children reflected in these different understandings of the child's right to religion. This chapter should be read in conjunction with that by Friedrich Schweitzer (in this volume) which considers children's religious rights from an educational perspective.

The religious rights of children in International Human Rights Law

In one sense the answer to the question of whether children have a right to freedom of religion is very clear: the right to freedom of thought, conscience, and religion is clearly stated in a number of foundational international instruments and is protected by those instruments without regard to the age of the rights holder. For example, Article 18 of the Universal Declaration of Human Rights states that:

> Everyone has the right to freedom of thought, conscience and religion; this right includes freedom to change his religion or belief, and freedom, either alone or in community with others and in public or private, to manifest his religion or belief in teaching, practice, worship and observance.

This right is reaffirmed in similar terms in a number of significant international and regional instruments, most notably Article 18 International Covenant on Civil and Political Rights (ICCPR). As the term "everyone" clearly applies to children, on a superficial level it is clear that children do possess a right to freedom of religion, but what this means in practice is much more difficult to discern. As with many general rights instruments, the right is written from an adult perspective with no independent consideration of the ways in which children experience such rights. Most notably, no consideration is given to the child's developing abilities and experience as she matures nor to the relationship between the rights of the child and the rights of her parents.

For parents to possess the same right to religious freedom; for devout parents the responsibility to bring a child up to know, understand, and participate in their religion is among the most important aspects of the parents' *own* right to religious freedom. This understanding of parental religious freedom is bolstered by the fact that many religions place obligations on parents to bring their child up with knowledge of and participation within that religion. For these reasons, many national legal systems recognize parents as having significant discretion in the way in which they direct their children's religious upbringing, with protection from state interference with parental autonomy save in those cases in which there is parental disagreement or the threat of significant harm to the child (Ahdar and Leigh 2013). The notion that the human rights of parents require such protection in determining the religious upbringing of their children has been particularly evident in the jurisprudence of the European Court of Human Rights (Langlaude 2014). That Court has recently reaffirmed that parents are protected in the transmission of their beliefs to their children, provided that they do not cause harm, even if that transmission is carried out in an insistent and overbearing manner that caused the child unease, discomfort, or embarrassment.[2] While in many situations the protection of the religious freedom of their parents will also protect that of the child, the potential for tension between such a strong parental right and the child's own religious belief is evident but unaddressed.

The United Nations Convention on the Rights of the Child

The failure of general human rights treaties to address the particular needs and interests of children is by no means limited to questions of religion. It was to address this lacuna that the UNCRC was drafted, to give explicit consideration to the particular position of children. The UNCRC recognizes the religious identity and interests of children at a number of points within its text. The connection between children's religious identity and the religion of their families is particularly noted in Article 20(3) which obliges the state to pay due regard to the importance of the child's religious background and continuity in upbringing in making arrangements for caring for children who cannot remain with their families. The child's place within religious community is also recognized in Article 30, which protects the right of children in minority groups to profess and practice their religion in community with others within that group. It is, however, Article 14 that is central to the protection of the child's right to religion in the UNCRC. Article 14 states that:

1. States Parties shall respect the right of the child to freedom of thought, conscience, and religion.

2. States Parties shall respect the rights and duties of the parents and, when applicable, legal guardians, to provide direction to the child in the exercise of his or her right in a manner consistent with the evolving capacities of the child.

3. Freedom to manifest one's religion or beliefs may be subject only to such limitations as are prescribed by law and are necessary to protect public safety, order, health, or morals, or the fundamental rights and freedoms of others.

This Article raises, but does not resolve, the tension between the evolving capacity of the child to freedom of thought, conscience, and religion and the rights of parents to provide direction to her in that freedom. It might even by argued that the Article fails to give children an independent right to freedom of thought and religion but instead predicates that right on the right of the parent to provide direction. The initial draft of the article was much more clearly centered on the child as an autonomous religious actor with the freedom to make independent religious choice. That draft (Van Bueren 1998: 156; Langlaude 2007: chapter 4) would have included the following:

> This right shall include in particular the freedom to have or adopt a religion or whatsoever belief of his choice and freedom either individually or in community with others and in public or in private to manifest his religion or belief

This drafting was based on Article 18 ICCPR and was clearly based on the notion of the child as able to make religious choices at variance with those of her parents. Certainly the same wording in the ICCPR has been interpreted by the Human Rights Committee such that:

> the freedom to "have or to adopt" a religion or belief necessarily entails the freedom to choose a religion or belief, including the right to replace one's current religion or belief with another or to adopt atheistic views, as well as the right to retain one's religion or belief.[3]

The view that a child might have a right to reject the religion within which they had been brought up was so controversial that it appeared to have the potential to jeopardize the entire Convention, leading to the negotiation of the much more equivocal adopted text. Nonetheless, the text remains controversial, as demonstrated by the large number of reservations and interpretive statements that have been attached to it by various countries. Some states, notably Belgium and the Netherlands, have attached interpretive declarations stating that they will interpret the right consistently with Article 18 ICCPR to give the child the right to choose their religion once capable of doing so. In contrast, a large number of Islamic states have entered reservations on the basis that the freedom of a child to choose their religion runs counter to national law[4] or the provisions of Shari'a law.[5] Further, both Poland and the Holy See have stated that the provision should not be interpreted so as to undermine the authority of parents. For these reasons, it seems that the apparent agreement formed in Article 14 UNCRC disguises continued fundamental disagreement as to the nature of children's religious rights.

Interpreting Article 14 United Nations Convention on the Rights of the Child

This brief history of Article 14 might be read as suggesting that the right to religious freedom that it contains is minimal and contingent on the stronger rights of the child's parents. The watering down of the article from the clearer statement of freedom in Article 18 ICCPR, the continued reservations to this reduced wording, and the role of parents in Article 14(2) might all support such a conclusion. Nonetheless, the subsequent interpretation of the provision has emphasized the importance of recognizing the right as one of the child herself and of respecting the child's freedom in exercising that right. Indeed one leading commentator on Article 14 (Langlaude 2008) argues that the interpretation of the right has gone too far in considering the autonomy of the child and neglects the importance of understanding children's religious freedom as rooted in relationships with family and community.

A particularly important aspect of this debate is the interpretation of Article 14(2) and the relationship between the rights and duties of parents and that of the child. As noted above, many legal systems give strong protection to the discretion of parents to bring their child up according to their own religious convictions. From this perspective the inclusion of Article 14(2) might appear to subject the child's religious right to that of the parents. This would, however, be a misreading for two reasons. First, it should be remembered that for many children, particularly younger children, the religious interests of the children and the parents will be complementary and in such cases the protection of the parents' religious freedom will be the strongest means of protecting that of the child. This is consistent with the preamble to the UNCRC, which recognizes the family unit as "the natural environment for the growth and well-being" of children. Second, it is clear that the requirement to respect the rights and duties of parents is only recognized in so far as that direction is consistent with the evolving capacities of the child. Where a child has attained the capacity to make religious decisions for herself, there is no requirement to respect the parents' inconsistent provision of direction. On this basis the primary right remains that of the child, with the parental rights and duties recognized insofar as they are compatible with that primary right. This reading is consistent with the general duty to have regard to the developing capacities of the child in Article 5 UNCRC and her rights of participation in Article 12. Although the UN Committee on the Rights of the Child ("the Committee") has not always been consistent in its interpretation of Article 14 (Langlaude 2008) it has tended to favor this interpretation of Article 14 as centered on the child's ultimate freedom of choice. A good recent example of this approach can be seen in the Committee's direct criticism of India's failure to allow children to choose a religion different from that of their parents.[6]

Conclusions: Children's right to religion in practice

It seems clear then that children do have a right to religion in international law and that while this right will often take the form of protecting the religious family from state intervention, ultimately the right is that of the child and may be exercised in a manner that conflicts with the parents' own religious convictions. There has been concern that such an approach leads to undue state intervention in the private decisions of the family but it is not at all clear that this is the case. Human rights law tends to operate by providing the outer parameters for legitimate state action, not be prescribing the precise means by which the right must be implemented. In relation to Article 14 these parameters appear to give significant latitude to the state. The duty on the state in Article 14(1) is phrased as a duty to "respect" the right of the child rather than a duty to "ensure" or "take measures" to protect that right. While the Committee has interpreted the duty to "respect" the right of the child to include taking positive measures such as ensuring that children's freedom of choice is recognized in legislation, it does not appear to extend so far as positively ensuring that the child has the tools and knowledge to make a full and informed choice regardless of their parent's views. This is most clearly seen in relation to education, in which international law has generally protected the rights of parents to ensure that the religious and moral education of the children is in conformity with the parents' convictions, so far as that is consistent with the child's right to an education.[7] The practical reality of the lives of many children mean that the religious convictions of their parents are likely to remain a dominant influence.

Notes

1 See Fortin (2009 chapter 1, for an introduction to this debate).

2 *Vojnity v Hungary* [2013] ECHR 426 esp at [37].

3 Human Rights Committee, General Comment 22 at [5].

4 For example, Malaysia and Algeria.

5 For example, United Arab Emirates and Iraq.

6 Committee on the Rights of the Child, Concluding Observations, CRC/C/IND/CO3-4 at [45].

7 ICCPR Art 18(4); European Convention on Human Rights Protocol 1, Article 2. See too Schweitzer in this volume.

References

Ahdar, R. and Leigh, I. (2013), *Religious Freedom in the Liberal State*, second edition, Oxford: Oxford University Press.

Fortin, J. (2009), *Children's Rights and the Developing Law*, third edition, Cambridge: Cambridge University Press.

Langlaude, S. (2007), *The Right of the Child to Religious Freedom in International Law*, Leiden: Martinus Nijhoff.

Langlaude, S. (2008), "Children and Religion under Article 14 UNCRC: A Critical Analysis," *International Journal of Children's Rights* 16: 475–504.

Langlaude, S. (2014), "Parental Disputes, Religious Upbringing and Welfare in English Law and the ECHR," *Religion and Human Rights: An International Journal* 9: 1–30.

Van Bueren (1998), *The International Law on the Rights of the Child*, The Hague: Martinus Nijhoff.

44

Child Labour and Moral Discourse in Brazil

Maya Mayblin (2010)

Maya Mayblin is Lecturer in Social Anthropology at the University of Edinburgh. Her research explores the history and practice of popular Catholicism in Northeast Brazil. Here she explores the moral dimensions of child labour as a cultural practice in the village of Santa Lucia, and how participation in child labour relates to local constructions of childhood as a period of uncertainty and transition.

The dangers of playing and 'Doing Nothing'

In accordance with the spatial and comportmental changes wrought by puberty, children are expected to manifest a change in attitude towards childish occupations. As children become older, their play (*brincadeira*) comes under scrutiny from adults. Parents are forever trying to prevent older children from joining in the games of younger siblings. On any typical afternoon, close kin and neighbours will gather in the shade of one another's doorsteps to sort beans, plait straw for hats, and exchange gossip. As they do so, an assortment of younger and older children will dart from courtyard to courtyard, playing tag, rolling marbles in the dirt, and climbing the skinny guava tree in the centre of the village. During such times parents call out intermittently to older children, ordering them over to the shade of the doorsteps to lend a hand with whatever task they are involved in. Women frequently talk about the need to teach their daughters an occupation such as crochet or embroidery in order to *parà-las de brincar* (stop them from playing). As one woman told me in reference to her 11-year-old-son: 'I got so anxious watching him pass the day playing that I asked my father-in-law to let the boy look after his horses. Well, thank God, now he has some proper work'. Play in older children is perceived as problematic for various reasons. The main reason being, however, that older children are much too *sabido* (knowledgeable about the world). In Santa Lucia, play is an ambiguous kind of activity indulged in by children and adults alike, and deemed to be both creative and potentially sinful. The danger of play, it is said, is that it can lead to *malandragem* (mischievous immorality). Indeed this concern over the concept of play maps onto a wider preoccupation with the creative but dangerous potential inherent in all unstructured, imaginative, and open-ended forms of social interaction .... The risk for younger, more innocent children is considered innocuous, and in full adults, is considered to be easily controllable. However, for jovens, who are between innocence and knowledge, play is neither innocuous, nor readily controllable.

However, if parents are anxious about the problems of play, they are equally as worried by the idea that their jovem 'does nothing' (*faz nada*). Whereas nobody notices what a younger child is doing, adults maintain a constant suspicion that their older charge 'do nothing'. I became accustomed to asking women how they were, only to hear that they were deeply anxious because one of their children was 'doing nothing'. The weight of parental anxiety in this sense often seemed in excess of what jovens actually did or did not do to arouse it. An interesting case in point would be Jeferson, the 15-year-old son of Ivanulda. When I saw Ivanulda, she would complain at length about the fact that her son was *fraco* (weak), and did nothing all day, not even properly attending school. Much like other parents I knew, Ivanulda was apt to compare her son's 'weakness' with her own *força* (strength). 'Look at me', she would exclaim, 'Everyday, even when I am tired, I prepare the dinner, wash the plates, feed the animals, and sweep the house'. Ivanulda's perception that her son 'did nothing' stood in splendid contrast to her own sense of activity and endurance.

Hard as I tried to understand it, Ivanulda's anxiety seemed a little excessive. For as far as I could tell, Jeferson was an obedient, polite, and helpful boy who never caused much trouble – at least not by the standards of trouble I had seen other adolescent boys cause their parents. One day I was present as Ivanulda, her sister, and Otàvio (Ivanulda's brother-in-law), were discussing the problem of Jeferson. At one point Otàvio hinted, jokingly, that he could resolve the problem by paying for Jeferson to visit a prostitute: 'The boy is at an age where he needs to lose his virginity' he declared. Ivanulda laughed and reminded Otàvio that Jeferson had already had several girlfriends. *Ele ja è sabidinho!* (he is already knowing/cunning), she proclaimed. Nevertheless, and to my amazement, Ivanulda was not actually opposed to the idea that her son sleep with a prostitute, her only suggestion was that it was also high time Jeferson started accompanying his father to work in the family field. Everyone nodded. What Jeferson needed most, they all agreed, was to cultivate his own patch of crops.

Although the solutions suggested to Jeferson's problem appeared to strike in opposing directions (i.e. sleeping with a prostitute is, in local terms, an inherently selfish and sinful kind of activity, whereas working the land is geared towards others and thus virtuous) both kinds of experience are necessary for a person to live successfully and productively in the world. It is thus easy to see why such opposing ideas arose simultaneously: whatever spiritual pollution would accrue to Jeferson through the former activity would be counterbalanced with the more spiritually productive pursuit of labouring for the household.

Before going on, however, it is necessary to point out an important difference between Santa Lucian conceptions of jovens and Euro-American conceptions of teenagers. In Santa Lucia, as in many other parts of the world, parents are used to conceptualising youth as a stage of life characterised by difficulty and danger. In the West, adolescence is generally perceived as a time of hormone driven rebellion. Parents worry about teenagers experimenting with sex or drugs and fear that they will suffer the consequences of immature decisions. In Santa Lucia, by contrast, there is no concept of hormone-driven 'teenage rebellion'. Interestingly, many Santa Lucian adolescents claim to disapprove of young people known to them who go against their parent's wishes. As one adolescent boy I spoke to put it: 'Why would I go against my father when it is he who will give me land to work, and to live on?' In such a context, young people have a vested interest in *not* rebelling against their parents, as parents are a means, rather than an obstacle, to establishing independence.

As in the example of Ivanulda discussed above, parents are apt to point out that their *jovem* is already cunning and knowledge at the same time as worrying that they are weak and 'do nothing'. The problem jovens pose for their parents, I suggest, is not linked to the notion of hot-headedness or rebellion, but to the perception that while jovens are acquiring adult-like knowledge about the world, they lack the tools to handle it appropriately. That is, they have not yet established full moral personhood. In the following section, I will explore how Santa Lucian people deal with this problem through the idiom of labour.

Labour

Today, as in the past, both boys and girls will remain closely linked to the domestic sphere from birth until about eight years old. Life until this time involves going to school, playing on surrounding terrain, and for girls especially, performing small domestic chores. As soon as they are able to girls start performing tasks such as watering plants in the *horta* (garden), helping to look after younger siblings, lighting the stove, laying the table for meals, drying plates, helping to wash clothes, mincing corn, feeding poultry, and fetching items such as bread and cooking oil from the village store. From 8 to 10 years onwards, a girl will perform additional tasks such as fetching water, killing and plucking chickens, cooking food, and sweeping the house. Up until about 8 years of age, boys are relatively free of chores. Their only tasks are to help out watering plants, feeding poultry, and running to the local store for goods. From 8–10 years upwards they take on tasks such as grooming horses, taking cattle to and from pasture, bathing and milking cows, feeding swine and taking lunch out to older kin working in the *roçado* (cultivated fields).

Between the ages of 8–10, boys and girls undergo a change, both in terms of increased responsibilities and in accompanying status. Coincidentally or not, it is precisely at this stage that older kin start to take note of whether or not a child is showing signs of becoming a *trabalhador* (hard worker). Boys and girls who are good at performing their tasks and, most importantly, who appear to enjoy them, will be singled out for praise. When talking amongst themselves, adults will often draw attention to the quantity and quality of the help received from children in the 8–10 bracket. They will comment that a particular girl is *muito trabalhadeira* (very hardworking), already able to do all the things her mother does, or that a particular boy is *muito trabalhador* as he never fails to get out of bed to feed the animals, even on the coldest morning. Children who register little interest or aptitude for household tasks are just as likely to be singled out but for teasing and criticism. As a friend of mine regularly commented of her 10-year-old daughter in the presence of friends and neighbours 'This one here is terrible for work'.

Such singling out for praise and criticism is linked to a significant event that occurs around this age: the participation in labour away from the domestic sphere. From 8–10 years of age, both boys and girls are encouraged to accompany their parents to the fields, and/or up until recently, the Casa de Farinha. Only a generation ago, a child upon reaching the age of eight, would receive the present of a hoe (*enxada*) from his father. The hoe given to a child of this age was special for being smaller and lighter than the one used by an adult. Such hoes were not fashioned specially for children, they were simply old ones worn down from years of use by adults. If the handle was too long for the height of the child, the father would cut it down to the correct size. The receiving of one's first hoe in this way used to be, I was told, something of a rite of passage. Various older people I talked to remembered clearly when they had been given their first hoe. The day following its presentation, the child would be expected to leave for the field along with all the other working members of the family. Although these days children do not receive hoes specifically for their birthdays, from the day they decide to follow their parents into the fields *para trabalhar mesmo* (to *really* work) as people say, an appropriately sized instrument will be found. The traditional age for starting to work is no longer 8 years, as it was in the past, and varies somewhat among individuals. The factors that affect whether at all and how much a child labours will also vary. What is generally true, however, is that children are encouraged, but never forced, to labour. Parents say that the decision has to be the child's own, and my data from children themselves appears to support this claim. Whereas some children I knew had begun working from the age of eight, others had not started until they were fifteen or even older ....

I want to suggest that in addition to its economic and material functions, the *roçadinho*, as with other forms of labour such as scraping manioc in the Casas de Farinha, offers a moral counter to the problems of playing and 'doing nothing'. In other words, we need to think about the practise as part of an overall strategy for dealing with the spiritually problematic nature of being-in-the-world. Viewed in relation to the songs and narratives produced by adults, which constitute most types of physical labour as the supreme expression of moral consideration for others, children's labour becomes meaningful, not merely because of its financial potential, but for its role in developing an essential characteristic of moral personhood: that of *coragem*.

Coragem

All kinds of purposeful activity, especially that associated with agriculture, that which is considered *pesado* (heavy), is thought to require one essential human quality: *coragem*. The word *coragem* is translated literally as 'courage'. But this literal substitution of one term for its English cognate fails, as translations often do, to convey the richness of what is signified in the local context. *Coragem*, in Santa Lucia, is not simply the ability to disregard fear, it is physical strength – a bodily state of being that enables one to do things that are either fearful, boring, uncomfortable, or difficult.

In practice, *coragem* can be used in a variety of linguistic contexts, some of which appear to emphasise its physiological properties, others which describe it more as an emotional or psychological state. The former sense arises when the word is used to allude to a bodily technique or particular muscle development needed for a certain kind of activity. An example would be when I was discovered by my host mother, trying in vain to wring large amounts of water out of a heavy, sodden blanket. 'Do you not have the *coragem* for this task?' she asked me. She then placed her broad sturdy hand, muscular from domestic work, next to mine and began to wring with me, demonstrating the right force required. 'You have to squeeze with strength', she said through gritted teeth, wringing a gallon of water out of the material. The latter sense of the term occurs in reference to the psychological willpower and motivation one needs to confront a difficult, tedious, or uncomfortable task. This becomes evident when people say they lack the *coragem* to move far from their families, or simply the warmth of their bed in the chill of early morning.

The highly differential contexts in which the term is used suggest, once again, its flexible application. However, in relation to its application to any purposeful activity described as labour or *trabalho*, a continuity of meaning occurs. One man explained it as follows:

Why does one need *coragem* to work? Because if you leave the house early when it is still dark, lift a heavy *enxada* (hoe) all day, work alone, sun hot on your head, you need to have *coragem*. My work is finished for the day. But if I lacked *coragem* this morning, I never would have gone to the *roçado* at all.

In this context, it becomes clear that *coragem* is an attitude that allows a person to perform work that is, in some way, mentally, emotionally and physically challenging. This attitude could be further defined as an embodied state combining both the ability to endure mental tedium and lack of financial reward with the ability to endure physical discomfort and pain. Although *coragem* in this sense is most commonly associated with work in the fields, it is also commonly spoken of in relation to the flourmill and domestic work. Indeed, *coragem* is thought essential for enduring the *fedio* (monotony), of predominantly female tasks such as washing clothes, washing dishes, sweeping the floor, and the like. The practical aspect of the concept was impressed on me several times during my fieldwork through my own labour experiences. In particular, I was often struck by my own inability to endure simply the tedium and monotony of women's work. Especially tiresome is that which pertains to the flourmill, which involves squatting for hours on low stools in semi-darkness, often in silence, while peeling manioc after manioc and tossing the peeled roots into baskets. Although they clearly did not relish such work, the women I worked alongside in the mill did not seem to mind the tedium, and would attribute their tolerance to the fact that they had started when young and so 'learnt' to endure it.

The presence or absence of *coragem* is there at birth. Most people are born with it, but a few are born without it. However, even if a person is born with it, this is not enough for it to develop; it needs to be nurtured by parents by accustoming their children to labour. Speaking to my friend Dimas one day about why he had started milking cows at the age of eight, he told me that it was partly because he wanted to and partly at other people's urging that he did it, in order to develop the right muscles in his forearms. He pointed out some of the muscles on the underside of his forearm and told me that his had developed differently from mine as I had never milked cows as a child. He added that it was impossible to learn this skill properly as an adult because it was too painful. His father, I was told, had initially been reluctant to let him milk the cows because, as a learner wastes a lot of milk, they risk allowing the milk dry up. His father had conceded, however, knowing that if his son did not start young, he would not have the *coragem* to do it when older.

Santa Lucian people often reiterated to me the belief that if a person is to develop the right level of *coragem* necessary to confront life successfully when older, they need to have started working by the age of 14 at the latest. If pushed, people accept that not working in childhood will not prevent a person from working in adulthood, but they claim that such a person will never have the attitude needed to stick with difficult work for very long, and will be likely to give up at the first hurdle. This, I suggest, is because *coragem* is perceived locally as a skill, like reading and writing, that requires a long period of time to develop. A common phrase uttered by older people when asked whether or not they attended school is *minha educaçao era na enxada* 'the hoe was my educator' ....It is true, they say, that a person can learn, in theory, the right way to plant a field or raise an animal. Equally true, they admit when pushed, that with a few days' practise anyone can learn how to milk a cow or swing a hoe. But what they maintain that a person cannot learn – either in theory or with a few days of practise – is how to endure the conditions of work: the climate, the rhythm, the discomfort, and the solitude; how to take all the difficulties and still return the next day, and the next.

45

Mitzvah Girls

Ayala Fader (2009)

*A*yala Fader is Associate Professor of Anthropology and Co-Director of the Women's
Studies Program at Fordham University. In her ethnography she chronicles the
ways Hasidic girls are taught to conform to societal expectations, while sublimating
their own desires. In this excerpt she explores how the girls react to these efforts by
both enforcing societal norms themselves and finding acceptable ways to embody
alternative roles and considers moments when the young girls find ways to flout the
boundaries of their non-liberal community.

Tsini the troublemaker

When a girl challenges authority figures repeatedly or in more serious ways, teachers
and mothers can become frustrated and resort to more dramatic forms of public
shaming to underscore the severity of the transgression. By describing a girl's defiant
behaviour as similar to the behaviour of Gentiles, adults make clear that such behaviour
will not be tolerated. This form of discipline is illustrated by the case of Tsini, a little girl in
the first grade, who, according to students and teachers alike, was a real troublemaker.
For most Hasidic girls, the desire to be a troublemaker is most safely enacted in make-
believe play. Little girls playing school often claimed the role of troublemaker. There is
a certain thrill, apparently, to play at being 'bad'. When kindergartners played school,
one girl was usually the teacher, another was a student, and the third was often the
troublemaker who inevitably was soundly reprimanded. Girls often acted out their parts
with gusto, and I never heard any commentary about girls choosing to play this role.

Tsini, however, was a troublemaker in real life. She was tall for her age and stocky, with short brown hair. Her clothing was sloppy, her uniform wrinkled, her blouse often not tucked in and her shoes scuffed. She was also the baby in the family, the last of ten children. Her mother was a third-grade teacher in the same school. When I asked Mrs Silver about Tsini, she told me that Tsini was 'wild and spoiled', perhaps because she was the family baby, but also because she had a *leybedik* (lively) nature which she 'couldn't help'. Indeed, she was an impulsive, moody girl, one minute throwing her arms around Mrs Silver and proclaiming her everlasting love, and the next, losing her temper and openly defying her teacher. Tsini was one of the few students to ever sit in the *tshive-benkl* (chair of penitence), and also to wear the red mitten showing that she had hit another girl. Other students, aware of Tsini's behaviour, often did not want to be her partner on line or play with her, and so Tsini was frequently alone.

One afternoon in class, the other girls had, as instructed, taken out pencils and were waiting for Mrs Silver to give them paper to do an assignment. Tsini was dreamily doodling on her desk, oblivious to Mrs Silver's instructions. Mrs Silver very dramatically called attention to Tsini's activities ... the other students chimed in and supported Mrs Silver, who allowed for an unusual level of calling out, perhaps implicitly encouraging other students to condemn Tsini's behaviour ....

Mrs Silver: 'Why does your desk look like a ... first, you have to clean your desk before you get paper. Go to the bathroom, take a wet paper towel .... It looks like a desk in a public school .... Have you ever been by a train station? Have you seen Gentiles, how they write on trains, on houses, on stores, on gates?'
Student 1:   'That's how they mess ... .'
Student 2:   'They write ... .'
Mrs Silver: 'They go around with spray. They take the spray and they scribble on the desks. They don't care if it's a scribbled up desk'.
Student 3:   'Right, it's like ... .'
Mrs Silver: 'They go around ... a house, they see a nice wall. They spray and write their names. A girl who writes on her desk, it's almost like the same kind of thing ... .
You can take a paper towel and if it doesn't come up, then you can bring soap from your house the next morning. You'll need to bring a small bag of soap, or I'll call your mother and tell her that she should bring a rag ... .'

Tsini tried to clean the desk with a paper towel, but it did not remove the doodling. Mrs Silver then called Tsini over and, in a whisper, read a letter she had written to Tsini's parents. Meanwhile, the other students stared at Tsini, who showed little emotion.

Mrs Silver's disciplining of Tsini was, in fact, the most severe I saw during my time in her class. By drawing public attention to Tsini's doodling, Mrs Silver emphasized the gravity of Tsini's offense, comparing Tsini's behaviour almost, but not quite, to that of a Gentile child who goes to public school, writes graffiti, and 'doesn't care'. Observant Jewish children always have to care about what they do and say because

God is always watching. As Von Hirsch (1995) similarly noted in her work with haredi caregivers in England, the phrase 'I don't care' is a particularly loaded one and elicits strong reactions from parents and teachers alike.

Defacing a desk was seen by Mrs Silver as a form of defiance and disrespect to authority: the authority of the school, its teachers, and ultimately, the whole community ... A number of times I heard mothers and teachers contrast Hasidic schools and children to Gentile children who go to public schools in the neighbourhood ... Mrs Silver's evoking a host of practises that define Gentile children emphasize how the moral boundary separating Jews from Gentiles can be threatened when Hasidic girls are *khispehdik* (wilfully defiant). Further, Mrs Silver suggested that Tsini's mother would have to come into school and scrub the desk in front of everyone. Tsini's behaviour not only has the potential for shaming her but also for shaming her parents and her family name. This serves as a warning to girls about their responsibility to respect their parents and 'make them proud'. Tsini's behaviour and discipline reminded the rest of the girls of the danger of not controlling oneself and not fitting in to the expectations of authority figures.

After witnessing some of Tsini's conflicts in class, I tried to broach the subject with Tsini's mother, Morah Margolis, whom I knew from time spent during recess. During one recess I told her that I had noticed Tsini had been having a hard time. She sighed and told me that it was tough for Tsini to sit still and focus in class. Then she told me how difficult it was to be different 'by us' (meaning among Hasidic Jews). Tsini's mother was a bit of an outsider herself, having been brought up in a Litvish household and marrying into an Hasidic family. She seemed to feel the pressure of fitting more than some other women. Perhaps this was because, as a woman in her mid-forties, she also had grown up in a less religiously stringent environment where she went to the movies and the library. She told me ... 'by us, you don't rock the boat. You have to fit in' ... some of the women I met acknowledged that one of the sacrifices of being a Hasidic woman includes 'not rocking the boat' either by asking for too many explanations, being too curious, wanting information that only boys need to know, or by being defiant.

Too old to ask

Hasidic adults expect that by early adolescence children should know that questions and requests cannot even be asked. Gitty described her impatience when her eleven-year-old brother asked her if their mother was going to have a bay; she responded, 'Ask a better question'. 'The others [her other siblings]', she told me, 'knew already not to ask, but my brother...'. Her brother was old enough to have known, she implied, that it was not modest or appropriate, especially for a boy, to talk about having babies. In fact, Gitty was able to reel off a battery of responses that immediately ended a questioning sequence. She reported that in her family when a child inappropriately asked 'Why?'

in English, an adult purposely reframed the question as the letter 'y' and responded with the letter 'z'. If a child asked in Yiddish, '*Fur vus?*' (Why?), the answers might be '*Azoy vi ikh hob gezugt*' (Because I said so), '*Azoy iz*' (That's how it is), or '*Nisht dan business*' (Not your business). Perhaps it is significant that the more playful silencing of questions in English, and the more serious shutdown of a child's questioning is in Yiddish, which, as I discuss later on, is considered by all Hasidism to be a more moral, more Jewish language, a language especially suited to ethical self-formation.

Parents' and teachers' refusal to answer certain kinds of questions or tolerate defiance does not mean that questioning or defiance simply stops as children become increasingly responsible for fulfilling the commandments. Part of growing up is learning the contexts in which questioning or challenging is more acceptable. Girls in school figure out early on that defiance will be less offensive to adults when it takes places during afternoon English classes. Substitute teachers and teachers of secular subjects, mothers reported to me, confront significantly more defiance than the Yiddish teachers who teach religious subjects. Once, during recess at Bnos Yisruel, some of the teachers laughed remembering how girls had so upset a Russian Jewish substitute teacher by writing 'Happy Christmas' on the board in Russian, that she cried. Boys are also notorious for tormenting their English instructors, although they would never think of such behaviour in their religious studies. Adults give less weight to secular subjects generally taught by outsiders to the community or by less religiously stringent Jews, and children and teens take the opportunity to be defiant in contexts with less potential for threatening communal authority.

Similarly, curiosity can be satisfied when the questioner is safely ensconced in Hasidic life (i.e. married) or when the context of the questioning is of less consequence to the Hasidic community. For example, married women can ask and find answers to more questions than unmarried teens or children. When I expressed surprise to an observant but not Hasidic friend that Gitty was asking me many questions about dating, my friend quickly asked if Gitty was married. When I said she was, my friend seemed relieved. She explained that asking questions out of curiosity was fine, especially once someone is married and part of a tight set of social relationships and responsibilities. If she were single and asking, my friend said, then she would be worried that Gitty was looking for something outside the community.

Indeed, the question about who made God that Esty had so wanted to ask as a child was answered when she was a married woman with children. She told me she went to an inspirational lecture for women and heard a rabbi offer an explanation for that very question. His explanation was that as humans we cannot expect to understand all of God's workings. Although to me this did not seem like an answer at all, she told me the answer had satisfied her. Perhaps the main issue was that her question had been acknowledged as legitimate, by a rabbi no less. She had been assured that there was a reason; she was just not yet able to understand it. I met another Hasidic young woman who told me that to answer some of her questions she'd gone to a summer class for Jewish returnees to the faith. There, in context with women who had grown up as secular Jews, she felt comfortable asking some of her more challenging questions that would have been unacceptable at home. Satisfied, she was able to return and participate in her own Hasidic community.

Those who continue to ask inappropriate questions or who cannot or will not fit in sometimes leave their communities and their families. A story reported in the *Village Voice* (July 1997) described four Hasidic boys who left their Brooklyn communities. At the time, all the Hasidic women in the bungalow colony I was visiting in the Catskill Mountains had either heard of the article or had read it. This was not unusual. Whenever an article or a book appeared about Hasidic Jews, no matter the publication, the material circulated in the community, as Hasidic Jews are concerned with and carefully monitor how they are portrayed in the media. The boys profiled in the *Voice* article left for different reasons. For example, one had been gay and another was not a strong scholar and could not find a place for himself. In each story, except for the boy who came out and seemed to be much more comfortable in an openly gay community, the boys spiralled out of control once they left their families. They often got involved in drugs or had other substance abuse problems the article reported. During my stay in the bungalow colony, Rifky and I joined a circle of women who were chatting, sewing, and relaxing on the lawn in chairs under a big tree surrounded by summer bungalows. The women started to talk about the article. Most knew the families of the boys, and they agreed that the boys had problems as a result of their parents' troubled marriages. They lamented that Hasidic dirty laundry had been aired in public to Gentiles and Jews.

In contrast to the *Voice* story about the boys, I spoke with two young women from different Brooklyn neighbourhoods, both of whom had broken with their communities. Both gravitated to higher education when they began to question their faith, and this ultimately led to difficult, though satisfying decisions. Miriam, who grew up in Boro Park in a Hungarian Hasidic family, had a crisis of faith at a relatively young age. She told me that one Sabbath, when she was nine, she sat under a table and methodically ripped up pieces of paper (a forbidden activity during the Sabbath). She ripped and held her breath, waiting to see if God would strike her down. When nothing happened, her whole world changed. She left her community as a young woman and went to a university, pursuing a degree. The background here is that her parents were divorced, and her mother too, had moved away from her Hasidic faith. Her mother's religious journey was a support to Miriam's own questions.

Chani, another Hasidic girl from a different neighbourhood and Hasidic circle, left just at the point of matchmaking (in the last year of high school when girls are between seventeen and nineteen years of age). Chani's parents, in contrast to Miriam's, were returnees to the faith. This meant that in their social world they were never quite as elite as those who were *ffb* or *frum* (religious) from birth. Chani was a top student and valedictorian of her school. She told me that as she grew up she increasingly felt there was hypocrisy in the community, and she simply stopped believing. She, too, left her family to live with a non-observant relative and went on to higher education. For both these young women, aside from attending a teachers' seminary, higher education was not an option.

Those who do fit in are always theorizing about why some leave the community. Most blame the children's parents or the lure of materialism. When there is not a clear person to blame, Esty, Rifky, and other women I met reminded one another that humans cannot always understand God's plan, but there *is* a plan. To echo an address given by the principal of Bnos Yisruel at a school assembly, '*Me tur nisht freygn oder complainen*' (We're not allowed to ask or complain).

Curiosity and authority

Hasidic women teach girls which questions they may not ask, what desires they may not have, whom they may not challenge. This happens in everyday exchanges when children's questions or behaviour challenge categories of belonging that are considered God-given. Women's responses to transgressions include appeals to a higher authority, silence, shaming, and comparison to the most unethical subjects, Gentiles – all effectively ways to end an interaction. A powerful means by which authority is shored up is through participation of peers in public disciplining....

The consistency across socialization contexts means that children are presented with reverberations of a similar moral message from all the Jewish adults, older siblings, and even the peers in their lives. This consistency makes it exceedingly difficult to continue to ask certain kinds of questions, as evidenced by the painful conflicts of Hasidic 'rebels' or those who leave (Levine 2003; Winston 2005). In question-and-answer exchanges between adults and children, curiosity is cultivated in ways that do not leave much space for challenges to hierarchies of authority, although children and young adults do find chinks in the system. The cultivation of non-liberal curiosity and relationships to authority are rooted in a particular form of faith that is enacted in sociological hierarchies of age and gender. Though all children must learn to give way before adults, girls must simultaneously put the needs of their brothers and fathers before their own, something they experience in everyday interactions with their siblings, parents and teachers.

In this... Foucault's notion of ethical self-formation shows the political implications of moral discourse between adults and children; in other words, how the cultivation of a non-liberal femininity, where girls learn to use their autonomy to discipline themselves, is part of a construction of a Hasidic alternative to their perceptions of Gentile and secular North America. A Jewish girl has to learn what Gitty called *tsirkhaltn* (to rein herself in). When I asked Rifky about this, she said that she felt a better way to think about self-discpline might be that a girl has to learn to 'channel' her desires, questions, and needs so that they match what is expected of her. Hasidic women cultivate this by trying to limit the situations where inappropriate curiosity or defiance can occur. They also cultivate a fear in children – which Kulick and Schieffelin (2004) note is the inverse of desire – of being like Gentiles.... In these interactions of ethical self-formation, Hasidic women engage with modernity's formations of the self but subtly shift the terms: they focus on discipline instead of freedom, faith instead of reason, and action instead of desire.

References

Kulick, Don and Schieffelin, Bambi B. (2004), 'Language Socialization', in A. Duranti (ed.), *A Companion to Linguistic Anthropology*, 349–368, Malden, MA: Blackwell.

Levine, Stephanie Wellen (2003), *Mystics, Mavericks, and Merrymakers: An Intimate Journey among Hasidic Girls*, New York: New York University Press.

Von Hirsch, Eva (1995), 'The Jews of Gateshead, England', PhD dissertation, University of Linkoping, Sweden.

Winston, Helle (2005), *Unchosen: The Secret Lives of Hasidic Rebels*, Boston: Beacon.

Author Index

Subject Index